Official Certified Ethical Hacker Review Guide

Steven DeFino

Intense School, Senior Security Instructor and Consultant

Contributing Authors

Barry Kaufman, Director of Intense School

Nick Valenteen, Intense School, Senior Security Instructor

Larry Greenblatt, Intense School, Senior Security Instructor

COURSE TECHNOLOGY
CENGAGE Learning™

Australia • Brazil • Japan • Korea • Mexico • Singapore • Spain • United Kingdom • United States

COURSE TECHNOLOGY
CENGAGE Learning™

Official Certified Ethical Hacker Review Guide
Steven DeFino
Barry Kaufman
Nick Valenteen
Larry Greenblatt

Vice President, Career and Professional Editorial: Dave Garza

Executive Editor: Stephen Helba

Managing Editor: Marah Bellegarde

Senior Product Manager: Michelle Ruelos Cannistraci

Editorial Assistant: Meghan Orvis

Vice President, Career and Professional Marketing: Jennifer McAvey

Marketing Director: Deborah S. Yarnell

Senior Marketing Manager: Erin Coffin

Marketing Coordinator: Shanna Gibbs

Production Director: Carolyn Miller

Production Manager: Andrew Crouth

Content Project Manager: Jessica McNavich

Art Director: Jack Pendleton

Cover photo or illustration: Digital Vision

Manufacturing Coordinator: Denise Powers

Copyeditor: S4Carlisle Publishing Services

Proofreader: S4Carlisle Publishing Services

Compositor: S4Carlisle Publishing Services

For product information and technology assistance, contact us at
Cengage Learning Customer & Sales Support, 1-800-354-9706
For permission to use material from this text or product,
submit all requests online at **www.cengage.com/permissions**
Further permissions questions can be e-mailed to
permissionrequest@cengage.com

Library of Congress Control Number: 2009938744

ISBN-13: 978-1-435-48853-3
ISBN-10: 1-435-48853-9

Course Technology
20 Channel Center Street
Boston, MA 02210
USA

Cengage Learning is a leading provider of customized learning solutions with office locations around the globe, including Singapore, the United Kingdom, Australia, Mexico, Brazil, and Japan. Locate your local office at: **international .cengage.com/region**

Cengage Learning products are represented in Canada by Nelson Education, Ltd.

For your lifelong learning solutions, visit **course.cengage.com**

Visit our corporate website at **cengage.com**

Printed in the United States of America
1 2 3 4 5 6 7 12 11 10 09

Contents

List of Try It Out Exercises

The "Try it out" exercises in this book represent exercises that are designed to help the student become comfortable with a few important elements before attending the intense lab environment of the official training experience.

For quick reference, the following is a list of the exercises. You might want to use this as a checklist and make sure to try each one before your training date. Some of these exercises will be expanded on, and the student should be prepared with questions as a result of trying them.

Chapter One: Ethical Hacking
1. Research hacker culture
2. Research the vulnerability databases

Chapter Two: Hacking Laws
3. Research intellectual property law

Chapter Three: Footprinting
4. Utilize the RFCs to understand network ranges
5. Banner grabbing
6. Collecting data
7. Competitive intelligence gathering
8. Watch "Privacy is dead, get over it"
9. Obtain a Who is record
10. Attempt a zone transfer

Chapter Four: Google Hacking
11. Visit Google Labs
12. Setup Google reader
13. Google search examples

Chapter Five: Scanning
14. Read RFC 826
15. Scanning a local segment
16. Angry IP
17. Read RFC 1574
18. Read RFC 793
19. Read RFC 791
20. Demo Core Impact
21. Read RFC 792
22. Read RFC 768
23. Using Netcat as a scanner
24. Using HPing as a scanner
25. Using Nmap as a scanner
26. Download and try graphical scanners

Chapter Six: Enumeration
27. Creating a NULL session
28. Changing the Restrict Anonymous key setting
29. Using the Netstat and NBTStat tools
30. Run the SMB Client command
31. Finger a user
32. Finding the SUID bit

Introduction

I have been teaching Certified Ethical Hacker (CEH) classes since version 3. Since then I have come to really appreciate the design of this course. I have seen firsthand, time and again, the unexpected benefits it can have on those who work the program correctly.

The CEH Exam (312-50) is developed by EC-Council, a member based global organization that certifies individuals in e-business and security skills. The exam is part of the CEH certification process and is the first step in becoming an LPT (Licensed Penetration Tester). This review guide covers Certified Hacker Exam #312-50, Version 6.1.

The most valuable piece of advice I can give from experience in terms of knowing what CEH is and how to make it work for you is: Remember that this is a concepts based course. Any attack or penetration test will involve improvising at some point; no class or courseware can tell you what exactly to do in those moments, but the experience of becoming CEH certified will demonstrate what is possible and set the necessary skills for practice and development.

EC-Council certifications are recognized in over 60 countries. As of August 2009, CEH has passed the IDA internal review and received favorable votes from the majority for four of the five CND categories on Directive 8570.1. Pending the change document to be released from DOD, CEH will satisfy four out of five Computer Network Defense categories. They are also an approved preliminary applicant for ANSI 17024 standards; ECEs are an ANSI 17024 requirement.

Also, the CEH can be obtained via many learning modes including live classroom training and online learning via the iClass option. iClass is EC-Council's live, online, instructor-led training platform. iClass makes EC-Council's entire catalog of vendor neutral IT Security certifications available to you in multiple schedule formats, dates, and times. Live classroom training is typically a five-day format that is run "bootcamp" style and gets the process done in short order.

For those pursuing their "Masters in Information Security," EC-Council owns the EC-Council University, a degree-granting licensed university in New Mexico, United States. EC-Council University is credited to be the world's first to have a Master of Security Science program.

In summary, I personally know the officers at EC-Council work tirelessly to further the reach and influence of this certification. They are always looking to make sure the value of your achievement increases over time, for all of those who have already met the challenge and for those who are about to.

It is time we dive in and get started....

—Steven DeFino

In This Introduction You Will Learn...

- how to approach the CEH course
- how to use this book
- how this book maps to the official courseware
- how to pass the exam and become certified
- about the authors and contributing authors to this book

How to Approach the CEH Course

- What is "Ethical Hacking"
- Embrace the spirit and intent of the CEH program

What is "Ethical Hacking"

EC-Council defines the term "ethical hacking" as "The use of hacking skills for defensive purposes." This begs the question "What is hacking?"

Many papers, essays, and discussions have been given on the topic. As expected, hacker is a recursive concept; people can hack the topic of hacking and never get to the end of it. To be successful with the CEH course, here are a few helpful tips and attitudes that should be adopted:

- Be curious about and respectful of the creative and intellectual works of others.
- Think of ways to repurpose tools and resources to get more out of them in order to meet objectives or discover entirely new things.
- Do not take control of what isn't yours and that includes P0wning B0x3n just because you can.
- Accept being mentored and mentor somebody else. Often this happens at the same time. Be patient and open minded.

Everyone starts somewhere to learn a new skill. Ethical hackers put their outcomes to good use, and help to improve something in the process.

Embrace the Spirit and Intent of the CEH Program

The great thing about studying information security is that everything you learn, experience, or create will sooner or later become useful. Ethical hacking develops your critical thinking and troubleshooting skills.

CEH really isn't just about attacking; it is also about performing in unfamiliar circumstances. It is about not getting flustered during times of trial and error. Its also about not feeling lost when there is no procedure to follow.

A willingness to look at technology from unusual perspectives is a real advantage in this class and experimentation is critical. CEH takes a point of view that might not be the same as traditional approaches in each respective discipline.

Information security certification programs tend to be considered "a mile wide and an inch deep." CEH certainly fits this description. The topics cover the entire range of accepted networking models and outlying material as well.

The work begins once you become certified. Doors are opened and new questions emerge. The design of this program is not based on the idea of trying to encapsulate one large topic into small areas but to set up a framework that will make a new career or expand an existing one possible.

How to Use This Book

- Intended audience
- Features of the book
- How to use this book for pre-study and post review

Intended Audience

EC-Council requires that authorized formal training be attended in order to qualify to take the exam (a waiver can be requested in writing from EC-Council). This book is intended for people that have met the minimum pre-requisites for CEH and intend on taking the class and exam. It is therefore both a preview and a review guide.

Due to scheduling or other resource challenges, sometimes meeting all pre-requisites prior to training is not possible. This book is designed to help a student identify what areas seem comfortable as well as those that will require more work. Students should be prepared to communicate this information to their instructor so that guidance can be provided.

Features of the Book

The layout of each chapter is designed to provide the following mechanisms that are ideal for a review guide:

Introduction

Each chapter is introduced in a way that links it to the ongoing context of the class and sets the tone for how to approach the ideas within it.

High, Medium, and Low Level Objectives

The topic headers provide structure and organization for the chapter and promote scanning and review.

"Try it Out Challenges"

In-line with the text, when they are most relevant, the exercises are suggestions on additional materials or activities that support the information being discussed. Occasionally exercises should really be taken a step farther. This encourages the habit of not just absorbing raw data, but also pausing and considering the importance to a hacker.

Conclusion

Each chapter is finished with a brief discussion of what is important in the discussion, what points to take away, and what maintains the context. String the introductions and conclusions from each chapter together and a high level business language view of the class will emerge.

Practice Questions

Each chapter has 15 practice questions with answers and explanations. They are all multiple choice and similar to the real exam in terms of balance (easy and unfairly hard questions), wording (sometimes short, sometimes scenario based) and mixing concepts from modules in the same question.

These questions may or may not directly be represented in the chapter text. Part of the drill is to get the student used to encountering material that might seem unfamiliar, but still remaining calm, using reasoning when possible, and taking a guess. This is necessary for the real thing, as the CEH exam is too difficult to rely on memorization alone.

Cheat Sheets

Sometimes memorization drills are necessary. For the convenience of this particular tool, they have been provided on the website that goes along with this book. (Go to *www.cengage.com/*

coursetechnology and search for this book.) Students are encouraged to print the version without answers and try to fill it in without looking at any reference material.

How to Use This Book for Pre-Study and Post Review

This book provides just enough background information to help the student enter the training environment more comfortably. We seek to provide the perspective that will best help the student prepare for the exam. We did not intend on this review guide to be a replacement for the classroom kit or a training process. An exam review guide is in the same way an adventure tour guide is not the actual hike down the trail but he will help you avoid the poison ivy and eat the tastiest berries. To be successful in this program you have to experience the material and not just memorize it.

Prior to class, approach this book in a "spiral." The information in this class is only linear at a high-level view. The details are interconnected and can involve several parts of the book at once. To avoid repetition, everything needed for every chapter can't always be mentioned inline.

> On the first run through, preview the table of contents, then scan each page of the book front to back, paying attention to only headers and what your eyes happen to catch.
> On the second pass through, read the introductions and conclusions for each chapter. Start generating questions and writing them down.
> On the third pass through, read everything. Start noticing how some chapters connect to others. Try some of the exercises and start doing the practice questions.

The official CEH courseware clocks in at 2666 pages in over four printed volumes, a lab guide, and Gigabytes worth of tools and additional materials. Every chapter has a few additional study questions for classroom discussion. It is the complete reference and designed to remain on your bookshelf for on-the-job use for years to come.

How This Book Maps to the Official Courseware

- Side-by-side map
- Description and "take away" points of each chapter

Side-by-Side Map

If you want to use the exam review guide alongside the official kit here is the way we have mapped the chapters of this book to the modules in the official course materials:

Exam Review Guide		Official Courseware	
Chapter 1	Ethical Hacking	Module 1	Ethical Hacking
Chapter 2	Hacking Laws	Module 2	Hacking Laws
Chapter 3	Footprinting	Module 3	Footprinting
Chapter 4	Google Hacking	Module 4	Google Hacking
Chapter 5	Scanning	Module 5	Scanning
Chapter 6	Enumeration	Module 6	Enumeration
Chapter 7	System Hacking	Module 7	System Hacking

Chapter 8	Trojans and Backdoors	Module 8	Trojans and Backdoors
Chapter 9	Viruses and Worms	Module 9	Viruses and Worms
Chapter 10	Sniffers	Module 10	Sniffers
		Module 15	Session Hijacking
Chapter 11	Social Engineering	Module 11	Social Engineering
		Module 12	Phishing
		Module 13	Hacking Email
		Module 21	Physical Security
Chapter 12	Denial of Service	Module 14	Denial of Service
Chapter 13	Buffer Overflows	Module 24	Buffer Overflows
Chapter 14	Web Servers and Applications	Module 16	Hacking Web Servers
		Module 18	Web based password cracking
		Module 17	Web Application Vulnerabilities
		Module 19	SQL Injection
Chapter 15	Hacking Wireless Networks	Module 20	Hacking Wireless Networks
Chapter 16	Cryptography	Module 25	Cryptography
Chapter 17	Hacking with Linux	Module 22	Linux Hacking
Chapter 18	IDS, Firewalls, and Honeypots	Module 23	IDS, Firewalls and Honeypots
Chapter 19	Summary of Optional Modules	Modules included on official courseware DVD	
Chapter 20	Penetration Testing	Module 26	Penetration Testing

Description and "Take Away" Points of Each Chapter

Each chapter in this exam review guide is designed to tell part of a story. The following short descriptions of each chapter will show the organization of this book and help create the intended "big picture" view of the CEH program.

Chapter 1—Ethical Hacking

The first chapter of a broad ranging information security course is always about setting the tone, and establishing the fundamentals such as vocabulary, context, and most of all, why this information is important.

Take away: The attack model CEH teaches provides the structure for the rest of the course. Use it as a compass when navigation through the concepts of this course.

Chapter 2—Hacking Laws

The laws are always far behind technology, but it is wrong to assume there aren't any that are enforceable. The rapidly innovating world of information technology is a moving target that makes creating laws difficult, and precedents are set that are quickly obsolete. This chapter focuses on fundamentals that must be understood by all ethical hackers.

Take away: Hacking can get you into trouble, and successful prosecutions are more and more common. Know how not to cross the line.

Chapter 3—Footprinting

The first step of any attack is reconnaissance and information gathering. This chapter goes beyond the obvious and provides a checklist of ways to learn as much as possible about a target. Using both passive and active techniques, this is the most important step of the attack process.

Take away: How to use both public information and active techniques such as DNS scanning to know your target.

Chapter 4—Google Hacking

The most powerful passive resource available must be looked at in depth. Google does most of the active work for the attacker. It can also be used as an attack tool itself. This chapter goes beyond just describing search syntax, and explores all of the tools and utilities necessary that go along with managing all information the attacker gathers.

Take away: How to use Google advanced search syntax to be creative and pick apart a target, locate possible vulnerabilities, and uncover additional opportunities.

Chapter 5—Scanning

Once the attacker knows the outside addresses and, if possible, the inside topology, the network must be footprinted and all operating systems and services identified and verified. This is a difficult step, as defenses such as traffic filters and intrusion response systems will affect the attacker's view of the network and opportunities for attack. Technical knowledge of scanning techniques, the protocols involved and why the network looks different to an attacker than it does to an designer, engineer, or administrator are covered in this chapter.

Take away: IP, TCP, UDP, and ICMP will be mastered to understand how to map a network and understand the traffic related defenses. Success with CEH depends on this chapter.

Chapter 6—Enumeration

The attacker is getting eager to start doing some damage, but the disciplined ones know there is still some work to be done. The live hosts, access points, and roles each host has needs to be better understood. The enumeration chapter is about user accounts and logical topologies. In order to develop a real strategy, the attacker must know what is happening above Layer 4.

Take away: How Windows file sharing and domain service protocols can be exploited to further explore the environment as well as similar functions on other operating systems. Begin to understand how the gaining access step starts to come into focus at this point in the course.

Chapter 7—System Hacking

Finally, the target is well enough understood to begin the gaining access and mainlining access phases. Perhaps a privileged user account can be compromised. Maybe economic espionage is possible. The attacker may have noticed unpatched systems exist that can be attacked from commonly available exploit tools. This chapter explores these vectors in detail.

Take away: How password cracking, covert channels and direct attacks work. Realize they can involve a lot of trial and error. Sometimes they are too noisy, or the opportunities are just not available. They can be worth the effort due to ease of execution and benefit.

Chapter 8—Trojans and Backdoors

If it is hard to attack the target directly, maybe the target will come to the attacker. This chapter builds on the system hacking chapter and shows how techniques can be combined together to gain and maintain access to systems. The chapter explores one of the oldest yet still very much relevant daily security concerns.

Take away: How to create Trojan horses and install illicit servers. Collections of exploited targets can be collected into groups of cooperative victims for more sophisticated attacks. The attacker doesn't want these installations to be repaired; hiding them and clearing tracks is also explored.

Chapter 9—Viruses and Worms

If hosts that are of value to the attacker cannot be precisely targeted, the strategy may turn to attacking as many as possible, in the shortest amount of time, to the greatest effect. If one piece of code can be written that will then do all the work for the attacker, all the better. Knowing there are others in the world that will capture your code, create a variant, and sent it back out may amplify the results. This chapter explores a category of automated, self powered attacks.

Take away: How viruses work, the different risks and the lifecycle of this form of attack. Many types of viruses are understood and how this attack vector has evolved from the earliest incidents to modern day outbreaks.

Chapter 10—Sniffers

Observing traffic is a piece of the puzzle between all of the techniques explored so far. It can be used for information gathering, compromising sensitive data, or as a step in a sophisticated control technique. On the defensive side, sniffing is a powerful troubleshooting, analysis, and testing technique. This chapter shows how to make the rest of the information in this course observable to the most detailed level. It shows how the importance of understanding the higher level concepts such as protocols and the expected events of a technique can lead the way to both more efficient attacks, as well as more effective countermeasures.

Take away: How to use sniffers in both hub and switched environments to detect sniffing attacks, and use this information for both attack and defensive purposes. The information in this module is critical to utilizing information from the previous chapters to begin thinking about tuning traffic filters and intrusion monitoring systems.

Chapter 11—Social Engineering

The greatest weakness of any network will be the human element and the most cost effective countermeasure is training. This chapter shows how humans can be deceived, misinformed or led to bad judgment. They can also simply be taken advantage of even if they are not doing anything wrong. Without proper and continuous training, awareness fades quickly and attackers can sense this over time and be attracted to these vulnerable targets.

Take away: The principles of social engineering and how attackers will combine this technique with the technologies that have been explored up to this point.

Chapter 12—Denial of Service

Sometimes the objective of an attack is to embarrass the target. Reputation is perhaps the most valuable asset to any organization. Since "non-techies" don't understand the concept of DoS or DDoS attacks, it is easy to create a sense that a network is not trustworthy simply by making its services inaccessible. There are other reasons for these attacks as well; it might be as simple as an attacker or virus author testing out or proving a theory. This chapter looks at how Denial of Service attacks are set up and how botnets that were possibly setup by worm droppings or socially engineered installations of malware can coordinate in a large scale event.

Take away: How one host can render another inaccessible with a single packet, or how many hosts can target a victim all at once using the principles of amplification and reflection.

Chapter 13—Buffer Overflows

This chapter takes a step back to look at the principles behind one of the most dangerous and consistently occurring vulnerabilities in software. It is one of the reasons much of the attacks explored in previous chapters are successful. The explanation approaches the topic not with an assumption the reader has a programming background, but from a perspective that anyone with some experience in IT can get the hang of. This area of attack is a specialty on its own that takes years of concentrated effort to master, but everyone needs to at least grasp the basics.

Take away: The fundamental concepts behind buffer overflows and reverse engineering.

Chapter 14—Web Servers and Applications

Web applications are a distinctly difference risk because their owner wants them to be as accessible as possible, unlike internal systems which can be more tightly controlled. This chapter discusses the different levels of exposure: from n-tiered models to platform architecture, as well as the principles behind the most common attacks that take place every day against these systems.

Take away: How the various attacks vectors against web servers, web applications, and databases work. For the exam, it is critical to be able to recognize in packet dumps and log files what each of the discussed attacks look like.

Chapter 15—Hacking Wireless Networks

Wireless networks are cheap and easy to install. They are also a return to the days of hubs, only worse because the signal can't be completely controlled like bounded media can. Wireless represents an opportunity for the attacker to access the network itself, from there all other attacks discussed in CEH are possible and essentially the same.

Take away: The unique concepts of wireless networking compared with wired physical topologies. How attacks against WEP works and how the improved technologies work is also discussed.

Chapter 16—Cryptography

This chapter lays out the fundamentals of cryptography that every security professional should know. It ties in with many other topics in this course, on both attack and defensive fronts.

Take away: How the cryptosystems are assembled using an interaction of symmetric, asymmetric, and one-way function techniques. The puzzles and solutions of cryptography that are relevant to other areas of the CEH program help tie many topics together.

Chapter 17—Hacking with Linux

One of the most frequently missing prerequisites of students coming into a CEH program is a comfort level with Linux. This chapter is the shortest path to getting started and highlights what is necessary to understanding the way to learn more about Linux as you go forward after CEH. Turns out, the key to becoming comfortable with Linux is very similar to the approach that is most helpful to mastering the concepts in the CEH program itself. You can't be afraid to try stuff, mess around, and break things. Safely of course.

Take away: How to get around the Linux command line, file system, and run a basic script. The CEH exam will have some Linux on it, and it will also be necessary to tell the difference at times simply by looking at port scans, log files, and scripts.

Chapter 18—Ids, Firewalls, and Honeypots

This chapter seems to be about defense and countermeasures at first, but since this is an attack class the idea it really to understand them well enough to detect them, avoid them, and a confuse them. Snort and IPTables are looked at because they are always present in Hacker's favorite operating systems; the ones that are free.

Take away: How to recognize and write snort rules and IPTables ACLs. The covering tracks phase of the CEH attack model is addressed.

Chapter 19—Summary of Optional Modules

The official CEH courseware includes incredible amounts of information beyond what is considered the coverage of the official training curriculum. These modules are included in the DVDs that come with the kit, and they address many topics that move hacking forward from the fundamentals constructs that appear in almost every attack, to the cutting edge topics that you will likely be applying your certification to on the job in the years to come. This chapter briefly describes each of these modules, and yes, some of this information might show up on the test.

Take away: Get the basic idea behind topics that reach beyond the CEH and extend this course to additional areas of attacks and threats.

Chapter 20—Penetration Testing

Applying your CEH skills in a defensive manner will likely involve performing a penetration test. There many types that can be ordered by the client depending upon need and objective. The next class in the track, ECSA/LPT, addresses this topic in detail. This chapter provides a preview of that course, and for those that stop at CEH this is the minimum that you should know before introducing your hacking skills into a professional situation.

Take away: The basics of penetration testing: the types, the legal requirements, and the reporting procedures.

How to Pass the Exam and Become Certified

- Assumptions on the exam
- How the exam works
- How to become certified

Assumptions on the Exam

The exam assumes that all pre-requisites for the CEH class have been met.
- 2 years of experience in the information security field
- One of the following certifications or equivalent training
  - Security+ or CISSP
  - Network+ or CCNA
  - Microsoft MCIPT or MCSA

There are some questions that reach back into those areas and may not be discussed during the CEH class itself. The following is a list of topics that a student be comfortable with prior to training. If there is only one or two items or you just feel out of practice on a couple. Be prepared to discuss this with your instructor.
- You know the OSI model up , down, and sideways
- You know how to work with binary and hex
- You know how to subnet and how CIDR works
- You know your port numbers, protocol IDs, and common acronyms
- You know the basics of risk management, BCP, DRP, IRP, and policy writing

This is not an administration course. These are all optional items and are only listed because it would be extremely helpful if you can also perform one or some of these tasks:
- Build and work with virtual machines; install and configure operating systems
- Set up basic network services such as DNS, DHCP
- Set up a Windows domain and include email services
- Set up and configure a web server, database server, and build a basic website
- Configure a router and basic firewalls
- Have a basic comfort level with a Linux command line. User level is sufficient.

In order to work through some of the "Try it out" exercises, access to a machine with a virtual machine product such as VMWare or Virtual PC is recommended. Instructions for the set up of this are beyond the scope of this book. At some point during training, the student should make sure they pick up this information. Working with the CEH tools and techniques depends upon having a safe lab environment available.

How the Exam Works

The exam is 150 question multiple choice questions. You have four hours to complete the exam. A score of higher than 70 percent is required to pass.

The exam can be delivered by VUE or Prometric testing centers (Exam EC0-350) or right in the classroom at the conclusion of training via Prometric Prime (Exam 312-50). It is up to the students to make the proper arrangements working with their training provider in regard to schedule and payment.

If you are taking the exam at a date after the training has concluded, it will be necessary to prove that you attended training or you can apply for a waiver. The application to receive an eligibility voucher number (required at the time of test registration) is on the EC-Council website.

You will know the result of the exam immediately. If a passing score was achieved, a .pdf version of the results page and an email will be sent to you. EC-Council will then send an official welcome package by certified mail to your address in about 4–6 weeks.

Contact information where EC-Council can reach you will be provided by you at the time you register or schedule the exam.

The current cost and additional information can be obtained on the official EC-Council website at: http://www.eccouncil.org

How to Become Certified

Attending training and passing the exam certifies you.

There is a requirement, however, to maintain the certification through ECE (EC-Council Continuing Education) units. (EC-Council is an approved preliminary applicant for ANSI 17024 standards, ECEs are an ANSI 17024 requirement).

When you receive your welcome package it will contain a letter with a registration number that allows access to the EC-Council Portal. This portal is for EC-Council certified professionals only. It contains discussion forums, links to tools, training videos, and much more. The welcome package will also contain an official certificate, decal, and legal permission to use the EC-Council logo on your business materials.

Through the portal you can access the "ECE Delta" system to report your credits. A complete explanation is provided by the FAQ on that page. It is an easy process. You are required to report 120 units every three years with a minimum of 20 per each of those years. Without reporting, you will be required to retake the exam to maintain the certification.

About the Author and Contributing Authors

- Author and Contributing Authors
- Acknowledgments
- About EC-Council
- About Intense School

Author and Contributing Authors

About the Lead Author

Steven J. DeFino, ECT, CTT+, SCNP , CISSP, ITIL (and a variety of CompTIA), travels the United States as the senior security instructor with Intense School and consultant with Vigilar Professional Services. He is the EC-Council "Instructor of the Year" for 2006 and 2009 and EC-Council "Certificate of Excellence" winner in 2008. Steven has been teaching technical and management classes since 1998 covering a range of topics from Cisco, Linux, Web Application Design to Project management and has experience in all of these areas over an adventurous 20 year career in the field. He has authored or maintained over 30 course curriculum, and is a frequent contributor to blogs and other professional resources. Steven is a proud husband and father, raised in San Diego, California but currently living in Salt Lake City, Utah.

About the Contributing Authors

Barry Kaufman, CISSP, CEH, QSA, is the Founder and Director of Intense School, a leading IT and InfoSec Training company. Barry holds a BS from University of Connecticut and an MS from the University of Bridgeport. Barry has over 15 years in IT and InfoSec, and has managed and teamed on over 120 pen tests, web assessments, vulnerability assessments, PCI audits/gap analyses, as well as other technical audits. He has served as Director of Professional Services for Vigilar, Inc., an Atlanta-based security firm. As Founder of Intense School, he was an original developer of the Professional Hacking training program, and has overseen the development and delivery of CEH training to over 1,000 Security Professionals, as well as other security training to over 10,000 professionals. As a security professional and professional educator, Barry is committed to security training led by instructors with real expertise and passion. Having established elite teams of security testers/hackers for large and complex assessments, he believes that certification is a credible way of establishing appropriate baseline skills.

Nicholas J. Valenteen, CISSP, CEH, CISA, is a computer security consultant who spends his time developing information security courses and presenting them throughout the United States. Nicholas has earned a BS in Marketing from Bentley College and a MS in Information Assurance from Norwich University. He has been working in information technology since 1980 and has been focusing on information security topics since 1997. Nicholas has been delivering training classes on IT and InfoSec since 1995, and has developed courses in network management, networking, information security management, and penetration testing. He delivers classes on these topics, and has been helping security professionals pass the CISSP and Security+ exams since 2002. A firm believer in the value of hands-on experience, Nicholas relies on real world experiences to enhance the quality of his classes.

Larry Greenblatt, CEH, ECSA, CISSP, CISM, is the founder of Internetwork Defense, a training and consulting company based in Pennsylvania. He has been in the IT field for 26 years and has worked with several fortune 1000 companies and government agencies as a network engineer and security compliance consultant. Today Larry is one of the world's foremost CISSP and CISM instructors, having trained over 2000 thousand people over the course of 12 years through both Intense School and his own consultancy. Larry has been involved in martial arts most of his life and holds several black belts in multiple arts including kick boxing, Tai Chi, and mixed martial arts (MMA). Larry is also an accomplished musician and plays several instruments including guitar, mandolin, bass, and exotic stringed instruments like the Chinese pipa and guzheng. Larry integrates all of these skills and arts into his training and has one of the most effective, entertaining, and memorable presentation styles in the industry.

Acknowledgments

These days the ability to work on just one project at a time is almost non-existent. Writing a book like this requires not just the effort of its author and contributors, but many others that make time between their other commitments to help however possible. Sometimes this help comes from creating time or resources. I would like to thank Barry Kaufman and Michelle Ruelos Cannistraci (Senior Product Manager for Cengage) for being flexible about the schedule and anyone else who had to work a little extra to make that work. Clearly Steve Helba, Jessica McNavich and many others at Cengage/Course Technology work together well as a team; I was always appreciative of the feedback and assistance they provided. Lastly, thanks to Sanjay, Haja, and Steven with EC-Council for tireless work making CEH what it is and for many years of friendship and support.

This book is dedicated to my wife Amberlee and to my daughter Krya, for setting aside a lot of their own needs at times to support projects like this and the entire career they are a part of.

About EC-Council

The International Council of E-Commerce Consultants ("EC-Council") is a leading international member based organization offering various information security and e-business certification programs and training. It is the owner and developer of globally recognized certification programs including the Certified Ethical Hacker (CEH), Computer Hacking Forensics Investigator (CHFI), and Licensed Penetration Tester (LPT) among others. EC-Council certification and training programs are currently being offered in over 60 countries around the world.

EC-Council certifications are recognized worldwide and have received endorsements from various governments including the US National Security Agency/CNSS Training Standard and Federal Government via the Montgomery GI Bill.

Over the years, EC-Council has trained over 60,000 individuals with some 25,000 of them being certified.

Individuals who have achieved EC-Council certifications include personnel from some of the finest organizations around the world including the US Army, the FBI, Microsoft, IBM, the United Nations, etc.

EC-Council has been featured in internationally acclaimed publications including *The Herald Tribune*, *The Wall Street Journal*, *The Gazette*, *The Economic Times* as well as in online publications such as *ABC News*, *USA Today*, *The Christian Science Monitor*, *Boston* and *Gulf News*.

EC-Council owns the EC-Council University, a degree granting licensed University in of New Mexico. EC-Council University is credited to be the world's first to have a Master of Security Science program.

For further information, please visit *www.eccouncil.org*

About Intense School

Intense School has been providing accelerated IT training and certification for over 12 years to more than 45,000 IT and Information Security professionals worldwide. As the founders of the accelerated training format, Intense School employs Expert Instructors who are industry-recognized leaders, authors, and experts in their fields.

Over the years Intense School has been honored with many prestigious Industry awards. Intense School has been honored with several awards including the Windows IT Pro Readers' Choice winner for Best Boot Camp Training and SC Magazine Awards for Best Security Training Program. Most recently Intense School has been recognized by EC-Council as 2009 #1 Authorized Training Center in North America.

Delivered in classrooms, at customer locations nationwide, online via Intense Online or through self-paced study, Intense School offers training on a variety of topics, including Information Security, Ethical Hacking, Forensics, Firewalls and more.

Intense School's dedicated Federal team has trained thousands of Government information and IT security personnel, empowering these professionals to maintain peak performance of both their skills and the technologies they oversee. Intense School serves all Government agencies through our GSA schedule, (GS-35F-0037P) that includes more than 200 courses delivered via multiple methods to accommodate demanding schedules. Intense School accepts GSA Smart Pay and GCPC credit cards, and participates in GSA Advantage.

The intense intensive approach is ideal for busy professionals in the IT and Information Security community, providing deep hands-on training coupled with exam preparation on several topics including CEH, ECSA, LPT, CHFI, CISSP, MCITP, CCSP, Security +, PMP, ITIL, VMware and much more.

ETHICAL HACKING

Introduction

This chapter defines ethical hacking and describes where this discipline fits into the methodology that is established throughout the CEH (Certified Ethical Hacker) exam.

This module sets the tone for the rest of the course.

These general concepts and vocabulary items must be instinctive for students while they study the rest of the material. To be successful on the exam it is extremely important to maintain a positive mindset and to understand the context of the material.

To Pass the CEH Exam You Need to . . .

- know the definition of ethical hacking
- know the concepts of threat modeling
- know the five phases of an attack
- know the concepts of vulnerability research and testing
- master the CEH Cheatsheets and practice questions!

Know the Definition of Ethical Hacking

- What is ethical hacking?

- Hacker classes

- Insider jargon

  - Try it out: Researching hacker culture

What Is Ethical Hacking?

Hacking creates the activities of curiosity. Hackers want to know how things work and are always taking a critical view about what they learn. They ask, "What else can be done with this?" or "How can this idea be combined with something else?" or "How can we take this a step farther?"

Hackers also want to know how to break things. Often, the best hacks are not based on exploiting bugs or flaws, but instead are based on wondering if the designer of the product or application truly thought of every scenario the technology could be subjected to.

Ethical hacking is about doing all of this with a defensive mindset. Our objectives are not to cause mischief, to seize control of what does not belong to us, or to superimpose our point of view onto an organization. Rather, we are looking for ways to protect our organization's assets and to facilitate improvement in any way we can.

Hacker Classes

Black hats

Black hats are usually described as the "bad guys."

White hats

White hats are what we are in the CEH class.

Grey hats

Grey hats are the most interesting hacker class. They could be hackers for hire, or they could be talented individuals that believe in full disclosure. Either way, there is a purpose of some sort behind their decisions that leaves room for philosophical argument.

Full disclosure, for example, is very controversial. If hackers innocently run across some information about a weakness in a system, they must decide what to do with that knowledge. They could publish it to a website or discussion forum, or they could go to the source of the problem and risk legal action for doing unauthorized research.

Hacktivists use their skills to fulfill a personal or group agenda. What makes them unique among other hacker types is that, in order to make their point, they must often not remain a secret. Suicide hackers are those who desire to get caught as a part of the process.

Insider Jargon

Other vocabulary terms exist within our field that can be very mysterious to those who do not study information security or its subcultures. The media, for instance, often uses these terms in very incorrect or silly ways.

TRY IT OUT

Researching Hacker Culture

Use your favorite search engine to research the following questions:

What is a "133t", "l337", or "1337"?

What are the terms "P0wn3d", "B0x3n", and "L@m3r"?

What is a "Script Kiddie"?

What is the significance of the number 2600?

What is meant by the phrase "All your base are belong to us"?

There are 10 kinds of people in this world. List them.

TRY IT OUT CHALLENGE

- These are only a few questions that could be asked. A good online reference to use for this sort of thing is "The Urban Dictionary" (http://www.urbandictionary.com/)

Know the Concepts of Threat Modeling

- Threat modeling and risk management
- Motivations and opportunities
- Different types of attack

Threat Modeling and Risk Management

A sense of how risk management works is considered prerequisite knowledge for the CEH curriculum. To set the tone for this course, it is helpful to cover a few of the basic concepts in terms of what will be covered on the CEH exam:

- Threat modeling is about determining the security issues that are most important to an organization and then identifying the possible events that could affect those issues.
- Risk management is about determining the proper course of action to take when threats are identified.

In both cases, senior management must be committed to diligent efforts in the way of assessing, planning, monitoring, testing, and following through. This part of running an organization is at the heart of the information security industry. Where the effort is lax there is usually an opportunity for an attacker to strike. The objective of the ethical hacker is to properly assess, test, and monitor all security controls and be able to provide the organization with reliable advice on what can be done to improve security levels.

Important risk management vocabulary for the CEH exam:

Threat:	Potential events, neither good nor bad, just possible
Weakness:	A flaw that leaves an asset vulnerable to attack
Exposure:	A point of access to a weakness
Vulnerability:	An instance of the exposure of a weakness
Exploit:	The act of taking advantage of a vulnerability

Motivations and Opportunities

As networks become more secure, they are often also harder to use. It is very difficult to achieve the proper balance. If a network is too secure the users will become attackers just to do their jobs. A culture of buy-in to these efforts must be driven by the leaders of organizations.

Business drivers, such as rising energy costs and competition for specialized skills, increase the demand for telecommuting solutions and mobile devices. As the perimeter of the network becomes harder to define, increased opportunities for attackers are created.

The tools of the trade in the attacking community have also become easier to use and obtain. For convenience purposes many tools are self contained on USB devices or can be run from within virtual machines. Framework tools have been designed to allow a tester to pick and choose between delivery and payload modules and the tool then assembles the exploit script automatically. Websites that exist to distribute exploit code number in the hundreds if not thousands. Some "hacking" skills are in fact becoming standard and expected knowledge for even casual computer users.

Attacking is big business. The situation is made worse by countries where certain activities either are not illegal or are out of the government's control. In many cases attackers can operate out in the open, selling their exploits on auction sites or even through store fronts. The challenge of enforcing jurisdiction on a globally connected network that has no central authority guarantees these problems will continue. Information warfare between governments and industrial espionage between corporations are also growth industries in the security field.

As long as security is seen as a cost and not as an enabling investment, many organizations would rather be compliant than secure. They are perfectly happy to do the minimum necessary to avoid paying fines or penalties, seeing that as a greater risk than anything an attacker could possibly do. In the meanwhile, botnets are setup with worldwide reach whose millions of hosts are joining these malicious networks from behind the firewalls of Fortune 500 companies. Low budgets are not the leading cause of weak security.

Different Types of Attack

Successful attacks can happen for many different reasons and can exploit weaknesses at all layers of the OSI model. Six broad categories can be used to begin to organize the discussion:

Social engineering and physical attacks

Social engineering is considered to be the most dangerous attack vector because human nature can be exploited without the need for high cost or much skill. Physical access is always possible in some way, even if the event comes from Mother Nature herself.

Network-based attacks

Many of the network protocols we use every day were not designed with security in mind. Layers of solutions have been added to mitigate these risks but they can also increase the complexity of the network. Denial of service attacks do not make the attacker much money save for extortion attacks, but they can cause great damage to the victim's reputation.

Operating system attacks

The underlying operating system of any host is vulnerable if unnecessary services are enabled and the accessible services are not properly patched. Bastion hosts (systems that have been hardened to withstand attack) and security appliances can reduce this risk but often at a higher cost than using general purpose servers and hardware.

Application-level attacks

Patching the operating systems is not enough and applications are often left to run for years without attention. Most applications receive input data from a user or other sources, and if the code to handle this input is not written carefully buffer overflows and complete system compromise are often the result.

Shrink wrap and malicious code attacks

Programming code is often reused whenever possible to reduce costs and to complete projects more quickly. Vulnerabilities that exist within the code are then spread to other applications. Worse yet, malicious code can be injected into these resources intentionally. Many other forms of malicious code exist that will be covered extensively in other chapters.

Misconfiguration attacks

Leaving systems at insecure default settings or relaxing the security levels of a product while troubleshooting a problem can leave vulnerabilities that go unnoticed for years. Overworked administrators or undertrained personnel may have the best intentions but can only do so much to properly secure a system.

Know the Five Phases of an Attack

- Reconnaissance
- Scanning
- Gaining access
- Maintaining access
- Clearing tracks

Reconnaissance

The first and most important step in an attack involves finding out as much information as possible about the TOE (Target of Evaluation). A passive information gathering approach is taken and will not raise any alarms. Patience and creativity are also necessary as this can be the longest phase of the attack.

Scanning

During the process of passive discovery, the technologies used by the TOE and a few configuration items such as external network blocks and other internal information will be known to the attacker. It might be necessary to obtain an insider perspective for a complete scan. Social engineering or physical attacks will aid the attacker in achieving this objective.

The goal of scanning is to learn as much technical data about the systems as possible. Live hosts are found and the network is footprinted. Then access points on each live host are determined. Finally, the services that are available are confirmed and the operating systems of each platform are verified. Policies and user information is gathered and, finally, vulnerabilities are assessed.

Gaining Access

If the first two phases are completed thoroughly and accurately it might be possible for the attacker to pick one exposure and exploit it correctly on the first try. This would be ideal for the attacker because the less noise made the better, as long as the objective is met.

There are many vectors (a fancy security word for choices) that the gaining access step might come from. The attack might be direct or indirect. A victim might volunteer to be attacked or be completely uninvolved. All resources, including poorly configured countermeasures and monitoring devices, are fair game if they can be used at this point.

The biggest question is whether or not completing this phase satisfies the requirements of the attacker. If not, it will be necessary to move to the next phase.

Maintaining Access

A computer could be the target of a crime or simply be used as an accessory while committing a crime. Sometimes it is necessary to compromise a host in order to perform "Vulnerability Linkage," which is also referred to as "Staging " or "Pivoting" off of one host to attack another. If an attack cannot be performed from the attacker's present location he will need a better place to attack from.

An attacker might want to establish a monit oring point, or it might be required to have repeated access to valuable data that changes over time. This phase is an extension of the gaining access phase and the skilled attacker will perform this step in a way that does not draw attention. If the goal is to maintain access over a long period of time, it is important not to break anything or the backdoor could be fixed.

Clearing Tracks

Clearing tracks is about more than just erasing evidence. It is also about not attracting attention in the first place. An attacker that does not follow all five phases of this methodology correctly risks making more noise than necessary.

Compromising log files is only the beginning. IDS (Intrusion Detection Systems) and firewall evasion techniques are challenging but often possible if the attacker has done her homework about the target.

Know the Concepts of Vulnerability Research and Testing

- The emerging research industry
  - Try it out: Researching the vulnerability databases
- The testing process
- Types of tests

The Emerging Research Industry

Security research is fast becoming a collection of highly specialized areas. Web application testing, software analysis, network testing, and forensics after the attack are just some of the high demand skill sets emerging in the information security field. Each requires its own dedication and discipline as both networks and attacks become more sophisticated.

TRY IT OUT

Researching the Vulnerability Databases

Visit two of the most prominent vulnerability databases and become familiar with what they offer:

http://cve.mitre.org

http://www.osvdb.org

Research the CVSS and become familiar with how it works:

http://www.first.org/cvss/

TRY IT OUT CHALLENGE

Perform a Google search on "Sample Penetration Testing Reports" and download two or three sample reports.

- See how they use the scoring or index systems you just researched (if they do).
- Look for what you like and don't like about each as if you were a busy customer.

There are both professional researchers working in controlled environments and underground researchers working at home or wherever their portable computers can find access. There are legal risks in doing certain kinds of research, but that does not stop most people. The motivations for putting in the time range from the joy of pursuing a challenge to gaining profit from the enterprise.

To get a sense for the growing community effort involved, begin researching the world of professional penetration testing while you pursue your CEH. This will also help you maintain the intended defense-oriented view of hacking and reveal areas of information security you might be very interested in but didn't know even existed.

The Testing Process

There are many reasons an organization might order a test. If compliance with a standard is mandated, they will perform yearly audits that involve vulnerability assessments. In other cases, threat levels need to be tested because something in their risk management process raised a concern.

Tests are conducted both internally and externally. They can be outsourced to a third party or management by an in-house team separated from the administrators. There is no one test that is better than the other, it is always a matter of cost versus value. Clients that order the test must have a clear reason for why they are doing a test and must select the best product for the task.

In all cases, a formal project management process must be followed for both complex tests and simple tests. It is critical to avoid "scope creep." It is also critical to have the proper tracking of everything that happens. The risk is worse than just wasting time and money; incomplete penetration tests can leave behind exposures that no one will think to go back and fix.

For the CEH, know this basic outline of the testing lifecycle. Rather than memorize it, make sure you can visualize the steps until you are comfortable with the order.

1. Determine the type of test required
2. Charter a project using formal project management methods
3. Draft all required legal documents
4. Approve the testing outline and strategy (in writing of course)
5. Test the communication channel, and make sure that if something goes wrong the test can be paused and the problem can be reported
6. Conduct the test
7. When the test completes, create a report
8. Securely deliver the report and archive or destroy all original copies according to client agreements
9. Schedule a follow-up test if appropriate
10. Review the entire process and look for opportunities to improve the next one

Types of Tests

For the CEH exam it is important to know the various testing types and under what circumstances they might be ordered.

Black Box tests

Black Box tests are ordered when the client wants the most realistic type of test possible. Only the sponsor of the test knows it is taking place and often times will only have contact with the testing team through a liaison.

No information is given to the team prior to the test. All they really know are the rules of engagement. For example, social engineering and physical security testing might be permitted, but no Denial of Service is allowed.

This test can be very risky and great care must be taken on the part of both the client and the consultant to protect each other and themselves. There are legal concerns as well as a great risk in something going wrong during the test. A clear communication plan and rollback procedure must be clearly established.

White Box tests

White Box tests are perhaps the most common and least invasive. Often times only the scanning phase is conducted and commercial vulnerability assessment tools are used to obtain a baseline of the present condition of the network. Many compliance standards require regular White Box tests as a routine part of yearly or quarterly audits.

Grey Box tests

Grey Box tests are specialized for a specific objective. The client might want to order a test for a particular vulnerability that was discovered during a White Box test that needs to be confirmed. Other times a particular aspect of the present security policy might be tested to see if users are compliant.

Conclusion

The CEH course is about the attack process. The primary difference between the attacker and the penetration tester is that in a business environment certain rules must be followed. Here is a brief list of just some of the contrasts:

- Pentesters will be legally bound by the "Rules of Engagement"; an attacker is limited only by nerve and imagination.
- Pentesters will be constrained by using only tools that are on an accepted list of well-known industry standards or what they have been able to license; attackers will use anything that suits their needs.
- Pentesters have a time constraint; attackers can take all the time they want as long as the target remains valuable to them.
- Pentesters have to "pull punches," meaning they usually cannot take full control of machines or cause damage; attackers only care about not getting caught or about having their access points repaired.

- Pentesters have to be able to clean up after the engagement; attackers often don't care what you discover about them after they have met their objective and have moved on to other targets.

The details involved in the pentester's perspective will be covered in the ECSA/LPT course should you pursue the full LPT certification. For the CEH exam it is important to focus on the tools and skills of an attacker, and the vocabulary and mindset of this chapter should carry through the following chapters.

## CHAPTER TWO

HACKING LAWS

Introduction

One of the best parts of choosing information security as a technical discipline is that you get to be philosophical at times. It is not enough to just know how to configure a server, follow a procedure, or troubleshoot an anomaly; you have to pay attention to what the trends and risks are and be prepared at all times to inform senior management about risk with reasoned advice.

Be curious about these legal issues and keep a diligent watch on them using current events' information such as the news outlets and RSS feeds. Professionally, this is an extremely powerful and important area.

On the exam, you will need to know what the legal acts do and be able to identify them, but you will not be asked to solve legal paradoxes or offer advice. The idea is that you know the risks and penalties for hacking in an unsafe manner.

To Pass the CEH Exam You Need to . . .

- know the legal issues of ethical hacking
- know the challenges of legal enforcement
- know the ins and outs of protecting intellectual property
- know the important legal statutes
- master the CEH Cheatsheets and practice questions!

Know the Legal Issues of Ethical Hacking

- Where does curiosity end and invasion begin?
- What differentiates white hat hacking from black hat hacking?

Where Does Curiosity End and Invasion Begin?

Computer hacking is generically defined as intentionally accessing a computer without its owner's authorization. Hacking also includes exceeding one's authorized permissions.

The Computer Fraud and Abuse Act states that whoever "intentionally accesses a computer without authorization or exceeds authorized access" is in violation of federal law. If a user compromises any type of an access control, even if it is an easily guessed password, it is considered hacking. If a user violates the terms of a warning banner displayed on a system, it is considered hacking. If anyone is caught performing either of these activities, the owner of the system as a victim may choose to press charges against the unauthorized user.

What Differentiates White Hat Hacking from Black Hat Hacking?

Black hat hackers and white hat hackers use the same techniques to gain access to a computer or a network. Both types of hackers can use any technique that is readily available in order to break into a system. However, the distinction between the two types of attackers comes from what each will do with the information that they gain as a result of their hacking activities.

Black hats will use whatever information they discover to their advantage; examples are theft of intellectual property, fraud, or some form of digital vandalism, such as defacing the website. white hats will use the information to improve the overall security architecture of the flawed system. The white hat hacker will typically present this information to the system's owner along with recommendations on how to improve the overall effectiveness of the system's security controls.

Know the Challenges of Legal Enforcement

- Legal Precedence
- Jurisdiction Issues

Legal Precedence

Until as recently as 1984, there were no U.S. laws in place outlawing crimes committed against or with a computer. In that year, the previously mentioned "Computer Fraud and Abuse Act" was passed; this legislation gave law enforcement agencies a weapon to fight computer crime with. Over time, this law was improved and other computer crime laws were passed which provided law enforcement with more *teeth* to address the ever increasing problem of computer crime.

Complicating the challenge of prosecuting computer crimes was the fact that companies would not report computer crimes when they occurred; the victimized organization would simply clean up the mess and proceed as though nothing had happened. When companies had identified the perpetrator of an attack and had proof of that individual's guilt, they would not pursue prosecution in a court of law.

The main reason for this lack of action on behalf of the victims was because going public with an IT security breach would be embarrassing to the affected organization. These companies believed that they would lose credibility in the eyes of their customers as well as with the general public if news of a successful attack came to light.

Another common reason that companies would not pursue prosecution against the guilty party was because the time and effort was not worthwhile on the part of the victimized organization. The perception by management was that going to court was often times too much trouble for the company to bear. They knew the law had not caught up with technology and each court case could take years to complete. There was a general lack of precedence to work from.

Jurisdiction Issues

A common source of attacks against private networks is the Internet. Hackers can attack websites or any other systems on the public domain with relative impunity because of the ease with which they can hide their true identity. The use of spoofed IP addresses, sites that *anonymize* the true identity of a user, and forged user accounts are all techniques that attackers use to disguise themselves.

Many attacks against domestic systems originate from international sources. It is difficult for a law enforcement agency to investigate a crime and prosecute the perpetrator if that individual is caught. In the U.S. any financial computer crimes such as those launched against banks are investigated by the U.S. Secret Service. All other computer crimes are investigated by the Federal Bureau of Investigation.

Know the Ins and Outs of Protecting Intellectual Property

- Obligations of an organization to enforce their rights
- Proprietary code and acceptable fair use
- Understand open source licenses
  - Try it out: Research intellectual property law

Obligations of an Organization to Enforce Their Rights

IP (Intellectual Property) is represented in many forms, and all of them are protected by federal law. Owners of any IP must take precautions to secure their property in order to enjoy the protection of law. The four most common examples of IP are copyrights, patents, trademarks, and trade secrets.

The first three examples are protected after the owner completes a registration process. The owners of a patent or a trademark must register their IP with the federal Patent and Trademark Office. An author of an idea must register with the Copyright Office in order to be protected by copyright law.

A trade secret is information that gives a particular company an advantage in its marketplace. An example might be the formula for a soft drink or the technology for a particular integrated circuit processor.

The owners of a trade secret must also take steps to protect their property. The owner must implement security controls to maintain the confidentiality of this secret; violation of these controls to access the trade secret represents a criminal act. If a trade secret is inadvertently published by an error on the part of the owner, then it is no longer protected under IP law.

Proprietary Code and Acceptable Fair Use

Proprietary code is typically a vendor's product offering which is sold commercially. This type of software is almost always protected by an End User License Agreement (EULA). This agreement defines the terms by which users of the software are legally bound after they purchase the product. The primary stipulation of the EULA is to prevent copies of the software from being illegally distributed. Proprietary software is the legal property of one party. It is protected by law within these licensing agreements.

In contrast to software protected by licensing agreements, there are applications which can be used on a limited basis for free by individual users. The developer of an application who chooses this arrangement usually requires a user to register the free copy of the developer's software. The developer may *request* that certain conditions be met by the user that are part of acceptable usage; the typical request is that the users not resell the software without the permission of the developer. These terms may be included in a "Read Me" file that accompanies the application, or they may be printed on the label of the application's package. It is recommended that the users of this type of software review these terms of usage before installing the code on their system.

Understand Open Source Licenses

An open source license is one that makes the source code of a computer application available to whoever is interested in enhancing the application's functions. This type of license generally does not require the author of the application to be compensated for such modifications. However, such licenses may have restrictions that may include preserving the name of the program's author.

A popular example of open source software licenses are those approved by the Open Source Initiative (OSI) based on a set of requirements called the Open Source Definition (OSD). The OSI is an organization dedicated to promoting open source software. Creation of this organization took place in 1998 after Netscape Communications Corporation published the source code for Netscape Communicator. The OSD defines the conditions that must be met for the free distribution of an application's source code that receives the approval of the OSI.

Popular open source licenses also include:

- GPL (GNU (GNU is Not UNIX) Public License)
- The BSD (Berkeley Software Distribution) License
- The Apache Software License
- MIT License

In the area of creative works there are two major licenses to become familiar with as well:

- Creative Commons (ShareAlike License)
- Copy Left (An example is the GPL)

Viral licenses require the original license to follow the work as it is shared. Usually, modification of an open source work is allowed, as long as the original attributions are retained, the modifications are stated, and the new work is not allowed to become proprietary. In other words, one cannot take a protected work from someone that intended it to remain open and close it up as an original.

In 2003, SCO sued Novell and other Linux vendors over ownership of code that IBM had donated to the Linux project. Their claim was the code belonged to them and IBM had no right to give it away. In 2007, Novell was awarded a decision that gave them ownership of UNIX and has since stated "There is no UNIX in Linux."

The reason this story is landmark to the discussion of intellectual property is that SCO could make the claims without having to reveal the source code in question during the process. They stated that revealing the code would be giving away their trade secrets to the press if that code were published. Some felt this meant an accusation could be made with impunity while hiding under a protective umbrella of other copyright laws.

This is a gross oversimplification of the case, and it is just one of many other examples to choose from. Hackers should spend time to understand and to learn the works of people that protect, in some ways, the rights to "hack."

TRY IT OUT

Research Intellectual Property Law

Read this true story that efficiently explains the origins of the open source movement and why they felt it was necessary. It is written by the person it happened to.

http://oreilly.com/openbook/freedom/ch01.html

Lawrence Lessig has written some fantastic books on the subject of IP. The book, *Free Culture*, is distributable free of cost or available for purchase through the bookseller of your choice.

http://en.wikipedia.org/wiki/Free_Culture_(book)

Scroll down to the bottom of the page and use the link to "Free Culture Download page for PDF version." A video presentation can be viewed here:

http://w2.eff.org/IP/freeculture/free.html

Know the Important Legal Statutes

- The "Computer Fraud and Abuse Act"
  - 18 U.S.C. Section 1029 "Fraud and Related Activity in Connection with Access Devices"
  - 18 U.S.C. Section 1030 "Fraud and Related Activity in Connection with Computers"
- The "Computer Misuse Act" of 1990 (United Kingdom)
- The "Freedom of Information Act"
- The "U.S. I-Spy Act"
- The "Patriot Act"
- California SB 1386
- FISMA (Federal Information Security Management Act)
- DMCA ("Digital Millennium Copyright Act")
- SOX ("Sarbanes-Oxley Act")
- GLBA ("Graham-Leach-Bliley Act")
- HIPAA ("Health Insurance Portability and Accountability Act")

The "Computer Fraud and Abuse Act"

The "Computer Fraud and Abuse Act," written in 1986 and amended in 1996, is the primary U.S. federal anti-hacking statute. It prohibits several forms of computer activity and makes them federal crimes. It is illegal for a person to knowingly access computers belonging to the federal government, to a financial institution, or to any protected computer involved in interstate or foreign communications in order to obtain classified information without authorization or access through the use of excess of authorization. Any activity that affects the proper use of the previously mentioned computers is also illegal.

Accessing a protected computer without authorization with the intent to commit fraud is a crime, and so is causing the transmission of code that intentionally damages a protected computer. The trafficking of stolen computer passwords violates this law, as well as the transmission of communications containing threats to cause damage to a protected computer.

These acts range from felonies to misdemeanors with corresponding small to large fines and jail sentences. Section 1029 of Title 18 of U.S. Code entitled "Fraud and Related Activity in Connection with Access Devices" and Section 1030, "Fraud and Related Activity in Connection with Computers," are recent enhancements to this law.

The "Computer Misuse Act" of 1990 (United Kingdom)

The United Kingdom passed the "Computer Misuse Act" in an effort to prevent certain unethical computer activities.

This law is comparable in scope to the U.S. "Computer Fraud and Abuse Act." The "Computer Misuse Act" outlaws hacking into other people's systems, misusing software, or helping a person to gain unauthorized access to protected files. This law was passed as a result of the 1984 R vs Gold *case*, which was appealed in 1988. The defendants in this case were accused of fraud and forgery after they managed to access an e-mail box belonging to one of the British royals.

The defendants argued that they were not using the compromised information for personal or financial gain, and consequently were acquitted. The appeal was successful, inspiring parliament to create a law that would make punishable the behavior committed by the two defendants.

The "Freedom of Information Act"

Section 552 of Title 5 of the U.S. Code is the "Freedom of Information Act" (FOIA).

FOIA allows any citizen the right to request access to personal records maintained by any federal agency. These agencies are required to disclose personal information upon receiving a written request, and they are expected to protect the privacy of this data. FOIA applies only to federal agencies and does apply to personal data held by Congress, the courts, or state or local government agencies.

The "U.S. I-Spy Act"

The "U.S. I-Spy Act," formally known as the "Internet Spyware Prevention Act of 2005" (H.R. 744), was passed by Congress. This law makes illegal any activity related to the unauthorized use of spyware, phishing, and other methods of using the Internet to obtain sensitive personal information without someone's knowledge. It imposes penalties on anyone convicted of using malware to obtain protected information.

The "U.S. I-Spy Act" defines "protected information" as first and last names, home or other physical addresses, e-mail addresses, telephone numbers, Social Security numbers, tax identification numbers, driver's license numbers, passport numbers, other government-issued identification numbers, credit card numbers, bank account numbers, and passwords or access codes associated with credit card or bank accounts. The bill was reintroduced in March 2007 to prosecute anyone who produces spyware.

The "Patriot Act"

The "U.S.A. PATRIOT Act," commonly known as the "Patriot Act," is an Act of Congress that President George W. Bush signed into law on October 26, 2001. The acronym stands for "Uniting and Strengthening America by Providing Appropriate Tools Required to Intercept and Obstruct Terrorism Act" of 2001.

The act expands the authority of U.S. law enforcement agencies for the stated purpose of fighting terrorism in the U.S. and abroad. Among its provisions, the "Patriot Act" increases the ability of law enforcement agencies to search telephone, e-mail communication, medical, financial, and other records; eases restrictions on foreign intelligence gathering within the U.S. expands the Secretary of the Treasury's authority to regulate financial transactions, particularly those involving foreign individuals and entities; and enhances the discretion of law enforcement and immigration authorities in detaining and deporting immigrants suspected of terrorism-related acts. The act also expands the definition of terrorism to include domestic terrorism, thus enlarging the number of activities to which the "USA Patriot Act's" expanded law enforcement powers can be applied.

California SB 1386

California Senate Bill (SB) 1386 came into effect in July of 2003. Essentially, it requires any entity conducting business in California that possesses an electronic version of individuals' personal information to notify said individuals of any breach of security relating to that data. The law describes the breach as any unauthorized access to personal information that is not encrypted.

This law also applies to any organization, regardless of their physical location, that has customers in California as well. Several other states have adopted laws that are similar to California SB 1386 in an effort to prevent identity fraud.

DMCA ("Digital Millennium Copyright Act")

The "Digital Millennium Copyright Act" (DMCA) is a U.S. copyright law that was passed in 1998. It criminalizes the production and dissemination of technology intended to circumvent measures that control access to copyrighted works. Also, it outlaws the act of circumventing an access control, whether or not there is actual infringement of the article's copyright. In addition, the DMCA heightens the penalties for copyright infringement on the Internet.

The DMCA amends U.S.C. Title 17 to extend the scope of copyright law; it also limits the liability of the Internet service providers for copyright infringement affected by their users. This law implements two 1996 treaties of the World Intellectual Property Organization (WIPO). WIPO represents 120 countries working together to protect intellectual property on a global level. The practice of implementing techniques that protect against unauthorized duplication is generically referred to as Digital Rights Management (DRM).

SOX ("Sarbanes-Oxley Act")

The "Sarbanes-Oxley Act" (SOX) of 2002 is a federal law enacted in response to a number of major corporate and accounting scandals including those affecting Enron, Tyco International, Adelphia, Peregrine Systems, and WorldCom. These scandals, which cost investors billions of dollars when the share prices of the affected companies collapsed, shook public confidence in the nation's securities markets.

The legislation establishes new or enhanced standards for all U.S. public company boards, management, and public accounting firms. It does not apply to privately held companies.

SOX contains 11 titles, or sections, ranging from additional Corporate Board responsibilities to criminal penalties, and requires the Securities and Exchange Commission (SEC) to implement rulings on requirements to comply with the new law.

The "Sarbanes-Oxley" Act establishes a new quasi-public agency, the Public Company Accounting Oversight Board (PCAOB), which is charged with overseeing, regulating, inspecting, and disciplining accounting firms in their roles as auditors of public companies. The act also covers issues such as auditor independence, corporate governance, internal control assessment, and enhanced financial disclosure.

GLBA ("Graham-Leach-Bliley Act")

The "Graham Leach Bliley Act" (GLBA) requires financial institutions to develop privacy notices and to give their customers the option to prohibit banks from sharing their information with nonaffiliated third parties. The act dictates that the board of directors is responsible for many of the security issues within a financial institution, that risk management must be implemented, that all employees need to be trained on information security issues, and that implemented security measures must be fully tested.

It also requires these institutions to have a written security policy in place.

HIPAA ("Health Insurance Portability and Accountability Act")

The "Health Insurance Portability and Accountability Act" (HIPAA) has been mandated to provide national standards and procedures for the storage, use, and transmission of personal medical information and health care data. This regulation provides a framework and guidelines to ensure security, integrity, and privacy when handling confidential medical information.

HIPAA outlines how security should be managed for any facility that creates, accesses, shares, or destroys medical information. People's health records can be used and misused in different scenarios for many reasons. As health records migrate from a paper-based system to an electronic system, they become easier to maintain, access, and transfer, but they also become easier to manipulate and access in an unauthorized manner. Traditionally, health care facilities have lagged behind other businesses in their information and network security mechanisms, architecture, and security enforcement because there was no real business need to expend the energy and money to put these items in place.

HIPAA mandates steep federal penalties for noncompliance. If medical information is used in a way that violates the privacy standards dictated by HIPAA, even by mistake, there are monetary penalties of $100 per violation, up to $25,000 per year, per standard.

If protected health information is obtained or disclosed knowingly, the fines can be as much as $50,000 and one year in prison. If the information is obtained or disclosed under false pretenses, the cost can go up to $250,000 and ten years in prison, which is the same as if there is intent to sell or use the information for commercial advantage, personal gain, or malicious harm.

Conclusion

Over the last several years, the legal issues surrounding hacking have gone from almost non-existent, to "just finally starting to get it," to being in the controversial area of favoring influential elements rather than upholding interests of the common good. There is no shortage of debate on these topics and they are almost always driven by requirements and goals rather than by true objectivity. An attacker will keep this well in mind, and will wonder "am I trying to solve the problems of the world or exploit them?"

For the CEH exam you will need to demonstrate a basic understanding of these issues and the names of the laws that were mentioned in this chapter.

In real life, you will want to apply the skills of this class in a way that neither limits your career nor subjects you to setbacks. The concept of "ethical" is relative to each person, but in this course the line is very clear. Do not P0wn3d what doesn't belong to you.

## CHAPTER THREE

FOOTPRINTING

Introduction

Footprinting is part of the reconnaissance phase of an attack and mostly involves passive information gathering.

Footprinting is something that occurs every day. Competitive intelligence gathering is a common practice among businesses trying to gain an edge. Entrepreneurs considering new ventures will perform footprinting research to determine the level of opportunity as part of the business plan. A hiring manager will footprint prospective employees, a customer can footprint businesses before seeking their services, and people can research each other before going out on a date.

An entire industry of security testing exists around the footprinting phase alone. Businesses hire firms to perform footprinting to research their reputation, celebrities research to find out if their brand is being abused, and executives hire consultants to perform a penetration test on their identities.

To Pass the CEH Exam You Need to . . .

- know the information gathering methodology
- know several different passive information gathering techniques
- know how to use DNS and the Regional Internet Registrars
- master the CEH cheatsheets and practice questions!

Know the Information Gathering Methodology

- Unearth initial information
- Locate the network range
  - Try it out: Utilize the RFCs to understand network ranges
- Ascertain active machines
- Discover open ports and access points
- Detect operating systems
- Uncover services on ports
  - Try it out: Banner grabbing
- Map the network
  - Try it out: Collecting data

Unearth Initial Information

Once the TOE (Target of Evaluation) is determined, the first steps of footprinting include basic Internet searches and research through other more creative sources.

Information about people within the company might be used in social engineering attacks. Technical information will assist attackers with forming a strategy for internal scanning and eventually for gaining access. For the attacker, the goal of this step is to learn as much as possible about the target.

Do not determine what is important or not at this point, just gather data. It is critical that this step be conducted as thoroughly as possible. Valuable information gained at this stage makes shorter work of the remaining steps of information gathering. Often, it is impossible to know how accurate the rest of the information is without data gained initially that can verify the findings.

Locate the Network Range

The attacker needs to know what external access is possible to the target. The whois record for the target's domain might reveal an assigned network block. DNS walking techniques will uncover hosts that are possibly accessible. Traceroutes to these hosts might reveal additional infrastructure.

It is often very helpful if the attacker understands the basics of routing and IP subnetting. The target organization might be splitting an address into additional subnets. These subnets might be accessible behind the perimeter.

The sum total of all connected networks under a summary address within the control of one organization is called the AS (Autonomous System). Traffic on the Internet can be routed to the target's ISP (Internet Service Provider) using the ASN (Autonomous System Number) of the ISP, which then routes the traffic to the AS of its customer. If a large organization is registered as an ISP and has been issued an ASN, their whois record might show this information. It is likely that the IP block they have been issued spreads out to serve other organizations or customers.

TRY IT OUT

Utilize the RFCs to Understand Network Ranges

RFCs (Requests for Comment) are the documents that describe the open protocols we use every day in networking. For the CEH exam, it is helpful to read several of them. Many will be mentioned throughout the course. Follow the links to read the following RFCs that relate to locating network ranges.

RFC 1393—Traceroute using an IP option

http://tools.ietf.org/html/rfc1393

RFC 1918—Address allocation for private Internets

http://tools.ietf.org/html/rfc1918

RFC 1930—Guidelines for creation, selection, and registration of an Autonomous System (AS)

http://tools.ietf.org/html/rfc1930

Ascertain Active Machines

Once the ranges of addresses have been determined, it is important to know what hosts are actually reachable and responsive. A large organization may have been issued a class B range, yet have only a dozen or so hosts visible from the Internet. It would be useless to perform complete vulnerability scans on a range that is 99 percent vapor.

The attacker wants to be careful not to exploit vulnerabilities on hosts that don't belong to the target unless it was discovered during initial information gathering that a connection exists between them, such as the case with extranets or VPNs.

Since load balancers and server clusters will affect the results of these scans, gathering initial information will help analyze the results of this step.

Discover Open Ports and Access Points

Once the responsive hosts are determined, the next step is to find out if there are a variety of options for access. Do not take for granted that expected services exist on these ports, just look for all the ways traffic can be sent from the point of attack toward the targets.

Traffic filters will affect the results of any port scan; from the traceroutes the attacker should have some idea where these firewalls are located. When you are sending traffic into a network segment the open ports on the firewall are a subset of what might be accessible on the hosts on the other side.

There is a difference between what ports are open on a system and which ones can be reached from the point of the scan, which is what the attacker is trying to determine at this point. It might be necessary to gain access to better positions on the network.

Detect Operating Systems

From the list of accessible ports, clues present themselves about the operating system that is running on each target. Examples of these cases will be covered in the scanning chapter.

The value of this step is simply that it doesn't make sense to scan a host for vulnerabilities that are operating system dependant if the OS itself is not known. This information also gives the attacker an idea of what software is running behind the services once they are confirmed. For example: If an open port 80 really is a web service, and the OS is Linux, then the software running the HTTP protocol is likely to be Apache.

Uncover Services on Ports

This step goes hand in hand with detecting the operating system, but all services are adjustable. Services can live on any port their administrator wants them to live on. Verifying the services on ports involves both making sure the expected service is truly there and identifying what is listening on less familiar ports.

For example: Perhaps port 43671 happens to be open. What service lives there? A quick Google search might not reveal anything interesting and, according to *https://isc.incidents. org*, there is nothing in the CVE (Common Vulnerabilities and Exposures) for it either. (At the time of this writing.)

Try to Telnet into the port and throw a couple carriages (press enter twice). Maybe you still don't see anything. Try slashes or other special characters. This is mysterious. Perhaps it is an illicit server or a low interaction honeypot. If so, you should get off that host now.

Banner grabbing is the most common way to determine if a service on an accessible port is actually what is expected. It often reveals information about the service which can help in determining the operating system as well.

TRY IT OUT

Banner Grabbing

This exercise can be done from either a Linux or Windows host, but it will be easier in Linux because what you type can be seen. Open a command shell and connect to a host that has an open port 80 (any web server).

```
telnet [target ip] 80
```

Issue the HTTP commands that will give you a banner grab.

```
GET / HTTP/1.0
```

Hit enter twice and view the results.

TRY IT OUT CHALLENGE

Whenever you connect to a port using Telnet, the best results come from issuing commands that the listening service will understand. Research a couple of other TCP protocols through the RFCs for commands that would work in a Telnet session.

Map the Network

This step just means the attacker takes everything that has been gathered and organizes it. There is too much information about the target at this point to keep it all in your head, so document it. Draw diagrams, make lists, and organize notes.

TRY IT OUT

Collecting Data

A typical attacker will not want to use expensive software like Microsoft Office. The open source suite "Open Office" could certainly be used for many things and is available for both Windows and Linux systems.

Many other freeware tools exist to compile a complete set of documentation tools. Many of them will even run directly from a USB key. Take a few moments to compile a collection of freeware tools that would allow you to document everything found during the reconnaissance phase of an attack. Use your favorite search engine to locate the tools but be careful where you download them from. A great place to start is: *http://www.snapfiles.com*

- A tool for drawing network diagrams
- A screenshot utility
- An outliner (hierarchal organizing of text)
- A Gantt chart maker (for scheduling)
- A document viewer (.pdf, .doc, .xsl, .ppt)
- A file encryption tool

Know Several Different Passive Information Gathering Techniques

- Competitive intelligence gathering
  - Try it out: Competitive intelligence gathering
  - Try it out: "Privacy is dead, get over it"

Competitive Intelligence Gathering

Industrial espionage is alive and well. Businesses are constantly trying to find out what other businesses are doing and what they know while the working folk that get traded between them cross-pollinate the database naturally.

There are many reasons for conducting this research that are both heavily driven by business and by the interest of attackers. In this area it is hard to tell the difference. As a result, sometimes "attack" is confused with "persistent, resourceful, or just doing your homework."

This fact guarantees that there is almost always a lot to be learned about a target. Gathering is big business while communicating that information is basically free.

Search engines like Google can only index what their spiders can see as they crawl. As large as they are, the estimated percentage of what has actually been indexed is in the single digits by some accounts. The "Darknet" is the term used to describe what the search engines cannot reach. The important thing to remember is that information gathering is not just about Googling. The following is a brief list of a few other ideas that will be covered on the CEH exam.

- Press releases
- Job sites
- Chamber of commerce
- People searches
- Edgar Database (Securities Exchange Commission)
- Financial information
- Competition
- Citizen journalists
- IP Address Location
- Domain information
- Traceroute
- Layer 4 Traceroute
- E-mail tracking
- Offline browsing (harvesting)
- Robots.txt
- Old copies of a website
- Advanced Google searches
- USENET

TRY IT OUT

Competitive Intelligence Gathering

Pick a publicly held organization to perform passive intelligence on. Be sure to visit at least the following sites:

Financial data: The Edgar Database

http://www.sec.gov/edgar.shtml

Archived websites: The "Way Back Machine"

http://www.archive.org/index.php

Determine Web server information: Netcraft

`http://news.netcraft.com/`

Look for leaks about internal processes: The Consumerist & Wikileaks

`http://consumerist.com/`

`http://wikileaks.org`

Search USENET: Google Groups

`http://groups.google.com/`

Look for rumors: Yahoo

`http://finance.yahoo.com/`

TRY IT OUT

"Privacy Is Dead, Get Over It"

Search on Google Video or YouTube for a video entitled "Privacy Is Dead, Get Over It," which is a talk given by Steve Rambam, a private investigator. He discusses footprinting and personal information leakage that anyone can perform, not techniques that require special clearance or licenses. The video is approximately 113 minutes and is a must view.

Know How to Use DNS and the Regional Internet Registrars

- What do we expect to find here?
- Understand the Regional Internet Registrars (RIRs)
- Using Whois
  - Try it out: Obtain a whois record
- Understand the SOA
- Records within the zone file
- Understanding DNS (from the attacker's point of view)
  - Try it out: Attempt a zone transfer

What Do We Expect to Find Here?

When businesses want to be found easily they need to participate in a directory system. IP addresses on the Internet are hard to remember and change often, so a better solution is to purchase a "domain" and to map accessible hosts to IP addresses through a worldwide directory known as the DNS (Distributed Name System).

When a domain is purchased, a record is kept regarding the owner of the domain. It is a violation of the ICANN (Internet Corporation for Assigned Names and Numbers) terms of service to have incorrect information in this directory, and if caught the domain could be forfeited.

Regional responders called CERTs (Computer Emergency Response Teams) rely on the contact information within these documents to notify organizations when they are the unwitting participants in security incidents such as denial of service attacks.

This also means that the information within a whois record should reveal important contact information that an attacker might use as well. There are services (for a fee) that will proxy this information so the VIPs (Very Important People) can remain anonymous without risking having the domain ownership taken away.

Many companies bought their domains several years ago and have long since forgotten that every ten years there is a renewal process. This is important for two reasons: If the attacker tries to use the TOC (Technical Point of Contact) in a social engineering ploy, yet that person hasn't worked for the company in several years, he will look like an idiot. Otherwise many domain kiters (domain tasters) lurk with automated tools that will catch, within moments of expiration, that your billion dollar domain has expired. They will gladly return it to you for a fee which is conveniently about a $1 dollar less than the court costs of suing them for it.

Understand the Regional Internet Registrars (RIRs)

ICANN issues domain names through Regional Internet Registrars. Customers purchase domains through third party companies that ultimately process the transactions through these entities:

- ARIN — North America
- APNIC — Asia Pacific Region
- LACNIC — Southern and Central America and Caribbean
- RIPE NCC — Europe, the Middle East, and Central Asia
- AfriNIC — Africa

Using Whois

Whois is somewhat like a "whitepages for the Internet." When a domain is purchased a record is kept that contains important information about the ownership of that domain. Technical and administrative contacts are documented along with the IP address of the primary and secondary name servers that host the zone for the domain.

A *zone* file is nothing more than a text file that contains information records about how to contact hosts within a domain. For example, to reach the web server within the domain "example.dom" there would have to be a record of what IP address that server can be reached at. This record is stored in a file that is accessed through a DNS server when a client needs to know how to reach it. The first step in this process is establishing the authority through which the domain exists. Look for the "NS record" within the whois document. This represents the "Name Server" for the zone, the IP address of where the best information possible about the domain can be found.

TRY IT OUT

Obtain a Whois Record

Open a command shell in a Linux host and try using the whois command.

```
whois [example domain]
```

TRY IT OUT CHALLENGE

Make sure that in your whois record you can locate the following pieces of information:

- Technical and administrative points of contact
- Network block (not always given)
- Name servers (NS records)

Understand the SOA

The Start of Authority (SOA) is the best place to obtain information about a domain for reasons discussed later in this section. On the CEH exam it will be necessary to understand how an SOA record works. It is not necessary, however, to know how to administer DNS or create a zone from scratch. Focus on the fields in the example below:

```
lab.dom. IN SOA ns.lab.dom. (200030432 172800 3600 1209600 3600)
```

200030432	is the serial number
172800	is the refresh rate
3600	is the retry timer
1209600	is the expiry timer
3600	is the time to live in cache

- The serial number increments by one every time the zone is updated. The secondary DNS server checks the serial number to see if an update is needed. Attackers want to compromise the primary server because this is where the zone file is always managed.
- The refresh time is how often the secondary looks for an update.
- The retry timer is how long the secondary will wait for an update if the primary did not respond to the last request.
- The expiry timer is how long the secondary server will tolerate not hearing from the primary before it considers the zone to be dead.
- The time to live is the amount of time this record should remain in the cache of other servers that remember these records.

Records Within the Zone File

When an attacker is manually asking for resource records from a Start of Authority, the following record types are the most useful:

A	Host	Host name to IP address
MX	Mail	Host name of the mail exchanger for the domain
CNAME	Canonical	Alias name for a host
PTR	Reverse	Host name for an IP address
SOA	Start of Authority	Defines the zone

Understanding DNS (From the Attacker's Point of View)

Every host in a domain is represented by an information record in a zone file. A client application such as a web browser also has the ability to call a *resolver* when it needs DNS information to complete a connection. The resolver first checks to see if it already knows the required answer. If not, it asks the locally configured DNS server. If that server does not have the answer it can forward the request to another one and eventually an answer should be provided back to the resolver.

If the resolver already knows the answer it will be held in one of two places: the hosts file or in cache. The hosts file contains static entries of host names to IP address mappings. Attackers that target the clients will often try to rewrite the hosts file because it is the first place the resolver will look. For example, when a host tries to contact *www.virusupdate.com* to obtain the latest updates to its antivirus software, it might end up at 0.0.0.0 which is nowhere. Since an answer was found, no further effort from the resolver will happen. The resolver does not realize the client went to nowhere because that is not in its job description.

Rewriting the hosts file on the client is a common time-honored technique of malware. Another one is to poison the cache. If a resolver learns of information, it will remember the answer for a short while in case it is asked again within a short time period. The problem is that sometimes it will accept answers to questions it didn't even ask! An attacker spews out lies and the resolver simply believes them without question.

If the resolver cannot find an answer for the client locally it must reach out to a DNS server. If the local server has the answer it will just respond back. If not, the server then is obligated to ask for help. This is where it gets complicated.

There are two ways a server can ask for assistance. The first is called *recursive query*. The resolver asks one server, who asks another if it doesn't know, and so on until someone finally knows the answer. In this sequence, a full answer to the original question is required. If attackers simply throw in thousands of requests that there are no answers to, the DNS servers in the recursive chain will be kept busy for awhile.

The other way to do it is called *iterative query*. If the resolver wants to know how to reach *www.example.com,* it will ask from the top down. Starting with one of the 13 root servers that run the worldwide DNS, it asks, "Do you have advice on how I can find 'com'?" Once the reply is given it will ask that resource, "Do you have advice about example?" Then it will ask the final resource, "Who is www?" In this sequence, the DNS servers can give advice rather than complete answers, but it places a large burden on the root name servers.

So we are back to cache. The most efficient way to answer questions is not to go to the original source each time but to the nearest person that has an answer. All of this information leads to an understanding that DNS from the attackers' point of view has to do with their objective.

If they want to hijack a network they poison the DNS cache where they can. When a victim tries to visit certain websites the resolvers will be happy with what they learn and inform the client of the answer. Host "www" in domain example.com is at IP address [1.2.3.4] or the address of the malicious website that has been copied from the original but augmented with bad stuff and placed on a compromised server.

If the attackers are not yet at that stage, and they are still in the information gathering phase, they will be looking for a zone transfer or will be scripting out a way to enumerate the hosts and sub-domains of the zone.

Obtaining a zone transfer is gold to attackers because it saves them days' worth of work. Most DNS servers are not vulnerable to entire zone transfers but it is so easy that it is certainly worth a shot.

TRY IT OUT

Attempt a Zone Transfer

Open a command shell in a Windows host and use the "nslookup" command.

```
nslookup
> server [IP of DNS server to query]
> ls -d [example domain]
```

Open a command shell in a Linux host and use the "dig" command to attempt a zone transfer.

```
dig @[IP of DNS server to query] [example domain] AXFR
```

Open a command shell in a Linux host and use the "host" command to attempt a zone transfer.

```
host -t AXFR [example domain] [IP of DNS Server to query]
```

TRY IT OUT CHALLENGE

Make sure that in your whois record you can locate the following pieces of information:

- Change the command arguments to query for different types of records.
- Setup a DNS that you know is vulnerable to zone transfers and try these tools. Then fix the server so it will not give out zone transfers and try again.

Conclusion

As we discuss the information gathering methodology and move into scanning and enumeration, the line between internal and external networks becomes blurry. The attacker must have a clear point of view; a good position to scan from. For the CEH exam, just roll with the punches. When given scenario questions, do not read into them. Just imagine you are in a short conversation with coworkers and you are late for a meeting. Provide the most direct answer to whatever they are asking and keep moving.

Information gathering is the cornerstone of every attack. It is not the most fun, and it takes a lot of patience. The reconnaissance and scanning phases of an attack or Black Box penetration test can take up to 80 percent of the total time spent on the engagement. As we move forward in this book the reasons for this amount of time needed will become clearer.

In the CEH program it is always important to be "connecting the dots." Five thousand hacker tools and websites by themselves might give attackers an advantage because they know of resources that might penetrate the defenses of the target. But without some imagination and critical thinking the tools are just toys. A hacker is always asking, "If I do this, what could I then do next?"

GOOGLE HACKING

Introduction

Google hacking *means using the extraordinary power of Google's Internet indexing enterprise in order to obtain information about potential targets. The sublimely simple interface of Google, introduced in 1997, is the front-end of a massive global network of servers that cache, index, and categorize the entire Internet, $24 \times 7 \times 365$. It swallows anything it finds, whether or not the owner meant it for public consumption.*

Google is not the only search engine on the web, but it is the largest. A good security tester should use several search engines, but will probably use Google more than any other. This is part of the information gathering phase and will be combined with techniques that were discussed in the previous chapter.

With the use of a limited number of search operators and querying techniques, an attacker can freely use this huge array of computers in order to determine a wide range of information about a target. Think of the Google database as a form of Open Source Spy Network and Warehouse. It is a spy network that is tireless.

To Pass the CEH Exam You Need to . . .

- know what the Google toolset offers
- know what you are looking for
- know about some of the other Google tools
- master the CEH cheatsheets and practice questions!

Know What the Google Toolset Offers

- Why is Google an essential hacker's tool?
- Basic Google hacking techniques
- Google querying syntax

Why Is Google an Essential Hacker's Tool?

Google is an essential hacker's tool because it provides a degree of mobility and anonymity while a hacker is footprinting a target. There are two aspects of Google that specifically support this: Google's caching feature and the Google language translation page.

Google maintains three copies of everything that its crawler can find. This provides enough redundancy that nothing they find is ever lost. The crawler (also called a spider) returns to popular domains so often that new content is often indexed within minutes of being accessible. A query of the contents in Google's cache does not register on the target's log files. However, whether Google will admit to keeping records of searches or not, it would be naïve to assume they don't. Google is an advertising company.

Further stealth activity is provided by the Google translation page, *www.google.com/translate*. By typing a URL into the field provided, Google will pull up the entire contents of the web page, albeit translating it based on the language choices you have made. As far as the target website knows, however, the query is made from Google's servers, providing you inadvertently with a free anonymizer service. Want to purchase a malicious website toolkit from a company in Russia but can't read the Russian website? No problem.

Basic Google Hacking Techniques

Google hacking is both easy and complex. Young children don't know of a world that isn't searchable and almost instinctively use Google without hesitating. Unfortunately, this also opens them up to a very adult world far sooner than desired, and in some cases to things even parents do not imagine exist. Although Google provides a filter, it can be toggled on and off so easily that its main use is to keep adults from accidently encountering material they would simply prefer not to see.

The complexity is in understanding a range of techniques, ways of combining those techniques, and understanding the world of vulnerabilities in an ever-expanding landscape of new possibilities. The more visible something is, the more Google will pay attention to it. Its spider favors indexing files that are linked from other files. What separates Google *hacking* from just querying is having the creativity to dig beyond the presented results of a basic search in order to find things of higher interest to the attacker.

First, we will look at the core techniques and then we will get into key information that testers, hackers, and students studying for the CEH exam ought to know. Knowing a few techniques behind structuring an appropriate query can yield great rewards.

The following is an exam-relevant, but not comprehensive, list of techniques that leverage Google's indexing mechanism.

- Basic information grinding
- Link exploring
- Group tracing
- Finding directory listings
- System/application versioning
- Directory traversal
- Incremental substitution
- Extension walking

Basic information grinding

There are several obvious ways to leverage Google in order to support target profiling and mapping. An easy way to assess the scope of a target is to use the *site* operator as follows: *site:example.dom*. This will return everything indexed at the example.dom domain.

You can also refine your search by combining the other techniques discussed in this chapter. For now, experiment with tuning the search by asking for all pages on the website except the ones containing *www*. This employs the Boolean operator NOT, also expressed with a "-" sign as in "*site:example.dom –www.example.dom*".

Link exploring

If the target links to another site, there may be some kind of trust relationship that may be exploitable. The link operator "link:" can be used to determine all sites that link to the target site.

Group tracing

"Google Groups" is an archive of Usenet purchased from DejaNews in 2001 that continues today. Usenet, an application on the Internet that dates back to 1979. Is a discussion-based service where people post messages arranged into *newsgroups*. Usenet operates using a unique protocol (NNTP) and client-server software. It is typically blocked from direct access from most business networks (TCP 119) but is completely accessible through the Google website.

Usenet was once commonly used for free community-based technical support. An administrator would post a question and seek the advice of other readers of that newsgroup. Social engineering techniques were also common place as attackers coerced more information from the original poster until source code, entire log and configuration files, or other forms of sensitive information were posted. Forever.

When participants argue over Usenet it is called a *Flame War*. Many administrators have been drawn into this waste of time that generates information the attacker can use if it isn't too old. Contact information is also often posted in these discussions.

Presently the overwhelming amount of Usenet activity is in the *alt.binaries* hierarchy. This area is used to transfer large binary files that have been encoded into multipart text messages. It is a prime source of leakage of intellectual property such as warez (Pirated software). Much of this material is also riddled with malware itself.

Finding directory listings

Google attempts to index the entire publicly accessible Internet. In doing so, it catalogues the existence of pages that allow directory browsing. Such pages have the text *index of* in the title as well as the terms *parent directory, name,* and/or *size* presented in the body.

Asking Google to return all pages that have *intitle:index.of "parent directory"* will yield a list of mostly pages which allow directory browsing. Of course, this is giving away too much information.

System/application versioning

Systems and applications can be fingerprinted by how they respond to requests. In many cases, applications advertise their presence in the way they publish web pages. For example, if you know that a vulnerable version of application *x* publishes web pages that say "Powered by Application *x*," then the attacker may be one step away from an exploit.

Directory traversal

This involves exploring a target's indexed data to find and *traverse* into directories of interest. For example, investigate the results of the following query: *intitle:index.of inurl:"/admin/*"*, and you will find the ability to browse potentially interesting directories with titles like "admin." Now *traverse* to other directories by abbreviating the URL, and you might be presented with paths to directories that are not necessarily indexed, but might be of even more value.

Incremental substitution

With this technique, the attacker looks for potential numerical patterns within a query result in order to guess at files in locations that are not being indexed. For example, if the results provide a filename of */xx/yy/users01.doc*, the attacker may want to test for the existence of a *//xx//yy/users02.doc*.

Extension walking

This technique takes advantage of the tendency to name files in the same location similarly. For example, developers will rename a file to save it for future reference rather than commit the changes. This is often done by renaming the file extension to ".*bak*", and can lead to locating files with source codes, database info, or other tidbits that were not intended for public consumption.

Google Querying Syntax

You will see the term *Advanced Operators* applied to some Google elements. This is largely because they are on the advanced page on the Google search engine in a GUI format. Here's a quick list of the pertinent Google query operators (note that there are more, but they are less relevant to those using Google for security/hacking reasons):

Operator	Example	Resultants
BASIC SEARCHES		
Using **OR** or | (note: the word *OR* must be capitalized)	*cracking passwords OR WEP*	Results on cracking passwords or cracking WEP.
" "	"default password"	The exact phrase default password.
the − (minus) sign preceding one word	hacker -golf	The word *hacker* but NOT the word *golf*.
the + (plus) sign	hacker +cracker	Forces the inclusion of the word *cracker* in the search
the − (minus) sign joining two words	fortune-telling	All forms of the term, whether spelled as a single word, a phrase, or hyphenated.
RESTRICT SEARCHES		
	site:irs.gov	Returns every indexed page within the domain irs.gov
filetype: or **ext:**	filetype:pdf "elite hacker"	Finds all pdfs indexed with term *elite hacker.*
link:	link:www.2600.com	Finds all pages with links to www.2600.com.
ALTERNATIVE QUERY TYPES		
cache:	cache:www.irs.gov	Shows Google's cached version of the U.S. Internal Revenue Service home page.
related:	related:www.2600.com	Finds websites related to the 2600.com website.
RESTRICT SEARCHES TO SITES WHERE QUERY WORDS APPEAR		
allintitle:	allintitle: Google Advanced Operators	Search for pages with titles containing *Google*, *Advanced*, and *Operators*. All query words must appear in the title of the page.
intitle:	cracker intitle:index.of	Searches for pages with *index of* in title (note that a period is a wild card, and can represent any character) and the word *cracker* on the page. Interestingly enough, Google will also include results with just the word *crack*.
allinurl:	allinurl:index.of cracker	Searches for pages containing *index of* and the term *cracker* in the URL.
inurl:	exploit inurl:crack	Searches for pages in which the URL contains the word *crack* and the word *exploit* on the page.

Know What You Are Looking for

- Types of information an attacker wants

Types of Information an Attacker Wants

Good hacking is part art and part science. Sometimes the most valuable data in a security test is found by just stumbling into the right stuff. That said, the main goal of Google hacking is to find information about a target's potential vulnerabilities. In some cases, what a developer puts out as a feature soon becomes vulnerable and might expose a system to information disclosure, manipulation, or destruction.

Google hacking queries can roughly be categorized into the following areas:

- Advisories and vulnerabilities
- Vulnerable files
- Vulnerable servers
- Web server footholds and login portals
- Sensitive directories
- Error messages
- Network data
- Sensitive e-commerce data
- Various online devices

Advisories and vulnerabilities

These searches can help locate vulnerable servers. In many cases these are product- or version-specific. Vendors will post information about vulnerabilities and provide a patch or a work-around. While this is helpful for organizations with great patching policies and procedures, these warnings/advisories provide an endless supply of potential points of entry for malicious attackers. There is an ever-increasing number of specific searches that will help you find these vulnerable systems. You just need to know what may be unique about the published pages of these systems.

If you know that a vulnerable version of application *x* always has a directory in a searchable URL called */buggyapp/*, then query Google for *inurl:buggyapp*, and see what sites show up.

Vulnerable files

Some applications or platforms produce files by default that contain vulnerabilities and/or sensitive information or produce files that are clear indicators of the existence of such vulnerabilities. Also, some administrators may think that sensitive files are not web-accessible when, in fact, they are. Such files can contain high value information like passwords, usernames, and other critical data mistakenly (or intentionally) published on the web.

A very simple exercise is to Google for *username\userid\employee.ID.* Also try *password\passcode.*

Vulnerable servers

These searches reveal servers with specific vulnerabilities. Keeping an eye on vendor vulnerability reports (such as from secunia and bugtraq) and then researching the searchable signatures of these systems are ways some hackers look to take advantage of the gap between the report and the time to patch.

A real common tag for many servers is "Powered by." Searching for "Powered by application *x*" is a simple way of finding loads of potentially vulnerable servers.

Web server footholds and login portals

These queries are used to find administrative or login pages for various services. Consider them the front door of a website's more sensitive functions or of a user's personal data.

For example, you can try: *"inurl:/admin/login.asp"* to find several servers with potentially vulnerable login portals if you combine it with the site: operator.

This of course can be narrowed down, but think of the attacker's comfort in knowing that a door can easily be located that might succumb to a brute force attack and allow remote administrative login.

Sensitive directories

Google can help you identify directories that can be mined for important data, potentially exposing the target to social engineering or network attacks. Obviously, a simple query of *inurl:admin* will yield a potentially rich set of targets.

Error messages

Some default and some custom error messages provide significant information useful to an attacker, such as databases that will give you critical namespace information. Just a basic query of *intitle:error\warning site:example.dom* (translation: return all pages on the *example.dom* site with the word *error* or *warning* in the title) can be a good start.

Network data

Firewall logs, honeypot logs, network information, IDS logs, and other data from network and security devices can be essential in further penetration. Knowing what to look for (and having Google do all of the dirty work for you) facilitates proper mapping of the target. For example, to locate Belkin Cable/DSL routers, try *intitle:"wbem" compaq login,* which locates HP Insight Management Agents. Another favorite of Google hackers today seems to be the search for Internet-accessible security cameras using *inurl:"ViewerFrame?Mode=refresh".*

Sensitive e-commerce data

Google can be used to run queries that reveal online shopping data such as customer data, suppliers, orders, credit card numbers, credit card data, and more.

Various online devices

Google can help identify the presence of printers, video cameras, and various other devices accessible via the web.

Know About Some of the Other Google Tools

- Google labs
  - Try it out: Visit Google labs
- Google reader
  - Try it out: Setup Google reader
- Search examples
  - Try it out: Google search examples

Google Labs

It has been said that the employees of Google are given 20 percent of their work time to pursue ideas of personal interest that relate to their positions with Google. Because the company celebrates innovation and creativity, many projects come to light from these efforts that are a bit off the beaten path but tap into the main Google database all the same.

TRY IT OUT

Visit Google Labs

Visit Google labs and explore the current projects.

```
http://www.googlelabs.com/
```

Google reader

One of the best ways to stay in touch with an overwhelming amount of daily information is to scan the daily RSS feeds. There are many standalone tools for this, but Google reader provides one of the best. With the addition of the Google Gears plugin the feeds can be downloaded and read offline.

TRY IT OUT

Setup Google Reader

You need to create an account with Google first, then log into:

```
http://reader.google.com
```

To get started, visit the following sites and locate the orange "RSS" button or a link that says "Feeds." Click the link and copy the URL to your clipboard. Return to Google reader and in the upper left corner click "Add a Subscription." Paste the URL into the box. Once you have collected several of your favorite sites you will want to view this every day (you can collect hundreds, but here are three to get started).

```
http://www.theregister.com
```

```
http://www.schneier.com/blog
```

```
http://www.slashdot.org
```

Google search by number

Typing in certain types of numbers or other symbolic data can automatically provide results. These include:

- Area codes
- Weather [zip code or city]
- Zip code
- Package tracking
- Flight tracking
- Vehicle information
- Patent search
- FAA airplane registration numbers
- UPC codes
- FCC equipment IDs
- Time [city]
- [food], [city]
- [name], [city]
- [value] [unit of measurement] to [unit of measurement]

Google alerts

One day this author received an e-mail from a company officer that noticed my name had appeared in an article and was indexed on Google. I knew he was too busy to be doing searches on my name specifically, but it turns out he didn't have to. Google alerts allow you to put in keywords so that if new content appears they will e-mail the results automagically to the interested person.

This fact should make you think twice about posting those photographs of yourself taken at the political rally. Google alerts mean you have to stand by what you do or not do it at all. You cannot always know who is cyber-stalking you. Attackers can monitor anything they want and have the results delivered each morning to peruse with their morning coffee.

Google for educators

Many of these tools are dangerous in that they are so cool the attacker will get caught up in playing with them and just poke around for hours.

- Google Earth
- Google Maps
- Google Sky
- Google Sketchup

Google for business

Google provides an entire mobile office suite for business people on the go that includes full integration with the Android operating system that can run on mobile devices. Google wants to own everything we do.

It was mentioned earlier that Google is foremost an advertising company, so the risks to security for someone that volunteers to integrate these services is as much related to the drivers of marketing and the big business of information leakage as opportunities for malicious intent.

- Google Docs
- iGoogle
- desktop gadgets
- gmail, gtalk, video and voice communications
- Google moderator
- the Google G1 phone running the android operating system

The android operating system is designed to be ported to many devices. This includes home appliances and entertainment mediums. One day, Google might know what is in your refrigerator and what you are cooking in your oven. Android is an open source operating system so the possibilities are endless as long as the Google API (Application Programming Interface) is available to it. Couple this with fiber to the home, and other players like Cisco becoming entertainment companies, and it is easy to see how we are just getting started in terms of data exposure.

Google more

At this point it is a waste of dead trees to keep listing more Google tools. Visit the Google home page and look in the upper left corner. Find a link that says "More" and continue to explore.

Search Examples

Now that you know the basic concepts and techniques behind Google hacking, and you have an idea about what type of information you would want to look for as an attacker, it is time to dig deeper into what you can accomplish by combining different techniques and Google querying syntax. The following page contains the more interesting queries that CEH candidates should get to know.

TRY IT OUT

Google Search Examples

Search the Intense School website for information about CEH and Steven DeFino.

```
site:intenseschool.com "Instructor of the year" | "Steven DeFino"
```

(Continued)

The operator: keyword pair does not always have to come first. To look for places that serve stromboli in your area try this:

```
stromboli loc:[Example Street Address]
```

Now try some of these searches, substituting your own data for what is in the square brackets. Try to combine some of them in creative ways:

```
inurl:"ViewerFrame?Mode=refresh"
intitle:[keywords will appear in the title html tag]
inurl:[keywords will appear in the resource path]
phonebook:[555-555-5555]
ports 1..1023
dictionary:flotsam and jetsam
calculator: 42 * 1000
90210
```

From here, there are so many possibilities that we have to cut them off somewhere. Spend one evening of study carefully working through the information in this chapter. Mix and match operators and keywords.

The whitespace (space characters) matters a lot in Google searches. If you don't see the results you are looking for, then experiment with spaces and adding quotes around phrases. Google typically ignores words like *the* which is something to keep in mind as well.

Conclusion

Google's spider has been so effective that the entire notion of copyright law and intellectual property has been challenged. Google doesn't take ownership of a photograph, for example, but they own the data that represents the knowledge that the photograph exists and how it can be viewed online. They don't own your identity, but they do own the data that has been recorded from your every online move.

As web cameras become more and more commonly integrated with Google Earth, the physical world will soon be as easy to index as our data bits. The Google crawler is learning OCR (Optical Character Recognition) and facial recognition skills, so don't believe that locking data up in images will protect it for much longer.

Imagine how upset people would get if a government tried to accomplish what Google is doing. Every time people post information about their family vacations or the party over the weekend, or update their MySpace page or other social network profile, it is archived, and much of the time we volunteer the information.

The current trend of blogging and twittering, and the need people have to speak their minds on anything whether the thought is large or small, is fascinating to a Google hacker. People aren't anonymous when they want to be seen and they forget that everything they do will last long after they change their opinions.

Have you ever watched a 24-hour news cycle and wondered why everyone is reporting the same stories? Even the silly funny stuff on YouTube or something strange in the first five hits of a timely Google search is repeated inanely all day long as everyone copies from each other. Hackers rise above this noise and stay below the radar.

Use search tools to find the hidden nuggets of information that no one else is copying or selling. Keep a close eye on this topic; the next version of CEH might have more than one chapter about it.

SCANNING

Introduction

At this point attackers have conducted thorough reconnaissance of the target. They know as much as possible about the organization, partners, reputation, and company officers. They have friends on the inside, or perhaps got hired to work there just to be inside. They know the network technologies the organizations use and have queried DNS for as many hosts and IP addresses as they could find.

It is time to enter the scanning phase of the attack. In order to understand the challenge of scanning, and how to interpret the results of each scan, it is also critical to discuss the protocols in use. The CEH exam will test this knowledge heavily. Knowing something about the protocols also unlocks many other skills for the hacker; sniffing, hijacking, MiTM attacks, DoS and DDoS, intrusion detection, and traffic filtering are all related to this chapter.

This is a complex chapter and the explanation will take the following form: An overview of all the theory independent of tools and specific scans will be presented followed by specific examples using Nmap (Network Mapper) as the primary tool. Read through the ideas behind scans first, and then apply them to the examples.

To Pass the CEH Exam You Need to . . .

- know the scanning methodology
- know how ICMP works
- know the TCP handshake
- know the types of scans
- know about scanning tools
- master the CEH cheatsheets and practice questions!

Know the Scanning Methodology

- The caveats of scanning
- Describe the CEH scanning methodology
- Scanning on the local segment
  - Try it out: Read RFC 826
  - Try it out: Capture an ARP scan
- Host discovery on remote segments
  - Try it out: Read RFC 1574
  - Try it out: Angry IP
  - Try it out: Read RFC 793
- Service discovery
  - Try it out: Read RFC 791
- Vulnerability scanning
  - Try it out: Demo core impact

The Caveats of Scanning

Scanning is about position. The results of your scan will always be influenced by where you are scanning from.

Externally facing servers might not have much exposure. In fact, they should never have more access points than are absolutely necessary. The trend is for internal networks to be designed in a similar fashion. In the past, once attackers had achieved an inside position they could scan and footprint with impunity. On some networks, they still can.

The attacker wants to find out just how *loose* the internal network is before going through the trouble of gaining an inside position. This is why the previous steps of the information gathering methodology are so important.

There is, of course, an easier way to approach this whole thing. A botnet (robot network) is a series of compromised hosts that can report to a C&C (Command and Control) center. If it is possible to compromise a collection of hosts within an organization to report back out, attackers not only overcome the SPI (Stateful Packet Inspection) firewalls but have a position on possibly every subnet in the network.

Ironically, the administrators of vulnerability assessment devices face exactly the same problem. If they scanned from only one position on the network, there wouldn't be much of a scan and the assessor would not accept the report. Either the controls are disabled during a maintenance window (something attackers would love to find out during the "initial information gathering" step) or the scanners have to be placed throughout the network.

Much of what has just been discussed will be elaborated on in future chapters. For now, we need to look at the fundamental concepts of scanning because they will apply to each and every situation.

Describe the CEH Scanning Methodology

In the footprinting portion of the reconnaissance phase, attackers performed some trace-routes to hosts that were either listed in documentation or were discovered in DNS.

Using some basic knowledge of routing, the traceroutes will reveal gateways to other network segments. Attackers keep track of everything they find and incorporate some guesswork along the way as well.

After determining the network segments, the next step is to ascertain live hosts with a "discovery scan." Several different techniques might be necessary depending on where attackers are able to scan from, and what types of filters are involved along the way.

Once the live hosts have been listed, a port scan is conducted to determine access points followed by verification of the services on each discovered port. With knowledge of the services and operating systems, a vulnerability scan can be fine tuned for each host.

Two basic challenges exist for attackers in this case: having the best position on the network to scan from and avoiding excessive noise that will trigger intrusion alarms. During reconnaissance, attackers learn what the risk level of a vulnerability scan is and will use a variety of techniques to achieve better positions to scan from.

It is important to realize that reconnaissance, scanning, and gaining access are iterative phases. Attackers will repeat these processes; each time they will get more accurate and move deeper into the network. Maintaining access is accomplished by planting backdoors along the way, like hikers that setup several base camps as they climb a large mountain.

Scanning on the Local Segment

From the internal positions of the scan, attackers will first see who else shares the local network segment. Since this segment is also defined as a "Broadcast Domain" it is only necessary to send broadcast messages to each potential address on the local segment and see who responds.

ARP (Address Resolution Protocol) is the way hosts determine the hardware address a frame needs to be marked for. Knowing the logical address of a host only gives the sender a concept of who the packet is for. In order to accomplish physical delivery of a frame of bits, the logical address needs to be resolved into a physical address called the MAC (Media Access Control) address. The best way to do this is to simply ask. For instance:

"Hey everybody! Who has the address 192.168.1.1? Please tell AB:CD:EF:12:34:56."

"Hey AB:CD:EF:12:34:56! I am 192.168.1.1 and my hardware address is 12:34:56:78:90:12."

Everyone that isn't 192.168.1.1 simply ignores the request. If this is part of an ARP scan, then the process is repeated for each possible IP address on the local segment.

Read RFC 826

ARP is used on a local network to resolve logical addresses and find the physical addresses. Understanding its operation explains many topics in the CEH course including ARP scanning, defeating switches for sniffing, and ARP spoofing attacks.

```
http://www.ietf.org/rfc/rfc826.txt
```

Capture an ARP Scan

To perform this exercise and those that follow in this chapter, you will need a local network that you have permission to scan. A VMWare network that you own would work perfectly. Download and install Nmap (*http://www.insecure.org*) or just Backtrack Linux as Nmap will already exist.

Also download and install Wireshark (*http://www.wireshark.org*). Sniffers, Spoofing, and Session Hijacking of Chapter 10: Scanning for more details about packet sniffing.

Start a Wireshark capture, then open a command window and try the following:

```
nmap -sP -v [IP range of the local network]
```

Notice that even though you chose a ping scan, Nmap knows that an ARP scan is all that is needed because the traffic is local.

Host Discovery on Remote Segments

When the target is outside of the gateway there are many other options for host discovery. At this point the attacker is only looking for a response regardless of what the response is. There are two broad categories of discovery methods:

- ICMP scans
- TCP flag combinations

ICMP scans

The Ping tool (Packet INternet Groper) is the most common way to test connectivity to a host. It sends ICMP type 8 code 0 messages (Echo request) with a payload that is determined by the local operating system. If the target host is accessible it will respond with an ICMP type 0 code 0 (Echo reply) and return the same payload it received.

It is common for traffic filters (firewalls) to block all incoming ICMP type 8 messages and all outgoing ICMP type 0 messages. When performing a standard traceroute to a target the attacker might see * (asterisk) characters to indicate the average trip times. This is one way to determine the ping isn't working.

A "ping sweep" is when an entire block of addresses is sent the type 8 messages in hopes of seeing some responses. If no hosts respond at all the attacker needs to be more creative.

TRY IT OUT

Read RFC 1574

"Essential tools for the OSI Internet" is an RFC that describes ping, traceroute, and other discovery tools.

http://www.ietf.org/rfc/rfc1574.txt

TRY IT OUT

Angry IP

One of the easiest and simplest tools to use for a quick ping sweep is Angry IP. Download and install it from:

http://www.angryziber.com/w/Home

Look for the version that runs from a USB key and keep it handy at all times.

TRY IT OUT CHALLENGE

Notice the payload specified for type 8 messages is just "data . . ."—this means that each operating system can make this choice for themselves, and it turns out to be one of the ways an attacker can tell what OS sent the ping. Try to send pings from both Linux and Windows hosts using Wireshark and analyze what the chosen payload is for each OS.

TCP flag combinations

TCP port 0 exists but should always respond with an RST (reset) regardless of the flag combinations that are sent. Filters that exist between the scanner and the target hosts might drop some combinations but pass others. Attackers can send TCP segments with port 0 as the destination to every IP address on a network segment. This is often an effective way to discover live hosts.

If port 0 is also being blocked, try to scan a known host to find out what ports might be open on the firewall. Port 80 or 53 is quite common. Then send different combinations of TCP traffic through that port to each host in the range of IPs on the target network. The ACK flag by itself is a common choice.

When scanning through a filter, attackers need to determine what is allowed to pass and then construct a scan that matches. Otherwise, if the firewall is set to allow all traffic but might filter particular values, the scan simply shouldn't have those values.

At this point scanning is becoming complicated and confusing. The next move is to put down the tools and understand a bit more about the TCP flags and what each is supposed to do. This will be discussed later on in the chapter.

TRY IT OUT

Read RFC 793

It is essential to understand TCP flags for the CEH exam. In fact, moving forward, there are many things that require this document. Take a few moments to read this RFC. Pay close attention to the header diagram and read the description for each field.

`http://www.ietf.org/rfc/rfc793.txt`

Service Discovery

Once the available hosts have been determined the attacker needs to know what options are available for accessibility. The next series of scans will determine the open ports or, if that is not possible, verify what ports are closed, knowing the rest of them perhaps are open or are being filtered.

For the CEH exam it is assumed you know the port ranges; let's review:

0	Unused service, always closed
1-1023	Well-known ports, require root privileges to open
1024-49151	Registered ports, requires only user privileges to open
49152-65535	Ephemeral (dynamic) ports open and close often

It is also important to know the possible states a port can be in:

Closed	Not listening
Listening	Available for connections
Half-Open	Has received a SYN and sent the ACK, waiting for reply
Established	Has completed the handshake, session established

The CEH exam also assumes before attending CEH that many popular port numbers have been memorized. For a comprehensive list visit: *http://en.wikipedia.org/wiki/ List_of_TCP_and_UDP_port_numbers*

Finally, port scans are not the only important type of service discovery. It is also helpful to know what transport protocols a host will support. This is determined by sending IP packets with different values in the IP protocol field (in the IP header) and can help show when a host is a VPN gateway or actually a router.

The most important protocol ID numbers are:

1	ICMP
6	TCP
17	UDP
47	GRE

| 50 | ESP |
| 51 | AH |

Read RFC 791

It is essential to understand IP for this exam. Notice the protocol field that was just mentioned. Also spend some time reading about the DF and MF flags, as they will be mentioned in the denial of service chapter.

`http://www.ietf.org/rfc/rfc791.txt`

Vulnerability Scanning

This type of scan is highly specialized. The products that exist to serve this purpose are very competitive and usually involve proprietary technology. The scanner sends an SCP (Specially Crafted Packet) toward the target host and analyzes the response. Sometimes more than one packet is involved. The response may indicate the presence of a possible vulnerability.

Vulnerability scanners are prone to false positives. Since they do not actually perform an exploit the best they can do is indicate the likelihood of an exposed weakness. They create extra traffic with well-known signatures. Attackers know that using these tools is a great way to get caught unless they run the scan during a maintenance window or in the midst of enough decoy traffic to keep the security analysts busy.

Vulnerability scanners do not perform *vulnerability linkage*. This term refers to the fact that some weaknesses can only be discovered through a multistage attack. Some weaknesses depend upon others being exploited first. One step up from vulnerability scanning would be tools such as Metasploit, Canvas, or Impact. These tools can do linkage but might not be necessary or allowed in a White Box test.

Demo Core Impact

EC-Council has a special agreement with Core Security that entitles prospective students to 30 day evaluations of "Impact," the industry standard commercial penetration testing tool. Send an e-mail to "mike@coresecurity.com" and mention this book. Mike will hook you up with an engineer who will provide a short training session as well as a link to download your evaluation copy.

Know How ICMP Works

- ICMP explained

  - Try it out: Read RFC 792

- ICMP types and codes

ICMP Explained

Internet Control Message Protocol (ICMP) is used for a variety of reasons, not just for Echo requests. The header changes as appropriate to the message type. The codes further describe the type of message. The CEH exam will test you on several of the message types.

TRY IT OUT

Read RFC 792

ICMP is a critical protocol for the network hacker to understand. Many of the types and codes will be on the CEH exam. Take a moment and read through the RFC to become familiar with the various message types.

http://www.ietf.org/rfc/rfc792.txt

For a comprehensive list of ICMP types and codes visit:

http://www.iana.org/assignments/icmp-parameters

ICMP Types and Codes

Following is a short list of the most significant ICMP "type" and "code" values that must be committed to memory before taking the CEH exam:

Type 0 Code 0	Echo reply
Type 3	Destination unreachable
Type 3 Code 13	Administratively prohibited
Type 5	Redirect
Type 8 Code 0	Echo request
Type 11	Time exceeded
Type 13	Timestamp request

Know the TCP Handshake

- TCP flags
- TCP sessions

TCP Flags

By now you have read the TCP RFC and reviewed the header diagram. The flags indicate the nature of the payload being transported. They are important to understand for sniffing and scanning purposes; memorize them:

URG	This payload should not have to wait to be processed
ACK	Please send me more bytes of data
PSH	Don't buffer up a whole segment, send what you have now
RST	I'm confused and need to bail out of this conversation
SYN	Hello, I would like to synchronize with you
FIN	I am politely saying goodbye

TCP Sessions

A TCP session is established when two hosts complete a handshake. Two other fields, the "Acknowledgement number" and the "Sequence number," are also involved in keeping the session organized. Understanding this operation is important for the CEH exam.

The TCP handshake between two hosts (A, B) is a three-step process. Consider the following example:

1. A sends to B   Flag: SYN   SEQ=1
2. B sends to A   Flag: ACK   ACK=2   Flag: SYN   SEQ=500
3. A sends to B   Flag: ACK   ACK=501

This three-step process causes a pair of SYN ACK responses, one in each direction. This establishes synchronization and full duplex communication between the services listening on the target ports.

Every byte of payload data the two hosts send back and forth will be counted. In order to keep track of what needs to be sent next, TCP uses positive acknowledgements; hosts ask for more data and it is implied that everything previously sent has been received.

The sequence number field establishes the beginning of this byte count. If host A sends host B 100 bytes of data, then B would acknowledge 101 to ask for the next segment, unless they started talking at sequence 325747. In this case, the ACK would be 325848. The formula is SEQ + payload size + 1 = ACK for next segment. During the handshake, the payload size is 0.

To establish a session the hosts have to synchronize on where they are going to start counting the bytes they each send. The target port number is that number where a higher layer service is listening (or not) and the sending host selects a random port above 1023 to receive the responses.

Know the Types of Scans

- Normal port scans
- Inverse port scans
- Additional scan types
  - ARP scan
  - Protocol scan
  - Idle scan
  - FTP bounce scan
  - ACK scan
  - Window scan
  - Firewalking
  - UDP Scan
    - Try it out: Read RFC 768

Normal Port Scans

"Normal" scans look for open ports. There are two basic types: connect and stealth.

Connect Scans (Vanilla Scans)

Connect types do not modify the natural behavior of TCP. A SYN flag is sent from the scanner to the target's destination port. If the port is open, a SYN ACK is returned to the source port. The handshake is completed and a RST is immediately issued to drop the session. Because the handshake completed, a log entry will result.

When the port is closed a RST, ACK will be issued from the target and the scanner moves on.

Stealth scan

A stealth scan modifies the natural behavior of TCP by issuing an RST on the third step of the handshake rather than an ACK if the port is open. Since this prevents the target port from entering the established state, no log entry is recorded. Root privileges are required to run this type of scan since the behavior is non-standard. Consider the following example:

1. A sends to B   Flag: SYN   SEQ=1
2. B sends to A   Flag: ACK   ACK=2   Flag: SYN   SEQ=500
3. A sends to B   Flag: RST

Once the scanner sees the ACK return there is no need for further conversation. If the target port is closed, a RST, ACK is sent from the target as expected.

Inverse Port Scans

Inverse scans must be used when the scanner cannot send SYN flags to the target due to filters that are placed between the scanner and the target. The objective is to confirm closed ports because the open ports will not produce a response at all. A filter will drop a packet and not tell the scanner. Flag combinations that avoid using the SYN simply do not make sense in terms of producing a reply. Only closed ports are kind enough to tell us they aren't interested in the traffic.

Xmas scan

The Xmas scan, for example, can light up all six flags (like a Christmas tree) or just the URG, PSH, and FIN flags. The newer version avoids using the SYN, ACK, and RST flags because the presence of those flags in the scan would make for less accurate results. Setting the URG, PSH, and FIN flags says, "Hurry and send nothing, goodbye." An open port would ignore such a request. A closed port would respond with a RST.

FIN and NULL

The same can be said for other inverse scan types such as sending only a FIN, or sending no flags at all (NULL). These requests make no sense to an open port, so in a very zen-like fashion they say nothing back. Closed ports will always RST.

Now that you have the basic idea of the inverse scan down pat, it is time to discuss reality. Microsoft Windows hosts are not zen-like; they will respond with a RST when confusing traffic is received even on the open ports. Inverse scans only provide meaningful results when a Linux host is the target. For the exam, be careful about the words in the question. If it wants you to prove you understand the idea of inverse scans, then closed ports RST and open ports do nothing. If there is a specific mention of a Windows host then everything is a RST. Inverse scans are then still perfectly good for host discovery, but that is all.

Additional Scan Types

Scanning is a challenging step and can take weeks to complete (if the attacker is trying not to be caught). Scanning appliances can be installed by white hats to keep a vigilant watch for rogue infrastructure (hosts that shouldn't be there). Great care is taken to do this properly or the scanners won't really see anything.

In addition to the normal and inverse scan types, some other techniques can also be attempted. The following are very likely to appear somewhere in your CEH exam:

- ARP scan
- Protocol scan
- Idle scan
- FTP bounce scan
- Window scan

- ACK scan
- Firewalking
- UDP scan

ARP scan

ARP scans involve sending broadcast requests to each logical address within a local segment. If the host exists, it will respond with its MAC address.

Protocol scan

Using the protocol field of the IP header, the protocol scan looks for the transport services offered on a host. This is much different than port scanning, so do not confuse the two. Protocol scans happen at layer three and can be useful in finding VPN gateways or routers.

Idle scan

The idle scan is assuming two things: the IPID field in the IP header (RFC 791) increments by one every time a packet is sent, and the zombie is truly idle.

An idle scan involves three hosts: the scanner, the target, and the zombie. The scanner first sends a ping to the zombie, checking its IPID field value. It then sends a SYN to the target, spoofing the zombie's as the source of the packet. If the port on the target is open, it will send a SYN ACK to the zombie, who will then send a RST, since it didn't actually send the SYN and is confused. The scanner then pings the zombie again and finds that its IPID field has incremented by two.

If the port was closed, nothing would happen. When the scanner sends the ping to the zombie its IPID field would only have incremented by one. This is mostly a clever method to exploit the way IPID fields work, and many operating systems have since gone to a pseudo random number for this field. Another reason this scan might not work is if the zombie is not truly *idle*. If it is sending traffic to other hosts while being used in the scan, the IPID field will increment by more than one or two and the scanner cannot know what that means.

FTP bounce scan

The FTP bounce scan requires an FTP server that will accept "PORT" commands. This command could be used to perform a port scan from a compromised FTP server that may have had a better position on the network than the attack otherwise had. A great description of this attack is presented here: ***http://www.cert.org/tech_tips/ftp_port_attacks.html***

Window scan

The window scan is looking for a non-zero value in the window size field as a response from open ports on certain versions of BSD machines. An ACK is sent to the port and RST returns because they are not synchronized, but the window field will report a size. If the port is closed, the window size will be 0 and still a RST will be returned.

ACK scan

The ACK scan will only provide meaningful results as a port scan from target versions of Solaris. Otherwise, it can still be used effectively as a discovery scan, or possibly to determine the rules of a filter.

Firewalking

A firewalk scan is about determining the ACLs (Access Control List) of a router. The attacker aims the scan to one hop past the target filter. If the TTL expires on the receiving host it will send back a time exceeded, indicating to the scanner that the packet made it through the firewall. All other packets are simply dropped and no response is expected.

UDP scan

UDP doesn't have flags; in fact, it is almost too simple a transport protocol to discuss much. You should go ahead and read RFC 768 though just to be thorough.

When a UDP datagram is delivered in a packet, there is no response expected from a higher layer service. Some respond, some don't; it is all on the decision of the application developer.

UDP scans are at best inverse scans because closed ports are supposed to respond with ICMP port unreachable (type 3 code 3). If this type is filtered the scanner will still get no response.

TRY IT OUT

Read RFC 768

So we don't forget, go ahead and read the RFC for UDP at this point too:

`http://www.ietf.org/rfc/rfc768.txt`

A great description of ICMP type 3 code 3 (port unreachable) is provided here:

`http://en.wikipedia.org/wiki/ICMP_Destination_Unreachable`

Know about Scanning Tools

- Command line tools
  - Try it out: Using Netcat as a scanner
  - Try it out: Using HPing as a scanner
  - Try it out: Using Nmap as a scanner
- Graphic tools
  - Try it out: Using graphical scanners

Command Line Tools

Having explored the theory behind various scan types, we have to look at the tools the CEH exam is most likely going to ask about. Knowing some command line options is necessary in this area. The following will give you a good start. If you have Backtrack Linux handy and a network that you have permission to scan, spend some time trying these out.

TRY IT OUT

Using Netcat as a Scanner

Netcat is "The Swiss army knife of network tools." We will get a lot more use out of this tool later. Open a command window in Backtrack Linux and try the following command:

```
nc -v -z [target host] [port range]
```

TRY IT OUT

Using HPing as a Scanner

HPing is a packet crafter that can do a few other tricks as well. Open a command window in Backtrack Linux and try the following:

```
hping3 -V --scan [port range] [target host]
```

TRY IT OUT

Using Nmap as a Scanner

Nmap is extremely important for the CEH exam. Open a command window in Backtrack Linux and try the following commands:

Try a ping sweep.
```
nmap -sP -v [target range]
```

Try a list scan.
```
nmap -sL -v [target range]
```

Try a protocol scan.
```
nmap -sO -v [target IP]
```

Try to verify services.
```
nmap -sV -v [target IP]
```

Try a normal connect scan.
```
nmap -sT -v [target IP]
```

Try a stealth scan.
```
nmap -sS -v [target IP]
```

Try an inverse scan: Xmas.
```
nmap -sX -v [target IP]
```

Try an inverse scan: NULL.
```
nmap -sN -v [target IP]
```

TRY IT OUT CHALLENGE

Additional options are necessary to run Nmap correctly. The order these options are used usually doesn't matter. What is important is that you try them out and memorize them for the CEH exam.

-P0	Do not ping first, in case a host seems unreachable before it is port scanned
-n	No DNS lookups please
-T[1-5]	Adjust the timing of the scan; 5 is the fastest
-p [#]	Specify a port range
-I	Ident scan (Linux target)

Graphical Tools

Graphical tools also exist for scanning and have a variety of features. Some are simple whereas others incorporate many techniques into the same interface. If you have a network lying around that you have permission to scan, download and try the following tools.

TRY IT OUT

Using Graphical Scanners

Download and run the following tools:

Zenmap
```
http://nmap.org/zenmap/
```

Superscan 4
```
http://www.foundstone.com/us/resources/proddesc/superscan4.htm
```

The Dude—Network Scanner
```
http://www.mikrotik.com/thedude.php
```

Conclusion

The scanning phase of an attack is both interesting and very difficult. From a defensive standpoint the less you reveal to adversaries the better. Yet as we have seen in learning about both footprinting and scanning, accessibility is a business driver. Where is the balance?

There are several drivers that influence the exposure decision. Designing DMZs to meet business needs along with security concerns only begins the discussion. ISP (Internet Service Provider) support, load balancing, and tracking access are the concerns of the business end. The IT department is worried about monitoring and administering countermeasures which often involve entirely separate network segments and configurations.

Scanning techniques are about exploration. The results you get will always be influenced not just by your tools and approaches, but by your position. Understanding the protocols and how both successful and failed scans look are critical steps to the process. Use multiple tools and corroborate the results. There are likely many devices along the scan that will influence how the network appears to the attacker.

In some cases, the complexity of the network doesn't matter. It is about access. If a resource can be reached it can be attacked.

Study this chapter a lot for the exam. It is the precursor to several other subjects including protocols, intrusion detection, firewall evasion, and attack research. Each of these topics is critical to the entire LPT program, not just to the CEH exam.

## CHAPTER SIX

ENUMERATION

Introduction

Enumeration *is a fancy word for "a list of things." In the enumeration stage, the objective is to attack each target one at a time and figure out as much information as possible about its resources, including user accounts and groups, patch levels, network shares, and reachable processes.*

The exact technique used to compromise the target will be determined by the available services and operating systems that can be accessed. From the scanning steps they already know it exists, and what ports they can reach to talk to it. The next step is about exploring these hosts in detail.

Enumeration is about asking "I know the host is there. What can it do for me?"

To Pass the CEH Exam You Need to . . .

- know the value of the enumeration step
- know how to create a NULL session
- know the file sharing ports
- know what the "RestrictAnonymous" key is
- know how to recognize Windows SIDs
- know how to use the netstat and NBTstat tools
- know how to enumerate a Linux host
- know how to use SNMP for enumeration
- know how to use LDAP for enumeration
- master the CEH cheatsheets and practice questions!

Know the Value of the Enumeration Step

- The story so far
- The risks
- The approach

The Story So Far

1. The attacker has performed thorough passive information gathering.
2. The attacker has scanned the network for live hosts.
3. The attacker has scanned the live hosts for ports that are accepting services.
4. The attacker has fingerprinted the operations systems of each host.
5. The attacker has verified the services on each of those open ports on the live hosts.

The Risks

Enumeration creates noise. Unusual or frequent access to the ports discussed in this module could trigger IDS alarms. Operating systems can be configured to give up less information about themselves. Some guesswork will be necessary even after enumeration is complete, but, if the attacker is lucky, potential targets for an easy and precise strike will be revealed during this step.

The Approach

Using widely available tools, attempt access to the same protocols and services that hosts use to share information with each other. From system calls to directory services, there is a wide range of information that can be gathered simply by masquerading as a client and making the request.

Know How to Create a NULL Session

- What is a NULL session?
  - Try it out: Creating a NULL session
- Understanding the loopback design

What Is a NULL Session?

A NULL session is a way to get two hosts to talk to each other in a network environment where the hosts have no previous association. It uses a NULL string for the account name and no password. Once the NULL session is established the hosts can ask each other important questions about resources. Attackers can also do this manually.

Most operating systems talk to themselves all the time. They do this through the IP loopback address of 127.0.0.1. This is one of the reasons host-based firewalls are so problematic. End users keep answering "no" whenever the software warns, "Your computer is attempting access to 127.0.0.1, do you want this?" Eventually the host cannot hear the voices in its own head and loses direction.

TRY IT OUT

Creating a NULL Session

Open a DOS prompt on a Windows PC and type:

```
net use \\[target ip]\IPC$ "" /user:""
```

See what options are available with the 'net' command by typing:

```
net ?
```

Then try each one out; for instance, try the following command:

```
net accounts
```

Understanding the Loopback Design

The advantage of the loopback design is that it becomes easy to teach PCs to send questions to one another if we just change the IP address from the loopback to the remote host. This works when the request is coming in from another location because the receiver of the question doesn't know the difference between a source of 127.0.0.1 and somewhere else.

One of the earliest attacks against the windows SMB protocol was "Red Button," a tool that would access administrator privileges and extract large amounts of data. Some worms (such as "Zotob") rely on NULL sessions to propagate. New vulnerabilities in the file sharing protocols are discovered all the time, and they are a constant target of research for the latest versions of any operating system. The next thing we should look at is what exactly are the ports of interest in this sequence?

Know the File Sharing Ports

- What is the portmapper service?
- Computer names and host names
- Running SMB over TCP/IP
- The risks of NULL sessions

What Is the Portmapper Service?

Some services expect to have permanent listening ports available to them, such as port 80 for HTTP, while other distributed applications do not need this type of accessibility. Instead, they rely on the portmapper service to assist them with establishing connections in the ephemeral port range of 49151-65535. Often times once a suitable port is placed in the listening state and its status is communicated, a single UDP datagram is all that is needed to complete the message.

The portmapper has many names and is relied on for many things. Windows documentation will give names to port 135 like "RPC DCOM" or "DCE-Locator" and relies on its services for remote execution of code in a variety of services including the resource sharing protocols. In packet dumps on the CEH exam you may see port 111 in a packet dump, indicating the host is very likely a Linux-based platform. Make sure you can identify both port 135 and 111 correctly.

RPC-DCOM or portmapper is a critical protocol for many networks. It is not a solution to simply firewall it from access because many distributed applications, rely on this service. Tools such as *rcpinfo.exe* can be used to query hosts for what sort of applications the portmapper is assisting. The Microsoft implementation of RPC is widely known for vulnerabilities up to the most current versions. The exploits range from denial of service to complete takeovers. Although a patch exists for what the recent conficker worm exploited, it still gained world-wide penetration. Older exploits such as the classic MS03-036 and Blaster worms are still common as well. Patches, patches, and still additional patches are the only current remedy.

Computer Names and Host Names

NetBIOS is actually an API (Application Programming Interface) that resource sharing protocols can access in order to refer to computers by unique names. When you see the UNC (Universal Naming Convention) path such as *server**share* you are using the computer name and a share it offers. Computer names are not routable; they are expected to exist on a flat local area network and are advertised or discovered through broadcasts. Should a computer name need to be converted to a routable IP address such as IP, the service WINS (Windows Internet Naming Service) can be provided or a static file called "lmhosts" is used.

Do not confuse the concept of computer names with host names. A host name is in reference specifically to TCP/IP-related networking. When you discover computer names, try them as host names also since they are likely to have the same string value. Host names are resolved to IP addresses through either the DNS (Domain Name Service) or the static "hosts" file. DNS enumeration was covered in a previous chapter.

Running SMB Over TCP/IP

Microsoft offers the chance to run SMB directly over TCP/IP using port 445. Sometimes this port is referred to as CIFS (Common Internet File System). When a host is making both ports 139 and 445 available, 445 will be preferred and 139 will see a RST. If NetBT (NetBIOS over

TCP/IP) is disabled, then only 445 will be used. Isn't this less confusing? The Sasser worm enjoyed dining on port 445.

On port 139, a session between two authenticated hosts is established in order to exchange data through a technique called "named pipes." Like port 135, this port has several known exploits. One of the oldest is SMBDie, which demonstrated that a malformed request to a pipe could cause a BSOD (Blue Screen of Death). Remember to patch, patch, and then patch some more.

For Linux, a package known as Samba can be installed to provide the same functions but not necessarily the same vulnerabilities. Be careful regarding what OS the target is running before getting too excited. Largely, the SMB protocol is not documented (publicly at least), and the Samba team did much of their work based on reverse engineering.

The Risks of NULL Sessions

The very real risk of leaking out file share advertisements to public networks caused many administrators to attempt disabling access to port 139. Whether this is accomplished by turning off the file sharing services locally or through filtering traffic, this tactic creates additional problems in terms of legacy applications and services. Ultimately a lot of impact study on a local network needs to be conducted before a solid security policy on how to handle these protocols can be implemented.

At this point it seems that unpatched hosts, where these ports are accessible, represent targets for denial of service or worse. If the primary goal is to have patience, and continue to dig deeper, the information gathering potential of the enumeration step might yield even better results. Once a NULL session is created, and if we are lucky some user accounts are discovered, attackers will look closely at the identifiers of each user account to determine what level of privilege it might have.

Know What the "RestrictAnonymous" Key Is

- The importance of the value set for the key

  - Try it out: Change the "RestrictAnonymous" key setting

The Importance of the Value Set for the Key

One way to at least restrict some of what the NULL user session can access is through the registry key setting. There are three possible values:

"0" is the default for Windows 2000 and gives up everything

"1" is the default for Windows 2003 and gives up less

"2" is the most secure setting but makes a machine not very cooperative with others

The location of the registry key is:

```
HKEY_LOCAL_MACHINE\SYSTEM\CurrentControlSet\Control\LSA
```

TRY IT OUT

Change the "RestrictAnonymous" Key Setting

Open a DOS prompt on a Windows PC and type:

```
regedit
```

Using the pane on the left hand side, navigate to the registry key listed above. When it is found, double click on it in the right hand pane. A form will open that will let you see what the value currently is.

If you wish to change it, please observe the unusual warning about always backing up the registry first, and then reboot. Try to enumerate the machine with a variety of tools and note the differences.

Know How to Recognize Windows SIDs

- What is a SID?
- What are the values we are looking for?

What Is a SID?

Whenever a user is created in Windows a value called a SID (Secure Identifier) is assigned to the account. The SID represents the resource to the system and the username is only there for our convenience as human users. There are certain accounts that get created automatically by Windows and they can be identified by the SID regardless of what the account name is.

What Are the Values We Are Looking For?

S-1-5-21-<. . . . .>-500	Built-in local administrator
S-1-5-21-<. . . . .>-501	Built-in local guest
S-1-5-21-<. . . . .>-512	Built-in domain administrator
S-1-5-21-<. . . . .>-1000	Anything above 1000 are users that have been created

If the built-in administrator account is renamed, it is still easy to figure out which one it is. Tools such as user2sid can query a host for a SID when the username is known and the tool sid2user does the opposite. All of these actions take place over port 139 and the RestrictAnonymous registry does not cause ACLs to be applied to these functions.

Know How to Use the Netstat and NBTstat Tools

- Try it out: Using the netstat and the NBTstat tools
  - Comparing the tools

Comparing the Tools

One common test *gotcha,* regardless of the certification, is the confusion over the difference between these two tools. At this point, stop reading and find a computer nearby that is running the Windows OS. Open a command prompt and play around with the various switches of these two programs until you feel there should never have been an issue in the first place.

It turns out that many of the Windows-based enumeration tools are just fancy interfaces to what is provided already in the DOS command shell or through WSH (Windows Scripting Host). For instance, the "net" command is also very powerful. However, some tools can get by the pesky ACLs and registry settings, so experimentation is a must. What could matter is the ability to report (make a list) and get around any ACLs (RestrictAnonymous) that might get in the way.

Know How to Enumerate a Linux Host

- Understanding the Samba package
  - Try it out: Run the SMBclient command
- "I fingered the user but there was no plan"
  - Try it out: Finger a user
- User privileges in Linux
- The importance of the SUID bit
  - Try it out: Finding the SUID bit

Understanding the Samba Package

If the Samba package is installed in order to integrate with other Windows hosts, the same principles of enumeration apply to Linux hosts as to Windows. Attackers are looking for shared resources using tools like "SMBclient" and "showmount," which will display what directories have been shared or mounted onto the file system from other hosts. NFS (Network File System) is also a common way for Linux hosts to share directories.

The showmount command can query a host for any directories it has exported. One challenge that administrators face when using NFS is the need to have equivalent local accounts on every system. If there is a lot of NFS going on there is likely a directory service also being used to manage a large amount of users across several systems. The attacker might also get lucky and discover too much root access going on as that is the easiest (and extremely dangerous) way to get a system of shares up and accessible.

TRY IT OUT

Run the SMBclient Command

Try this out on a Linux client with the Samba package installed and ignore the fact that you don't know the password on the remote host.

```
smbclient -L [remote host]
```

Now connect to one of the shares. The extra backslashes are necessary because of the way the Linux shell interprets them. This time, it is necessary to provide a password.

```
smbclient \\\\[remote host]\\[share] -U [username]
```

This will give you a command shell. Use the help feature of the command to see what actions are now available. Enter a question mark.

TRY IT OUT CHALLENGE

- You can get the manual page of any installed program in Linux by running the command man [program name]
- Man page the SMBclient tool, and if your Linux system has the NFS services installed try the showmount tool. Take a look at the options and try some things.

"I Fingered the User but There Was no Plan"

If the finger daemon is running, an attacker will attempt to "finger" a user to determine personal information and login times. The plan file is something that could be setup to reveal information about the user.

User Privileges in Linuxs

Linux uses a very simple UID (User ID) and GID (Group ID) system where UID and GID "0" is always a user with root level privileges. Different usernames can have the same UID, effectively making them the same user as far as the system goes, but for logging and auditing purposes it is still common to use the assigned usernames for each different account.

Service processes such as "named" (naming daemon or DNS) run under the ownership of a user account that often has the same name. An attacker that has gained access to a Linux system might try to create an account that will blend in, such as username "dns" and assign it a UID of 0 to ensure it always has privileges. They might also clear its password using the passwd –d command, hoping that none of this will look conspicuous during an audit.

The Importance of the SUID Bit

Another way to hide a user's escalated activity is to set the SUID bit for a common tool (the SGID bit works the same way but for a group rather than the user). This causes the program to run with the permission of its owner, not the user actually running it. For instance, if a common utility such as "ps" is run by Mallory, a member of the users group, but the file is owned by root and the SUID bit is set, then the tool will run as user id 0 and not with Mallory's ID. The attacker would have replaced the ps binary with something that can do harm, knowing that sooner or later a user will run the tool and the escalated privileges will ensure the harm is carried out.

Administrators must baseline their systems for utilities that need to have the SUID bit turned on so they can tell when it has happened to a file that it shouldn't have. The find command can be used on a regular basis for this search, so look out for the possibility that an attacker has replaced the find command with a version that will not support the options needed for such a search.

Finding the SUID Bit

Open a terminal on a Linux host and dump a baseline of the current SUID and SGID commands into a file. It will take some time to go catch up on "Burn Notice."

```
find / -type f -perm +6000 -exec ls -l {} \; > baseline.list
```

Imagine it's a week later and you want to check again:

```
find / -type f -perm +6000 -exec ls -l {} \; > newsearch.list
```

Run the diff command to see if anything has changed:

```
diff baseline.list newsearch.list > changes.list
```

Take a look at the file:

```
cat changes.list
```

Know How to Use SNMP for Enumeration

- What is SNMP?
- Risks of SNMP

What Is SNMP?

SNMP (Simple Network Management Protocol) is a protocol that is used for centralizing network management. It is an open protocol that is quite complex. Usually a commercial tool is deployed, such as Solarwinds, that knows how to speak SNMP. The basic idea is that agents are deployed onto managed systems and NMS (Network Management Stations) then process the information that is collected. A Master Information Base (MIB) is configured with the knowledge of what on the network needs to be monitored. Threshold values are configured for certain network events and traps are sent to the NMS whenever they are exceeded.

Risk of SNMP

An attacker is particularly interested in the MIB because that is where the data is stored that describes the resources being monitored. What an attacker needs to know is something called the "community string" which by default is set to the letters "PUBLIC." This string of characters acts as a shared password; the SNMP clients that can provide this string are considered trusted and will be able to make read only queries.

If the attacker is lucky, all it will take is a default configuration attack, meaning that if the target host has SNMP enabled but the community string has not been changed, then many of the built-in SNMP objects will be visible for enumeration. The SNMP protocol standard comes with a number of network items already mapped, along with the flexibility for administrators to create their own. These maps are called OIDs (Object Identifiers) and at first glance they look a bit strange:

OID Example: 1.1.2.6.1.2.4.2.3.1.1.4

Really this is just a map that shows how to travel down a hierarchal database. Starting with node 1, go to child 1, then child 2, then child 6, then child 1, and so on until the proper object or property is found. Using a tool like snmputil, attackers can query a host for information if they know both the OID and the necessary community string. If the attacker does not know the string, he will first guess the default. If that doesn't work the next step is to hope a newer version of SNMP is not deployed to sniff the string from the network since by default it is in clear text. Because this vulnerability is so widespread, the SNMP protocol has been updated to support better authentication that includes encrypting the community string.

The easier thing to do is use a commercial tool that already knows the common map. A social engineering or information gathering technique would then be needed to obtain the community string. On the CEH exam, look for the term OID and something that looks like the above example inside of a log file or screenshot of a packet dump.

Know How to Use LDAP for Enumeration

- What is LDAP?
- What is LDIF?

What Is LDAP?

LDAP (Lightweight Directory Access Protocol) is a subset of the ×.500 specification for directory services. It solves the puzzle of how to send data that refers to objects in a hierarchal structure across the network. In other words, if someone was to refer to "Gabriel" that would not mean that much. If we included more information about Gabriel within a serial string of characters we could move this data easily in a packet across the network knowing who or what Gabriel actually is. A DN (Distinguished Name) would be assigned that is unique to Gabriel and is his alone. Even if there are other Gabriels in the world, this string is his.

What Is LDIF?

Using LDIF (LDAP Data Interchange Format), Tom's place in the directory would look something like this:

UID=Gabriel Fischer, OU=Musician, OU=Guitar, DC-celticfrost, DC=com

Unfortunately it is very difficult to organize objects in one perfect way. Should orange be in the OU (Organizational Unit) color or should it be in the OU food? It depends on context, and at the same time is true in both cases. Since the attacker is just enumerating and not debating the nuances of information science, it is only necessary to learn whatever can be learned and reach conclusions about it later.

LDAP is an open protocol. It is supported by many operating systems including the popular Microsoft Active Directory. It runs as a service on port 389 and, in the absence of having a convenient administration tool like the Microsoft Management Console plugin, it might be possible to access the directory using a command line client such as *ldap.exe* or a java-based tool like jxplorer.

Conclusion

Enumeration is really about finding out as much as possible about each host on the network. Each operating system has its own services that can be accessed during this process and there are a variety of tools to work with to accomplish this. Once the information has been thoroughly collected, the next step is to formulate a strategy for gaining access.

The attacker will target the weakest points of the network to setup the maintaining access phase. If direct communication is not possible, techniques such as Trojan horse applications and social engineering will be used to bring the connection back to the attacker.

This would be a good time to completely review the recon naissance and scanning phases of an attack.

Take a blank sheet of paper and brainstorm as complete a list as you can make about all the work that is involved and what concepts have been discussed so far. Then go back through the first six chapters of the book and see how close you got to covering the objectives.

SYSTEM HACKING

Introduction

To a large degree, the rest of this course is about the gaining access and maintaining access phases of an attack. Assuming the reconnaissance and scanning phases were done properly, we should now begin exploring possible attack vectors.

During the enumeration portion of the scanning phase, the attacker might discover interesting user accounts on hosts with weak security configurations. If an account cannot be directly attacked, the next best thing is to see if there is a way to get the target to reveal more about itself during the course of daily activities. Finally, all information gathered must be hidden safely away, stored, or leaked without the chance of being caught with it. This is the focus of the current chapter.

To Pass the CEH Exam You Need to . . .

- know password cracking techniques
- know eavesdropping and privilege escalation
- know the techniques of Steganography
- master the CEH cheatsheets and practice questions!

Know Password Cracking Techniques

- Understanding password protection
- General approaches to password cracking
- Recovering passwords from hashes
  - Try it out: Calculating password combinations
- Obtaining password hashes
  - Try it out: Read RFC 1510

Understanding Password Protection

Passwords are the least expensive and easiest to implement form of authentication credential. They are also exposed to a number of different attack techniques. The greatest challenge of using password protection lies in achieving the balance of risks involved.

Consider the following statements:

- Password cracking and password recovery are the same activity. The question is about what role the attacker is playing: a "white hat" (defense oriented hacker) attempting to save company data or a "black hat" (offensive oriented attacker) attempting to complete the gaining and maintaining access phases.

- Passwords that are extraordinarily strong are unwieldy, difficult to remember, and cannot be recovered if lost. A management system for strong passwords must be created and then it must also be protected.

- Some systems generate a strong encryption key passed on a password value that is, in turn, used to encrypt the data. Breaking the encryption is unlikely, and guessing the password might not be practical. Having to change passwords will mean having to archive old ones or data could be lost.

- Before selecting a strong password, it is necessary to accept whether losing all access to the data is worth the risk of choosing a lower quality password.

- With hardware becoming cheaper and storage cost almost a non-factor, the ability to attack passwords will continue to increase exponentially. Since this is the most common form of access control, the motivation is high in continuing to develop attack techniques.

The activity of password cracking is both art and science. There will be times a password simply is not practical to crack. But due to the difficulty of managing this form of credential there is also often a chance a weakness can be found somewhere in the system. Default passwords and weak passwords that are protecting network resources that have not been properly risk managed are surprisingly common.

General Approaches to Password Cracking

There are four types of password cracking attacks:

- Passive online attacks
- Active online attacks
- Offline attacks
- Non-technical attacks

Passive online attacks

This form of attack involves sniffing passwords from the network traffic. On an Ethernet network this has become more difficult in the years since most organizations have replaced their hubs with switches. Wireless networks are a full circle return to a hub-like environment, however. With the right hardware, passive online techniques are still possible.

Active online attacks

In order to overcome the switched environment, an active attack such as a MiTM (Man in The Middle) technique can be used to capture credentials between two or more target hosts. ARP (Address Resolution Protocol) poisoning is the most likely vector but the attacker must be in the broadcast domain to make it work.

Session hijacking and replay attacks were once used in active online attacks but each has become more difficult over time. Session hijacking is difficult because changes have been made to protocol implementations that make the many steps required difficult to accomplish. Replay attacks involve sniffing a login sequence from the network wire and resending those packets to the server at a later time. Replay attacks are mitigated by using multifactor authentication, timestamps, and challenges that can be associated with each captured packet, rendering them unplayable at a future time.

The most efficient and effective active online attack is simple password guessing. The attacker would have performed thorough reconnaissance and enumeration information gathering steps in order to know where guessing has the best chance of working.

In a guessing attack, knowing something about the target user is helpful also. If the password is based on a hobby interest or if cognitive passwords (answers to pre-chosen questions must be provided) are involved the guesses will be more accurate. This information can also be added to a dictionary file if automating the guessing attack is possible.

In September of 2008, then presidential candidate Sarah Palin was the victim of a form of password guessing attack. The attacker used the password recovery system and guessed at the cognitive passwords to achieve a password reset. He then logged into her account. (*http://www.huffingtonpost.com/2008/09/18/sarah-palins-e-mail-hacke_n_127553.html*)

Offline attacks

Passwords should never be stored in the clear text. Usually they are placed through a hashing algorithm and the result of that calculation is stored. In order to avoid the same password always producing the same hash result, a salt value is added to the hashing calculation. This salt is a nonce (one time value) that is generated differently depending on the implementation. If attackers can obtain a database of the hashes for each user of a system, they would also have to know something about how the salt is implemented.

Luckily, many password-cracking tools exist that know how popular implementations work and can perform a variety of password attacks easily. Those techniques will be discussed later in this section.

Non-technical attacks

The method involves social engineering or physical eavesdropping. Sometimes the easiest way to obtain a password is simply to ask the victims for it, perhaps offering them something in exchange such as technical assistance.

Shoulder surfing is the visual observation of someone entering his credentials. It is even possible to install a WiFi connected webcam in a hidden but strategic location and observe the keystrokes remotely, or use a small video camera that must be retrieved at a later time. Such cameras disguised at common ink pens are easily purchased and can record hours of video.

Hardware keyloggers can be obtained easily from sources on the Internet and are easy to install. They record every keystroke and provide a report to the attacker that is easily searched. They are undetectable through software controls but, as is also the case with small cameras, require two instances of physical access: one to install the keylogger and the next to retrieve it.

Password guessing is also applicable in non-technical attacks. A system might still have the default password configured or a published maintenance hook (a way for technicians to obtain access without the assistance of an onsite administrator). Many vendors have been caught posting repair manuals online, forgetting the maintenance hooks are there for all to see.

Recovering Passwords from Hashes

The basic idea of a hash is that a *message digest* of string data is calculated, producing a *fingerprint* that represents the data but does not reveal what the data string was. It is impossible to reverse a hash, just like capturing a person's thumbprint cannot reveal her entire physical appearance.

Hashing algorithms are used to compare data. If you have several files that are each 1 Terabyte in size and want to see if they are the same or not, the easiest way is to hash them and compare the results. If each file produces the same digest they are exactly the same as each other, bit for bit. Yet you would not expect to extract 1T of data from a 128 bit hash.

Passwords are stored as hashes because while the password itself cannot be guessed from a hash, we can tell if the credential provided at login time is the same as what was selected in the past to be the password.

There are several methods that can be used to recover passwords. In all cases, it is not about reversing the hash, but about finding a value that produces the same fingerprint and hoping the system will accept that credential. This event is called a *collision* and is the primary weakness of hashing algorithms. For the CEH exam, it is essential to understand these concepts. They can be mixed and matched. A combination of these techniques will be common but there is always a tradeoff.

The simpler the attack the faster a result will be returned . . . sometimes within seconds. The more complex the attack the longer the amount of time that will be necessary, sometimes in the trillions of years. This is where the art of password recovery comes in. The well-used "P@ssw0rd" could be found in seconds in a dictionary attack, moments in a guessing attack, and eons in a brute force attack. You just never really know.

The CEH Exam References the Following Types of Password Cracking Attacks:

- Dictionary attack
- Syllable attack
- Rule-based attack
- Hybrid attack
- Offline brute force attack
- Rainbow attack
- DNA attack

Dictionary attack

A list of words are hashed and compared with the captured hashes. Dictionary files are easy to obtain on the Internet for almost any language.

Syllable attack

Instead of using full words, phonics or portions of words can be combined together and hashed. Passwords that are combinations of dictionary words or phonetically spelled words are vulnerable.

Rule-based attack

Rules are created such as "substitute character 'a' or 'A' with '@'". A language called *regular expressions* can be used in very powerful ways to perform these substitutions on strings of dictionary or syllable attack variations.

Users might append a one or two digit count to their passwords (pass01, pass02, pass03 . . .) if they are asked to change them often so numeric rules can also be used in this attack.

Hybrid attack

This attack simply describes a combination of the other attacks with additional techniques. Characters will be shifted or transposed, and case can be flipped. Example: P@ssw0rd, @ssw0rdP, P@SSW0Rd, rdsw0sP@ . . .

Offline brute force attack

Rather than base the attack on dictionary or phonetic strings, a brute force attack uses different random combinations. The difficulty in performing this attack lies in selecting an appropriate character set. Too small of a set will miss the password while too large of a set could make the attack impractical without the aid of additional techniques.

Rainbow attack

A rainbow table is used as a technique to solve the *time-memory tradeoff* problem.

If it takes 1^{18} years to brute force one hash, imagine having to start all over again for the next one. Since all of that work was done, why not store the hashes in a lookup table as they are computed? Each subsequent crack would then take only seconds.

A strong administrator level password would be 1.46×10^{29} combinations of up to 15 characters, round it to 16 Bytes per combination, and it turns out to be a very large amount of space indeed.

Using a less absurd combination, a 6-character password set would require roughly 2.5 Terabytes of storage if the 88-character set is assumed. 340Gs would be needed if only case and digits were considered. Both are certainly achievable within reasonable budgets. It would be nice, however, if the process were more portable.

We want to get the lookup table down to a size that can be carried around on an average laptop, even if it will take some time to lookup string combinations. Complete rainbow tables for LM or NTLM hashes range from 3–128Gs in size (*http://project-rainbowcrack.com/table.htm*).

The drawback to rainbow tables is that several are required for different circumstances. Salting the password before it is hashed renders the rainbow tables ineffective because you would have to have a table for each possible salt.

Salting a password usually does not require the salt to be kept a secret, and it needs to be generated by the authentication system each time in order to validate the user's credentials. Capturing the salts or knowing how they get built allows the attacker to use brute force techniques. A rainbow table is an efficient lookup method that will not fit every situation.

DNA attack

Distributed network attack (DNA) involves using the power of parallel processing. A DNA client is installed on a group of hosts that wish to participate in the effort. A section of the possible combination space is downloaded to each client that will work on the computations in the background or during idle time, such as when the screen saver is on (*http://www.freerainbowtables.com*).

TRY IT OUT

Calculating Password Combinations

Using Google or a calculator, try the following calculations:

If a password can have only digits (0–9) and must be 4 characters long (like a PIN number), enter into Google the following statement:

10^4 = ?

If a password can have only lowercase characters and must be 4 characters long, try:

26^4 = ?

If a password can have both digits and lowercase characters and must be 4 characters long, try:

36^4 = ?

If a password can have lower- and uppercase characters and digits and must be 4 characters long, it becomes:

62^4 = ?

Add special characters !@#$%^&*()<>?+-[]{}\/| ';" (26 additional characters listed)

88^4 = ?

Increase the length of the password to 6 characters:

88^6 = ?

Increase the length of the password to 8 characters:

88^8 = ?

Increase the length of the password to 15 characters:

88^15 = ?

By now the pattern is becoming clear. Increasing the character set has a huge effect, and lengthening the password by one character increases the possibilities by a factor.

Every computer is different in terms of the number of password combinations it can try every second. Choose a benchmark such as 1,000,000 and divide the numbers above by that amount to estimate the amount of time an exhaustive attack would take. The CEH exam will ask about extremes: will a particular scenario take a few seconds or a trillion trillion years? You have to be able to recognize the circumstances.

Now imagine a single computer built specifically to perform these calculations using the GPU (Graphics Processing Unit) of easy-to-obtain graphics cards. Elcomsoft demonstrated 55 trillion calculations over the course of a few days using common off-the-shelf computer hardware. Actual numbers vary widely according to the report you find and, of course, many variables in a given experiment would change this number dramatically. For now we are just playing around with estimates.

Imagine 10,000 desktop supercomputers running DNA software. A strong 15-character password might be cracked in about 60–90 days. Now imagine someone with a lot of resources setting up something like this to run behind a simple web-based application that would allow users to copy and paste in a hash (for a small fee) and be e-mailed the results when the password is cracked. (Hint: Sites like this already exist.)

If you play around with it for awhile, you'll see that having 1,000,000 not so powerful PCs is not as good as having a moderate number of very powerful ones. The work Elcomsoft has done is extremely significant. Like many things in information security, *proof of concept* speculation is much different than actually doing it, but the data owner has to perform risk analysis on the damage caused by the one time an attack is successful.

Obtaining Password Hashes

Hashes can be obtained through network sniffing or by copying them from a stored database. Some tools, such as PWdump or FGDump, can access these databases from remote locations if the user already has a privileged credential. Physical access to a machine and, best yet, the ability to boot the host to an alternate operating system (bypassing all local controls) usually yields the best results. 0phtcack, for example, is a Linux-based distribution that is designed specifically for this purpose and integrates easily with a variety of rainbow tables that understand the ways most common operating systems store passwords.

For the CEH exam, know that Windows hosts store passwords in multiple places: the SAM (Security Accounts Manager) file, a "Repair" file that is a backup of the SAM, in the registry, and in memory (LSA Secrets) as current credentials are cached. On a Linux machine the hashes are stored in the /etc/shadow file and are salted first.

Extensive research on each of the following algorithms is recommended additional reading. Wikipedia has excellent articles on each of these topics. At least be very familiar with the following implementations:

- LM (LAN Manager)
- NTLMv2
- Kerberos

LM (LAN Manager)

- Uses DES in ECB mode (Data Encryption Standard in Electronic Code Book mode).
- Divides every password into two halves of seven characters each. This results in two 56 bit keys that encrypt a static string and the result is stored.
- If a password is shorter than seven characters the second half will always be NULL characters and will produce the same result every time.
- Passwords longer than 14 characters cannot be stored as LM credentials. 14 NULL characters are used instead and will always produce the same result.

NTLMv2 (NT LAN Manager version 2)

- Uses MD5 as the hashing algorithm
- Incorporates a challenge protocol that results in HMAC-MD5
- Is still commonly used for hosts that do not belong to a domain

Kerberos

- Kerberos is a protocol that was developed at MIT and is implemented in many operating systems, each with its own variations.
- A Kerberos pre-auth key is vulnerable to network sniffing at the time a client first authenticates to the server.
- Kerberos cannot defend against the user credentials being compromised locally.

TRY IT OUT

Read RFC 1510

It is recommended to review Kerberos technologies and pick up some of the vocabulary involved. Start by reading RFC 1510.

`http://www.ietf.org/rfc/rfc1510.txt?number=1510`

Additional recommended reading:

`http://www.securityfocus.com/infocus/1554`

`http://www.kellys-korner-xp.com/win_xp_passwords.htm`

Know Eavesdropping and Privilege Escalation

- Privilege escalation
  - Try it out: Creating a user from the windows command line
- Keyloggers
- Spyware
- Rootkits
- Covering tracks

Privilege Escalation

The goal of the attacker at this stage is to gain and maintain access to any target that will provide an advantage. This is either a host with better access, important data, or user accounts that have high privilege. We have just discussed cracking passwords, but there are other ways, too.

If attackers can convince the target users to click a link in an e-mail that takes them to a site with code that exploits their browser, there is a chance the user will be surfing as administrator at the time. Home computer users do this probably 95 percent of the time. Home computer users with laptops that they are allowed to bring to work are a great find.

Another way is through a Trojan horse application (discussed in the next chapter). An attacker can take a tool such as the exploit "x.exe" (creates an administrator account named X with X as the password), bind it with a useful utility or a cartoon animation, and convince the target to install it.

It is not always necessary to create an administrator account. Sometimes it benefits the attacker to create a normal user and then run certain applications from it that have escalated privileges when performing certain functions. In Linux, this could be to run tools that have the SUID bit set. In Windows it could be a lot of things. Creating and being logged in as administrator or root accounts is noisy and should draw some attention. The attacker will have to be creative about it.

> **There are three different types of privilege escalation:**
> - Vertical
>   - A lower privilege is promoted to a higher privilege.
> - Horizontal
>   - A user of the same privilege is created.
> - De-escalation
>   - A user performs functions at a downgraded level.

TRY IT OUT

Creating a User from the Windows Command Line

Use the net command to create a user account:

```
net user [username] [password] /ADD
```

Now check the default setting for this account:

```
net user [username]
```

Keyloggers

Keyloggers can be used in either hardware or software form. Software keyloggers are usually a part of a larger surveillance package, discussed in the spyware section later in this chapter.

Hardware keyloggers are undetectable other than by visual inspection. They are inexpensive and extremely easy to use but are not an option if the victim is using a laptop with an integrated keyboard (although embedding hardware keyloggers in such places has been demonstrated).

One popular example is "Keyghost" (*http://www.keyghost.com*). It sits between the keyboard connecter and the PC and looks like a noise filter. Once attackers retrieve the keylogger, they install it in their own machine and use a keystroke sequence to dump the contents. Another challenge for the attacker is the physical access is required twice; if the keylogger is ever noticed, hopefully major changes to physical access policy will result.

Hardware surveillance is a security threat that is growing daily and becoming more and more frightening. It by no means stops at keyloggers. What was once the subject of spy movies and junk in the Johnson Smith catalogs many of us grew up with is now very much a reality. Unlike those X-ray eyeglasses, these things actually work.

The best way to hide surveillance hardware is to use what is already expected to be there. Some spyware applications target the built-in hardware that now comes standard on most portable computers. They can activate the camera and voice recorder at will. The easiest way to record a person in public is to activate the cell phone camera and pretend you are "texting." So many people "tweet" these days that it would never raise alarms.

Spyware

Many of the attack tools that are discussed in the CEH course have commercial equivalents.

It is difficult sometimes to distinguish between "attack tools," "hacking tools," and "justifiable spying." The truth is, as long as people want to observe their teenagers, spouses, or employees, there will be a market that guarantees the malware (Malicious Software) we have to deal with will not only exist, it will thrive. The sad part is, this malware costs businesses billions of dollars a year.

The market behind spyware is driven by paradoxical values. This assures a solid business model. Commercial companies often require their software to "phone home" to a license server. Unless you perform a packet trace you will not know exactly what that message entails. Access ports can be opened on your system and might have high privilege, creating exposure to buffer overflow exploits as resources are downloaded and processed. The legal fine print will not be clear about this and when the user clicks "agree" all bets are off in terms of who is held accountable.

Spyware is the subject of many social engineering attacks as well. Sites that warn of impending doom and offer a convenient tool for $29.95 to remove the threat have been circling our e-mail in-boxes for decades now. Sometimes they are themselves the spyware once installed.

A common social engineering of spyware attacks is the Trojan horse. The play on the subjectivity of convenience products is possibly the most powerful example of this technique. Consumers will spend up to hundreds of dollars a year on various anti-malware and identity theft products while at the same time volunteer to be spied on when they download freeware, sign up for discount clubs, and celebrate that Google has finally installed a webcam on their street.

Even commercial software is getting into a regular practice of spying on its users. This is often justified as "Licence enforcement" or "Demographic data to improve the product." Once enough data is collected it can then be sold to generate additional revenue. Users must read the EULA thoroughly for all software they use, but even then enforcement is only possible if someone is motivated enough to sue over it. Some companies will take this risk and violate their own EULA.

Spyware is a hacker's paradise and is not going away any time soon. The amount of damage incurred has become a personal decision; the spyware authors certainly don't see themselves as accountable when the victim can be blamed for their own choices.

Rootkits

Rootkits are a form of malware that seeks to give the attacker control of the operating system itself. A variety of techniques are used to hide processes, intercept system calls, or modify authentication services. The ultimate objective is to accomplish the maintaining access phase of an attack, ensuring that backdoor access is available to the attacker.

Rootkits do not provide *root* or *administrator* access initially. Usually the attacker must already have that level of privilege to install the rootkit. Typical installation vectors are buffer overflows against common clients, Trojan horses, or "remote access reverse shells" that were run in the context of the privileged user.

The rootkit is a collection of files that replace existing system binaries. Once the underlying operating system has been modified, the rootkit files can allow ordinary users to perform privileged activities through the backdoors that have been created and hidden from dectection.

The most common type of rootkit is the kernel level rootkit. Many operating systems such as Linux use LKMs (Loadable Kernel Modules) that allow for code such as device drivers to be installed and removed on the fly. This architecture can be used by a rootkit to install itself in a way that allows it to operate at "Ring 0," the most privileged protection level.

If the malicious code operates at the same level as the kernel, it can intercept all calls made by scanners to avoid detection. It can masquerade as a legitimate service. As a result, some antivirus products have to install a rootkit to protect their own functionality.

In addition to drivers and LKMs, rootkits can target libraries (DLLs in Windows) and installed applications. Some rootkits have been demonstrated that can be installed via firmware, and some products ship from companies to unsuspecting customers in the already "rooted" condition.

Hypervisor rootkits modify the boot order of an operating system. They start a virtual machine and run the local OS within it. This means the rootkit completely wraps the OS and has complete control over everything including hardware.

Once a rootkit has been installed, the system is considered untrustworthy. It requires great skill and persistence to completely clean out a rootkit, and even then it is difficult to verify that the system has been restored. The only accepted countermeasure against rootkits is to rebuild the system.

Covering Tracks

The majority of this chapter is about covertly storing data, processes, or activities. Covert channels can be encrypted network traffic, hidden processes within the system, or ways to store and forward information that bypasses filters and detection controls. Sometimes however it is good enough to simply "stay under the radar" or delete files before the attacker leaves a system.

The best way to avoid being caught is to avoid doing things that attract attention but might still achieve the attacker's objective. Most users are more interested in experience and usability than in security. Most enterprises are more interested in achieving compliance and letting that define them as secure. So if the attacker has enough patience and discipline, he can remain undetected simply because no one is paying enough attention to notice.

Files such as temporary Internet files, browser history, the recent documents list, and the recycle bin can be automatically removed on restart or at scheduled intervals. Many tools are available for download that perform this function.

The major browsers—Internet Explorer, Firefox, Opera, Chrome, and Safari—all have privacy modes. With IE8, using the keyboard shortcut Ctrl+Shift+P launches a new window in what some people like to call "Porn mode" because it keeps no traces of what activity was conducted during the session. It should be assumed, however, that all online activity can be traced to an IP address, without the use of "anonymizer" services or proxy servers such as TOR (The Onion Router network). This information can be subpoenaed by the courts if deemed necessary.

These privacy modes are not perfect, so before relying on them it would be a good idea to investigate in each browser exactly what that term means.

Know the Techniques of Steganography

- Steganography and encryption
- (ADS) Alternate data streams
  - Try it out: Alternate data streams
  - Try it out: Execute a binary from an alternate stream
- Hiding data within media files
- Other places to hide messages

Steganography and Encryption

Hiding data on a system is an important skill for system hacking. The attacker may have collected a number of passwords, off-shore bank account numbers, or contact information for team members. Perhaps the leaking of proprietary secrets is the attacker's very objective and not necessarily control over resources.

It might be necessary to hide malicious source code inside of a media file. Leaking company secrets might be the objective. Whatever the case, the attacker wants to make sure that common data scans and network filters will not detect the data.

Steganography is about hiding information inside of other information. Encryption is about obscuring the meaning of data. The fundamental difference is that encryption doesn't try to hide; good encryption looks like a random mess of characters and can be hard to notice, but it can usually be seen. The value is that the observer won't have any sense of it.

Steganography does nothing to draw attention to itself. Without sophisticated analysis it is often impossible to tell that a message has been hidden inside of another file that is in plain view. If done correctly, there is no reason to think anything is there.

Combine the steganography and encryption together, and you have an incredibly powerful way to store and move data with confidentiality and integrity in a way that is often completely undetectable.

(ADS) Alternate Data Streams

The Microsoft file system format NTFS (NT File System) supports a feature called alternate data streams. Every file in NTFS is listed in the MFT (Master File Table), and the data for all file attributes is stored there. "$NAME" for instance is the name of the file, and $DATA is the content of the file. If the file is too large to fit into the MFT directly (each entry is 1024k) then pointers, called external attributes, are stored in the $DATA stream to where else in the volume the data can be found.

The HPFS (High Performance File System) used in other operating systems gives every data file two data streams. Applications written for those systems expect to pull meta-data from one stream and data from the other stream. This is fundamentality incompatible with systems that use NTFS, since only one data stream is available and the attributes are accessed entirely differently. Porting applications between the two systems would mean a lot of extra work, if even possible on some occasions.

The easiest way to solve this problem would be to give the NTFS a way to support a second data stream. So that is what they did. Unfortunately, they didn't teach Windows Explorer how to see the streams. Any scanning of the hard drive that depends upon using Windows Explorer will miss the alternate streams completely. Normally, this is not a problem for Windows-based applications, and a program that uses the alternate stream will already know what the second stream is called, so it will be accessed directly.

The best thing to do at this point is demonstrate the principle.

TRY IT OUT

Alternate Data Streams

On a Windows computer that you know has a hard drive volume formatted in NTFS, open a command window and change the root of the volume. Create a notepad file:

```
c:\ notepad.exe test.txt
```

Enter some text into the file and save it. Close the notepad window. Now create an alternate stream and put some data into it.

```
C:\ notepad.exe test.txt:altstream
```

Notepad will again ask if you want to create the new file. Answer yes, type some data into it, save it, and close it.

Open My Computer and look on the C drive. Only "test.txt" will be available. Return back to your command window and open each stream using the same two commands above. The alternate stream is there, but where is it in Windows Explorer?

It is important to keep a couple things in mind about alternate streams. This data is not meant to be moved. If you copy the test file to a USB key or send it as an e-mail attachment the ADS data will be lost in the copy. Also, what you name the files does not matter at all, but it is often more reliable if file extensions are used as you'll see in the next example.

TRY IT OUT

Execute a Binary from an Alternate Stream

In the same command window used in the previous exercise, copy a small executable into an alternate stream. In this example we will use calculator, but you could try other things as well.

```
c:\ type c:\windows\system32\calc.exe >> test.txt:calc.exe
```

Now execute calculator from the alternate stream:

```
C:\ start ./test.txt:calc.exe
```

Again look at Windows Explorer and notice the file sizes have not changed. Windows Explorer will report 1k (because the MFT entry for the file is 1k and there is not enough data in the file to require external attributes). Right click on the test.txt file and look at the properties.

TRY IT OUT CHALLENGE

Look at Windows Explorer and notice that there are three file sizes reported:

- 1k because it has an MFT entry
- 4k because the file takes up one cluster
- a handful of bytes for the actual data

Shouldn't there be quite a bit larger file size after having put an executable in its alternate stream?

Hiding Data within Media Files

There are many ways to hide data inside another file if the format of the carrier file is well understood. Binaries can also be encoded into character formats and then embedded as string data.

Text files such as office documents use a markup language to describe the structure of the data within the file. Data can often be hidden outside of the root container or within the root container but not within other markup. For example, the following XML document illustrates the concept:

```
<xml>

<object>

This text     <item> Data 1</item>

is in ignored<item> Data 2</item>
```

```
space <item> Data 3</item>

</object>

</xml>
```

If the application that parses this document only looks at the path "object/item/element" it would only find: Data n. The additional text would be ignored. It is also possible to place character data between the nonprintable control characters of simple files like those notepad reads.

Messages can be hidden inside of music and video files by taking advantage of the way the compression algorithms work. The data is hidden in the distortion that naturally occurs when converting an audio signal into lower bitrate. It is done in such a way that the audible threshold is not exceeded. The encoded data will not affect how the media sounds.

Hiding information within images is quite simple and works best on detailed images such as an oak tree full of leaves living next to a stream. Each pixel is represented by bits of data. If the image has only 256 possible colors only one byte per pixel is needed. For 16 million colors three bytes are required. The LSB (Least Significant Bit) can be odd or even aligned with the bits of a message we intend on hiding:

We want to encode a string "secret" whose first character "s" in ascii is:

01110011

Pick 8 pixels in an 8 bit color depth image. In our example might have the values:

01101001 10011001 00110100 01101001 11011001 01100111 11101110 10011101

The least significant bit of each pixel works out to be:

11011101

In order to encode the character "s", some LSBs will have to be flipped:

01101000 10011001 00110101 01101001 11011000 01100110 11101111 10011101

Five of the eight pixels were changed, and in each case only one of 256 possible steps. If the images were using 24 or deeper colors the changes would be statistically even less impactful. We could encode every third pixel only, and therefore we could encrypt the string "secret" into something like "$F^Sw3jgni2K" before encoding it. Considering the possible variations, it is easy to see how difficult this form of steganography would be to detect.

Encoding messages within image files does have two drawbacks. Although the file size will not change, if a hash of the original image can be compared with the encoded image we would at least know it had changed. The other drawback lies with compression techniques that are "lossy." Recompressing an image that has already been encoded will lose data, if it was encrypted first that could make the message impossible to achieve.

Other Places to Hide Messages

Physical steganography has existed for centuries and with a little creative thinking it is easy to see the possibilities are endless. From messages hidden behind paintings to strange ads posted in classified ads the techniques could be sophisticated or extremely basic.

The printing industry has commonly used watermarking techniques to hide data that allows documents to be tracked or authenticated. Color copiers embed a series of yellow dots throughout every document that indicate the manufacturer and serial number of the printer that produced the image.

There are several places data can be hidden on physical storage devices. These methods are easily detectable using forensic tools, but if no one thinks there is any reason to look in these areas they could easily remain unnoticed:

- RAM slack
  - The space from the end of file marker and the end of a sector
- File slack
  - The space from the end of file marker and the end of a cluster
- Inter-partition gaps
  - Unallocated hard drive capacity
- White noise volumes
  - Encrypted data can be hidden within large areas of data that look like fragments or noise from previous files.

Conclusion

This chapter built on the enumeration efforts from the scanning phase and looked to exploit possible opportunities to gain access to user accounts. Sometimes users are the target because they have important data that logging in as them instantly provides access to. Other times, attackers will need to escalate their privileges by compromising an administrator level account or creating one via a weakness on an accessible server.

It might be possible to simply social engineer a victim into installing an illicit server or have them click a link to a browser drive-by exploit. The entire hacking process for the white hat, however, involves much more than that. Along the way troubleshooting and other problem-solving skills are developed along with a greater awareness of security threats.

Some commercial software embeds backdoor code in order to collect usage data and enforce licenses. Chances are high that your laptop is talking to several machines on the Internet while you watch YouTube and so on. Which ones are malicious or legit is hard to tell and, in some ways, is a matter of opinion.

This is the point where, for most students, the class starts to feel overwhelming. The trick to managing the scope of this class is to take it a chapter at a time, keeping the relevance of the information to attacking in mind. However, don't think you are supposed to know everything simultaneously.

As you continue through the course, notice areas of system administration that are outside the scope of this exam but are certainly skills that would aid the attacker or pentester. Once your CEH exam has been completed, plan on working toward more depth in the areas that interest you the most. For now, focus on developing the skill of being able to recognize when further research is necessary, and pick up the important information regarding the objective at hand rather than trying to become an expert in everything.

After repeated exposure to this material, your expert-level knowledge will happen on its own. Just keep after it.

TROJANS AND BACKDOORS

Introduction

This chapter and the "Viruses and Worms" chapter are tightly connected in a family we call malicious code and builds on some concepts that were introduced in the system hacking chapter. The CEH courseware recognizes three categories of malicious programs:

1. *Trojans and Rootkits*
2. *Viruses*
3. *Worms*

In the wild, malicious software might be categorized any number of ways. In fact, most malicious software contains a combination of several payloads, making it extremely difficult for security researchers to create a universal naming system.

To add further confusion, commercial applications are often Trojan horses. This assertion depends a lot on the user's point of view. Some people believe the following: "If I have nothing to hide, then I don't mind if a police officer pulls me over and searches my personal belongings." Other people say: "Since I have done nothing wrong, I should not be treated as though I have." In terms of computers, the question is "Should legitimate customers be treated like they are software pirates?"

There is also the business end of the Internet that is often taken for granted. Advertisements drive the cost and revenue models of most online companies. There is high motivation to track patterns and target messages. Competitive intelligence depends on it. The data has to be collected somehow. The advertisements have to be served, and smaller organizations have to fight hard to be noticed at all.

To Pass the CEH Exam You Need to . . .

- know what Trojan applications can do
- know the infection vectors
- know how to build a server

- know how to detect an infection
- master the CEH cheatsheets and practice questions!

Know What Trojan Applications Can Do

- The definition of Trojan horses
- Types of Trojans

The Definition of Trojan Horses

A Trojan horse can be defined as any of the following:

- An illicit program enclosed within a valid program. This illicit program performs other functions that the user does not know about and probably does not need.

- A valid program that has been altered by the placement of malicious code within it and performs other functions that the user does not know about and probably does not need.

- Any program that appears to perform desirable and necessary functions but also performs other functions that the user does not know about and probably does not need.

This class of malware usually consists of two parts: the client and the server. A victim host will be a server that provides data such as keylogging files, screenshots, or packet captures back to a client being controlled by the attacker. Even file system browsers and command shell access can be provided to the client of the malicious server.

Let's clarify some terminology before continuing. *Malicious code* is a broad category that could include rootkits, illicit servers, viruses, and worms, or a combination of them all. *Trojan horse* is simply one of the many delivery mechanisms for malicious code. This chapter is also focusing on illicit servers because they are the most common payload of a Trojan.

Another important aspect of malware infections is to define the target or objective of the attacker. Many of the basic concepts are the same, but the techniques will change. If the target is just one user or system, then a single attack that provides backdoor access is all that is needed. Usually the attacker picks victims for this specific reason, and determines the best way to compromise them in one attempt.

If the objective is on a larger scale, then the attacker must cast a wider net of exploits persistently over time until enough victims are collected. These hosts act as *Zombies* doing whatever the attacker commands them to do. The reason behind botnets (Robot Networks) varies from information theft to setting up a distribution network for other malware or pirated materials. The most recent botnets have a level of sophistication that most could not have anticipated only a few years ago.

Types of Trojans

Once again, remember that these concepts are not separate. Malicious code can include one or a combination of these capabilities. A Trojan horse can be defined as any of the following:

- Remote access Trojans
- Data sending Trojans
- Destructive Trojans
- Denial of service Trojans
- Proxy Trojans
- FTP Trojans
- Security software disablers

Remote access Trojans

The remote access Trojan installs an illicit server with enough features to allow the attacker complete control of the system. Since the compromised host is a server, the attacker must connect to it from a client, and firewalls might prevent this. The attacker has two options: Find a port the firewall will pass and configure the illicit server to listen on that port, or get behind the firewall and run the client from there.

Data sending Trojans

This server collects data about the usage of the system and sends it back to the client (attacker). Keystrokes, cached credentials, screenshots, and Internet connections are common categories of usage collection.

Destructive Trojans

This type of malware destroys files on the system. It might target system files such as .dll or .ini files or it might go after data files such as office documents. Destructive Trojans often activate as "Logic Bombs" rather than as illicit servers. A logic bomb is malicious code that activates on the trigger of an event such as date and time or a keystroke combination.

Denial of service Trojans

This type of malicious code requires a cooperative effort from other infected hosts to attack a single target with excess traffic. The target can be either a host, in the sense of sending it confusing traffic, or a network segment, in the sense of creating enough traffic to use all of the available bandwidth.

Proxy Trojans

Proxy servers make requests on behalf of a client. They initiate new connections to the target. Attackers can use a proxy server to hide the point of origin of the true attack. They can make purchases from stolen credit cards, launch commands to a botnet, and virtually anything their proxy is designed to do. Ultimate responsibility for the attack will be blamed on the owner of the network segment the proxy lives on.

FTP Trojans

File Transfer Protocol (FTP) is ideal for transfers of large files. FTP servers are setup secretly to move pirated movies, music, video games, or large applications.

Security software disablers

Malicious code can specifically target anti-malware tools and personal firewalls. Some even take the time to replace the icon in the system tray to appear as if the software is running normally.

Know the Infection Vectors

- Ways a Trojan gets into a system

  - Try it out: Configure an Autostart script

  - Try it out: Research the two letter TLDs

- Startup methods for Linux

  - Try it out: Using the $PATH variable

- Startup methods for Windows

  - Try it out: Using the $PATH variable in Windows

Ways a Trojan Gets into a System

Many attack vectors are possible in terms of delivering malware. Most involve a combination of social engineering, carelessness on the part of the victim, and exploitation of vulnerabilities within the system.

- Instant messenger applications
- IRC (Internet Relay Chat)
- Peer to peer, BitTorrent, file sharing, and Usenet
- E-mail attachments
- Physical access
  - Try it out: Configure an Autostart script
- Browser drive-bys
- Filesharing on the local network
- Fake programs, untrusted sites, and "shrinkwrapped" code
  - Try it out: Research the two letter TLDs
- "Free stuff"

Instant messenger applications

IM applications are a common target for social engineering attacks. If a contact is being masqueraded or if the user opens her IM to accept invitations for strangers, the acceptance of download opens them to a lot of risk. A successful password guessing attack would be all that is necessary to begin the process.

IRC (Internet Relay Chat)

The DCC (Direct Client to Client) protocol can be used to transfer files over IRC. New users to IRC are often the targets of social engineering attacks and can be convinced to accept the download. A file could be renamed to "list_of_sites.txt .exe" (space characters inserted) that will look like a plain text file in many IRC clients.

Peer to peer, BitTorrent, filesharing, and Usenet

The common filesharing networks are still very active because they are easy to use and populated with people that do not understand what they are doing. They are looking for free stuff as fast as they can get it without regard to legal issues. The shame of it is that these technologies, particularly in the case of BitTorrent, Usenet, and IRC, were not designed for this purpose. They do not promise anonymity. Victims take their chances as they could easily be attacked not only by trojanized files but by groups of lawyers from groups like the RIAA.

E-mail attachments

E-mail presents so much risk that we have an entire chapter on it. Some e-mail systems completely block all executable code without exception, but this usually causes people to exchange files through means they are even less familiar with.

If someone wants to share a file they will find a way to do it. Online services that provide temporary hosting for files and other resources are easy to use and are often free for small files. Many users give no thought, however, to whether or not those files are being stored, searched, archived, and "repurposed."

Physical access

USB thumbdrives are just high capacity floppy discs. Data both going out and coming in has become such a problem that some organizations are disabling USB interfaces altogether, but then steps need to be taken to allow the other devices to work when needed. USBs can be configured to auto run in the same way that CD-ROMs are often designed. All it takes is a properly written text file.

Tools such as hacksaw and slurp.exe can even run as U3 applications. They will copy files from the host they were inserted into, compress them, and even upload them to another server so they don't fill up the USB key. Many media devices such as iPods can also perform these tasks (podslurping to be exact).

Of course the tables could also be turned. Using "USB Dumper," a host PC can sense the insertion of removable storage and dump all of its contents to the host. This tool can be installed automatically from a USB drive first. Other tools are combined with USB Dumper to include compression and sending to e-mail or FTP. The Trojan part of the delivery is whatever means the attacker uses to convince people to insert keys into a compromised host (for a demonstration video visit: *http://www.graspr.com/videos/Hak5-Episode-2x03*).

TRY IT OUT

Configure an Autostart Script

At the root of a USB drive, place an executable of your choice. Create a file called "Autorun.inf" with the following text:

```
[autorun]
open=example.exe
icon=example.ico
```

Eject the USB key and remove it. Reinsert the key and the example.exe file should launch.

Browser drive-bys

Many home users surf the Internet as administrators. If the browser they are using has a buffer overflow vulnerability and they visit a malicious site, the exploit will have administrator rights when it runs. These weaknesses exist in not just the browser itself, but in any media plugins or other BHOs (Browser Helper Objects) such as .pdf, .jpeg rendering, and Active X controls.

Filesharing on the local network

On some peer to peer networks or even on older domains, the default hidden file share for the root of a system drive, \\victim\C$, is available to the everyone group with writeable permissions. The attacker simply uploads a script to the share and then sets it to start whenever the machine is rebooted. Sometimes, denial of service attacks are launched just to make the reboot happen sooner.

If the hidden shares are not available to the attacker, then planting Trojans in the public share drive on the network is the next best step. Any shared directory on the network that can be written to will do. UNC (Universal Naming Convention) links to fileshares can be placed inside e-mails just like links to web pages. One click and having the user run the file is all it takes.

Fake programs, untrusted sites, and "shrinkwrapped" code

Google ads make it possible for sites to engineer higher placement in the search results. If a user looks for a popular utility, chances are good that the first several sites listed will not be the official source of the tool, but rather several entries for common file download sites. Some of these sites are perfectly legitimate, if not irritating and difficult to use. It is possible to sneak in sites that host trojanized versions of tools and the victim would not know it.

Many download sites use deceptive advertising practices to make the actual download link confusing. The ads are placed and worded in such a way that they appear to be what the user was looking for, and the host site for the advertisement has likely done absolutely nothing to vet the source for legitimacy. Again, the victims have no idea what they are really clicking on unless they know exactly what to look for.

It would not be accurate to make a blanket statement like "avoid all websites with a .cx, .nl, .to, or .de top level domain" (just to name a few). But it is wise to be on the lookout for download sites with similar names to established .com domains that come from unfamiliar TLDs and avoid them. Also, stay away from any site that promises "Warez", "Serialz", or "Keygenz". These sites operate in places where their activities might not be illegal or where the government has no ability or care to do anything about it anyway. Many small countries or territories such as Christmas Island (population 1,402 people) make their TLDs available for purchase around the world through agreements with Verisign.

TRY IT OUT

Research the Two Letter TLDs

There is a nice article at Wikipedia that explains some of the background stories of the two letter domains. Take a moment to investigate this and realize where some of this material might actually be coming from. Click the links to articles about some of the places.

`http://en.wikipedia.org/wiki/Country_code_top-level_domain`

In some cases simply visiting "warez" sites will subject your browser to dozens of attempted drive-by exploits in addition to anything that is available for download. Do not research these sites on a computer you care about.

"Free stuff"

Users that are looking for hardware drivers, clip art, ringtones, music lyrics, "wavs" (short mp3 files that are bits from movies or T.V. shows), screensavers, or basically anything with the word "free" in front of it find themselves in a never ending labyrinth of pop up ads and links that go nowhere. These sites could be just annoying or could be full of trojanized material.

Forum messages on social network sites, free technical support discussions, and blogs can contain links to files a poster makes reference to. Never directly download a file from such a location; always try to go to the original source of the file and get it from there. Although that is not foolproof, it is the best practice.

Once the trojanized file has been accepted, it must be launched without the attacker having to interact with the target. The first access is usually not the best way to sustain control of the target host. The objective is to plant backdoors that allow the attacker to return at will.

If the Trojan was installed as an application, the code would already have made the necessary configurations. If the attacker has to plant the files on the system, this process can be scripted or performed manually. The challenge for attackers is gaining enough privilege, having their changes blend in or be hidden via a rootkit, and not causing so much damage to the target host that it gets repaired. The best Trojan horse attacks occur without the victim either being aware of it or detecting it.

There are many ways to cause applications to start automatically on both the Linux and Windows platforms.

Startup Methods for Linux

The Linux operating system boots up according to scripts that can be located in different parts of the operating system. The most common location is in a directory called "rc#.d" where # represents the runlevel number. The full path to the directory that contains the scripts for runlevel 3 would then be /etc/rc3.d/*. These scripts are often run through a series of shortcuts (symbolic or hard links) that exist somewhere else. The point is that there is enough complexity in this for an attacker to hide quite a bit of mischief.

The problem with making changes to built-in scripts is that the next time a system is updated it is possible these scripts could be overwritten. So the distribution vendor usually provides a script called something like /etc/rc.local. References to commands or scripts anywhere on a system can be called from here and will be run each time the system starts.

Another way to start programs automatically would be to replace existing binaries with modified versions that include the malicious code or call it from elsewhere. Since Linux is an open source operating system, it is easy to get the code, make changes, recompile, and have at the ready. For someone that doesn't want to do all of that work, Linux rootkits are widely available if you know where to look. The hard part is getting the access and privilege to make these changes.

If malicious code were to be copied to a system with the same file names as common tools, then attackers can attempt to place the file in a directory that is earlier in the path system variable. When a user executes a command, such as "ls," the shell looks in all the directories mentioned in the $PATH variable, and the first one encountered will execute.

TRY IT OUT

Using the $PATH Variable

On a Linux host, open a command shell and issue the following command. Notice what the current search directories are.

```
echo $PATH
```

Start creating a script by entering (if nano is not available try pico):

```
mkdir /etc/foo
```

```
nano /etc/foo/ls
```

When nano opens the file, write, save, and quit the following:

```
#!/bin/bash
```

```
echo "It worked!!"
```

Give the new file execute and set the suid bit to ensure that it executes with the root UID even when a user runs the command.

```
chmod 4755 /etc/foo/ls
```

(continued)

Add the directory to the beginning of the $PATH variable so it will execute before the real "ls" command and export it.

```
PATH=/etc/foo:$PATH
```

```
export $PATH
```

Run the "ls" command

```
ls
```

TRY IT OUT CHALLENGE

This demonstration is not a realistic attack for a number of reasons, but it is meant to show a few necessary commands and techniques. Attackers would be stealthier, as ethical hackers; can you modify the lab in a more realistic fashion?

Startup Methods for Windows

Many freeware tools exist that will detect, list, and, in most cases, help a user control the startup programs in Windows. Some of the more important ones are:

- Windows defender
  - (Built in to Vista)
- msconfig
  - (Built in to most Windows installations)
- Autoruns
  - (*http://technet.microsoft.com/en-us/sysinternals/bb963902.aspx*)
- Hijack this
  - (*http://www.trendsecure.com/portal/en-US/tools/security_tools/hijackthis*)
- Winpatrol
  - (*http://www.winpatrol.com/*)

Depending on the flavor of Windows, there are different places for startup configurations to hide. In generic terms (not specific for each version of Windows) here are some of the most commonly used:

- Auto-start folder
- Win.ini
- System.ini
- Wininit.ini
- Winstart.bat

- Autoexec.bat
- Config.sys
- `[HKEY_LOCAL_MACHINE\Software\Microsoft\Windows\CurrentVersion\ Run] "Info"="[path to the executable]"`
- `[HKEY_LOCAL_MACHINE\Software\Microsoft\Windows\CurrentVersion\ RunServices] "Info"="[path to the executable]"`
- `[HKEY_LOCAL_MACHINE\Software\Microsoft\ActiveSetup\ InstalledComponents\KeyName] "StubPath"="[path to the executable]"`
- `[HKEY_CURRENT_USER\Software\Mirabilis\ICQ\Agent\Apps] "Info"="[path to the executable]"`

Currently, installed applications that create registry keys with auto-start capabilities are common targets for malware. Keys that masquerade as incomplete installations are another way to do it. These are some of the reasons that the possibilities are endless, so it is a good idea to use a utility that stays up to date. Before simply deleting everything you find, be aware that false positives are possible as well.

TRY IT OUT

Using the $PATH Variable in Windows

There are actually many ways to set the execution path variable in Windows. Along the way, it would be helpful to become familiar with some of the other environment variables available. Visit and review the following site:

`http://vlaurie.com/computers2/Articles/environment.htm`

Modify the basic idea of the previous Linux exercise to fit a scenario that will work on a Windows host. The principle concepts are the same.

Know How to Build a Server

- Overview of the illicit server process
- Binding or wrapping malicious code
- Features of a typical illicit server

Overview of the Illicit Server Process

The following steps are involved with a typical illicit server attack:

1. The attacker finds a server generator on the Internet and downloads it.
2. The attacker uses this tool to configure the settings and capabilities of the server and compile it.

3. The malicious server is then "wrapped" into another program that will seem like a legitimate file. This creates the Trojan.

4. The attacker then spreads the Trojan, whether targeted to one individual or randomly spread across hundreds or thousands of targets.

5. The infected machines announce their presence by connecting to a chatroom, or sending an e-mail or an instant message. On an inside job the attacker might scan for the targets.

6. That attacker uses the client portion of the illicit server to connect to infected victims, or communicates with them through the chatrooms or instant messaging.

7. At this point the attacker has taken control and is only limited by what the illicit server can do.

The CEH exam might require you to have memorized a few of the default ports used by popular illicit servers. Most of the time the attacker can change these settings, but for the exam it will be important to be able to recognize attacks from log files, packet dumps, and IDS alert files. The first clue is usually the ports involved in the session.

Ports used by common Trojans:

Back Orifice	31337 or 31338
Sub Seven	27374 or 6711, 6712, 6713
ICQ Trojan	1033
Tini	7777
Senna Spy	13000
MStream	9325
Deep Throat	2140, 3150
Netbus	12345 or 12346
Whack-a-mole	12361 and 12362
Netbus Pro	20034
Girlfriend	21544
Qaz	7597

Binding or Wrapping Malicious Code

A legitimate need for some applications is to combine data and executable files into a single file that can be used during an installation sequence. Since a given program could have a number of data files, library files, and executables we don't want to ask the user to work with each of them separately and follow elaborate instructions. A script can be included in the package to perform all of the steps.

Creating a Trojan horse is simply using a tool that *wraps* or *binds* a number of files into a *packfile* to combine together legitimate and illicit server executables into a believable application. There are many tools that accomplish this task easily; *elitewrap.exe* is one example.

Some illicit server tools have binders in them already, and attackers can create their Trojan all in one step.

Features of a Typical Illicit Server

Every Trojan generator or illicit server application works differently in some way but they usually also have a lot in common. Once you figure out a couple they get easier to do.

For the CEH exam, be sure to understand how these features relate to illicit servers:

- Command interface
- Documentation
- Lamer tools
- Social engineering
- File browsers and reverse shells
- Desktop control
- Notification and chat
- Bots

Command interface

The GUIs are usually very nonstandard with artwork, hard-to-look-at color schemes and fonts, new terminology, and places to click that are not intuitive and are buggy or unstable. Some Trojans offer a command line interface that is more flexible and could be accessed more easily from a pivot point in a multistage attack.

Documentation

You are very lucky if there is any documentation to follow; at the most you get a readme file with a few hints. Do not bother asking much or e-mailing the author. If you are a stranger to a newsgroup, e-mail list, or the author of the tool it is likely you will mostly be insulted rather than be helped.

Lamer tools

Lamer tools are common features of an illicit server. They constitute functions like opening the CD-ROM tray, changing the screen resolution, replacing the desktop with a fake background image, switching the mouse buttons, and disabling the task bar.

Social engineering

Some servers allow the attacker to configure dialog boxes with the OK or Close buttons, for instance. This makes the installation of the server more believable when the victim accepts the file and tries to run it. By not having to bind the server with another full application, the total size of the illicit server is kept small.

File browsers and reverse shells

These features allow an attacker to search through the file system of the target. The reverse shell connects back to a listening port on the attacker's host, creating a TCP session that overcomes stateful inspection firewalls.

Desktop control

A small efficient VNC (Virtual Network Computing) server might be established on the target machine that allows the attacker full control and access to the target's desktop.

Notification and chat

Once the target is infected the attacker must have a way of knowing about it. The server will be configured to send e-mail, initiate an ICQ or other instant messaging session, or report into a chatroom. Some servers provide a way for the attacker to chat with the target victim. In the case of an extortion attack, for example, the attacker might threaten to encrypt all the user's files if they don't follow instructions.

Bots

The illicit server might be accessed from both its corresponding client application, a simple telnet command shell, or through commands in a chatroom. Configuration options include which IRC server to connect to, a login password, and a nick (nickname used in the chatroom to define the bot).

Be careful not to leave default settings as this would be considered the ultimate script kiddie mistake. Who is to say the default setting won't reveal the attack to someone else and at the same time be an attack against the attacking host?

Know How to Detect an Infection

- Staging and testing

  - Try it out: Use Netstat to look for current connections

  - Try it out: Use troubleshooting tools to baseline a system

Staging and Testing

Before attackers use a tool they should know exactly what it does. In most cases, this step is skipped or attackers write the tool themselves and know what it does. The idea of staging an infection intentionally is an important white hat activity. It teaches how to perform the attack, how to verify how it could work, what exactly it did, and how to defend against it.

Using a methodical approach will be more effective than just poking around, although sometimes that is useful, too.

Build two baseline hosts. One is worst-case scenario and the other is best-case scenario. Virtual machines can work well unless the Trojan specifically looks for VMs and alters its behavior accordingly. Snapshots save time and they are easy to keep backed up for reducing initial build times.

The worst-case scenario machine is vulnerable. The attack should work against it. Figure out how to perform the attack and try your idea. Trial and error is expected at this point. Take note of information revealed during failures. Remember that hacking is about figuring things out for better or worse; now is not the time to get frustrated; rather, it is the time to pay attention and be creative.

When intentionally infecting a host machine for forensic purposes, use *marker strings* whenever building illicit servers. For example, the server creation tool might let you configure what the name of the process will be when it runs. If it were called "svchost" it would just be one of the six or so that is already running. This is good for an attacker, but hard for research. Name the process something that will stand out and can be searched for.

When the attack is successful, explore what it might have affected. Assuming a Windows host is the object, look for these elements:

- Processes and dependencies
- Windows on the desktop
- Open ports
- Registry entries
- Look through startup methods and things that might affect DNS resolution
- Have a sniffer running and sample some traffic

TRY IT OUT

Use Netstat to Look for Current Connections

In either a baseline Windows or Linux host, open a command shell and baseline the current network access points. Better yet, compare a Windows and Linux host to each other.

```
netstat -an
```

Enable or install a network service and try again. The idea is to compare and notice differences.

The CEH curriculum includes over 14Gs of tools, code, and reading materials that directly apply to what has been discussed so far. It is a safer and time-saving way to obtain lab samples rather than search for yourself. The live classroom will also provide an opportunity to look at these tools and perform these attacks.

In the meanwhile, baselining your machine and getting used to what normal activity goes on in a typical system will give you a head start.

TRY IT OUT

Use Troubleshooting Tools to Baseline a System

Download and install these "bread and butter" tools and try them out. Use a test machine if possible and be careful where the tools come from. The research is part of this exercise. Think about how each of these tools could be used.

fport

tcpview

process viewer

Insider

(continued)

What's running?

Rootkit revealer

Wireshark

Packetyzer

Spyware S&D

Window Watcher

Regmon

windiff

hasher

Conclusion

How much of your computer belongs strictly to you and how much right do others have to control your system when you are connecting it to a global network? If you are walking down a street in a public place, can someone stop you for a conversation? Of course, it happens all the time. Computers are an extension of this, only better. You can ask for directions to Luigi's pizza parlor and be given directions to "Lemmy's Lingerie" and have your pockets picked along the way there.

It is understandable if you connect to a public network and expect privacy, but it is not reasonable.

Be paranoid on the CEH exam. Unlike other certifications that test perfect scenarios of well-intentioned CEOs with unlimited budgets to test plans for measuring and assessing security and compliance, this one is darker and more direct. It assumes that weaknesses still exist in spite of all these plans. It assumes that weaknesses still exist in spite of all the plans to plan an analysis of a plan that will eventually become a plan to secure the network. Do not question likelihood because this test is not about your well-defended position. It is about the ones that are open and what could be done to them.

Having made that point, the biggest difference between the secure network and the insecure network is the motivation and creativity of attackers. Some networks are not worth the effort, some are. What if even the most secure network on planet earth could be breached by a simple pickpocket-type attack from a simple vulnerability?

This brings us to the topic of viruses and worms, which is covered in the next chapter.

VIRUSES AND WORMS

Introduction

Viruses and worms are among the most controversial topics in the computer hacking community. The following open-ended questions can keep security professionals debating for hours:

- Are viruses on the decline because there is less money to be made, or because anti-virus practices have improved so much?

- Is there really a difference between a virus and a worm since by some technical opinion a worm contains a virus anyway?

- What would be the best way to formalize an industry accepted ontology, or a standard naming system for viruses? Is this even a good idea? Is it viruses or virii?

- Is it ethical to teach virus writing or to create them at all? Can there be good viruses? Should positive acknowledgement be given to the clever ideas that have been incorporated into viruses?

Regardless of how you would answer any of these questions, we agree the topic is very important to the world of information security and risk management. In terms of studying for the CEH exam, take the most traditional road and focus on the importance of certain characteristics of viruses and worms as they relate to information security.

To Pass the CEH Exam You Need to. . .

- know the history and evolution of viruses and worms

- know the types of viruses and worms

- know about virus detection and removal

- master the CEH cheatsheets and practice questions!

Know the History and Evolution of Viruses and Worms

- History of viruses
- The basic structure of malicious code
- Characteristics of infections
- Lifecycle of replicating software
- Differences between viruses and worms
- Motivations for creating malicious code

History of Viruses

Like many concepts in information security, proof of concept studies often comes long before any actual working examples. As early as the 1970s computer scientists worked with the idea of self-replication code as well as countermeasures such as other code that could combat the original infections. Some of these experiments, such as "Creeper" and "Reaper," worked across the network while the "Wabbit" virus used up system resources. Even non-malicious code such as the ANIMAL virus demonstrated viral concepts while intending to be a basic game the end user could interact with and is considered the first Trojan.

Even though the term *virus* was coined in 1983 by Fred Cohen, the CEH exam will consider the first actual working virus found in the wild to be an outbreak called "Elk Cloner" that began in 1981. It targeted Apple II systems and propagated via infected floppy discs that stored the operating system.

In 1986 the first IBM PC-compatible virus—a boot sector virus called "Brain"—was released. In that same year the "Virdem Model" was created by the Chaos Computer Club. It is a demonstration of self-replicating code placed in the COM format, and is a common executable file type in the DOS OS.

In 1988, a virus known as "Festering Hate Apple ProDOS" spread via BBS (Bulletin Board Systems). BBS was a widespread technology used both in business and personal applications and was the arguable precursor to Usenet or even the World Wide Web before the Internet became available for mainstream use. In that same year, the first worm, known as "Morris," infected machines connected to the Internet. The Morris worm was an experiment in replicating patches, and exploited buffer overflow vulnerabilities in DAX and BSD UNIX systems.

In the late 1980s and early 1990s the advent of multipartite viruses (code that can infect using multiple means of exploitation) and polymorphic viruses (code that can encrypt itself to evade detection) were created, such as "Tequila." In 1992, the Michelangelo virus represented the first mass hysteria that amounted to very little actual damage as the mainstream media began to cover stories about malicious code in the news outlets. Virus construction kits came onto the scene, which promised to provide a person without programming skills the ability to create malicious code with a variety of features.

In the mid-1990s we saw the first "Macro viruses" and the continued development of polymorphic techniques. In 1998 the CIH Chernobyl virus proved that hardware could be attacked as it targeted system BIOS (Basic Input Output System) chips that were becoming increasing rewritable while installed on the system board. The CIH virus hid itself in the gaps between other instructions within executable "PE" files and therefore did not change the size of the files it infected. It also overwrote the first two sectors (1024K) of the primary hard disk, wiping out the partition table and the backup sector.

The late 1990s saw an explosion of malicious code as Windows 95 and 98 had become commonplace in almost every business and home. The Melissa worm targeted e-mail systems and caused denial of service conditions; the Netbus and SubSeven (Sub7) elicit servers were released and sparked mass availability to create Trojan horse applications.

Another event in the late 1990s was the introduction of virtual machine technology into the common market. The Java programming language is designed to work inside of an environment that can be made cross-platform. The "Strange Brew" virus proved Java was vulnerable and because the virtual machine runs on many systems the potential for infection is almost limitless.

The early 2000s was perhaps the beginning of virus activity that caused widespread financial damage and sparked the need to improve security practices in this area. To name a few, ILOVEYOU, Sircam, Code Red, Nimda, and Klez were all released during this period. Code Red II demonstrated "variants and copycat code" as it was a rewrite of the original worm and fixed several of its programming errors to make it spread more efficiently. Nimda (*admin* spelled backwards) exploits holes left behind by Code Red and Sadmind.

In 2002 the concept of RAT (Remote Access Tools) was building on the demonstration of Netbus and Sub7. Beast integrated the client and server into one binary and could infect hosts running Windows XP. The term RAT also came to be known as Remote Administration Tool and some of them, such as Netbus, became commercially sold products. Rather than spread and cause damage on their own, RATs set up a service on the victim's host that could be accessed by a client run by the attacker. This provided real-time capability of keylogging, screen capturing, depositing files, and even pivoting other forms of attack from the victim's location on the network.

In 2003, a series of worms focusing on denial of service attacks were released. The "SQL Slammer," "Blaster," and "Sobig" worms received media attention for their ability to spread rapidly, and the "Welchia" and "Sober" worms built on the carnage they left behind.

In 2004 the DoS attacks continued with "MyDoom" and "Sasser." The illicit server category of malware continued with Nuclear RAT and could reach Windows 2003 servers. Later that year, "Santy" exploited websites that used a WWW based popular bulletin board system written in PHP by using Google searches to find its victims.

In 2005 the publishing company Sony BMG decided to attack their legitimate customers with a rootkit that would not only prevent fair use of CDs they published but would also "phone home" and indicate to a server whenever the disc was placed into a computer for listening. The rootkit was spread using their CDs, making this a virus outbreak. In an interesting irony, although Sony claimed it would stop at nothing to protect intellectual property rights, it was found that Sony violated the GPL of the LAME (LAME Ain't and MP3 Encoder) encoder it used in the proprietary player that was installed.

From 2007 to the present, viral outbreaks have largely been about depositing payloads that attempt to setup "botnets" (Robot Networks) for large-scale attempts at crimes such as identity theft, extortion, and illegal bandwidth usage for spam and other advertisement distribution. The Storm worm was estimated to infect 10 million computers worldwide. The Koobface worm has entered into the social networking space targeting MySpace and Facebook. Worms have also been released for Twitter.

The Conficker worm has an undetermined size at the time of this writing, but is capable of infecting versions of Windows up to the as yet released Windows 7. On April Fool's Day, 2009, the Conficker worm had a logic bomb that was supposed to activate while the world waited, having no idea what it was going to do. Not much happened (like with Michelangelo), but soon after the worm was discovered to have the ability to patch itself and to learn new capabilities.

The Basic Structure of Malicious Code

There are three phases of a viral attack:

- Infection phase
- Spreading phase
- Attack phase

Infection phase

A weakness in a system is exploited during this phase. The exploit can come in the form of buffer overflows or of any simple logic errors in which attackers understand the sequence of expected steps better than the application developer and can inject code into a process.

Direct viruses infect their hosts by executing as standalone applications. Logic bombs lie in wait until an event triggers the executable. TSR (Terminate and Stay Resident) programs execute at various stages, even after the initial host application has been closed.

Spreading phase

How the spreading phase works depends on whether the malicious code is a virus or a worm and what its objective is.

A virus that is looking to drop code or breach data integrity will spread through file shares, portable storage, e-mail, and boot sectors. Worms typically involve denial of service objectives and can spread using network protocols with the user having to trigger them.

Attack phase

Many modern malicious code examples incorporate several types of payload. A *dropper* is code that leaves behind other malicious code that completes the gaining access and maintaining access loop. They can also incorporate encryption and morphing techniques to evade detection algorithms. As stated earlier, they are paying as much attention to us as we are to them.

Characteristics of Infections

The following is a list of common symptoms or characteristics of viral activity. It is critical that standard incident response procedures be observed. Hoax viruses are specifically designed to exploit overreaction and poor analysis of these events. False positives can be as costly as actual breaches depending on what the attacker was trying to accomplish and how wise the response was.

- Malicious code can possibly reside in computer random access memory and replicate itself as a matter of a host application performing normal functions.

- Malicious code can possibly leave random access memory and copy itself to secondary storage, waiting for another event to call it back out of dormancy.

- Malicious code can possibly copy itself to the boot sector of a file or setup an auto-start from removable media.

- Malicious code can transform itself through an efficient encryption engine (polymorphic) or by rearranging its instructions, mixed with some decoy mnemonics performing significant steps between the attack opcodes (metamorphic).

- Malicious code might alter its host to avoid changing the file size or affecting other detection criteria.

- Malicious code can encrypt the files it targets, and hold them for ransom.

- Malicious code might slightly break a host, causing unexpected events such as displays that turn upside down or change resolution and cause spontaneous kernel panics (BSOD or Blue Screen of Death in Windows), which mimic common driver compatibility issues.

- Malicious code can possibly redirect the I/O (input/output) stream of an operating system functions in order to avoid detection.

- Malicious code can possibly trigger events within its own code. It can make system calls. If installed with a rootkit it can even completely hide from the operating system kernel.

- Malicious code can possibly use I/O processes that both involve memory access and network access to spread. They can access the features of an operating system to access resource shares and directories to facilitate their propagation.

- Malicious code can possibly have a *nuclear* feature that simply allows remote attackers to ask their victims to self-destruct themselves (by the millions, perhaps, because it would be better to destroy botnets than to leave them in enemy hands).

At the time of this writing, the "torpig" botnet, which from early 2008 is considered responsible for more than half a million bank account thefts, surfaced again in researchers' labs. They were able to seize over 70G of stolen data. Botnets do not go away when they aren't in the news any more. The attackers do not care about arguments over patching or about what is outdated. They find victims and keep them for years.

Lifecycle of Replicating Software

The CEH exam recognizes a six-step virus lifecycle and helps to explain in general terms how an infection can so quickly spread.

1. Design
2. Replication
3. Launch
4. Detection
5. Incorporation
6. Elimination

Design

A researcher discovers a vulnerability using a combination of computer language, processing theory, and knowledge of a particular platform. A proof of concept is drafted and then tested. The code can be only a few lines, and the cleverness is often in how easy it looks to everyone else once the attack is demonstrated.

Replication

A virus needs to replicate itself to spread. This is either accomplished in a self-sufficient form (worm) or with the aid of user action. Utilizing existing files is a convenient way to guarantee spreading because users will interact with them eventually. Hiding within critical resources also makes detection and response a challenging process. Part of the defensive puzzle is how to remove the virus without destroying the host.

Launch

User actions are often depended on for these type of infections. The range of such infections has expanded from inserting floppies to inserting a USB key (on second thought, maybe this hasn't changed all that much). Since several vulnerabilities in the rendering engines of popular browsers have been discovered, user action can be as simple as visiting websites. If they have escalated privileges at the time, then it is all the better for the attacker.

Detection

The hardest part of having a response plan to avoid infections is often about avoiding overreacting. Anyone who plays the role of technical support for family members is well familiar with the phrase, "Can you spend all weekend fixing my computer, it did something strange and I think it has a virus."

In business, IRP (Incident Response Planning) and DRP (Disaster Recovery Planning) are mandatory processes. A measured, reasoned approach makes the largest difference between success and failure. Detection is a necessity of due diligence, and organizations that do not perform detection procedures can face liability risks that exceed the damage of a viral outbreak.

Incorporation

An amazing effort is at work in regard to the fight against malicious code that involves commercial researchers, academic researchers, and private individuals with a variety of motivations. Each is in a race against time to be the first to exploit an opportunity and to understand the possible defense vectors.

Conficker is clearly demonstrating that the more sophisticated attackers are as much infiltrating the white hat world as we have always tried to penetrate theirs. The incorporation phase of the malware lifecycle is extremely competitive and each situation is unique.

Elimination

Assuming the good guys win the incorporation battle, the elimination step is about installing countermeasures and mitigating damages. It is often said that no virus ever completely disappears; it just slows down. Diligent monitoring is necessary following the elimination of any threat, particularly self-spreading code.

Differences Between Viruses and Worms

- A virus requires a user-initiated event to spread and must have a carrier. A worm can execute itself and can include its own spreader.
- A virus typically affects files such as executables or can hide in media files. A worm typically does not target data but carries out its own agenda.
- Viruses are difficult to remove without affecting the infected body. A worm can usually be removed without damaging a system.
- Viruses have fewer spreading options because they target data and rely on external vehicles. Worms have almost limitless spreading possibilities because they can provide their own services and even protocols.

Motivations for Creating Malicious Code

Historically, the reasons people have created viruses is fairly clear. Viruses started off being written as curiosities and exercises in the power of computing. As their capabilities matured, the intrigue created a strong motivation for further exploration. Eventually, the bad guys and the good guys saw business opportunity and became adversaries.

Presently, these motivations and several others continue to drive the malware industry:

- Research
- Pranks
- Vandalism
- Industrial espionage
- Extortion
- The spreading of payloads with increased capabilities

Know the Types of Viruses and Worms

- Approaching this section for the CEH exam

- Classifying and naming viruses

- Virus types: terms and definitions

Approaching This Section for the CEH Exam

For this section of the chapter, it is most important to focus on the terminology. Do not expect that every example of malicious code will be "one or the other" as these are not mutually exclusive ideas. Any example of malicious code could incorporate one or several of the concepts mentioned in this list of vocabulary.

Classifying and Naming Viruses

Classifying viruses is a difficult task. There is no system that is recognized universally when it comes to computer viruses. Some of the possible ways to categorize viruses and worms are:

- How does the spreader work?

- How does the virus store itself?

- What sort of damage does the virus do?

How does the spreader work?

Viruses can attach themselves to other files, or copy themselves through means such as network resources or boot sectors of removable storage. Worms can carry their own *tftp* or *http* servers and spread through native clients.

How does the virus store itself?

A shell virus wraps its code around the infected file and then calls the original file as a function. Add-on viruses just place themselves at the beginning of an executable and run when the application is called. Intrusive viruses completely overwrite the original file, usually corrupting it in the process. Cavity viruses hide within the executable.

What sort of damage does the virus do?

Some malicious code causes a denial of service by simply wasting resources. This could include network bandwidth or filling up storage space with useless files. Other viruses steal data by looking for types of strings and copying them from files. Some viruses intend on corrupting data. There are also those that seek to destroy the host by making it unusable after a restart or even by scrambling critical firmware code within the hardware.

A typical name will look something like this (from Symantec): "W32.Sens.A" Indicating the target platform is a Windows 32bit operating system, the name of the virus is "Sens", and we are currently discussing variant "A". Some researchers will intentionally not name the virus after anything that describes a signature within it, so as not to give credit to its author or encourage celebrity among those that release malicious code. Once a virus is captured, variations or copycat viruses soon make their way to release. Researchers must determine when it has changed enough to be a whole new virus rather than a variant of a previous one.

Virus Types: Terms and Definitions

For the CEH exam, be sure you are very familiar with each of these virus types:

- Hoax
- MBR (Master Boot Record) virus
- Cavity virus
- Multipartite virus
- Network virus
- Source code virus
- File infector virus
- Macro virus
- Polymorphic virus
- Metamorphic virus
- Stealth virus
- Tunneling virus
- Camouflage virus

Hoax

False alarms can trigger overreaction and possibly hysteria. They are considered possibly as damaging as the real things. When one person tells five friends, then each of them tells ten friends, the e-mail traffic can cause wasted time and network performance issues.

A hoax is a social engineering trick that can also attack the reputation of a product because some people will continue to believe the hoax was real long after it is disproven.

MBR (Master Boot Record) virus

The bootable volume of a floppy, hard disk or USB key contains a small program in the first available sector (Cylinder 0, Head 0, Sector 1) that loads enough code into computer memory to give the processor something to start doing. Usually the next events involve accessing the active partition from a virtual file system, loading an operating system kernel, and turning control of the remaining boot process to the OS.

A boot sector virus overwrites this code and completely controls the system during startup. It typically copies itself into memory and will infect the boot sector of any other secondary storage media that gets inserted. If the intent of the virus is to damage the computer, it will start to erase the hard drive the next time the system is started.

Cavity virus

Many executable binaries have places where other executable code can hide. A cavity virus is also a file infector in that it seeks out these vulnerable programs and modifies them to host the malicious code. This does not necessarily affect the original program execution, and it also does not cause an increase in the size of the original file. Cavity viruses target critical system files that were once never expected to change and therefore were not often scanned.

Multipartite virus

This type of virus can infect systems through more than one means. For example, a multipartite virus might be both a "program virus" and a "boot sector" virus, attacking specific executables to drop a destructive payload while copying itself via boot sector copies.

Network virus

A network virus spreads itself through protocols that communicate across the network. File shares and e-mail are common vectors. In operating systems like Windows, the applications can use common libraries to access objects such as the contact list database which the user configured through his e-mail client. If a virus knows how to access this library, it can generate the e-mails and spread to every address without the local user knowing anything happened at all.

Source code virus

As project deadlines get tighter and tighter, programmers look toward as much reusable code as they can find. Scripts downloaded from the Internet can have malicious code inserted either by the original author or someone else that has compromised the script. The spreading mechanism in this case is the advertising and sharing of the code.

File infector virus

A file infector targets specific files such as executables or data files. Office documents are a common target because they are likely to be copied or e-mailed as attachments. Once the file is infected, a "data diddler" will try to change the contents of the file, sometimes with random bytes grabbed from RAM (Random Access Memory).

Macro virus

The Visual Basic scripting language is powerful and versatile. Being able to automate the process across large collections of data documents or applying reliable and repeatable changes with the click of a button saves time and money. The more adaptable the API (Application Programming Interface) is, the more opportunity will be present for malicious code.

The common social engineering technique that assists the spreading of infected files is to rename the filename extension to hide the fact that it is a script. "Example.vbs" can be renamed to "example.txt.vbs" making it look to the victim as if it was simply a harmless text file.

Polymorphic virus

In order to avoid detection, a virus can change its appearance to the anti-virus scanner. Polymorphic viruses change themselves with encryption. A small and simple key-generating engine ensures that each time it changes not only will it not look the same but it will be able to decrypt itself the next time it activates or spreads. It is not necessary to be too elaborate. In this case confidentiality is not a long-term goal so the method of encryption can be very straightforward, such as XOR (Exclusive OR) streams with a short key.

Although it is not possible to detect a polymorphic virus directly using signature analysis, the decryption engine can be detected. Different viruses could use the same decryption engine, so further analysis would always be necessary.

Metamorphic virus

This type of virus rewrites itself. The process works basically like this: Imagine two separate lists of instructions. The first is the malicious payload, and the other is a set of nonsense instructions that don't break the code but don't do anything useful either. Blend them together to form one list with instructions from the second list inserted into the first at various places. This would be done in assembly instructions and ensures neither the signature nor sequence of events is ever the same. The following example serves as a simple visualization:

List one:

1. Load into memory
2. Launch a command shell process
3. Search for all .xls files in the local documents folder
4. Delete all .xls files that were found
5. Echo random bytes from memory redirected into new files named f009(x).eml
6. Do once each time the user right clicks the mouse

List two:

1. Begin counting to 1024
2. Stop counting at a random time, load the value into x
3. Subtract x from the time of day
4. Overwrite x with random data from memory

Example of new copy of the virus (1)

1. Load into memory
2. Begin counting to 1024
3. Launch a command shell process
4. Search for all .xls files in the local documents folder
5. Delete all .xls files that were found
6. Stop counting at a random time, load value into x
7. Subtract x from the time of day
8. Overwrite x with random data from memory
9. Echo random bytes from memory redirected into new files named f00(x).eml
10. Do once each time the user right clicks the mouse

Example virus (2) – Child of the previous generation:

1. Load into memory
2. Launch a command shell process
3. Begin counting to 1024
4. Search for all .xls files in the local documents folder
5. Stop counting at a random time, load value into x
6. Subtract x from the time of day
7. Delete all .xls files that were found
8. Overwrite x with random data from memory
9. Echo random bytes from memory redirected into new files named f00.eml
10. Do once each time the user right clicks the mouse

Stealth virus

Stealth viruses hide themselves from "the immune system" (meaning anti-virus counter-measures), but copy themselves to temporary locations, leaving the infected files to appear clean when they are scanned.

Tunneling virus

A tunneling virus hides itself from anti-virus applications by intercepting the interrupt handlers of the operating system. It can make sure the scanner never knows it is there.

Camouflage virus

A camouflage virus pretends to be a genuine application. It masquerades as having characteristics the anti-virus scanner is looking for in terms of what allowable code is.

Both tunneling and camouflage viruses are rare because modern anti-virus software hooks deep into the kernel, essentially as a rootkit. They also perform much more than simple signature detection.

An important element of a virus is how small it can remain while still accomplishing its objectives. Part of remaining undetected might include not breaking the system it has infected or not slowing itself down with complex operations while it spreads. There are many types of viruses built to accomplish many different objectives.

Know About Virus Detection and Removal

- Virus construction kits
- Prevention and incident response
- Virus detection techniques

Virus Construction Kits

Programs have been created that generate malicious code simply by asking the user to configure a few options. Some even have graphical environments with drop-down menus and *wizards* that help someone with no knowledge of viruses whatsoever create a malicious application.

When these types of tools are discovered they are called PUPs (Potentially Unwanted Programs) and most anti-virus scanners will detect and eliminate them. Many hacking tools are considered PUPs; this practice generates some controversy within the defense community.

Prevention and Incident Response

Prevention is the best first response. User education on how to properly handle e-mail attachments and how to communicate suspected breaches is critical.

All traffic that comes in or out of the network should be scanned. This is a process known as "Sheep Dip." The name comes from the practice of never letting a sheep join the flock without first going through the flea bath, because all it takes is one infested sheep to affect the whole flock.

Standard incident response procedures apply when infections are detected. It is critical that these procedures be tested and rehearsed regularly to ensure the most effective and rapid resolutions are achieved. The following is a brief review of an incident response model. The actual terms vary from text to text; focus on the basic framework and visualize walking through the process:

1. Detection
    *   Monitoring systems notice that a breach has occurred.
2. Notification
    *   The proper personnel are notified and arrive on scene.
3. Assessment
    *   An assessment of the situation is taken. A measured response is determined.
4. Containment
    *   The breach is prevented from spreading further.
5. Eradication
    *   The malicious code is neutralized or removed.
6. Reconstitution
    *   All affected services are restored.
7. Lessons learned
    *   The total response lifecycle is reviewed and feedback is given to risk and continuity planning.

Virus Detection Techniques

Analysis and detection tools include the following:

- Commercial and freeware anti-virus scanners
- Host- and network-based intrusion detection systems (IDS)
- Dissemblers and debuggers
- Utilities for forensics and troubleshooting

Commercial and freeware anti-virus scanners

Several commercial anti-virus software products are available and this space is extremely competitive. What you want to look for during evaluation is: How often are new signature updates published? Will the interface be intrusive to the user? Does the software uninstall correctly if we decide to remove it?

There is also confusion over the marketing words being chosen to describe the products. Viruses, worms, malware, Trojans, and PUPs are all different classes of risk and various products handle each differently. An all-in-one solution will usually involve cost, but each class can also be handled with separate freeware utilities.

Host- and network-based intrusion detection systems (IDS)

A class of tools called SIVs (System Integrity Verifier) can keep a database of the file sizes, access times, and hash calculations of critical files on a system. If anything about the files changes, that change is logged. An example is "Tripwire" on the Linux platform. Windows operating systems have a limited SIV feature built in and will attempt to restore an affected file from a CAB (Cabinet) archive, or ask for the original install media if the CAB is not available.

Detecting virus and worm activity involves setting up a series of checks. Signatures, which are essentially recognizable sequences of data bytes, are looked for and compared to a database of known byte combinations Checksums are kept of files to detect changes in the data. Rules based approaches to look for unusual network activity are part of the process as well. Heuristic scanning focuses on behavior characteristics and is useful when the malicious code is metamorphic or polymorphic.

Dissemblers and debuggers

Tools such as the commercial "IDA Pro", or the freeware "OllyDBG," allow the analyst to take a byte-for-byte look at every instruction and step an application takes when it executes. These tools are also used for reverse engineering and breaking license enforcement within applications (making "keygens"). Many researchers say this method of research can be better than having the original source code.

Utilities for forensics and troubleshooting

Many tools such as those in the pstools set can be extremely useful for an analyst. When infecting a host intentionally for research, use name-generated files with easy to distinguish patterns such as "MMMNNNMMM" that are unlikely to occur naturally. Search functions of these forensic tools can then look for processes, registry keys, files, libraries, window names, and other dependencies.

File comparison tools such as the classic "Windiff" tool are also helpful. Commercial products exist that can make short work of comparing "before and after" snapshots of virtual machines. Some malware will detect and decide not to infect virtual machines for exactly this reason.

Conclusion

One of the key elements of this section is to remember that overreaction is not helpful.

Spontaneous reboots and the malfunctioning of typical widgets (the desktop quits responding, shortcuts stop working) is sometimes caused by badly written applications or driver conflicts. When the computer hard freezes, there is no movement of the mouse, or any other limited response exists, the most likely cause is an overheating CPU. The dust bunnies in the fan need to be blown out with compressed air. Spontaneous reboots can be caused by RAM chips simply needing to be cleaned and reinserted.

Having a proper response system is the best antidote for viruses. Prevention and preparedness can neutralize this form of attack almost 100 percent if ongoing discipline is made a matter of strict routine. The idea of a single small file bringing down an entire enterprise is too enticing for there not to be continued effort given to the discovery of these vulnerabilities. Once a virus is wild it is forever present. It may be slowed down or dormant because of countermeasures, but it is certainly capable of becoming active again when the opportunity arises.

SNIFFERS, SPOOFING, AND SESSION HIJACKING

Introduction

In the networking environments of today, administrators can no longer just run a sniffer for troubleshooting reasons as too much sensitive data is flowing on the network. Voice data and other media can easily be sniffed and reconstructed into files. Network infrastructure changes, such as Layer 2 switching, have made sniffing much more difficult, but often still not impossible.

Network sniffing is a crucial part of research and being able to understand exactly what attacks do. Even if sniffing is not a part of the attack itself, it is important to be able to stage attacks in an environment that would allow the researcher to analyze the traffic that various tools create. For this reason, many tools incorporate an encryption layer to avoid this and any other intrusion detection services. This is why, from a defensive point of view, it is important not only to mandate encryption for some things, but also to forbid encryption in other places on the network.

Attackers might not be discouraged by the countermeasures against sniffing. Spoofing, MiTM (Man in The Middle), and session hijacking are all possible work around techniques when passive sniffing is not possible.

The Try It Out exercises in this chapter are only here for example and should not be run on hosts without express permission. In addition, they should only be run on hosts in controlled environments. Sniffing is no longer something that a person can just do without regard for policy or other risk factors.

To Pass the CEH Exam You Need to . . .

- know how sniffing works
- know how to use packet capture tools
- know how to exploit vulnerable protocols
- know how session hijacking works
- master the CEH cheatsheets and practice questions!

Know How Sniffing Works

- Passive sniffing

- Active sniffing

  - Try it out: Research advanced ARP procedures

Passive Sniffing

Sniffers are also called protocol analyzers, but that label really depends on the tool itself. Some only display or collect, while others can calculate statistical details and provide reports. Another common activity is to reconstruct captured traffic to view the data as a complete Layer 7 file rather than as a network conversation.

A sniffer does not interact with the packets that it captures; it simply displays the packets or collects them into files for later analysis. There are a variety of reasons for capturing traffic: Trojan horse malware, troubleshooting tools, and network forensics are a few of the types of tools that need to sniff traffic.

A passive sniffing tool can capture packets sent from or received by the network interface of the host it is running on. Doing this generally does not require elevated permissions or special techniques. Sniffing all traffic within a network segment, regardless of who the source and destinations are, is more complex.

Active sniffing on a local network segment requires three elements: The user of the sniffer must have privileges, the NIC must be in "promiscuous mode," and the NIC must be able to see all network traffic.

Elevated privileges are necessary in order to install or activate the promiscuous mode driver for the NIC. This driver essentially tells the NIC to ignore the first 48 bits of the Layer 2 frame header. This field contains the hardware address of the NIC; normally the NIC would ignore all network frames that were not addressed to it. In order to capture packets, the NIC must be told that even the frames not meant for it must be processed.

For wired NICs, promiscuous mode drivers come from two libraries: "WinPcap" for Windows and "LibPcap" for Linux. Each library is typically installed with common sniffing software such as Wireshark, but can also be downloaded and installed separately. For wireless networks the equivalent concept is called "monitor mode." Most wireless NICs either have monitor mode capabilities disabled in the firmware or require specific drivers for that particular wireless device.

If the NIC is on a host that is accessing the local network through a hub device at Layer 1, then all packets will be visible. Most modern networks use Layer 2 switches to reduce the collision segments and manage traffic more efficiently. In this case, active sniffing techniques will be required. Wireless networks are essentially working on physical hubs. This is one of the reasons manufacturers make it hard to access the monitor mode capabilities of their wireless network interfaces.

Active Sniffing

Active sniffing is necessary when the host attempting to capture traffic cannot "see" all of the packets. There are some techniques an attacker can use to capture packets under this circumstance. Because they are active techniques, they do create some noise, and attackers will be most successful if they know who their targets are up front and do not try to sniff everything. Here are the techniques covered on the CEH exam:

- ARP poisoning
- MAC flooding
- MAC duplicating (spoofing)

ARP poisoning

In order to detect conflicting IP addresses on a network, hosts will accept unsolicited ARP replies called "ARP announcements" or "gratuitous ARP." When a new host comes online, it will announce itself to the network. It says in essence, "Hey everybody, IP address 1.2.3.4 has hardware address AA:BB:CC:DD:EE:FF." If any other hosts have the same IP address, the conflict will be detected. (These are example addresses, of course.)

There are other reasons for gratuitous ARP as well. Clusters use them to announce when an IP has been moved to a different NIC, and hosts can announce themselves this way to the port on a switch they are connected to so the switch doesn't have to learn through unknown unicast frames.

ARP spoofing is when a host sends gratuitous ARP messages that intentionally mislead everyone. Consider the following example (addresses abbreviated for illustration purposes only):

	IP Address	Hardware Address
Attacker	10.3	YY:YY
Victim Host	10.5	AA:AA
Network Router (gateway)	10.1	BB:BB
Remote Machine	20.20	Doesn't matter

Sequence of events:

1. Attacker tells the victim "Hey, AA:AA, the MAC address of 10.0.0.1 is YY:YY."
2. Attacker tells the router "Hey BB:BB, the MAC address of 10.0.0.5 is YY:YY."
3. Victim needs to send some traffic to the remote machine:
    a. It sees in its cache that it already knows the MAC address of the router. It creates a frame for YY:YY with the destination IP of 20.20.
    b. The frame arrives at the attacker's NIC. It is copied or altered, and the attacker then creates a new frame:

    destination MAC address BB:BB and IP address 20.20

4. The router forwards the packet along and eventually 20.20 replies back. The router must now deliver the reply packet to the victim.

   a. It sees in its cache that it already knows the MAC address of the victim. It creates a frame for YY:YY with a destination IP of 10.5.

   b. The frame arrives at the attacker's NIC. It is copied or altered, and the attacker then creates a new frame: destination MAC address AA:AA and IP address 10.5.

This is also called an "ARP poisoning" or ARP MiTM (Man in The Middle) attack. Steps 1 and 2 above have to be repeated many times and at intervals to make sure the target machines do not lose this information from their caches. It is easy to detect the ARP spoofing because of the unusual amounts of gratuitous ARP messages present on the network. The switch itself is transparent in this attack and plays no role.

MAC flooding

Switches that learn about what NICs are connected to which interfaces must store that information in memory. This is called a CAM (Content Addressable Memory) table. There is a limited amount of memory space available for this information. The attacker floods the switch with enough ARP traffic to fill the CAM, which causes the switch to fail safe or enter "hub mode." This happens because the switch can no longer learn about new hardware addresses and doesn't want to bring the whole network down.

The countermeasure for MAC flooding is to configure port security on the switch. Limit the number of addresses it can learn on each interface or how much memory each interface is allowed to use.

MAC duplicating (spoofing)

Attackers configure their NIC to have the same MAC address as another NIC on the network. As demonstrated by the ARP spoofing attacks, it is possible for two hosts with the same MAC address to exist on a local network segment. The layers above 2 don't care at all and the switch might forward frames out every interface that seems to have that MAC address living there, not just one.

Some hardware devices such as wireless access points are configured with an ACL (Access Control List) that allows only hosts with certain MAC addresses to associate. An attacker can sniff these MAC addresses from clear text management frames and learn what addresses need to be spoofed. With this information attackers can attempt to associate with the access point and join the network.

TRY IT OUT

Research Advanced ARP Procedures

Read the RFC on ARP messages:

http://www.ietf.org/rfc/rfc3927.txt?number=3927

Read the RFC on resolving IP address conflicts:

http://www.ietf.org/rfc/rfc5227.txt?number=5227

Know How to Use Packet Capture Tools

- Command line tools
- Working with capture filters
  - Try it out: Using tcpdump
  - Try it out: Research advanced Wireshark capture filters
- Graphic tools for packet analysis
  - Try it out: Experiment with GUI-based graphic analyzers
- Working with display filters in Wireshark
  - Try it out: Research advanced Wireshark display filters

Command Line Tools

The primary command line tool for packet capturing is "tcpdump" (named "Windump" for the Windows version). Many others also exist such as "tshark" (the command line version of Wireshark) and special purpose sniffers like those in the dsniff suite (mailsnarf, urlsnarf, and more) that look for specific data only.

It is important to be able to work with the command line sniffers. If you have to run one from a remote host, it is possible that all you will have is a command shell access. Packets can be dumped into files and opened by the tools that provide a graphics interface later. The other reason for command line sniffers is that less overhead could mean a more accurate capture.

Working with Capture Filters

On the CEH exam it will be necessary to recognize the difference between a capture filter and a display filter. It will also be necessary to read a filter and determine what it does or to pick the best one from a list, given a scenario of objectives.

Capture filters tell the sniffer what to pick up or what to ignore. The benefit is that you won't get data you aren't supposed to have, that would be harmful, or that simply is not interesting. The downside is that if your filter is not quite right, you could miss something important. Capture filters are ideal for when you can be specific about what you want to detect and capture.

The syntax for capture filters is straightforward. We are looking at specifically the "tcpdump" syntax because that is what the CEH exam will cover. Most capture rules can be read almost like an English sentence. For example, "Capture only traffic that happens between the James and Kirk computers" would look like "host james and host kirk".

There are three elements to a capture rule: the operators, the keywords, and the variable data. The trick is building a statement using these elements. A few are given as reference here:

Operators

is	==	when equal to
and	&	all of these things
or	|	any of these things
not	!	other than this
gt	>	greater than
lt	<	less than

Keywords

host	the target object
net	the network ID
src	source
dst	destination
port	port
TCP	Transmission Control Protocol
ether	ethernet
IP	Internet Protocol
broadcast	Traffic sent to all

Variable data examples

192.168.1.1	host IP address
192.168.1.0	network id
0x42	The value 42 in HEX
0x56524659	The hex equivalent of the string VRFY
[0:2]	byte offset, start at byte 0 then start at byte 2

TRY IT OUT

Using Tcpdump

Open a command shell on a Linux machine and review the main page for tcpdump:

```
man tcpdump
```

Start the simplest possible capture:

```
tcpdump -i eth0
```

If you are using Backtrack Linux the tool will already be there. The "-i eth0" option just ensures you are listening on the first ethernet nic.

```
Press ctrl+c to stop the capture
```

TRY IT OUT

Research Advanced Wireshark Capture Filters

Visit the wiki for advanced Wireshark capture filters:

`http://wiki.wireshark.org/CaptureFilters`

TRY IT OUT CHALLENGE

• Put together a couple capture filters and try them out. The challenge is to create a filter with certain traffic in mind and then be able to generate that traffic to see if the capture worked.

• Use the –w option to write a capture file. Use that file after the next section to look at it in Wireshark.

Graphic Tools for Packet Analysis

Wireshark is the premier protocol analyzer that is free of cost to use. It used to be called "Ethereal" (pronounced Etheereeuhl, just like the English word, not eethuhreel); don't let the name be confusing in case it comes up on the exam or elsewhere. Wireshark runs the same way on both Linux and Windows systems, so getting used to it benefits in many circumstances.

Although there are many other tools available, Wireshark is probably the best known. These tools can help draw graphics and diagrams, and assist with creating a report that displays statistical analyses of network bandwidth. Wireshark allows you to right click on a TCP packet and choose "Follow TCP stream" to rebuild an entire Layer 7 protocol session. The tool "Packetyzer" has a built-in packet crafting tool that allows raw editing of any packets captured and will resend the traffic too.

In the official training that is required by EC-Council as a part of the CEH certification, an environment will be provided to experiment with several sniffer tools.

TRY IT OUT

Experiment with GUI-Based Graphic Analyzers

Using a Windows host that you have permission to install applications on and to perform a packet capture from, download and install the following tools. Make a comparison of each from a reporting standpoint.

We have already discussed this one:

`Wireshark`

`http://www.wireshark.org/`

(continued)

TRY IT OUT

This tool uses the Wireshark engine but provides a native Windows interface, which allows it to perform a few extra Windows-specific tricks.

```
Packetyzer
```

```
http://sourceforge.net/projects/packetyzer/
```

While perhaps not as feature rich as some of the others, there is a version of this tool that runs straight off a USB key.

```
SmartSniff
```

```
http://www.nirsoft.net/utils/smsniff.html
```

Less of a pure sniffer and more of a scanner, it can dissect protocols into usage reports and provide statistical data.

```
The Dude
```

```
http://www.mikrotik.com/thedude.php
```

This one is a special purpose tool for sniffing passwords. It also does a lot more than that and needs to be seen to be understood.

```
Cain and Abel
```

```
http://www.oxid.it
```

Working with Display Filters in Wireshark

Display filters have a different syntax than the capture filters. The operators are slightly different and the nouns in the expression are hierarchical (protocol.field operator value). If you wanted to only display captured packets that have a TCP destination port value of 80, there are a number of things to consider:

- Port of what protocol? Many protocols might have fields named "port" and Wireshark supports many protocols.
- Is the port a source, a destination, or doesn't it matter?
- Is "80" the decimal or hexadecimal value?

The expression would be either of these:

- tcp.dstport == 80
- tcp.dstport == 0x50

If you wanted Wireshark to only display TCP segments that included the SYN/ACK flags, the expressions would be:

- tcp.flags == 18
- tcp.flags == 0x12

The TCP flags field (RFC 792) is 8 bits (1 byte). The order is "nnUAPRSF" (nn=not used, URG, ACK, PSH, RST, SYN, FIN). To set the SYN/ACK bits the binary would be: 00010010.

It is critically important for the CEH exam that you can recognize decimal, hex, octal, and binary numbers. This is assumed knowledge. When you take your formal training class, ask the instructor to review the conversions and differences with you.

TRY IT OUT

Research Advanced Wireshark Display Filters

 Open Wireshark and start and end a capture. Toward the top of the window just below the menu bar is a button called "Expression. . ."Explore the window thoroughly and notice the following:

In previous chapters you looked at several RFC documents that included header diagrams. Notice how each field of each protocol can be chosen for a filter.

There are hundreds of protocols that are unfamiliar to you. But once you get the hang of mastering IP, TCP, UDP, and ICMP, the process is the same. Obtain the documentation, understand the header fields, and interpret the situation.

Know How to Exploit Vulnerable Protocols

- Protocols that are vulnerable to sniffing
- Scanning for sniffers on your network

Protocols That Are Vulnerable to Sniffing

Many protocols send critical information across the network in clear text. While some sniffers exist to look specifically for these data, the general purpose tools like Wireshark show them equally well.

Protocols that send plaintext credentials across the network include:

- HTTP
- SNMP (community string)
- NNTP
- POP
- FTP
- IMAP

Many of these protocols have been updated or replaced with more secure options. Administrators requiring the use of older versions might setup encrypted tunnels such as SSH (Secure Shell) to protect them.

Scanning for Sniffers on Your Network

The best way to completely avoid detection is to use a "receive only" cable to connect the host to the network. This is a common practice that solves the problem at Layer 1 by removing the physical ability for the sniffer to reply to scans.

One technique for detecting a sniffer is to send traffic to a high enough layer protocol that would respond, while intentionally using incorrect addressing for a lower layer. Consider the following example:

	IP	MAC
Sniffer	10.0.0.1	AA:BB:CC:DD:EE:FF

The scanner sends traffic to IP 10.0.0.1 but spoofs the target MAC address of something random like A4:FE:65:D5:1F:6D. The NIC should ignore the frame because it is not correct. In promiscuous mode, that fact will be ignored and the packet will be passed up to Layer 3. Since the logical address does match, the networking software in the OS protocol stack will accept the packet and process it. If a higher layer has a way to disagree with the bits and respond, there will be a response. The sniffer is detected.

Know How Session Hijacking Works

- The importance of session hijacking
- The differences between spoofing, MiTM, and hijacking
- Types of session hijacking
- Countermeasures to session hijacking

The Importance of Session Hijacking

Session hijacking is about compromising the trust of two hosts, services, or accounts. Counter-measures are put in place to counteract the effects of eavesdropping (sniffing). These controls usually involve some type of authentication or session to be established. If the attacker can wait until that trust is established and then impersonate one of the parties, the blind system would have no idea it is giving or receiving data whose integrity has been breached.

Integrity is based on the knowing and verifying with complete certainty that the source of input data is solid. The processes that affect that data are not in control of an unknown third influence. The output is exactly what the system was designed to produce. Accuracy is different, and a separate topic altogether. This matters because attackers who are causing an integrity breach cannot assume that what they compromise is accurate. This is part of the dance, and why so many other steps to a graceful attack are necessary.

The influence that compromises integrity could be an attacker, an occurrence in nature, or a logic error in the program. If attackers can masquerade a natural or logical occurrence that would be useful. Even better would be if they can hide the integrity breach and make all parties believe nothing is awry.

The Differences Between Spoofing, MiTM, and Hijacking

Spoofing, a technique that is useful in social engineering, is the basic act of pretending to be something else. People are not always the essential parties. The problem with some authentication controls is they are based on hardware or protocol constructs and have nothing to do with user accounts or actual identities.

The inherent problem with spoofing is that the receiving host will reply to the party that seemed to have sent the data. Either the masquerading party has to become that party, or she must eavesdrop in. An additional problem could occur if the receiving host doesn't get the reply it expects after sending the data; it may try to send more data assuming an error has occurred. If the masqueraded victim receives these messages, he might get confused and create additional confusion through asking more questions.

Although spoofing has its place, it is often more of a component in an attack rather than the only technique.

An MiTM attack also involves social engineering. The attacker is able to transparently accept and send traffic to the true endpoints of communication. Much like sending important documents via a courier, the data is handed off, stored, and forwarded to the receiver. The transparent part is the trick. If the client sending the data knows it is using a proxy service, it is agreeing to this type of exchange. If not, the middle man must exploit a service at a lower level of the OSI model.

Application services, such as surfing the web, usually involve client/server interactions. If the client knows about a proxy server, it sends the data there and gets the response back from the proxy without worry. In this case, the client must be "proxified" in that it is fully aware of the man in the middle transaction. The human being user, however, might not be. Clients can be pointed to proxies without their user knowing or caring in the slightest, and this is the best MiTM attack vector. These proxies can be anywhere on the Internet, and this is a common technique of the malware exploits discussed in previous chapters.

If the attacker has to utilize lower layers of the network model, meaning that protocols must be manipulated to hijack traffic, greater skill and positioning is required. Earlier we discussed the ARP poison attack as an example of this. The victim is totally unaware of the attack, and therefore the attacker is considered transparent.

Pure session hijacking is the ultimate example of combining techniques to completely take over an established session after the authentication phase has completed.

In session hijacking, the following sequence of events takes place:

1. Tracking the connection
2. Desynchronizing the connection
3. Injecting the attacker's packet

Tracking the connection

The attackers must identify the targets and observe the characteristics of their connections. Predicting sequence numbers and windows sizes will allow the attacker to construct packets in advance of the attack. These packets will be injected at exactly the right time.

Desynchronizing the connection

If a server is presently communicating with an authenticated client, it is the client that needs to be knocked offline (assuming the attacker wants to impersonate the client). If this step does not happen correctly, the server will see echoes, traffic from both the real client and the attacker. The server will get confused and possibly drop the connection.

The client must be convinced it is no longer speaking to the server while leaving the server still expecting data. This can be accomplished using a variety of means.

Sending NULL data to the server spoofing the client's IP address as the source will cause it to expect traffic the real client is not prepared to send. Other techniques involving SYN/ACK and FIN fags can be used. The idea is to make the server think it is at a different place in the conversation, a place the attacker knows but the client doesn't.

The client is the DoS'd (Denial of Serviced) to keep it from attempting to recover. The attacker is spoofing the client address, so he needs to be able to sniff the traffic that comes from the server, since he is not really the destination of the traffic.

Injecting the attacker's packet

Packets can be injected at this point onto the network in the form of disruptive data that will be trusted or commands that continue the conversation.

Types of Session Hijacking

The official CEH courseware lists several types of hijacking, though some of them are arguably completely different forms of attack. This is one of those points where the precision of the terms is less important than the point behind them. Be very familiar with the vocabulary, however:

- TCP hijacking
- UDP hijacking
- RST hijacking
- Session tokens

TCP hijacking

This form of attack involves having an accurate understanding of the current state of synchronization between two hosts. The handshake must be observed, and sequence numbers must be set in the injected packets to be accepted inside of the current window.

Since this form of attack was discovered, RFC 1948 was written to suggest that ISN (Initial Sequence Numbers) are not incremented every four microseconds as suggested by RFC 792, but should instead involve a PRNG (Pseudo Random Number Generator). The quality of the randomness of the ISN greatly impacts the difficulty of predicting the number.

RST hijacking

This is a form of DoS attack. Packets are injected into an established TCP stream that convinces one side that the other is confused and wants to call it quits. All it takes is to set the RST flag, set the ACK number so it is in the window and, and spoof one side of the conversation. Ettercap is a tool that makes this easy as long as the initial synchronization was observed.

UDP hijacking

The UDP protocol does not involve the complexity of TCP. There are no flags or SEQ/ACK numbers to keep track of sessions. MiTM attacks and DoS attacks are much easier. The UDP protocol does not require the receiving host to respond at all, or acknowledge that there is even a source port to which a response can be given. All communication is handled at the application layer.

Session tokens

Whether or not an application uses the UDP or the TCP protocol, if the application layer requires an authentication or session token, it may be possible for the attacker to capture this token from the network or from a MiTM attack and replay the token to the server.

In stateless environments such as HTTP, session hijacking based on HTTP session tokens and CSRF (Cross-site Request Forgery Attacks) are examples of hijacking. The applications try to create a sense of "state" using unique strings that will be volleyed back and forth. Trust is established and then abused either by replaying a challenge or issuing commands that are trusted. The attacker can capture this information through a proxy server, or cookie stealing.

Countermeasures to Session Hijacking

Since the advent of the session hijacking attack, the TCP protocol specification has been modified to make sequence number prediction extremely difficult. Since it is a 32 bit field, there are about 4.3 billion possible values that can be chosen for the ISN. The attacker would have to sniff enough connections from a host to predict what an ISN would be in the future, even a PRNG (Pseudo-Random Number Generator) is sufficient to make this extremely challenging.

Circuit level gateway firewalls take this a step further by translating the ISN at the same time the network address and ports are translated when a host initiates an outbound connection. This in effect makes it a Layer 4 proxy server; the circuit level gateway is a man-in-the-middle but does not interfere with Layer 7 data.

Finally, IPSec (Internet Protocol Security) incorporates an integrity check that will not accept forged packets. Between all of these countermeasures, session hijacking threats are well mitigated, but the presence of the idea is important both from an academic standpoint, and to illustrate the importance of maintaining such countermeasures.

Conclusion

Sniffing, spoofing, and hijacking are advanced hacking activities in most networks. With the right tools, a good position, and an understanding of the protocols involved it can still be accomplished and is often extremely powerful. There are so many checks and balances between security, usability, design requirements, and company policy that there is almost always an opening somewhere if the attacker can find it.

For the CEH exam and almost any other security exam, the best approach is to assume default and vulnerable protocols and work the question from there. In other words, if a question asks about SNMP community strings in the clear and you believe "This is ludicrous, in my network this would never fly," go ahead and argue the point and get the question wrong if that makes you feel better. Remember, the exam is not about your network or your experiences. There is a chance the person sitting next to you has an entirely different view of the question based on the network he knows.

The reason tests are often set up this way is to ensure you understand that if one of your juniors comes along and decides that this control is unnecessary and disables or misconfigures it, the network will open wide its gates for any trespasser. The positive state of security in your network is not accidental. It is the product of a lot of hard work.

SOCIAL ENGINEERING

Introduction

*Social engineering is a hacking technique that focuses on the human factor.
The social engineer employs deception and other elements of psychology in an
effort to extract sensitive information or motivate a person toward an action or
response. The most valuable targets are not always the personnel component of a
security program. Sometimes an unwitting bystander can have the most valuable
information.*

*Social engineering can be broadly categorized in two ways: human-based and
computer-based. In previous chapters (System Hacking, Trojans and Backdoors)
we have already begun the discussion of computer-based social engineering.
This chapter will expand on that with a discussion about human-based social
engineering, then provide examples of how technology can be further incorporated
through, the use of e-mail..*

To Pass the CEH Exam You Need to . . .

• know about social engineering

• know about phishing scams

• know about hacking e-mail accounts

• know about social networks

• master the CEH cheatsheets and practice questions!

Know About Social Engineering

- The dangers and countermeasures of social engineering
- Types of human-based social engineering
- The elements of social engineering
- The three steps of reverse social engineering
- Social engineering using telecommunications

The Dangers and Countermeasures of Social Engineering

The goal of a social engineer is to obtain sensitive computer information from a human target. The objective of social engineering is to circumvent technical controls in an effort to breach a system. The particular danger of this type of attack comes from the fact that it focuses on what security experts consider the weakest link in any security program: the user. This is because users can make an active decision not to comply with the policies and procedures of an organization's security program.

To execute an effective social engineering attack, attackers must spend time identifying what sensitive information is needed to break into an IT system and what user has it. They then develop a plan to obtain the information. As attackers work toward breaking into a system, they may have to interact with multiple individuals to collect bits of seemingly unrelated data. These fragments of data seem harmless by themselves; however, when combined with other data they represent something that is of use to attackers. Upon determining who to get the necessary information from, attackers will then develop a relationship with the target. This relationship will include reasons that justify the target providing sensitive information to the attackers. In order for the attack to be successful, these reasons must be compelling enough for the user to make a decision to violate an organization's policies.

Preventing social engineering attacks is a very challenging task. Defending against social engineering typically involves two steps. First, an organization must implement policies that describe how its members are expected to act when someone queries them for any type of system information. Second, employees must be trained to recognize what activities could represent an attack and how to respond to them. Generally, users must remember not to provide sensitive information to a party whose identity they cannot confirm; they must share information with only those individuals that they recognize.

Types of Human-Based Social Engineering

The essential practice of supplying information only to known parties will address attacks that originate from outside of the organization. However, some surveys estimate that 70 percent of all attacks are "inside jobs."

Many organizations are large enough that frequent communication with unfamiliar people is necessary, and all it takes is for the attacker to understand how to properly introduce himself. For example: "This is Paul Massaro, the manager of store 467" (information easily obtained if there is a nameplate on the outside of the door of that franchise). Other common identifiers are employee IDs, project numbers, telephone extensions, building numbers, and the list goes on and on. This can be extremely effective from either an inside or outside position.

The motivation for a social engineering attack may be driven by revenge from a disgruntled employee. If an attacker is performing social engineering from within an organization, that person has an inherent advantage. In this case, the attacker may already be familiar with systems that contain sensitive information. The attacker may also have a pre-existing relationship with users or administrators of these target systems.

Another cause of these violations is for financial gain; insiders may recognize or develop an opportunity to commit fraud against their employer. There have been documented cases of employees sharing proprietary information with their employer's competitors. Whatever the reason might be, the circumstances are still the same: social engineering attacks originating from inside the organization are more difficult to prevent than those coming from outside because the attackers know what is most valuable and how to get it without having to use much guesswork. This helps them keep their profile low.

Social engineering attacks can be elaborate and take months to complete or they can be accomplished in one simple phone call or e-mail. One of the most basic motivations is for the entertainment of the attacker. They make prank calls, or attempt to gain information in order to impress friends, or record the calls and results for sharing with others.

Another thing to keep in mind is that some attacks are not the work of malicious intent, but rather carelessness, lack of respect for a process, or a way to gain an advantage. People trying to conduct what they feel are normal business activities are often the worst culprits. Many small attacks add up over time; the best attacks are often never identified, and their impact is never accurately measured.

The Elements of Social Engineering

There are many techniques that social engineers can use in order to establish a relationship with the target. Attackers may offer the target an opportunity to access something that is limited in its availability. This scam could involve the social engineer correcting a potential problem on the target's system, or the target can obtain access to some data of perceived value.

Other social engineering attacks involve the attackers making the target think they are talking to a high-level manager who needs access to the network immediately. Another social engineering technique includes attackers establishing rapport with the target or creating empathy on the target's behalf in an effort to access sensitive information. The only limitation to the variety of social engineering attacks is the attacker's lack of imagination.

According to ISOC (Internet SOCiety) there are six elements to social engineering. They are:

- Authority
- Scarcity
- Liking (similarity)
- Reciprocation

- Commitment (consistency)
- Social proof (validation)

Authority

People are highly responsive, often without question, to those they perceive as being in a position of authority. Wearing the uniform of a recognized symbol of authority is a simple way to exploit this characteristic of people.

Scarcity

People often desire an item more if they believe it is in short supply or will become totally unavailable soon, even when they don't need the item or didn't desire it much before learning of the scarcity. A sense of urgency can also be created using this technique, which furthers distracted thinking.

Liking (similarity)

People are often far more comfortable with those similar to themselves and will often not scrutinize their appearance or intentions as much. Normal checks and defenses are dismissed and an instant level of trust is given. These similarities can be cultural, or they can be based on common ground within a situation such as having the same problems at work, pursuing the same interests, or agreeing on matters far removed from their lives such as political frustrations.

Reciprocation

Sometimes also called "quid pro quo" or "something for something," this tool can be used in many ways. People have a tendency to want to return favors. If a gift is given or a promise is made and kept, the receiving party wants to reciprocate the giver with something of equal or lesser value. If not, intimidation or guilt can be used to cause the reciprocation response. A forceful "You agreed!" whether true or not, often makes the victim give up the object just to end the discomfort.

Commitment (consistency)

What people do today is likely what they will do tomorrow. This tactic involves a social engineer who can "read people" and know exactly who to use for what. Loyalty is a powerful trait for a victim to have when combined with authority or validation techniques.

The written word is a powerful medium used to access the true consistency of victims. While they may be on their best behavior in person, something about writing brings out the real emotions. It is certainly possible to misinterpret the emotions behind an e-mail, but it is also as easy to bend the meaning toward what the attacker needs, and then hold the victim to it.

Social proof (validation)

Dale Carnegie identified this trait in what is considered to be among the first "Personal Improvement / Sales Coaching" books on the market. People like to discuss themselves, and they enjoy it even more when whatever they say is validated. The social engineer will be nice and complimentary, not in an exaggerated way but in a way that seems charming and sincere. This disarms the victims and makes them think no harm could come from talking to such a nice person.

The Three Steps of Reverse Social Engineering

Reverse social engineering is an attack during which the target is compelled to ask the social engineer for assistance. There are different techniques for executing a reverse social engineering attack, but the results are always the same. The social engineer typically has a solution to an immediate threat or one that can potentially cause the target to suffer a dramatic loss.

One method for performing a reverse social engineering attack involves the hacker damaging the target's system and then conveniently being readily available to provide a fix. The "fix" always requires the attacker to have access to the target's system, typically with escalated user privileges.

Another method involves the social engineer recommending a software patch to the target for a system that the social engineer knows the target happens to own. Reverse social engineering attacks stand a greater chance of succeeding when they involve a timely current event, such as a known attack that happens to be in the latest news headlines. Reverse social engineering attacks are considered the most difficult to execute because they take a significant amount of planning and preparation in order to succeed.

The three principles of reverse social engineering are:

- Sabotage
- Advertising
- Assisting

Sabotage

In this case, the attacker will create a problem such as a paper jam in the printer or a DoS (Denial of Service) attack on a single host. The attacker can also make the target think there is a problem that doesn't really exist. The objective is to setup the next two steps.

Advertising

In this case, the attacker will advertise being an expert that can solve the problem faster than the authorized incident response personnel.

Assisting

In this case, the attacker will assist the victim with the solution.

Gaining information during a side conversation while the victim is distracted or installing malware along with the fix could be possible. Over time, reverse engineering might be repeated in order to establish trust or authority that gains the attacker a more inside position.

Social Engineering Using Telecommunications

Before the Internet flourished, the hacker's target of choice was the public switched telephone network. These individuals were described as *phreakers*, and their primary goal was making free long-distance telephone calls.

One of the most notorious phreakers was John Draper, who went by the name of Captain Crunch. One of his associates determined that a phreaker could activate a long-distance trunk line by blowing a toy whistle into the telephone receiver. This whistle could be obtained from a cereal box of the same name as Draper's phreaking handle.

Draper's claim to fame started when hackers learned of his ability to activate a trunk line without the use of the toy whistle. The exact frequency of the tone emitted from this whistle was 2,600 Hertz. An organization dedicated to hacking called "2600" was created; the organization publishes a quarterly magazine by the same name to this day.

Another hacking technique involving the telephone is *pretexting*. This is a social engineering attack that includes unauthorized individuals pretending to be someone they are not in order to obtain personal information. Private investigators and con artists have been using this technique for years not just to obtain phone records, but also to get access to bank records, credit card information, and other sensitive information.

A recent scandal involving pretexting included members of Hewlett-Packard's board members and private investigators attempting to uncover unethical behavior by the company's directors, who were suspected of leaking information. The fallout from the scandal resulted in the investigators being prosecuted and a shakeup within HP's senior management, including one board member losing his job.

Other attacks in the telecom industry are generically known as *slamming and cramming*. Slamming is the practice of changing a customer's long-distance carrier without the consumer's knowledge. During the phone wars in the early 1990s between MCI, Sprint, and AT&T, these three corporations pursued high-priced marketing programs to get new customers. Also, resellers of long-distance services used less-than-ethical methods to change customers' long-distance carriers.

Cramming is the fraudulent practice of adding charges to a consumer's phone bill using devious techniques. Organizations can piggy back charges onto the telephone company's billing procedure. Sometimes it is as simple as a $0.15 surcharge of some kind and other times it can be significantly more. The attackers know that the telephone company often doesn't want to get involved; they consider themselves a neutral billing party and just want to collect. The victim has to take the charges up with the originator, who is either very difficult to find or unreachable.

Know About Phishing Scams

- What is phishing and spear fishing?
- 419 scams (Nigerian fishing)
- Recognizing phishing scams

What is Phishing and Spear Fishing?

Phishing is the latest social engineering technique. E-mail is now considered to be the most common form of social engineering. Phishing uses spam e-mail to lure unsuspecting users into divulging sensitive information about themselves or their financial accounts. This type of attack is used to commit fraud against the attacker's victims.

The objectives of phishing attacks range from selling nonexistent products to acquiring personally identifiable information about potential victims. While the objectives are numerous, the attack methodology is always the same: potential targets are lured to unscrupulous websites selling products or services. Users always suffer some loss if they choose to interact with a phishing website.

These attacks are successful because certain users simply do not understand what phishing is, they are not clever enough to notice anything suspicious, and they almost always ignore security warnings.

A variation of phishing that has become popular lately is called spear phishing. This technique focuses on a particular subset of Internet users that happen to be customers of a popular online vendor. As with a traditional phishing attack, target users are lured to a hacker's website; however, targets are linked to a webpage which is mistaken for a familiar website, such as that of a financial institution or Amazon.com.

Spear phishing websites are identical in their presentation when compared to legitimate websites, and average users do not notice the subtleties that are typical of fake domains. Users provide their account names and passwords to the fake website and the system responds with a message indicating a failed login attempt. The frustrated user will leave the website, but not before the hacker captures a valid login name and password to a legitimate website. The hacker would then log in as the victim and commit some sort of fraud by masquerading as the authorized user.

In order to perform phishing, a hacker must perform three steps. First, the hacker must establish a domain name to which the target users will be directed to. Next, the hacker must configure the fake website to be identical to the legitimate one. By creating an exact copy of a legitimate website, potential victims will be unsuspicious while submitting their personally identifiable information to this page. The final step is when the hacker sends out the spam e-mail messages in an effort to lure users to the fake website. Several factors will determine how successful this attack may be, including the accuracy of the fake website when compared to the real one and the quality of the mailing list used by the hacker for sending spam.

419 Scams (Nigerian Fishing)

A popular phishing attack is generally known as the Nigerian prince scam, and is formally called the 419 scam. A more generic name for this attack is advance-fee fraud. In this phishing attack, the target is persuaded to forward a sum of money to the spammer in the hopes of realizing a significantly larger financial gain. The target may be directed to provide a personal bank account to which funds will be wired to. The 419 scam originated in the early 1980s as the oil-based Nigerian economy declined. The number "419" refers to the article of the Nigerian Criminal Code that outlaws this technique.

Recognizing Phishing Scams

Obfuscation is the process of deliberately making something difficult to understand. As it relates to the Internet, this practice can be applied to code as well as to URLs. Hackers use code obfuscation to disguise the true intent of malicious code, and phishing scams typically rely on this technique to hide the real name of the phisher's website. A common technique of URL obfuscation is to make a subtle change to the name of the malignant website.

Phishing websites can execute malicious code against anyone who happens to visit the website. These sites may transmit malware to the client in an attempt to create an unauthorized account to take control of the target system. The specific malware technique in this case is called a Trojan horse. Trojans can facilitate the attacker taking control of another's computer, and they can steal PII (Personally Identifiable Information).

A common practice of malicious software (often spread by Trojan horses) is to use the victim's computer to send spam or other forms of advertising material. This has not just been a practice of attackers; advertising companies have tried to go "legit," such as the infamous "180 Solutions," and find ways of tricking users into giving legal permission to have their computers used in this way.

Legitimate websites can also be compromised to perform this same pernicious act of infecting the systems of visiting users. Other hacking techniques applied to legitimate websites include redirecting a visitor from the proper site to a phishing website. Phishers can achieve this same result of redirection by compromising resource records or the cache of a DNS server. DNS queries return the IP address of the phishing site which has been illicitly associated with the domain name of a valid website.

Malicious hidden code resides in places other than websites. In e-mail messages, spammers are including code that will return a message to the sender whenever their spam message is opened. This allows spammers to validate the existence of a legitimate e-mail account, thereby improving the quality of their mailing lists. This reporting of the status of an e-mail account to the spammer is performed by a web bug, also described as a spam beacon.

Know About Hacking E-mail Accounts

- The dangers of online e-mail
  - Try it out: Using a disposable e-mail address
- The dangers of open relays
  - Try it out: Sending a spoofed e-mail

The Dangers of Online E-mail

Spammers strive to create a list of valid e-mail addresses to which they send their harmful messages. Personalized e-mail addresses tend to be more believable and therefore harder to recognize as spam. They can also use legitimate e-mail addresses from which to originate spam. Again, a message sent from a party known to the recipient tends to be perceived as more credible than one received from a complete stranger. Spammers also collect additional data about users to have the opportunity to perform spear phishing attacks. Security experts recommend that users offer their e-mail addresses to valid parties only.

Using a Disposable E-mail Address

Create a fake username for an e-mail address such as:

`ers45rteq21@mailinator.com`

The username can be anything you want, but something you can remember.

Visit the mailinator website and check your inbox using the address above

`http://www.mailinator.com/`

The Dangers of Open Relays

Spam is unsolicited e-mail traffic that is typically used to advertise the availability of products or services from an online vendor. More recently, spam has been used as a vehicle for committing fraud against unsuspecting Internet users. Spam is distributed by acquiring a list of legitimate e-mail addresses and exploiting an SMTP open mail relay. An open mail relay is an SMTP server configured to allow any e-mail traffic on the Internet to pass through it; an open relay is not for mail destined to or originating from specific e-mail accounts. This used to be the default configuration in many mail servers. This was the original method for sending e-mail across the Internet; however, open mail relays have become unpopular due to their exploitation by spammers.

Sending a Spoofed E-mail

This is an easy lab to do from a Linux shell but could also be done from a DOS prompt. Open the shell of your choice and telnet into port 25 of an available mail server:

`telnet example.dom 25`

Enter the following script (if using Windows you will not see what you type, and mistakes might cause you to have to start all over):

`helo`

`mail from:fake@mail.dom`

`rcpt to:[target victim account]@example.dom`

`data`

`Please visit the following link ASAP!`

`http://www.eccouncil.org`

`quit`

In order to combat spoofing e-mail and other attacks on these systems, administrators have had to incorporate a number of "afterthought" style countermeasures to protect the inherently insecure SMTP protocol. Following are two examples you must know for the CEH exam:

- Implement SMTP_AUTH (RFC 4954). Although spoofing is still possible, this extension to the SMTP protocol prevents open relay generated spam.
- Use a Layer 7 firewall to block certain SMTP commands. The VRFY command allows an attacker to verify the existence of particular e-mail accounts. The EXPN command allows a spammer to obtain additional addresses. RFC 2505 largely addressed this issue and most ISPs filter these commands also.

Know About Social Networks

- Why be paranoid about social networks?
- Popular social networks and their dangers
- Social engineering of physical controls

Why be Paranoid About Social Networks?

At first glance, social networks appear to be an entertaining way for users with common interests to interact with one another and to make new acquaintances. However, phishers view these websites as a potential source of data that could generate opportunities to commit fraud.

Personal details found in social networking sites can be used to commit identity theft. A social engineer may create a personality on a social network and invite unsuspecting targets to join the attacker's network in an effort to exploit their personal data.

It is not difficult to impersonate someone on a social network. Just sign up, fill in the profile, find a picture online to put in the profile, and start inviting people. While close friends might know the difference, a network of people two or three degrees removed might not.

Popular Social Networks and Their Dangers

Four popular social networks are MySpace, Facebook, LinkedIn, and Twitter. All four services have been victimized by some type of a social engineering attack. MySpace and Facebook members received a spam message inviting them to visit a fake login page. This page would steal the visitors' login credentials and scan their systems for vulnerabilities in various entertainment applications, such as image viewers and MP3 players.

Hackers created fake LinkedIn profiles that appeared to be created by celebrities. When unsuspecting users visited these profiles and clicked on posted links, they were redirected to hacker websites which attempted to load a Trojan horse onto the visitor's system. This Trojan would allow the attacker to take control of the infected system.

Phishing attacks have affected Twitter as well. Members received direct mail messages from other users inviting them to a website which appeared to be sponsored by Twitter that turned out to be a phishing site. This site was designed to steal the victim's Twitter account login information.

Both Facebook and Twitter account credentials have been collected by social engineers who believe that many users create the same account name and password for popular e-commerce websites. The attacker would use these login credentials to masquerade as the victimized user and make purchases on these commercial websites.

Social Engineering of Physical Controls

Social engineering techniques are used to compromise the logical access controls of an organization's network. These techniques can also be used to gain physical access to a facility. If attackers can gain physical access to that part of the building which houses sensitive IT resources, they can cause as much damage as if they were logged into a computer on the network.

Intruders may steal data processing equipment or stored data on portable media, and they could cause physical damage to sensitive IT assets. An attacker can also steal data from a powered up system by interfacing with a USB port on that target.

The most popular execution of physical social engineering is to perform activities that could lead to compromising the logical access controls of systems on a network. For example, following an authorized user through a secured access point such as a door requiring a badge for access is known as piggybacking or tailgating.

A social engineer may also masquerade as a service technician to enter a facility by presenting fake credentials to a receptionist or other administrator.

Social engineers can perform other tasks that may provide information for gaining access to an organization's IT systems. A common technique involves sifting through trash that has been discarded by a company in an effort to discover potentially sensitive information about that company's systems. This is called dumpster diving.

Another technique known as shoulder surfing involves the hacker observing authorized users as they enter authentication information into a keypad. Similar to this activity, social engineers may eavesdrop on conversations between employees in an effort to overhear sensitive data inadvertently divulged by a careless user. All of these techniques can be used to support a social engineer's efforts to bypass the technical and physical controls of a company.

Conclusion

Social engineering is considered the single most dangerous form of attack. Many successful attacks in some way incorporate social engineering on some level. Spam and phishing attacks convince victims to visit malicious websites. Impersonating a friend or colleague helps convince the victim to install a Trojan horse. Strangers participating in chatrooms, online forums, and blog comments are often trusted because of several principles of social engineering including reciprocation and liking (common interests).

It gets much more complex. There are too many business incentives for us all to master the practice of the social engineering principles just to compete in some environments. At the heart of social engineering lies information gathering and clever psychology.

The constantly eroding privacy of individuals in our society makes social engineering easier and easier. Add to this the fact that we are participating in so many things at once, and it is easy for an attacker to change a victim's perceptions of what the endgame of his own activities are. It is easy to get distracted. It is easy for us to simply feel we have no time to be concerned with the consequences of each correspondence we get involved in.

If you become a cynical or paranoid person, then it is hard to form colleague relationships in today's fast moving world. It is difficult to consider reasonable countermeasures to social engineering when there is an expectation that you have revealed far too much of yourself on a continual basis, because everyone else has already made a habit of it. Hiding makes you stand out.

Education remains as the best countermeasure, but best practices are getting harder, not easier, to establish.

Professional penetration testers are not always allowed to perform social engineering attacks, and some might argue it requires a person with a personality suited for the task to be successful. At the same time, social engineering in the form of industrial information gathering and, in many cases, the normal course of a business day is occurring all the time. Many people are social engineers; they have just never characterized their activity this way.

The stealthy nature and blurry lines of social engineering attacks have sparked a specialized form of attack known as "Identity Testing" or "PII Testing," which includes testing social networks along with the time honored forms of information gathering. Data from this research can be aggregated, and inferences about a person or organization can be reached from analyzing everything that is found.

Before attempting to test your own identity, realize that activity might cause you to inadvertently reveal data. For example, if you search for your own PII in any system, it may not have been there before, but now it is.

DENIAL OF SERVICE

Introduction

Denial of service (DoS) attacks are meant to embarrass the reputation of a company or make it impossible for its customers to reach its services. They can also serve as decoy events which cause an incident response team to become busy investigating the attack while the real harm is being done elsewhere.

The trouble with DoS attacks is that they don't generate income for the attacker. Extortion attacks are attempted but have a fairly low success rate. Still, DoS attacks can occur in industrial espionage situations where a company is trying to sabotage a competitor or as a last resort of frustration because all other attacks have failed.

If the attack is coming from an external source, the attacker must know the block of IPs and the live hosts of the target; otherwise much of the packets generated will go nowhere and accomplish nothing.

To Pass the CEH Exam You Need to . . .

- know the types of DoS attacks
- know how DDoS attacks work
- know how botnets work
- master the CEH cheatsheets and practice questions!

Know the Types of DoS Attacks

- The methods of DoS attacks

- Types of DoS attacks

- The DoS attack tools

The Methods of DoS Attacks

A denial of service attack can be as simple as a single packet of data that confuses the receiving host. A malformed request to a portmapper service or a null data packet with flags set in an unexpected way can be enough to bring down a server. This type of attack is also called an *asymmetric* attack because the target host and the attacking host need not have the same level of processing power. A simple computer can send DoS packets over a dial-up connection to a vulnerable million dollar mainframe.

Attackers read the RFCs and other documentation with critical thinking. Since most spec sheets just describe what is supposed to happen, the attacker wonders, "What if I create a packet or a scenario that isn't supposed to happen? Will the host know what to do or just puke?"

In cases where a full disruption due to the consumption of resources is needed there are two approaches: consume the resources within a host, or consume bandwidth on the network. Often times this action will require multiple attackers focusing on a particular host or network segment. Packets can even be bounced off of unsuspecting hosts that are volunteering to participate, not because they have been compromised, but because the attacker understands how the protocols work.

Another form of denial of service involves affecting the configuration of a service or client. If the host can be compromised, configuration files can be changed that make the service operate in such a way that it is not accessible.

Types of DoS Attacks

The following DoS attack types are considered basic knowledge for the CEH exam and questions will assume you understand how they work.

- Smurf and fraggle
- Buffer overflow
- Ping of death
- Teardrop
- SYN flood

Smurf and fraggle

A Smurf attack occurs when an attacker on an external network sends ICMP echo requests to the broadcast address of a network segment. The source of this traffic will be spoofed as one of the hosts inside the segment. This action causes each host in the broadcast domain to reply to the victim.

Smurf is an example of amplification. One packet can generate many other packets in the response, resulting in bandwidth consumption. The attacker will send a stream of these packets into a vulnerable network.

This particular attack is easily defended against. Hosts can be told not to respond to broadcast pings, as is the case with Windows by default. Routers can have ACLs that do not allow traffic to enter a network to which the source is on the destination segment. The outside interface of the router should never see such traffic.

Fraggle is a UDP version of the same attack. In this case, UDP packets are sent to the echo (Port 7) or chargen (Port 19) services of vulnerable hosts while spoofing the true victim's IP address. Chargen (Character Generator) and echo are part of the "simple TCP/IP services" packages on Windows systems and are also supported in Linux-based systems. Other protocols in the collection are discard, daytime, and qotd. Usually these services are not enabled by default, but they are useful in troubleshooting various network conditions. A simple scan reveals vulnerable hosts.

Buffer overflow

Computers do not react well to ambiguous conditions. If the program doesn't provide explicit instructions on how to handle input the result can be a kernel panic or BSOD (Blue Screen of Death). Destabilizing a system can be as simple as making sure it cannot understand the answer to a question. If the program asks for a person's name (assumed to be no more than 16 characters) and the attacker provides a string of 257 ASCII "A" characters, slashes, or random stuff, the receiving host might have no idea what to do with it and die.

"Fuzzing" is a technique that can be used to scan for buffer overflows that crash a system or provide backdoor access. Random strings of characters of various lengths are submitted to an application by the fuzzer. Automating this technique makes testing many applications at once trivial.

Ping of death

According to RFC 791, an IP packet cannot be larger than 64k in size. If this is true, developers would have no reason to set aside more than that much memory space to buffer and process a packet. The attacker uses fragmentation techniques to disguise a packet that is larger than 64k. The receiving host begins to reassemble the packet and doesn't realize until the buffer is full that there is more to the packet space to store it.

IP has no mechanism for dealing with situations like this as it is designed to be a stateless, unreliable protocol. The result on a vulnerable host is a system crash. ICMP is often used in this attack because it is easy to add as much data as necessary into the data field of an echo request message (Type 8 Code 0).

Teardrop

Reassembling a fragmented packet is accomplished using the IPID field, the MF (More Fragment) status flag, and a data field called "offset value." Each fragment of a packet will get a new IP header and the IPID field will be the same for each, indicating they are all fragments of the same packet.

Let's illustrate fragmentation using easy numbers. The first fragment is called the "0th" fragment. The MF status flag is set, and the offset value is 0, telling the receiver to load this fragment at byte 0 in the buffer.

If the 0th fragment is 1500 bytes in size it will occupy bytes 0–1499 in the buffer. The next fragment has the MF flag set and the offset value will be 1500. If it is also 1500 bytes in size it will occupy bytes 1500–2999 of the buffer. The next fragment will have an offset of 3000. This process continues until the MF bit clears, indicating there are no more fragments to reassemble.

In a teardrop attack, the offset fields are adjusted to cause overlap of the fragments when they are loaded into the buffer. If the 0th fragment is exactly 1500 bytes, it will occupy bytes 0–1499 as normal. The next fragment will not have the expected offset value of 1500. The attacker will set it to a smaller value, something like 1200, so when it is placed in the buffer at byte 1200, there is a 300 byte overlap. That data is simply overwritten. The next fragment should have an offset of 2700, but its offset will be set to 2400 instead. This process will continue until the MF bit clears.

The result of a teardrop attack is a datagram that is much shorter than it is supposed to be. In a vulnerable host the IP function will be confused by this and crash. A variation of this attack is called the "unnamed" attack, where the offset value is increased, causing the packet to expand instead of shrink.

SYN flood

In a TCP handshake, all three steps ensure an established and synchronized connection. In a SYN flood the attacker sends multiple SYN flags to begin the handshake process but never finishes with the last ACK. The victim is left in a state of waiting for each half-open port to move to the established state. They will eventually time out, but the attacker sends new traffic at a faster rate. Sockets are opened faster than they give up. This eventually uses up all available resources on the victim.

The attacker aims the SYN requests to an open port on the target hosts and increments their source port value each time so that each SYN is treated as a new socket. Since the return traffic is not necessary, the source IP could be spoofed, making it difficult to figure out where the attack is coming from.

Most current TCP/IP stacks have been updated to prevent these attacks from working. However, they are still covered on almost every security exam for academic reasons, since older host platforms might be at risk. Understanding these attacks is a valuable proof of concept discussion that relates to the importance of asking critical questions about the protocols, and what could happen if an attacker makes them misbehave.

The DoS Attack Tools

For the CEH exam, be familiar with the following DoS tools. Many of them are on the older side but still discussed for illustration purposes. Modern DoS tools are more or less based on the same principles:

- Jolt2
- Bubonic.c

- Land and LaTierra
- Targa
- Blast and UDP Flood
- Nemesy, Panther 2, Crazy Pinger, and Some Trouble

Jolt2

Jolt2 is an IP fragmentation attack against Windows 2000 and previous versions, along with many Cisco routers. Packets are sent that contain different amounts of data than what their length fields indicated. When the host cannot reassemble the packets correctly they use CPU effort trying, eventually resulting in 100 percent utilization.

Bubonic.c

Bubonic worked against Windows 2000 and Redhat Linux 6.2. TCP packets with random settings are sent to the host, and eventually cause a system crash

Land and LaTierra

The attacker sends SYN traffic to the target, spoofing the target itself as the source. The target responds to itself with a SYN/ACK but does not increment the ISN in the ACK field as expected. This, in turn, causes a resend of the same packet over and over.

When a target actually does send itself traffic, the ACK numbers increment properly, and the Land attack works because the attacker is a remote host. The LaTierra attack is based on the principle of a Land attack, but sends multiple packets to multiple destination ports on the target host.

Targa

Targa is infamous for being a so-called "All-in-one" tool that supports multiple DoS techniques including Land, Teardrop, and Nestea (exploits "Off by one" errors in Linux kernel 2.0.33).

Blast and UDP Flood

These tools can be used by administrators to stress test their servers. Of course, any tool like this can then be used to bring down a server that cannot handle the loads.

Nemesy, Panther2, Crazy Pinger, and Some Trouble

These are examples of *flooders*, which are a class of DoS tools that attempts to bombard a network segment with traffic.

Know How DDoS Attacks Work

- Creating the DDoS traffic
  - Try it out: Read about the GRC denial of service attack
- Structure of a DDoS network
- DDoS tools

Creating the DDoS Traffic

A distributed denial of service attack occurs when multiple attackers focus their efforts on a single network, domain, or host. Combinations of reflection and amplification techniques along with a large group of hosts under single control allow the attacker to generate enough traffic to make services unreachable for a few hours to several days.

Reflection occurs when traffic is aimed at a host with the IP address of the intended victim given as a source. The reflector sends response packets to the victim. From the victim's position the reflector will appear to be the source. DNS servers, HTTP servers, and most routers make perfect reflectors because they will always respond to certain types of traffic. An HTTP server, for example, will respond to a SYN with a SYN/ACK. The victim in turn might respond to what it receives with a RST, because it didn't actually send the initial SYN and was never expecting traffic. The additional packet that results is an example of amplification.

Other amplification attacks include sending DNS requests into a chain of servers that support recursive queries. The requests are random strings to which there is no answer, but each DNS server feels the need to ask its neighbor anyway. As many as 74 additional UDP packets can be generated from one request.

Tracing backscatter to determine the true source of a DDoS is difficult but sometimes not impossible. Backscatter is the traffic that reflects off the victim and heads back in the direction of the source. When the attacking reflector is discovered, the next trace attempts to determine the source of the initial sender. Some traffic will have been sent to the reflector from the attacker at some time that points back to him. If that traffic can be associated with the spoofed packets used in the DDoS, the source can be determined. For this reason, attackers often send their packets through proxy servers or use a multi-tiered botnet.

Unintentional DDoS attacks can occur also. If a website suddenly receives more traffic than it has been designed to handle it can be brought down. Thinking they are doing the business a favor, fans of a product might send a discussion link to a popular news aggregator such as Digg, Reddit, or Slashdot. If that link generates a spike of hits to the site, the web server or the web hosting service might not be prepared.

TRY IT OUT

Read About the GRC Denial of Service Attack

This story documents one of the classic and best explained stories of denial of service. Every step of the process from attack to research to defense is demonstrated, but you won't believe the ending.

www.crime-research.org/library/grcdos.pdf

Structure of a DDoS Network

Most DDoS networks consist of a number of *zombie* hosts that can be commanded from a central location called the C&C (Command and Control). Zombies are also called *agents* or *handlers* in the more complex systems.

Zombies are created in any of the ways previously discussed in the chapters of this book that discuss malware. Trojan horse applications, malware injected through buffer overflow exploits, scripts, and executables "dropped" by worm spreaders are examples of the most common vectors. Rootkits are also used to hide the process and library files that reside on an infected system. Essentially, any flaw in a system that allows access to attackers can become a zombie if that is the attackers' objective and that is the backdoor they plant.

A DDoS network can have two, three, or many more levels of hierarchal control. The attacker sends commands from the C&C to the handlers, who in turn command a number of agents. A multi-tiered approach gives attackers greater control of the activities of the network and allows them to launch the DDoS attacks from different locations asynchronously or at the same time for an all out assault.

Changing the source of the attack makes backscatter more difficult to analyze. The reflectors can be the same or can also change. Imagine a small DDoS network of 100,000 machines that is divided into ten segments of 10,000 apiece. The attacker needs only to directly communicate with ten handlers, who can then tell each agent to bounce traffic off 100,000 reflectors.

The result could be 1,000,000,000 packets focused on the victim, who might then try to respond at a minimum by doubling the packets sent on its local network segment. This is just one turn. The agents keep bouncing traffic. Modern botnets can change pivot points, promoting agents to become handlers. The symmetry of the network is adjustable.

DDoS Tools

For the CEH exam, be familiar with the following DDoS tools. Like the DoS tools listed previously, these tools are on the older side. Modern DDoS tools are more or less based on the same principles and it is imperative that networks be able to defend themselves from these attacks.

- Trinoo
- TFN, TFN2k
- Stacheldraht
- MStream
- Slammer
- MyDoom

Trinoo

Trinoo is a UDP flooder DDoS tool. The readme file uses the terms "Master" and "Daemons" instead of handler and agent, so watch out for this change on the CEH exam as well.

The attacker communicates with the Master on Port 27665, which in turn communicates with the Daemons on Port 27444. The target ports are randomized.

TFN, TFN2k

Tribal Flood Network can launch multiple types of DDoS attacks such as UDP floods, SYN floods, and ICMP directed broadcasts. Source ports can be randomized.

TFN2k is an update to the original code that includes bug fixes and features for making the backscatter and Master to Daemon traffic harder to detect and reverse engineer.

Stacheldraht

The word means "Barbed Wire" in German. This tool integrates Trinoo and TFN2k and uses encryption to hide the command traffic. The agents mostly infected Solaris hosts through a buffer overflow weakness in the RPC service.

MStream

This tool uses ACK storms to attack its target. ACK storms can sometimes cause stateful inspection firewalls to open because the flood of traffic makes them think they should have an entry in their state table that they really shouldn't.

Slammer

Slammer is a worm that is best known for its speed. Ninety percent of all infected hosts were thought to be compromised within ten minutes of its launch. The size of the attack doubled every 8.5 seconds, eventually resulting in a DDoS due to network congestion issues.

Slammer did not contain a malicious payload, but its scanner was only 376 Bytes in size which helped it spread so quickly. It attacked Port 1434 on the MDAC SQL server engine found in most Windows computers. A reboot of the system would clear the worm, but it was extremely likely that within minutes the worm would return.

MyDoom

MyDoom is a mass e-mailing worm. It spread through peer to peer filesharing networks such as Kazaa, and attempted to DDoS the *www.sco.com* and *www.microsoft.com* domains. It deposited a backdoor payload that would open Port 1080, 3128, 80, 8080, or 10080. It also attempted to overwrite the local hosts file to prevent the DNS resolver from locating certain anti-virus update sites.

Know How Botnets Work

- The evolution of botnets
- Defending against DDoS attacks
  - Try it out: Visit the CATCH team and regional CERT websites
  - Try it out: Connect to IRC

The Evolution of Botnets

Botnets were first created to automate repetitive activities on the IRC (Internet Relay Chat) network. A *robot* user could appear as a participant in the chatroom and interact with other users so the real owner of the chatroom did not have to be there 24 hours a day. The first example was the GM bot, which would play a game with users called "Hunt the Wumpus."

The first malicious botnet was set up through the spread of the "pretty park" worm, which is most famous for displaying the 3D pipes screensaver on infected hosts. This bot demonstrated the ability to steal information and receive updates from the botherder (the user that owns or has collected the botnet).

Subseven came next, and included features also common to RATs (Remote Access/Administration Tools). Most botnets were being collected via Trojans. E-mails with the malicious code attachments were sent to users along with clever social engineering to convince the user to run the code. SPIM (Instant Messaging Spam) also became a common vector as that technology grew in popularity.

It was quickly realized that DDoS attacks were far from being the only reason to set up a botnet. The SD Bot evolved botnets to a whole new level. The author provided the source code and tools for creating the illicit servers. Soon a small community of contributors participated and variants were created that added new spreading vectors and additional capabilities.

The Agabot malware added a multistage approach with modular code that could be updated on command. The first stage creates backdoor access and contacts the C&C (Command and Control) chatroom. The second stage downloads a module that turns off or blocks anti-malware scanners and firewalls. The third stage downloaded a module that would block the host from accessing update sites and online security services. The modular nature of Agabot meant that more and more variants could be created, and there is almost no end to the combinations of spreaders and payloads.

In 2004, a Lithuanian organized crime group paid a team of Dutch hackers to create a large botnet. The hackers figured that if the mob can make money with a botnet so could they, and they began to use their botnet to distribute adware for 180Solutions. At that same time the advertising firm was battling a lot of bad public relations originating from their methods. They were trying to be a legitimate business but used spam and peer to peer networks in their services.

180Solutions changed their policy to exclude botnet type delivery of their advertisement service and refused to pay the hackers for their work. So the hackers used the botnet to send a DDoS attack against the company, and attempted to extort payment. 180Solutions then got the FBI involved and, after the hackers were caught, filed a civil lawsuit against them.

Botnets are a mix of commercial interests, organized crime, and cyber warfare. The question isn't "if a lot of machines can be herded" but rather how many machines, how powerful will the malware be, and who will be using it for what purpose. Botnets are sold or rented by the hour. Botherders battle each other over taking ownership of the C&C. Recent botnets, such as Storm and Conficker, are sophisticated enough to adapt to defensive efforts. They encrypt their traffic and use proxy chains to make it difficult for researchers to figure out what they are up to at any given time, where the C&C is based, or what the actual size of the botnet is. Some botnets can now even be updated, patched or given new capabilities.

Defending Against DDoS attacks

The best defenses against DDoS attacks are simple: Try not to make enemies, and don't be cheap when it comes to the hardware you purchase for the network perimeter.

Many of the most damaging and costly DDoS attacks have happened either because attackers were trying to make a point and get attention, or because they were insulted and wanted to get back at somebody. In other cases, such as ones involving government offices or security companies, there is risk simply because of the jobs involved.

A well-designed network is your best technical defense. Make sure the attacker will have to really build up a lot of traffic in order to disrupt access to your services. Every router connected to the Internet is constantly being pounded on, scanned, and used as a reflector.

It is difficult to stop a DDoS attack once it has started. Usually the ISP must get involved and they can be reluctant to do so. Multi-agency efforts such as the CATCH team and regional CERTs assist at a higher level with keeping the Internet as a whole in a healthy state.

DDoS attacks are a waste of computing resources and usually affect many networks, not just the target. These organizations will keep your participation anonymous if you choose so, but reporting attacks and cooperating with defense efforts is part of good netizenship.

TRY IT OUT

Visit the CATCH Team and Regional CERT Websites

Take a few moments to visit these websites and notice who participates.

```
http://www.catchteam.org/
```

```
http://www.cert.org/
```

TRY IT OUT

Connect to IRC

The most popular IRC client for Windows is probably mIRC. It is not a free tool, but supports many advanced features. An evaluation copy is available.

```
http://www.mirc.com/index.html
```

The first time you run the client you will have to create a profile and determine your nick (nickname) which must be unique on the IRC network you have connected to.

Once connected to an IRC network, you will have to join a channel. Be careful as many of them are full of bots, lurkers (people not doing anything), or rude people. But not all of them are bad.

Refer to the help section of either client for a list of commands and other things.

TRY IT OUT CHALLENGE

- If IRC is completely blocked from where you are trying this exercise, you can download an IRC server called Beware IRCd. Default configuration works fine, just double click on the program and it is running. Use your IRC client to connect to 127.0.0.1 or whichever host you ran Beware IRCd on. You will be the only participant, but it may be a bit safer that way.

- Download the server here: *http://ircd.bircd.org/*

Conclusion

Denial of service tools are said to be on the decline because there isn't much financial incentive to attack in this manner. However, cyberwarfare, industrial sabotage, and extortion remain important motivators.

Denial of service attacks are not necessarily about exploiting a software weakness. They are also about understanding the normal operation and behavior of networking protocols and being able to generate either confusing traffic or just a lot of it.

Combining together the vectors of social engineering, Trojan horses, worms and viruses, botnets, and commercially driven equivalents, it is easy to imagine that potentially millions of hosts are currently connected to the Internet just waiting for commands. DDoS attacks can be launched from anywhere to bring down companies (1) or entire countries (2).

For the CEH exam, you will need to know the principles of multi-tiered DDoS attacks and some of the tools that have historical significance. These tools showed that it could be done, and modern attacks are based on many of the same ideas.

1. *http://searchsecurity.techtarget.com/news/article/0,289142,sid14_gci1188794,00.html*
2. *http://blogs.zdnet.com/threatchaos/?p=548*

BUFFER OVERFLOWS

Introduction

Buffer overflows are one of the "sexiest" forms of hacking because many of the "owning the bOx3n" type attacks seem to be based on them. Hunting for and creating buffer overflow exploits is a humbling endeavor. On some levels this might be the most intriguing aspect of the attack.

There is an ecosystem of security professionals researching in teams or as individuals that are racing to get the word out first. Vulnerability scanners are constantly updated to assess 0-day exploits (vulnerabilities that do not yet have a patch). Intrusion detection systems get signature updates minutes after examples are found in the wild. Commercial penetration testing products wrestle with the ethics of releasing 0-day exploit modules. Pressure is applied in all directions to be first to market without helping to publicize the vulnerability.

Many argue over whether or not buffer overflows are truly preventable. The very nature of some languages in computer programming lends to the risk. The constraints of time and budget placed on many software projects often require shortcuts or lack of emphasis on thorough testing. It may also simply be that clever hacking cannot be stopped no matter what anyone does.

For the CEH exam, you will be presented with some code; however, you will not have to be a programmer to understand it. The basics are sufficient for the scope of this certification. And we have tried to approach this chapter assuming as little programming background as possible from the reader.

As a defense practitioner, keep in mind the diligence required to defend against this vector is ongoing and never ending.

To Pass the CEH Exam You Need to . . .

• know the theory behind buffer overflows

• know how to work with overflow exploits

- know the tools for performing exploits
- master the CEH cheatsheets and practice questions!

Know the Theory Behind Buffer Overflows

- Defining buffer overflow vulnerabilities
- Assembly, machine, and interpreters
- A "proof of concept" illustration of the buffer overflow
  - Try it out: Read the original "Smashing the stack" article

Defining Buffer Overflow Vulnerabilities

A buffer overflow occurs when input given to an application exceeds the amount of memory that was set aside to store it. The input is still accepted, and it overwrites other critical data such as register counters that the CPU (Central Processing Unit) requires to manage the running of the program.

The input to the application could be either direct interaction (the application pauses to ask the user a question and the response is returned) or receiving a data file (such as a Web browser receiving a graphic image and rendering it on the Web page). It could also be a remote request that is supported on an open network service port. In essence, any time the application needs to receive data for processing, there must be a place in memory to store it (buffer) and program instructions loaded to handle it.

Assembly, Machine, and Interpreters

In order to be comfortable with the concepts of buffer overflows there are a few vocabulary terms that need to be addressed (pun intended, sorry).

- Machine, assembly, byte code, and high level code
- Disassemblers and debuggers
- Compilers and interpreters
- High order, low order
- Boolean logic
- Stacks, heaps, and registers

Machine, assembly, byte code, and high level code

Machine is the code that the CPU actually runs. It is seen in an   exploit script as a block of hexadecimal bytes that will load into memory and run exactly as they are.

Assembly is a language that uses commands of the CPU architecture directly. Abbreviations for instructions called "mnemonics" are used to represent the actual machine code. The mnemonics are specific to a CPU architecture. An "assembler" is an application that translates the assembly into machine code.

Byte code is an intermediary language used by languages such as Java and .NET that require a "virtual machine" interpreter to get to the machine level code. The virtual machine handles a lot of the "dirty work" of programming, such as memory and resource management. The programmer is allowed to focus more on the intended functions of the application and less on the mechanics of how a computer works.

High level code is written in a syntax that is more "human relatable" and must be compiled. Compilers are available for a variety of platforms and make the written code "portable" (written once but compiled for multiple systems). Source code written in high level languages is like having documentation on solving a problem if you know how to read the language.

Disassemblers and debuggers

Disassemblers turn machine back into assembly to make the code easier to analyze.

Debuggers run the code step by step at run-time or within a virtual machine that allows the analyst to observe what takes place with each instruction. The data stored in memory addresses and registers can be closely monitored as the program executes.

Some researchers feel that analyzing code through disassemblers and debuggers is even better than having the original source code. High level languages can often have very obfuscated statements (intentionally confusing), but looking directly at what is actually happening can be more accurate for "reverse engineering."

Compilers and interpreters

Compilers turn high level code into machine language. They also look for possible errors, dangerous functions, and ambiguities. If the high level language is not written perfectly in terms of syntax, the compiler cannot possibly do its job. This is one of the reasons some people get turned off by programming; a missing semicolon or unclosed quotation will cause the compiler to fail.

Interpreters run scripts and assemble the code into machine language "on the fly." There is a performance hit for this but the code is considered much easier to maintain. The real danger is that an interpreter has no way of knowing if the code can run or not in advance. It has to learn the hard way if something will not work. Programmers can use "try—catch" functions to help mitigate this risk, but only if they suspect at design time there could be a possible issue.

High order, low order

The "width" of a computer system is measured in the bits of a bus. If the CPU has physical pins that handle 32 signals at a time on its three busses (data, control, address) then it can handle 4 bytes of data with each cycle of the timer.

Some data such as "double words" are 32 bits long. The 4 bytes must load into memory in some order; consider this example: In the number 3467 digit "7" is the low order byte. The digit "3" is the high order. The whole value can load into memory in either direction without losing its meaning as long as we know how to process it.

Big endian systems would load the value as 3467.

Little endian systems would load it as 7643.

Why this matters has to do with interpreting what analysis tools show you. The researcher must know what the architecture is and how the tools they are using to observe the data will present it. They must also know whether certain data fields are 1 byte, 2 bytes, 4 bytes, or longer. This is particularly important in forensic work, but certainly becomes important in reverse engineering of code as well.

To add to this mess or perhaps to solve it, some architecture supports switching "endianness." The researcher must also keep this fact in mind.

Boolean logic

Essentially a computer is a set of billions and billions of two state switches (logic gates) that are either on or off, or that store an on or off state. Machine language is a hexadecimal representation of binary signals that essentially create circuits within this network of gates. The rules that govern what should happen in given situations are called the logic. Boolean logic is a way to understand how this works and how computer systems are designed.

Boolean functions include "AND", "OR", "XOR", and "NOT". The rules are expressed in truth tables. But for now, consider the logic on a more human level:

AND is the pessimist: if there is any doubt then the whole answer is false.

OR is the optimist: if there is any truth then the whole answer is true.

XOR is the realist: things that are different get attention while sameness is ignored.

NOT is the contrarian that does the opposite no matter what.

For a more technical understanding: Logic gates have two inputs, and a truth table tells what will happen for each gate:

Inputs	AND	OR	XOR
0 0	0	0	0
0 1	0	1	1
1 0	0	1	1
1 1	1	1	0

The NOT has only one input and inverts the signal.

Stacks, heaps, and registers

All data has to be placed somewhere, whether it is in non-volatile storage such as a hard drive or volatile storage such as RAM (Random Access Memory). If we put something somewhere we have to know where it is so we can find it again.

We also have to have a place to process stuff. Stacks and heaps are used for that. Registers are like the sticky notes on your monitor that help you track the current status of things. The small stuff matters. If the registers are corrupted, bad decisions get made. If the stacks and heaps are messed up, usually some sort of crash occurs and we reboot. The key to a buffer overflow attack is to get to those trusted sticky notes and misinform the processor.

A "Proof of Concept" Illustration of the Buffer Overflow

For this explanation, we are going to use non-realistic friendly numbers for the illustration. It does not matter what they are in reality and they will be different in every situation anyway.

When a program is loaded into memory, a "stack" or a "heap" is created to store the instructions. A heap is for the long-term running of the program as a whole and the stack is for temporary processes. We will just use the term "stack" for now. Registers are memory addresses that hold temporary values such as counters. These values tell the CPU things like how much memory we are using and what we should be doing next. Variables are places in memory where data such as user input and instructions are loaded into the memory space (push) and removed after they have been executed (pop).

The registers are set up at the bottom of the stack, which actually contains the higher addresses. "Bottom" is a confusing visual word in this case. Think of it this way:

Address	1000
	. . .
	. . .
Address	1500

In this example the bottom of the stack is address 1500 and the top is 1000. The ellipses represent instructions that are not important to us right now. If we need more room, the address at the top of the stack is decremented, which "grows" the stack like so:

Address	500
	. . .
	. . .
Address	1500

This gives us 500 more bytes to work with for program code. Initially, instructions are pushed onto the stack starting at the bottom and they "pile up" in a sense. Then as the program executes, the stack reduces in size as the instructions are popped off. Let's look at how the stack is set up as the program initially loads:

The counters (registers) are established at the bottom. Let's say we needed 100 bytes for them.

	1750
Registers	. . .
	1850

There must also be a place to keep variable data. Let's say we think we needed 250 bytes. The stack would now look something like this:

	1500
Variables	. . .
	1750
Registers	. . .
	1850

Finally, the instructions of the program itself push onto the stack. If we ended up with 500 instructions the stack would now look like this:

	500
	. . .
Instructions	. . .
	. . .
	. . .
	1500
Variables	. . .
	1750
Registers	. . .
	1850

As instructions execute there is a register that keeps track of what the next instruction that must be executed will be (the IEP register). This is in case a branching operation happens, such as figuring out an "if, then, else" function where a temporary stack is set up to run that function and the CPU needs to know how to come back to the main program code with the result.

Here is the fun part. The program asks the user for a first name, and the user inputs 300 bytes worth of data. Oops. The space set aside for variable data cannot hold this much, since it is only 250 bytes. Therefore, the remaining 50 bytes will overflow and replace the values in the registers, because data like this does not load the same way instructions do.

On the first try this will just crash the program. Once attackers notice what has happened they try something more deliberate. When asked for a first name, they input just the right amount of data to both overflow the variable space and place a particular value in the IEP register. The CPU will see that address and simply go there to find the next instruction. However, instead of returning to the correct part of the stack, the CPU ends up where the attackers want it to, someplace in the payload they have just given to the program.

Using the same numbers in the previous illustration, if the CPU thinks the next instruction is an offset of 250 from the bottom of the stack, it will execute what it finds at address 1600. This is smack in the middle of the variable area and not where the actual program instructions are loaded.

Knowing that it is difficult to be precise about this, attackers start the payload with a NOP sled (no operation). The classic example is a long series of 0x90 instructions in the machine code of the payload portion of the attack. This way, the CPU just executes "do nothing" instructions for a few clock cycles and then slides nicely into the shellcode, which is the remainder of the payload.

What the shellcode can be is dependent on how much room there is in the buffer overflow weakness. Shellcode as small as 24 bytes can be executed on the Linux platform. The idea is usually to start an execution process and feed it a command. This is all done directly in machine language. If more room is available, an entire binary can be inserted and launched. Netcat is a popular choice in this case because it is small, fast, and can open a TCP/IP socket that is now available to the attacker that knows what port number to connect a client to.

TRY IT OUT

Read the Original "Smashing the Stack" Article

In volume 7, issue 49 of the online hacker magazine, *Phrack*, a classic article was written by Aleph One called "Smashing the Stack for Fun and Profit." The article is represented at the link below. Take a moment to look it over.

```
http://insecure.org/stf/smashstack.html
```

Know How to Work with Overflow Exploits

- Understanding the risks
- Monitoring and detection
  - Try it out: Create a simple buffer overflow

Understanding the Risks

A typical buffer overflow exploit script is written in C and contains two main elements: the exploit and the payload. The exploit accesses the vulnerability which is the input the target application is willing to receive. The payload contains raw, pure machine language binary code that can execute as is when directly inserted into memory by the exploit code.

Researchers and penetration testers need to know the true origin of the code they download from the Internet. Attackers often could not care less. The problem is that it is extremely easy to embed additional backdoor code into any exploit; sure, it might do what it is supposed to, but it might do a whole lot more as well. Unless you look at the code line by line and then compile it yourself, and that includes the machine code, you cannot be sure what to trust (unless you write the exploit yourself, of course).

It is a common practice to intentionally bug exploit scripts to force the attackers to fix the bug and admire the handiwork of the exploits author in the process. Another common practice is the "proof of concept" approach that involves a harmless payload and is intentionally not stealthy in the execution of the attack. For the white hat hacker, this is not only perfectly acceptable but often preferred.

The next question is, "What privileges does the shellcode have when the exploit runs?" That depends on who was running the application or service that was attacked. If the exploit is successful the shellcode will take on the same security context as the user of the vulnerable application. This is why it is so critical not to surf the Internet while logged in with administrator rights.

Monitoring and Detection

There are a few basic things to look out for when considering buffer overflow vulnerabilities. These include:

- Requirements of design
- Dangerous functions
- Bounds checking
- Canary bytes
- IDS signatures

Requirements of design

Any application development project should be managed in accordance with relevant standards for the industry in which the application will be used. Although project management, testing, development, and maturity models are outside of the scope of CEH, they play an important role in the development community.

At the very least, make sure every application meets these criteria:

- No bypass of authentication is possible
- No input from users that can exploit vulnerabilities
- No "shrink wrap code" vulnerabilities

Shrink wrap code refers to shared program libraries and possibly to entire applications that are utilized in the creation of new products.

Dangerous functions

The most important technique in defending against buffer overflow vulnerabilities is to observe the best possible secure coding practices in the first place. In the language "C" strcpy() and strncpy() are considered vulnerable functions. Compilers exist that will root out the use of this and similar code; however, when programmers are used to a particular compiler they have worked with for 20 years and know how to keep it happy, it can be a hard political battle to get them to change. To be truthful, there must be a strong business case to even ask them; otherwise, the project deadline will be the priority.

Bounds checking

"Bounds checking" or "input sanitizing" is the detail of making sure that a user's first name should not be entered as 300 bytes (referring to our example). Whenever input is requested, criteria that ensures the input is clean must be enforced within the code. Clean is defined as meeting certain constraints such as not being larger than what the malloc() (Memory allocation) function was that set up the variable size in the first place. Special characters must be properly escaped as well, meaning they are not to be processed by the interpreter but rather ignored or seen literally as just characters.

Canary bytes

Canary bytes are placed by the programmer in the last four bytes of the variable space, also called the "stack frame." These are checked to see if an attempt has been made to overwrite them, which would be the case in a buffer overflow exploit. This technique could also be used as a troubleshooting measure when debugging code.

IDS signatures

Intrusion detection systems (IDS) can look for NOP sleds. However, there are many ways that a skilled and creative programmer can cause an application to do nothing for awhile. The CEH exam will likely stick with 0x90 and not expect intricate knowledge of assembly bytes for various platforms, but in the real world it is important to note there is a constant game being played in this area between the good guys and bad guys.

The CEH exam does not require you to be a programmer but it could show you some source code and ask about a few basics. Just to be sure, try to run the following example and look at the code carefully. If you have never written a line of C before, see if you can guess what each line means.

TRY IT OUT

Create a Simple Buffer Overflow

Open a command shell in Linux. Start a new file in a text editor such as pico, nano, or vi. For example, try:

```
nano overflow.c
```

Type the following:

```
#include <stdio.h>

main()

{
```

(continued)

(continued)

```
char *name;

char *dangerous;

name = (char *) malloc(10);

dangerous = (char *) malloc(128);

printf("Address of name is %d\n", name);

printf("Address of command is %d\n", dangerous);

sprint(dangerous, "echo %s", "Hello World");

printf("What's your name?");

gets(name);

system(dangerous);

}
```

Save the file, compile, and execute the script. (There will be some warnings, but ignore those because you are in too much of a hurry to correct them.) Run the program once properly. Now,

```
gcc -o overflow overflow.c

chmod +x overflow

./overflow
```

Notice the difference of 16 bytes in the memory address outputs. Run the program again. This time, when it asks for your first name enter:

```
1234567890123456cat /etc/shadow
```

Know the Tools for Performing Exploits

- Compiling scripts
  - Try it out: Disassemble the buffer overflow exploit example
- Using the Metasploit framework
  - Try it out: Use the Metasploit framework tool

Compiling Scripts

The previous lab example illustrated the command for compiling scripts. The command "gcc" (GNU C Compiler) is the classic tool for compiling. The command line tool for disassembly is "gdb" in Linux. For Windows operating systems two powerful tools are "IDA Pro" (not free of cost) and OllyDGB (is free of cost).

TRY IT OUT

Disassemble the Buffer Overflow Exploit Example

Since we did the example in Linux, let's follow through and see what it really looks like. Compile a new binary we can take apart:

```
gcc -S -o overflow.s overflow.c
```

See what the assembly looks like:

```
cat overflow.s
```

Now take a look at what the gdb tool has to say:

```
gdb overflow
```

```
disassemble main
```

For the CEH exam, you do not need to worry about knowing what all of this output means. Even so, you now have a basic idea of how programs can be analyzed for buffer overflow errors or be reverse engineered.

Using the Metasploit Framework

Metasploit is a powerful tool for vulnerability testing. It is mentioned in this chapter because of the reason this tool exists. It can be time consuming for a researcher to compile and run scripts with different combinations of exploit, payload (shellcode), NOP sled encoding, and basic parameters such as destination target IP address and port.

Metasploit is a framework tool that makes each of these components modular. It allows the tester to quickly select a combination of different things and let them run. It provides both a command line and Web-based interface.

The basic idea is as follows:

- Select an exploit
- Select a target OS or service version
- Select a payload
- Configure options
- Attack

TRY IT OUT

Use the Metasploit Framework Tool

The documentation for Metasploit use has been growing exponentially. Start with the source of the project, read a few blog postings, then download and try the tool.

You can also search YouTube for videos that illustrate the use of the Metasploit framework.

```
http://www.metasploit.com
```

Conclusion

It might turn out to be impossible to completely avoid buffer overflow vulnerabilities. The issue is perhaps at the heart of the application development process. Business case and time constraints are sometimes at odds with each other. Indirectly, it does not matter if weaknesses in software are preventable or not. There are forces at work in the world of programming that almost guarantee that vulnerabilities will always exist and there will always be someone somewhere trying to discover the attack vector.

Like actors, musicians, artists, and athletes, talented programmers have skills that involve a combination of creative and critical thinking that can only be applied after long hours of hard work and practice.

From the attacker's point of view, opportunity is the objective, not an assessment of the quality of any development program. It is possible to be relentless in this area and there is nothing that can be done to curtail the effort. The tools for exploitation are becoming more common and easier to use. The financial incentives for sharing this knowledge are real.

Attacking can range from the simplest social engineering trick to a complex and specialized buffer overflow exploit. The takeaway from this chapter is this contrast, and the lesson that a skilled attacker will not forget that the entire span of opportunity exists.

HACKING WEB SERVERS AND WEB APPLICATIONS

Introduction

Web application development is extremely tricky. The stateless Internet environment presents an entirely different set of challenges than desktop applications encounter. There are more users of unknown origin. There are mechanisms for overcoming the stateless environment for statistics gathering and marketing data analysis that desktop applications have never had. The client server architecture is fundamentally different because it is driven by the perception of user experience. In modern times, users have increasing expectations of these applications.

In an interconnected world, all vulnerable Web-based applications are dangerous. Attackers are looking for any opportunity they can find. Vulnerable websites can be used as mules in attacks against the true object of any attack. Just as we have discussed reflection in terms of protocols, think of vulnerable sites as potential social engineering reflections.

The first step is to understand a few things about how Web applications and the associated protocols work. Then we can look at the variety of risks and challenges involved with securing Web applications.

To Pass the CEH Exam You Need to . . .

- know how Web servers work
- know how Web applications work
- know the attacks and risks of Web applications
- master the CEH cheatsheets and practice questions!

Know How Web Servers Work

- The responsibility of a Web server
- The HTTP protocol
- Understanding requests
- URL encoding schemes
- Secure Sockets Layer (SSL)
- Authentication methods
  - Try it out: Research HTTP authentication

The Responsibility of a Web Server

A Web server is essentially a file server. It receives requests from a client application for a file and returns the result. Sometimes the file contains active code that must be processed first. This is best described in a multi-tier architecture model that follows in this chapter.

When users contact a Web server, they usually log in as anonymous users. In Windows this account is IUSR_<Computer Name> and in Linux it is usually the account "Nobody." In both cases the password is blank, and the user account should have extremely restricted access to the system as a whole.

The request a client makes is in the form of a URL (Uniform Resource Locator) and a series of header messages.

The HTTP Protocol

The Web server provides the HTTP service between the client and server. HyperText Transfer Protocol is essentially a "request/response" transaction that facilitates the simple exchange of a set of data. In the case of viewing a Web page, this data is in the form of a text file.

The fact that this file contains HTML is not important to HTTP. The data is passed to the client and the client must know what to do with it. This allows for multiple media types to be involved in a typical Web page viewing.

A client makes a GET request. The server is required to respond. The protocol header contains a code that indicates the nature of the response. The following is a sample of these responses:

Series	Meaning
100	HTTP 1.0 did not define 100 series codes and they should not be used
200	Everything is OK
300	Redirection, the resource is somewhere else
400	Client error, the request could not be fulfilled
500	Server error, the request could not be processed

Protocol header conversations are not normally visible to the user; the client processes them in the background. Using packet sniffers, proxy applications (such as Paros), or various plug-ins that are available for browsers, such as Firefox, the headers can be viewed and tracked. They can even be modified on the fly as is the case with MiTM attacks.

HTTP defines several methods the client can invoke. Some are considered safe, while others might have more powerful effects. The safe methods include:

- HEAD
- GET
- OPTIONS
- TRACE

The methods that cause "side effects" include:

- POST
- PUT
- DELETE
- CONNECT

We do not have to get into them all right know, but notice that GET and POST show up in different lists. These are the two principal ways in which forms that appear on Web pages are submitted. From the names of the other methods it is clear that HTTP supports multiple tasks. Downloading Web pages is only the beginning.

Understanding Requests

When an HTML form is calling the GET method, the names of the form elements are paired up with the input data (what you fill out) and appended to the URL in the form of a query string. Examine the following example string and the labels within:

http://host.domain.tld/resource/path/page.ext?form_item1=string1&formitem2=string2

The name value pairs passed from the client to the next page (the action attribute of the form) are separated by ampersands. The string to the left of the equal sign is the form element name, and the value to the right is what the user provided before clicking the submit button.

Hidden form field elements (not visible in the browser but can be seen in the source code) can carry name value pairs, too. For instance, a form that is tracking the number of login attempts made into a page might look like this:

http://host.domain.tld/resource/path/page.ext?attempts=2

Modifying either the URL or the source code of the page, then reloading and submitting, could possibly overcome the limitation imposed by the application. This is one of the most important characteristics of the GET method. Also notice that if credentials are included in the URL they would be visible.

Credentials are not just usernames and passwords. They can also be token strings, often implemented as "SessionID=asfdjwqjherj2hj2h34jqsd7343rq" or something similar. This token is generated on the server and passed back and forth between the client and server in order to establish "state."

HTTP 1.0 did not support "state." HTTP 1.1 added the feature. It is important for some Web applications to understand unique users and the time they spend on the website. A random string of characters can be used to make this easy. If attackers can sniff or otherwise capture this token they can become "you." They simply replace the token in their own request.

Knowing that IP addresses might change during the session and considering the original intent of the Internet to be stateless, it was a design choice not to consider additional elements outside of this token to establish a stateful connection.

The POST method, on the other hand, places the name value pairs in the HTTP header and can be protected by an SSL connection. Proxy servers can be used to perform man in the middle attacks; it is important when sensitive data is exchanged in the header that the SSL (Secure Sockets Layer) connection should be established first.

URL Encoding Schemes

The specification for URLs says that certain special characters are either forbidden from use or must be encoded because they already have special meanings. The space character, for instance, can not be used in a URL and can be substituted for with a plus sign. The ampersand, question mark, and equal signs are all parts of a query string (sometimes also referred to as a parameter string).

The most common way to encode characters is by using "percent encoding" which is a percent sign followed by a two digit hexadecimal representation of the original character. The following are just a few examples:

Character	Code
Space	%20
Dot	%2E
Slash	%2F
2	%32

Consider this URL:

http://www.example.dom/cgi-bin/search+page.pl?search=Intense+School

This URL could become the following UTL if certain characters were encoded:

http://www.example.dom/cgi-bin%2Fsearch%20page.pl?search=Intense%20School

There are other ways to encode URLs as well as to represent the address of the website itself. Some characters can be double encoded, and in certain cases triple encoding may work.

Since the client browser plays a role in this process along with the HTTP server, some attacks are better conducted directly through Telnet connections to port 80 on the Web server. Regardless, more is to be discussed on this topic when we get to the attack section of the chapter.

Secure Sockets Layer (SSL)

Secure Sockets Layer (SSL) was created by Netscape and later adopted into an IETF standard as TLS (Transport Layer Security) and updated in RFC 5246. This is the famous protocol that causes that little padlock icon to appear in your browser (unless one has been placed there by an attacker).

The server authenticates to the client in order to exchange a cryptographic secret. This secret is then used to create an encapsulation that encrypts the traffic of the resulting session. SSL operates at a lower OSI layer than HTTP; therefore, all traffic between the client and server are protected.

The server sends a digital certificate to the client. It is up to the client to validate this certificate for a level of trust. The client then uses the public key within the certificate to encrypt a symmetric key (generated randomly by the client) and sends it to the server. The server then decrypts the symmetric key with its own private key. This shared secret is then used to protect the rest of the session data.

SSL/TLS can be used to support a number of transport protocols. There have been several security issues identified with this technique, along with business-related pressures to continue adoption of legacy implementations.

The earliest installations of SSL employed the use of 40-bit encryption due to cryptographic export standards. While a government might not want to trade in weapons with enemies, commercial companies do not mind doing so at all. Under some pressure, certain standards have been relaxed, but this remains an issue when certifying an organization to conduct e-commerce. The PCI DSS (Payment Card Industry Data Security Standard), for example, has strict requirements in terms of protecting consumer transactions.

As SSL/TLS evolves, many potential customers with older browsers still require legacy support. In addition to this, there is still a lot of potential for this technology to be implemented wrongly. Attackers and penetration testers alike are always on the lookout for errors in this area.

Authentication Methods

Web server-based authentication is a critical part of separating the

- Basic
- Digest
- Application

Basic

In basic authentication, the username and password pair are encoded in Base64 and presented as username:password in clear text. The encoding is to support an extended set of characters.

Base64 encoding is taking the binary representation of a string and repackaging it into 6 bits per character. It is also a common way to send binary files over systems that are meant for text only, such as Usenet.

Digest

Digest authentication incorporates a nonce value (one-time generated string) added to an MD5 hash of the password. This design evolved to combat "chosen plaintext" attacks, which basically means that the attacker can take combinations of characters and attempt to reproduce the encrypted stream.

Additional features have been added to prevent replay attacks by ensuring the nonce value has a correlation with time. Replay attacks occur when credentials are sniffed from the wire and simply presented to the server again at a later time.

Application

Depending on the platform, there are authentication methods that are supported by either the Web server or by a custom-built application.

The Apache Web server uses a file called the .htaccess file to store credentials. The more recent versions of Apache have moved that file out of the website's file system, but earlier versions placed it in a potentially vulnerable place. The IIS Web server supports integrated authenticate with Windows domain services, in which the user account credentials are stored in the same way as they would be for local accounts.

Applications that have been custom built involve storing credentials in a database and checking that database for information provided by the user from a login page. In this style, it is up to the application developer to make sure hashing is properly implemented and that the SSL connection is established before the login process occurs.

Brute force password attacks can be conducted against these applications using tools like Brutus or Hydra, unless the developer has instituted a way to limit the tries. Typically, after three to five failed attempts, the attacker is diverted to a secondary page and required to enter a captcha.

Captchas are those distorted images that are required to determine the characters displayed and type them into a form. They present usability issues so alternatives must often be provided. Attackers can try alternative (non-graphic) browsers to reach those pages instead.

TRY IT OUT

Research HTTP Authentication

The basic and digest authentication schemes were improved and described in RFC 2617. Take a few minutes to look through this document.

```
http://www.ietf.org/rfc/rfc2617.txt
```

Know How Web Applications Work

- Presentation layer
  - Try it out: Learn more about building Web pages
  - Try it out: Use the Lynx browser
- Logic layer
- Database layer

Presentation Layer

The presentation layer is the code that gets processed in the visitor's browser. The role of the browser in a Web application is to resolve DNS addresses, make HTTP requests, receive the page and all resources that are referenced within the page, and, through a variety of rendering engines and plug-ins (also called BHOs or Browsers Helper Objects), render the content visually.

There are primarily three languages involved. Combined together they are sometimes called "DHTML" (Dynamic Hypertext Markup Language):

- HTML
- CSS
- Javascript

HTML

HyperText Markup Language provides a way to describe the structure of a page. It marks elements as being headers, paragraphs, and references to other resources. These elements which do not necessarily all look a certain way, but these marks are functional to the document as a whole.

CSS

Cascading Style Sheets (CSS) handle the look and feel of a Web page. Browsers have a built-in default style sheet that can be used to display marked-up page objects. The designer can also provide a style sheet of his own to define elements in accordance with a layered (cascading) set of style guide rules.

The flexibility of this design allows the same page content to be usable in a variety of browser clients. Marketing and business pressures often result in poor designs that override this flexibility in order to force a graphic and color scheme onto the visitor. This was not the original intent. Section 508 (*http://www.section508.gov/*) described accessibility standards for Web pages. The basic idea is that content should be accessible if users specify their own style sheet and the scripting functions of a page are disabled.

Javascript

A scripting language provides interactive elements to the document and can access the objects modeled by the HTML markup as well as objects that are built into the browser.

This is one of the ways various browsers have attempted to compete with each other over the years, much to the frustration of developers who must often write their pages to work in several different ways so as not to alienate their customers.

In recent years, a technology called "AJAX" (Asynchronous Javascript and XML) has completely transformed the client experience. Rich applications such as Google office and greatly enhanced multimedia have changed the way we work on the Web. The advertising world has also been revolutionized by this technology—targeted ads now become a part of the Web page and can react to how the visitor uses the website.

AJAX is a suite of protocols that uses the XMLHTTPRequest API to send HTTP requests and pass the results directly to the scripting object in the page on the client side. This enables continuous conversation between the client and server.

While HTML parsing engines were forgiving of sloppy code, the sophisticated nature of AJAX requires unambiguous object models created by the markup of page elements. XML (eXtensible Markup Language) provides the specification for *well-formed* markup along with the ability to create an entirely new vocabulary for describing objects. CSS is still used to define the visual properties of the page elements.

Although the programming of AJAX websites is much more involved than standard DHTML, many of the same threats still exist if the application is not coded properly. AJAX allows for server side validation of form data, which is a huge improvement, but XSS and SQL injection attacks are still possible.

TRY IT OUT

Learn More About Building Web Pages

One of the best reference and tutorial sites on the Web is the w3schools. Take some time to visit the site, look around, and use the "try-it-yourself" examples.

```
http://www.w3schools.com
```

TRY IT OUT

Use the Lynx Browser

Lynx is a command line browser that allows attackers to safely view dangerous Web pages (it does not support scripting or media elements that could contain malware) or surf the Web from a shell they have accessed on a remote host.

If you have a Linux host handy, Lynx is likely already there. If not, or if you need the Windows version, it can be obtained here:

```
http://lynx.isc.org/
```

Logic Layer

The logic layer processes active code within the pages requested through HTTP. When the client asks for a page that is recognized as having code that must be processed, the server runs the code and the expected output generates a full text string Web page that can then be provided to the client as the response.

The phrase "on-the-fly" describes the way in which the logic layer of a Web application creates Web pages in real time. A site like yahoo.com, for instance, does not have tens of thousands of pages like one might think. It may have only a dozen or so, but each one acts as a template of sorts that contains active code which initiates a connection to a database, makes a query, and delivers the results as a plain text file.

Any language can be used for the server side functionality of a Web application. CGI (Common Gateway Interface) is the specification that describes how to create the Web application to meet the unique needs of the Internet environment and cooperate with HTTP and other protocols. Examples of popular server-side languages include:

- PERL (.pl)
- PHP (.php)
- Active Server Pages (.asp /.aspx / asp.NET)
- Cold Fusion Markup Language (.cfml)
- Ruby

PERL (.pl)

PERL (Practical Extraction and Reporting Language) was originally designed to replace command line tools such as SED and AWK as a powerful set of string parsing libraries. Although PERL was meant to be used for sorting through large log files, for example, it turns out to be ideal as a CGI language due to the text-based nature of HTTP messages.

PHP (.php)

The acronym PHP is said to no longer stand for anything. It went from "Personal Home Pages" to "Hypertext Pre-processor" but essentially it is now just simply PHP. It was created from the ground up to be a CGI language. PHP has a very active community of developers and has had its share of security issues over the years. Its ease of use, however, facilitates powerful Web applications that can be developed in a relatively short time.

When a Web server is described as a LAMP, it runs Linux, Apache, MySQL, and PHP, PERL, or Python.

Active Server Pages (.asp/.aspx/asp.NET)

Active Server Pages (ASP) is the CGI language supported by Microsoft and the IIS (Internet Information Services) browser. The .NET version supports server side form validation and other enhanced features that make up for many of the shortcomings of the .asp libraries.

If the site is using .asp, the attacker will look for a file at the root of the Web directory called "global.asa". It represents the main configuration of the website and might contain hard-coded database connection strings and passwords.

Cold Fusion Markup Language (.cfml)

Macromedia (now owned by Adobe) is an industry leader of Web-based applications. Notably, the Flash platform has almost become the defacto standard in multimedia delivery. CFML (Cold Fusion Markup Language) was a tag-based syntax that allowed the developer to easily define reusable code functions that could simply be called at any time from these "tags."

Ruby

Ruby is a relative newcomer to the Web application space and seeks to take the idea of RAD (Rapid Application Development) to a whole new level by providing an API (Application Programming Interface) of many commonly used functions that can be reused with very little or no customization. An IDE (Integrated Development Environment) can be created that allows drag and drop functionality for programmers that need to create applications quickly.

In the cases of all of these languages, many scripts are provided on the Internet and the programmer rarely has to figure out how to reinvent the wheel. Remember that EC-Council refers to this as "Shrink Wrap Code." Vulnerabilities that exist in these resources propagate to any websites that use them. The developer must still analyze the code and ensure there are no backdoors, or no known issues. An attacker will look for obvious signs of code reuse and might be able to perform a Google search to locate additional vulnerable sites.

Database Layer

When a Web page is executed at the logic layer, it is often necessary to start up a session with a database server and pass it an SQL request. User credentials to content blobs can be stored in the database, and are populated through other applications such as content management systems.

If successful, the results that come back from the SQL request are processed by the logic layer and formatted into standard HTML as the document is prepared to be sent to the requesting client. Each time a logic layer script runs, a new session is established, and then is closed gracefully once the transaction is complete. A driver is necessary to establish this connection. Although there are several available depending on the database technology involved, the CEHv6 exam covers ODBC (Open Database Connectivity)

On a Windows system, the administrator can use the Data Connections applet in the Control Panel to setup a DSN (Data Source Name). From there, it is simple in the .asp code to construct an object based on the DSN, and pass it an SQL query. Regardless of the driver used, the point is the same: credentials are passed along with a session request (Layer 5) then an SQL query is submitted; there is a return, and the connection is closed.

If attackers can get the credentials the benefits are clear. Once the database technology is determined, attackers would connect to the appropriate ports with a front-end tool and have at it. Otherwise, it might be possible to manipulate the SQL query all the way from the presentation layer. This is the essence of SQL injection attacks.

Know the Attacks and Risks of Web Applications

* Banner grabbing
* Denial of service (DoS)
  * Try it out: Banner grabbing
* Password guessing
* Abusing the robots.txt file
* Offline browsing
* Hidden form fields
* Directory traversal
* URL obfuscation
  * Try it out: Explore URL encoding and obfuscation
* SSL attacks
* Cookie stealing
* Session ID hijacking
* XSS (Cross Site Scripting)
* SQL Injection

Banner Grabbing

Banner grabbing is conducted during the information discovery phase of the attack. It is for the purpose of determining the Web server and operating system versions.

Another important resource is *http://www.netcraft.com*. This service tracks version, OS, and uptime of Internet accessible websites.

TRY IT OUT

Banner Grabbing

This exercise can be done in Windows but it is clearer in Linux. Either way, simply enter the following:

```
telnet [target ip] 80

GET / HTTP/1.0
```

Hit enter twice.

Denial of Service (DoS)

If all of the other attacks fail, or if the objective in the first place is simply to embarrass the owner of the website or perform an extortion attack, a DoS or Distributed DoS is a possibility.

There are also attacks against unpatched Web servers that exploit both problems with modules provided by the HTTP service and issues with the underlying OS. A common occurrence is the Sasser worm which exploits a weakness in the Windows LSA (Local Security Authority) and renders the host inaccessible.

Administrators must always remember to disable unnecessary extensions. In the IIS server, these are called ISAPIs (Internet Server Application Programming Interfaces). The IIS Lockdown tool available from Microsoft can assist with selecting the correct modules to leave enabled based upon the role of the server.

Password Guessing

Unless the front door of the Web application is protected with a "try limit" there is nothing stopping attackers from spending all day guessing at password accounts. In some cases it is possible to get lucky and find a random person's account. If the attackers have performed thorough reconnaissance, they can make educated guesses and figure out the answers to cognitive questions that might reset or reveal the actual password.

Tools such as Brutus or Hydra can automate the guessing process. Looking at the source code of the page, determine the names of the fields associated with the login form. For example:

```
<form action=http://www.example.dom/login" method="post">

<input type="text" name="uname"/> <br/>

<input type="text" name="passwd"/> <br/>

<input type="submit"/>

</form>
```

In this case, the *uname* and *passwd* fields are of interest. A dictionary file with pairs of words can be thrown at this form automatically. The file should include obvious words like "test," "guest," "practice," and so on. With some dumpster diving or other means of collecting information, a company directory can be used to put together likely usernames. Then a dictionary list of common passwords can be used to audit the weak logins.

Abusing the Robots.txt File

All files on a site are organized into folders under its root directory. Robots (spiders) from search engines crawl the directories of a website looking for pages to catalog into the search engine.

Some files such as scripts should be stored in a directory that is inaccessible to the Web user login and instead is only accessible by the Web service that needs to call the library files from other active pages. Other directories might contain documentation or sample code that is not meant for public viewing.

The robots.txt file is supposed to tell a robot what it can and cannot index. It is placed at the root of the website. It also tells attackers where the good stuff is. Consider the following example robots.txt file:

```
User-agent: *

Disallow:/cgi-bin/

Disallow:/docs/
```

The first line says this file applies to all forms of robots. The other lines tell them what they cannot index. The problem with this is clear—it is up to the robot to be courteous enough to obey the directives.

Offline Browsing

Sometimes it is more efficient to download as much of the website as possible first, and then search through it offline for information such as keywords, e-mail addresses, names, and so on.

Tools such as "wget" and "black widow" are ideal for this activity. Also do not forget about archive.org and "The Wayback Machine," which archive old versions of sites.

Hidden Form Fields

Whether you are offline browsing or looking at the source code of a recent page, finding hidden form fields is sometimes great. They do not display in the browser window, but the value attribute can carry important data with the form submission back to the server.

In the early days, hidden form fields included prices! The attack simply modified the source code and submitted the page. Presently, hidden form elements might contain password hashes, retry counters, or other significant items. Consider the following example:

```
<form action=http://www.example.dom/login" method="post">

<input type="text" name="email"/> <br/>

<input type="text" name="comment"/> <br/>

<input type="hidden" name="token" value="34dfxadsf5dt6hfg"/>

<input type="submit"/>

</form>
```

Capturing the token using a proxy such as "Paros" would allow attackers to substitute this token with one generated from their own browser, and assume the login session of the other user.

Directory Traversal

One of the other functions of a Web server is to keep the anonymous user account confined to the file system of the website itself. In other words, the root of the website files is the root of what the user can see on the system. In navigating directories, the "../" characters mean "navigate to the parent" directory. On some systems it is possible to navigate to several parents and then drill down into the file system. For example:

http://www.example.dom/scripts/../../../winnt/system32/cmd.exe?c+dir+c:

Starting in the root folder on example.dom, move into the scripts folder (to pick up execute permissions), then come up three parent levels (which might place the attacker at the root of the drive), then drill down to where the cmd.exe utility is and invoke it. The query string passes a command to that shell, and since the result is a character stream, HTTP will return it to the attacker's browser. On a vulnerable host, a directory listing would be displayed.

This vulnerability potentially exists on both Windows and Linux systems. Filters are available to detect the "../" characters in the URL; however, there are two problems. First, if the programmer of the website decided to use relative links between pages, then the dot dot slashes will appear in the requests intentionally, and the filter will break the website. Second, there are many ways to hide the characters with encoding techniques. Consider the following examples:

%2E%2E%2F

%2E%2E/

%2E.%2F

%%32E%%32E%%32F

These are all equivalent strings once the URL encoding has been parsed, the final example is double encoded. The point is to see that there are thousands of ways to represent a directory traversal attempt. Scanners such as "n-stealth" have tens of thousands of traversal and xss attempts that can be sent to test a Web server for vulnerabilities.

URL Obfuscation

In addition to URL encoding techniques, there are different ways to represent the address of the Web server. This technique is commonly used in spam messages to convince the victim the link is safe. Consider the following examples:

http://eccouncil.org

http://superbank@eccouncil.org

http://64.147.96.106

http://0x40936606A

http://1083400298

http://superbank@1083400298

These are all equivalent addresses. For the CEHv6 exam, it is important that you can use a normal (not a scientific) calculator to perform the conversions. To convert a dotted quad IP address to its decimal form using the previous example, the formula would be worked out as follows:

```
(64*(256^3))  +  (147*(256^2))  +  (96*(256^1))  +  (106*256^0))  =

(64* 16777216)  +  (147*65536)  +  (96*256)  +  106  =

1073741824  +  9633792  +  24576  +  106  =  1083400298
```

TRY IT OUT

Explore URL Encoding and Obfuscation

There are actually dozens of ways to convey an IP address. Not all methods are supported by all browsers, but to get an idea take a look at the examples on this page:

```
http://www.pc-help.org/obscure.htm
```

SSL Attacks

Also referred to as a SSLMiTM attack, this attack begins as a social engineering exercise where a victim is convinced to accept a fake certificate. The website is often a spoofed site designed to masquerade as a common business, as an intranet page, or as a place the victim would be familiar with.

The browser will warn users that the certificate chain cannot be validated, but most users in this situation are not familiar with the idea. If the e-mail they were sent with the link was convincing enough, the victim will be focused on the urgency of visiting the site and will dismiss the warning as being a browse error. The padlock closes, the SSL connection is established, and users are certain they can trust the site with their passwords.

Once the attack is completed, users might be sent to the legitimate site in order to keep the appearance of the scenario intact.

Cookie Stealing

Cookies are small pieces of data stored on the client side (presentation layer) of a Web application. They can then be read back from subsequent pages loaded from the same domain. Netscape invented the cookie object in order to store authentication tokens, customization settings, and dates and times that would allow Webmasters to track usage patterns.

There are some constraints to using cookies. The original specification set out the following rules:

- Only the domain that set the cookie could read it.
- Browsers will only store cookies from 20 unique domains.
- Browsers will only store 200 cookies total.

These constraints were meant to protect clients from having their entire hard drive consumed by cookies. The data are stored in different ways according to the browser design, and they are not always encrypted.

Cookie stealing can be accomplished in the following ways:

- Physical access to a system might allow an attacker to simply copy cookies out to a file and walk away.
- Using a sniffer or proxy server, unencrypted cookies can be eavesdropped on and then substituted on the next page request.
- Companies can triangulate cookie tokens on the back end of an application.

Let's examine the latter possibility. If "techsite.com" sets a cookie on a visitor's system that contains a unique token, it can then share that token with an affiliate site such as an advertising partner. The advertisement itself will be downloaded from the domain of the advertisers, who then correlate the token they were given by "techsite.com" and write it into a cookie from their domain. From here, all activity can be tracked, and every link the visitor clicks builds up a database of preferences from which future ads can be targeted. This includes other websites that the ad agency partners with since they could always share the token with them as well.

There are many scripts and examples of using the document.cookie object in JavaScript. The aforementioned *http://www.w3schools.com* has some excellent tutorials on the topic.

Session ID Hijacking

Session IDs are strings of random characters that are associated with a visitor's present visit to a website. They can be set and stored in a cookie, transferred in the HTTP header, or even placed in the URL.

Session sidejacking is another name for the process of sniffing this session ID string from a legitimate user. Attackers then start a session with the same website and replace their own ID token with the one captured from the victim's session. Packet sniffers and proxy servers make this a fairly easy attack if measures are not taken to enhance the token with additional characteristics or to protect it within an encrypted tunnel.

XSS (Cross Site Scripting)

This attack was originally called a CSS attack, and on the CEHv6 exam that term might still be used. Since CSS stands for Cascading Style Sheets, the name of this attack was changed to XSS. Sometimes it is referred to as JavaScript injection.

Many actual XSS vulnerabilities are more complex than the following example, but the basic idea can illustrate the concept well enough. When an HTML form allows a visitor to submit special characters that are not "cleansed" or filtered, it is possible to interact with the code on the logic layer from the HTML form on the client side.

In the case of XSS attacks, the string of characters entered into the HTML form make it all the way through processing and back to the client side with no alteration at all. The client then executes it as presentation script.

Consider the following example: An HTML form is asking for a visitor's first name. In the field she puts:

```
<script>alert("FUBAR!")</script>
```

Then she submits the form only to find that on the resulting page an alert box indeed pops up and says "FUBAR!" She notices in the URL that there is a name value pair that includes the string:

http://www.example.dom/page.xyz?first_name=<script>alert("FUBAR!")</script>

She then examines the source code and notices that the injected script looks like something the client would try to execute rather than treat as a simple string of characters. She enters a different parameter into the browser address bar such as:

```
FirstName=<script>window.location=http://fakesite.cx</script>
```

Then she resubmits the page and is quite surprised by what she sees. The location property of the window object of the browser has changed, resulting in a redirect.

The final step would be to find a vulnerable site and inject a similar redirect attack. The URL can be obfuscated using encoding methods to hide the intent of the link. Send this link in a phishing e-mail and those who click on the link will have unfortunate results waiting for them. Other than not clicking, there is little the victim can do to stop this.

SQL Injection

SQL injection works from similar principles as XSS attacks, but involves SQL (Structured Query Language) being passed to the database layer of the Web application rather than round tripping back to the client. Once an SQL injection vulnerability is found, the only limitation to attackers is their skill with SQL queries. Attackers can sit there at the browser and submit SQL statement after statement until the entire backend is mapped, altered, viewed, and controlled.

On an HTML form, the attack tries something along the lines of a single tick character (single quote). If a 500 series error results from the HTTP server, indicating the logic layer script could not do its job, then there is a possible vulnerability. Next attackers try a string such as:

```
Blah' or 1 = 1 - -
```

The "blah" does not matter; it could be anything. The tick disrupts the code on the logic layer and the characters that follow are evaluated rather than simply passed through. The two hyphens cause the rest of the logic layer statement to be commented out and therefore ignored.

Consider the following line of code (it is all meant to be one line):

```
Set rst=Conn.Execute("select * from userinfo where username = '" &
Request.Form("username") & Request.Form("password") & " ' ")
```

There are two languages present in this code. One is Active Server Pages and the other is SQL. They are separated by nested quotes (alternating between single and double) so the server side interpreter can make sense out of each statement starting at the innermost nested statements first.

Once the tick and the hyphens are injected into the code by the evaluation of the statement Request.Form ("username"), the characters that follow have a completely different nature to them.

```
Set rst=Conn.Execute("select * from userinfo where username = '" &
blah' or 1 = 1 -
```

The return of this command will be a "true." The rest of the script is an if/else construct that says "If true then it is all good" else go to the failed login page. This exploit will result in a successful login. Once the vulnerability is discovered, nearly any SQL statement can be inserted instead.

Conclusion

Web exposure provides an attacker with many choices. The network layer must deliver traffic, the OS runs the protocol stack, the Web server provides responses, and the application might be poorly coded.

These attacks are sometimes called "blind" attacks because the attacker will not always see the result of the attack, only the HTTP response, which in some cases is an expected error. Regardless of the attack, cleansing input is the best way to prevent this risk.

Similar to buffer overflows, however, programmers might try their best to follow secure coding practices only to find the attackers remain one step ahead. The need to understand various programming languages and Internet protocols is enough to keep any security professional busy. Unfortunately, all it takes is one attacker to discover a vulnerability and share it with others on the underground to make for a very bad day for all administrators involved.

Web applications must be tested as a part of an ongoing program of risk assessment. Fortunately, many tools exist to help the security professional perform this task, but they must be used properly and their outputs analyzed correctly. For the CEHv6 exam, it is not necessary to become a skilled programmer in these languages; however, be prepared to look at some basic code and identify what kind of attack is taking place.

## CHAPTER FIFTEEN

WIRELESS NETWORKS

Introduction

Wireless networks have more advantages than simply being cheap and scalable. In the competitive modern mobile economy, wireless access is a utility right along with other things like running water and plumbing. It is impossible to do without this technology at this point.

Fortunately, everything you already know about networking still applies. Once access to the network is established, everything else is the same. Unfortunately, wireless networking extends physical exploits to unseen places and is very difficult to control.

In this chapter we will look at the technologies and opportunities an attacker is looking for.

To Pass the CEH Exam You Need to . . .

- know the basics of designing a wireless network
- know how WEP and WPA work
- know the important security risks of WiFi networks
- know the basics of Bluetooth
- master the CEH cheatsheets and practice questions!

Know the Basics of Designing a Wireless Network

- Basic categories of wireless networks
- Basic types of WiFi networks
- Setting up a WiFi network
- Antenna types
- Sniffing wireless traffic
- Security considerations

Basic Categories of Wireless Networks

Wireless technologies operate at Layer 1 of the OSI model and often incorporate additional Layer 2 protocols for framing and management needs. The goal is to create and provide access to an unbounded medium for data transfer. Wireless technologies provide an inexpensive and flexible way to establish communications very quickly. Challenges such as privacy and signal reliability must also be considered.

The following are broad categories of wireless technologies in use:

- Legacy technologies (Infrared, Microwave, RF)
- Wireless fidelity
- Cell phone technologies (CMDA and GSM)
- Bluetooth
- RFID devices

Networks of clients can either connect in an infrastructure configuration or in an ad hoc fashion. An infrastructure allows a group of clients to work together and share resources. The ad hoc networks are usually meant for temporary connections between two hosts. Most wireless technologies support either configuration.

For the CEH exam, focus primarily on the WiFi technologies.

Basic Types of WiFi Networks

The term WiFi actually refers broadly to a series of different protocols and versions. The IEEE (Institute of Electronic and Electrical Engineers) has assigned certain designations for different WiFi specs. On the CEH exam it will be assumed knowledge that you have memorized the following information:

IEEE	Distance	Speed	Frequency Range
802.11a	30M	54Mbps	5 Ghz
802.11b	100M	11Mbps	2.4 Ghz
802.11g	100M	54Mbps	2.4 Ghz
802.11n	+125M	+600Mbps	2.4 Ghz

Looking closely at the table, notice that 802.11a networks are not as resilient to noise and signal degradation as 802.11b. When 802.11g came along it gave us the best of both worlds with speed and reliability.

Additional IEEE specifications build on these and incorporate additional features:

802.11i is essentially a rewrite of the WEP protocol that upgrades the security to WPA(2). Both will be discussed later.

802.11e includes extensions that allow for quality of service for data streams such as streaming multimedia. WMM (WiFi Multimedia) is a subset of 802.11e.

802.11n is an upgrade that focuses on distance and reliability. Originally the speed was 108Mbps in the pre-draft version. New "n" devices have increased the possible speeds dramatically. The distance of 125M is also very much a debate, but some products have demonstrated reliable signals at a distance of up to 500M.

802.1x is an authentication extension that allows technologies such as RADIUS or EAP and LEAP to be used in the authentication of clients to the network. These technologies can be somewhat difficult to setup and keep going, but many commercial tools have made it easier and the approach can be extremely effective.

Before rushing out to purchase the latest and greatest hardware, consider all of the topics that are presented in this chapter and remember that risk management should play a key role in your decision. If someone lives in an apartment and only uses the Internet to check e-mail and surf a few Web pages, then basic or legacy hardware might be the best choice to reduce exposure. However, in order to overcome obstructions or get a strong signal from the bedroom to the tool shed in the backyard it becomes necessary to accept overkill.

Many people are replacing their televisions with Internet-based entertainment, and a growing number of business models are adapting to become entertainment options that compete with traditional TV and radio. Lifestyle might be the driving force for residential customers. In the business world, telecommuters that conduct online meetings as well as the growth of social networks that work best when mobile devices are connected everywhere are ensuring exponential investments in wireless technologies.

Setting Up a WiFi Network

WiFi networks have similar characteristics to a wired network that uses a hub as the concentrator (also called "star wired, logical bus" architecture), only it can be even more dangerous. Everyone within radio distance of the signal can see it, without requiring physical access to wiring. The hardware equivalent of the concentrator is called the AP (Access Point). Wireless clients must first associate themselves to an AP in order to participate in the network.

Since everyone in range is sharing the same signal space, they have access to multiple APs and peers. A shared string is used to create a logical group of participants. This string is called the SSID (Service Set Identifier) and the group of participants is called the Service Set. Part of associating with an AP involves presenting this string in a management frame.

If the administrator of a network wants it to be easy to find and join, the SSID is broadcast by the AP periodically in beacon frames. This is considered to be an *open* network. A *closed* network happens when the AP does not broadcast the SSID, causing each client to need to know the string in advance of associating.

The SSID is considered a shared password even though it is not necessarily much of a secret. The SSIDs are sent in clear text even on a closed network when a client is associating. An attacker with a wireless card capable of sniffing these management frames can discover this information easily.

Once a client has associated, additional agreements are made with the AP in terms of collision avoidance and other management parameters. The client is now ready to send traffic, and the upper layers of the OSI Model (Layers 3–7) come into play in the same manner as any wired network.

A typical infrastructure configuration will involve both wired and wireless clients participating in the same Layer 3 network segment. Those associating with the AP via their SSID string are using a different Layer 2 technology altogether than those that are wired up via Ethernet. Most "Wireless Router" products incorporate Layer 2 translational bridging to allow the 802.3 and the 802.11 devices to seem as if they are on the same network segment. As far as it goes from there, nothing is different. Each client must have or lease an IP configuration and be able to speak common protocols.

Sometimes the best way to access wireless machines is to physically connect to the router (if possible) and bypass the wireless part of the attack altogether. At the same time, successfully associating with the AP is the same thing in effect as plugging into the drop in the wall, even if the attacker is doing this from the parking lot or street.

Proper segmentation is critical in terms of defense. It is also important to consider higher layer authentication techniques whenever wireless access is going to be provided.

Antenna Types

The first step in understanding how to attack wireless networks and how to install them correctly is to consider antenna types. There are two broad categories of antenna:

- Directional (or unidirectional)
- Omnidirectional

Directional

Antennas are categorized by the signal pattern and power capabilities. Omnidirectional antennas send the signal in all directions at once on a single plane (sometimes referred to as a doughnut shape).

Directional antennas aim the signal in a more specific pattern. There are many kinds. A Yagi antenna, for instance, uses an array of dipole elements to more precisely control the direction of the signal. A dipole antenna is very common; it resembles the shape of the letter "T" with a feedline connecting to the center of the element. A reflector antenna is a dish-shaped assembly that focuses the signal to a small area.

Omnidirectional

To understand the coverage of an omnidirectional antenna, consider looking from overhead at a round picnic table. From the center all directions are possible; the diameter of the table depends on many factors, but there is always full coverage. Now, squat down beside the table and look at the edge. The thickness of the "table"—in other words, the perpendicular coverage—is also affected by many things. In discussing this topic we are looking for stable, reliable signal quality. Nothing says that the happy accident of a receiver picking up a signal outside the specified shape of radiation is still not possible.

Omnidirectional antennas are not like spheres. An isotropic antenna attempts all directions but is mostly theoretical or is mistaken for an assembly of omnidirectional antenna pointed at different angles.

The properly installed wireless network will achieve signal coverage with a minimum of leakage or dead spots. Fortunately for the attacker, many networks are simply omnidirectional units placed in the ceiling tiles or on top of a filing cabinet with nobody paying much attention to them.

Any laptop can be turned into a low power AP and would therefore create little suspicion. For a little more power (to the parking lot, for example), portable APs no larger than a deck of playing cards can be easily hidden under a desk and act as a DHCP server and router. Many operating systems will automatically connect to the strangest signal to which they can successfully associate. All of these elements add up to opportunity for the attacker.

It is important to consider that in addition to rogue radios, the signals we intentionally create cannot be controlled perfectly without expense and effort. In the correct natural conditions and in the absence of signal crowding (too many other APs in the area), wireless signals can travel several times farther than the engineering specifications expect.

Sniffing Wireless Traffic

Sniffing on a wireless network can be a bit tricky. Hardware NICs are easily placed into promiscuous mode by simply using widely available drivers. For wireless cards there is no "universal" driver set for this. The equivalent term is "monitor mode," and some wireless card chipsets do not support it at all. Others do in a limited fashion only.

If the manufacturer does not provide monitor mode drivers, then third party attempts have been made for many popular wireless products. Various Linux distributions such as Backtrack come with some ability along with tools such as Kismet. Firmware versions and a variety of factors will affect your success, so do some research before deciding on a particular combination. The AirPcap tools from Cace technologies can be purchased ready to use in monitor mode with an assortment of powerful open source applications preconfigured. (*http://www.cacetech.com*)

If you only need or want to see your own traffic, standard sniffers such as Wireshark will work; just uncheck the option for sniffing in promiscuous mode. There are also times when limited monitor mode has been achieved, but some or all management frames are not getting past Layer 2 and into the protocol analyzer where the attacker can see them. Lastly, some attacks require packet injection, and just being in monitor mode does not mean your wireless NIC will do that either.

Security Considerations

As discussed, signal leakage can expose data or provide greater exposure to possible connectivity from unauthorized clients. MAC address filtering can be configured, but as we saw in the sniffing chapter this address is easily spoofed. Additional layers of protection such as encryption will also help, but all best practices come at the price of administrative overhead. The attacker is always looking to discover the network that has not been given the proper attention.

Configuring an open or closed network is a simple setting in the AP itself. If it is determined that having a closed network is more trouble than it is worth, at least change the default SSID of the AP. Common SSIDs such as "Linksys" or "Tsunami" indicate to an attacker an AP point that is likely not administered properly in other ways as well. If additional authentication is not in use, this could also result in associating with the wrong network.

Regular audits of the surrounding area are also important steps. A baseline of existing SSIDs is a decent first step; even better is to develop signal profiles so that rogue APs might at least be detected. In this chapter we will continue to discuss detection and encryption issues.

It is important to keep in mind that when a wireless client connects to an AP only a hardware association exists. This has nothing to do with user accounts; in other words, there is no way yet to know who (attackers possibly) is actually operating the hardware that has just joined the service set. But without securing any network at the lowest layer possible, the higher layer authentication services are at risk. If attackers can see the network and transmit traffic, they can attack it.

Know How WEP and WPA Work

- WEP (Wired Equivalent Privacy)
- WPA (WiFi protected access)
- WPA2
  - Try it out: Generate a strong WPA2 PSK
  - Try it out: Research cracking WPA/WPA2

WEP (Wired Equivalent Privacy)

WEP (WiFi Equivalent Privacy) was designed to approximate the benefits of being on bounded wire in a switched environment. As mentioned earlier, the *hub-like* nature of wireless networks exposed them to risk that we thought had been fixed by using switches. In addition, signal leakage means the situation is even worse because physical access is difficult to control.

Configuring WEP starts with a pre-shared key. The AP is configured with this key and then each client that is authorized to connect is also configured with the same key. One key is shared, in advance of any connection, to as many clients as necessary. Immediately, we see that the key is not particularly secret and that changing it often would be a lot of administrative effort. But what WEP does do is help separate frames from different service set traffic, and makes sure that if someone is sniffing that person can't just see everything.

The pre-shared key is either 40 bits or 104 bits long. The access point transmits an IV (Initialization Vector) periodically to each associated client that is then appended to the pre-shared key. This generates an RC4 encryption key that will be either 64 or 128 bits long, depending on what has been configured. The IV itself is always 24 bits long.

The resulting key (40+24, or 104+24) is then used to encrypt the data portion of the WiFi traffic sent between the client and the AP using a simple XOR process. Each time the AP changes the IV, it is then transmitted in a management frame to the client so it knows how to encrypt and decrypt the traffic until the IV is changed again. The pre-shared key is never exchanged on the network, but the IV is in the clear and unprotected if the attacker can see the management frames.

When an IV is transmitted it is called an "interesting frame." Since the IV is only 24 bits, there are a limited number of them available before they will start to repeat. If the AP has not been restarted, its pseudo-random number generator will produce a set of IVs that will eventually repeat. In addition to this problem, some IVs are "weak" in that they introduce patterns of bits into the key stream.

For example, the 24-bit sequence of 110110110110110110110110 is one of the possible keys but has a pattern that effectively makes it a 3 bit sequence that just happens to be repeated eight times.

The flaws of the list of IVs being repeated and the presence of weak keys means that if attackers sniff enough interesting frames, enough statistical data will exist to extrapolate the likely bytes of the pre-shared key. This technique is formally known as the FSM (Flurer, Mantin, and Shamir) attack, and it takes advantage of the weak key scheduling algorithm in RC4 along with analysis of predictable IVs to compute the PSK.

WPA (WiFi Protected Access)

WPA (WiFi Protected Access) is a subset of the 802.11i specification. It is an improvement to the previous 802.11 specifications that addresses security. Three new features were added:

- Key mixing
- Rekeying
- Message integrity

Key mixing

WPA includes support for TKIP (Temporal Key Integrity Protocol). Unlike WEP, which only appended the IV to each key, TKIP mixes the IV into the key stream. This helps minimize the risk of *related key* attacks (the primary vulnerability of WEP).

Rekeying

WPA uses three keys: a master key, working key, and the RC4 key. The master key is shared between the client and AP and is used to generate new keys (working keys).

The RC4 key results from a new IV being mixed in. If the hardware supports it, it is possible to change RC4 keys for each frame that is sent.

Message integrity

WEP used a simple CRC (Cyclical Redundancy Check) to detect integrity breaches of each 802.11 frame. WPA uses "Michael" (MIC—Message Integrity Check), which computes integrity checks not for each frame but for the datagram passed to the Layer 2 protocols.

Michael protects against *bit flipping* attacks that a CRC was vulnerable to. If attackers made changes to the payload of a frame, it was possible to also make a minor change to the CRC calculation to compensate.

WPA2

The original WPA/TKIP specification is considered to be at the end of its design lifetime. WPA2 is the current specification. WPA2 uses AES (Advanced Encryption Standard) in CCMP (Counter Mode with Cipher Block Chaining) mode. It replaces both the RC4 and TKIP features of WPA.

The downside to WPA2 is that while WPA could be added to old hardware via firmware upgrade, the new encryption standards make that impossible. For this reason, the older standards of WEP and WPA are still widely used.

WPA2 in PSK (Pre-shared Key) mode is configured similarly as WEP is configured. A key of up to 64 bytes is entered into both AP and authorized clients. If a short key is used, WPA and WPA2 are still vulnerable to "offline brute forcing" attacks. Best practice is to use the entire 64 byte space for the PSK, in which case a brute force is extremely unlikely.

PSK can be difficult to distribute or to allow friends and family to connect to when they visit. Using *shared-key* mode instead allows a password or passphrase to be entered at the time a client connects. This configuration is vulnerable to password guessing or to brute forcing. If the owner of the network chooses something like the name of the AP, the SSID, her own last name, and so on then it won't matter how sophisticated the WPA2 standard is.

Since the AES key that is generated is the result of hashing a passphrase 4096 times, it is easier to use a pre-computed lookup table of common passphrases before attempting a true brute force.

TRY IT OUT

Generate a Strong WPA2 PSK

The following site is meant as a demonstration of how to generate long, truly random character strings. Several character sets are available. Take a few moments to read the page for a full explanation of how the generator works.

```
https://www.grc.com/passwords.htm
```

Research Cracking WPA/WPA2

The following site provides 33G lookup tables for download as well as a .pdf that lists the top 1000 most popular SSIDs (which are sometimes used as shared-key passphrases) as gleaned from analyzing over 17 million wireless networks found in the field.

```
http://www.renderlab.net/projects/WPA-tables/
```

Know the Important Security Risks of WiFi Networks

- Discovering wireless networks
  - Try it out: View a map of discovered WiFi networks
  - Try it out: Learn the warchalking symbols
- Common attacks against wireless networks

Discovering Wireless Networks

Tools such as Netstumbler (Windows), Ministumbler (Windows Mobile), and Kismet (Linux) make it easy to survey an area for the presence of WAPs (Wireless Access Points). Some brands of wireless PC Cards (PCMCIA) and USB cards have a special connector for adding an extended antenna that receives signals better. These antennas range from homemade "Cantennas" (Pringles potato chip packages or coffee cans have been tried) to commercial products that are extremely sensitive and can measure many aspects of signal quality.

Portable phones such as the iPhone and the G1 have applications for finding WiFi networks and can tell you the GPS coordinates. Tools such as "wi-spy" hardware include troubleshooting and diagnostic tools. Signal meters that can be carried on a keychain are available for just a few dollars.

View a Map of Discovered WiFi Networks

Attackers know that free WiFi is everywhere. Unsecured wireless networks exist on almost every street and, if not, then one will be right around the corner. Small towns are also great for free Internet access because residents are far more trusting and far less security conscious than those who live in large metropolitan areas.

```
http://wigle.net
```

For a list of registered "hotspots" that conform to the WiFi-alliance standard visit:

```
http://www.wi-fi.org/
```

While attackers will be active in discovering WiFi networks for obvious reasons, it is also an important activity from a defensive point of view. Walk the area of your organization and create a baseline of the discovered signals. When new networks appear, it is necessary to make sure someone has not setup an access point inside of your network. Perform regular audits of approved networks for proper security configuration.

When WiFi networks first hit the scene, the act of driving around looking for networks (wardriving) became a popular hobby. When a network was found, one could draw a symbol in chalk (warchalking) on the side of a building or utility box that would indicate to other wardrivers that a network was found and whether or not it was secured.

Almost any form of transportation can be referred to in this activity. Examples include "Warwalking," Warbiking," and "Warflying."

TRY IT OUT

Learn the Warchalking Symbols

For the CEH exam, you might have to recognize the common symbols used in warchalking. Visit the following website and at the bottom of the page find the link to a .pdf that provides a nice printable reference card that can fit in your wallet.

`http://en.wikipedia.org/wiki/Warchalking`

Common Attacks Against Wireless Networks

The nature of a WiFi network leaves it vulnerable to several specialized attacks and many other common attacks as well. For the CEH exam, be familiar with the following attacks:

- Default configuration
- Warkitting
- Brute forcing authentication
- Denial of service (DoS)
- Eavesdropping
- MiTM [Man in The Middle] attacks
- Basic network attacks

Default configuration

Most residential wireless products are designed to allow for the easiest installation possible. The default settings are for an open unsecured network that just magically works. In spite of the cartoonish installation instructions and the unnecessary DVD with the configuration wizard that many products include, many people are either not aware of the risks or simply are not interested.

Knowing this, it is important to always be on the lookout for default configuration honeypots. It is a common practice for attackers to setup a WiFi and see who connects. It is always dangerous to associate with unknown networks no matter how tempting it may be. Simply changing the SSID to something like "MelsCoffeeHouse" or "FreeMP3s" will attract connections like flies to. . . . Well, you get the picture.

Warkitting

Warkitting is a combination of Wardriving and Rootkitting. In this attack, the WAP has been configured to allow administrative access from the wireless interface. The attacker performs a firmware upgrade that includes backdoor access to the router even if its owner gets around to fixing the settings.

This is not usually a default setting. Most products will only allow administration from the wired interface, which just means attackers must access the WAP from that direction and can accomplish it through any compromised host on the network.

Brute forcing authentication

In wireless terms, a network that supports OSA (Open Systems Authentication) essentially consists of clients and APs that know the SSID. If the service set supports SKA (Shared Key Authentication) then something like a WEP key is required.

To cut down on administrative effort in configuring clients ahead of time, some APs will allow a password to be used from which the key is generated as if it had been there all along. Like any other password protected system, this entrance point is vulnerable to default passwords, guessing, and brute force.

Denial of service (DoS)

802.11b/g operates in the ISM (Industrial, Scientific, Medical) band where many other products also operate. Baby monitors and wireless cameras, cordless telephones, and microwave ovens all share this space.

RF (Radio Frequency) interference is an expected issue, and the 802.11 specification uses CSMA/CA (Carrier Sense Multiple Access/Collision Avoidance) along with hamming code signaling to be as *error tolerant* as possible. But nothing can overcome a flood of high-powered noise.

Microwave ovens affect WiFi networks the most on channels 8–11. If someone is heating up a burrito in the break room and the AP has also been placed there, a noticeable degradation in throughput will likely occur. The solution might be as simple as configuring the AP to use channel 1 or 6, or the AP might have to be moved farther away from the *nuker.*

"Jammers" are tools that will send out white noise at a high enough power to easily DoS a wireless network. They can be purchased or made using common electronic parts; even cheap cordless phones can be modified to become jammers. There is no way to prevent this, and this should be considered heavily in the risk analysis study prior to installing wireless technologies.

Eavesdropping

As discussed earlier, the hardest part about sniffing wireless traffic is to get the WiFi NIC into monitor mode. Failing an ability to do that, the next best thing is a MiTM (Man in The Middle) attack.

MiTM (Man in The Middle) attacks

In the 802.11 standard, management frames are sent in the clear even if encryption is protecting the data frames. This opens the network to a variety of spoofing attacks.

Attackers can create "De-authenticate" or "De-associate" frames that spoof the MAC address of any given client, causing a temporary DoS attack. When the wireless NIC attempts to reconnect, the attackers set up a WAP with a stronger signal that has the same SSID as the legitimate network. The client connects to the attacker.

Using basic operating system tools, attackers can perform all necessary network functions that make their access point transparent to the user. If attackers are running Linux, a DHCP server, a DNS forwarder can be set up using a tool called *dnsmasq*. If using a Windows server product, the process is just as simple. The next step is to turn on routing and forward all traffic. The victim will never know this is happening.

Basic network attacks

Since wireless networks operate at Layer 1 (physical) with Layer 2 protocols for framing link to link connectivity, all protocols at Layer 3 and above work exactly the same way they would on a wired network. TCP/IP could not care less about it.

One approach to protecting the internal network is to isolate the wireless segment completely using firewalls, and then implement a VPN (Virtual Private Network) service to authenticate the user of the associated hardware and encrypt all packets into a tunnel before Layer 2 can create the frames and links.

Technologies such as EAP (Extensible Authentication Protocol) can be used to accomplish enhanced control of the traffic. But if the underlying wireless network is left unprotected it can still be abused. Best practices at securing the WiFi link still apply.

Know the Basics of Bluetooth

• Describe the Bluetooth specification

• Attacks against Bluetooth networks

Describe the Bluetooth Specification

IEEE 802.15 describes PANs (Personal Area Networks). IEEE 802.15.1 is a standard based on Bluetooth. The protocol stack operates at the physical layer in the 2.4Ghz range.

The idea was essentially to replace the RS-232C serial cable standard with a wireless alternative. There is a complex alphabet soup of specs and standards surrounding this technology that can become confusing very quickly. For the CEH exam, focus on the basics and the risks.

There are three classes of Bluetooth devices:

Class	Power	Range
1	100mw	100m
2	2.5mw	10m
3	1mw	1m

There are different versions of the Bluetooth spec:

Version	Throughput
1	723Kbps - 1Mbps
2.0	2.1Mbps - 3Mbps
3.0	(still in development at the time of this writing)

Within the specifications there are several *profiles*. Devices that establish connectivity must support the same profile. Among the most common are HFP (Hands-Free Profile), HID (Human Interface Device), and A2DP (Advanced Audio Distribution Profile), all of which operate many of the devices we use every day.

Devices associate on a link by link basis to a host, much like plugging in a cable that is approximately 10 meters long. Because it is wireless, there is opportunity for spoofing and sniffing; in fact, *sniff* is a state of a device as it waits for data.

Two devices are "paired" based on the sharing of a link key. When the pairing is established, they share information about device name, device class, services supported, and additional technical information. From this combination a signature can be formed that allows the devices to cryptographically authenticate each other, at which time they are said to be bonded.

There are several different modes by which two devices can be bonded. When a symmetric key is involved it is often derived from a number (usually "0000") but many other factors are involved that make that number less important.

Attacks Against Bluetooth Networks

On the CEH exam there are two main categories of Bluetooth attacks:

- Bluejacking
- Bluesnarfing

Bluejacking

Bluejacking is mostly an injection technique. It does not involve the compromising of data but can be startling or embarrassing to the victim. Contact information in the form of a vCard or text messages could be the payload; therefore, social engineering is possible.

Bluesnarfing

In contrast to bluejacking, bluesnarfing does involve invasive measures. A connection is made that allows the attacker to view data stored on the remote device. The vulnerability that made this attack possible was patched in the specification itself, so the victim must either be a legacy device or be using an incorrect implementation of the standard.

Conclusion

With the popularity of WiFi long since exploding, it is no longer novel or surprising to find wireless networks. The question for the attacker becomes, "What is the level of security?" Some cities have attempted to make legal requirements for properly configuring WAPs, but this is clearly almost impossible to enforce. ISPs have all but given up on worrying about the prevention of sharing access points even though the practice results in tens of millions in lost revenue for ISPs.

On the "information wants to be free" topic, unsecured access points have been used as a defense in "John Doe" lawsuits. These are the lawsuits brought about by those who believe their IP (Intellectual Property) rights have been violated even if they are not exactly sure by whom. The customer who is said to have been issued the IP (Internet Protocol) address that was the source of the violation claims there is an open network attached to it and the perpetrator could have been anyone.

So why bother trying to protect WiFi? Maybe the strategy is to leapfrog over the whole concept and understand that, similar to the way long distance telephone service was once expensive and almost overnight became almost free, wireless access will soon be available anywhere, anytime, and by almost every computing device imaginable—for free.

Municipal WiFi will be unnecessary; the government will not have to provide this utility because the commercial products will give it away. It is essentially like providing a virtual front door that allows customers to enter the showroom who hopefully will purchase something.

This is the principal reason ISPs are trying to become entertainment media companies. So much is being done to compete with TV, cable, and satellite that ubiquitous Internet access is no longer a revenue sink, it is a priority.

## CHAPTER SIXTEEN

CRYPTOGRAPHY

Introduction

The subject of cryptography is one of the most challenging and fascinating areas in information security. It intimidates many students at first because they fear the math. Do not worry; the CEH exam will not require that. It is important to grasp the puzzles behind the proper use of cryptography and the design of complex cryptographic systems.

It is not enough simply to encode a message and send it. The problems of managing and exchanging secrets, binding actions to identities, and understanding the risks of cryptography (not just the benefits) are important to the attacker. Often the most effective attack against cryptography will not be direct, but will be against a weakness that was exposed because the entire system was not designed or managed properly.

In this chapter we will approach "crypto" in a way that explains the philosophy and challenges behind the various technologies and leaves the trivia out of it for now. The student should focus on the vocabulary and application of the ideas. Read this chapter slowly. You may notice we have taken more of a "spiral" style approach to explaining it. Expect to have to read it more than once. Each time the picture will become clearer.

To Pass the CEH Exam You Need to . . .

- know the basic concepts of cryptography
- know how symmetric encryption works
- know how asymmetric encryption works
- know how hashing algorithms work
- know about cryptosystems and key management
- know advanced attacks against cryptography
- master the CEH cheatsheets and practice questions!

Know the Basic Concepts of Cryptography

- Intro to "crypto"
  - Try it out: Meet Alice and Bob
- Algorithm classes
- Key management
- Basic attacks against encryption

Intro to "Crypto"

The word "cryptography" means "hide" and "write" (Crypt = Hide, Graph = Write). The art and sciences of cryptology date as far back as writing itself. All over the world, from China, India, and the western cultures in Egypt, Greece, and Rome, wherever there are written languages there have been encoded versions of the language to allow parties to share secret messages.

Typically cryptic messages were hidden to all but those who knew a secret key to unlock them. By sharing this secret key it was also possible to authenticate that the sender of a message was indeed the claimed trusted party since only trusted personnel would be told the secret key (e.g., "Open Sesame"). Such a system of sharing secrets becomes pretty cumbersome as the number of trusted partners grows. Perhaps the biggest problem in all of cryptology is the issue of key management.

One easy way to summarize the most important concepts of cryptography is to use the PAIN model (Larry Greenblatt). The PAIN (Privacy, Authentication, Integrity, and Non-repudiation) of cryptology drives the design and risk behind implementing all crypto systems. Keep these elements in mind throughout the rest of this chapter.

TRY IT OUT

Meet Alice and Bob

Because many concepts involve several interactive steps that need to be explained, there are traditional characters used to describe cryptography and each has a specific role to play. Take a moment to be introduced to Alice, Bob, Eve, and their friends.

http://en.wikipedia.org/wiki/Alice_and_Bob

Algorithm Classes

There are basically three classes of cryptographic algorithms:

- Symmetric (shared key, secret key)
- Asymmetric (public key)
- Hashing algorithms (one-way)

Symmetric (shared key, secret key)

Shared key systems have been very popular and it is pretty much accepted today that all crypto systems in the past were based on some form of shared key encryption. When users share a key the system is symmetric. The same key is used to both encrypt as well as decrypt messages.

The first challenge in using a symmetric system is how to initially share the secret key. For example, password authentication is basically a shared key system. The user is "challenged" to provide the correct secret after identifying himself. If the e-mail administrator sets up the initial password for the user, how would the password get to the user if the password is required to access the e-mail that contains it? The administrator could not simply e-mail the password because the user needs this password or "key" to log in first to get the e-mail.

Another challenge is the concept of non-repudiation. If Bob and Alice share a key to the file cabinet (assuming a perfect lock and no others know the secret key), not only could Bob share secrets with Alice, but if Alice opens up the cabinet and sees something she knows she did not place there, she could authenticate that Bob placed it in the cabinet. Since no one else should have the key this is a fair assumption. However, suppose Bob wanted to frame Alice and he places something malicious in the cabinet; she would not be able to prove that it was Bob, even though she would know he was lying. Bob could always claim that Alice did it and it would be a matter of his word against hers.

Asymmetric (public key)

Asymmetric encryption was successfully introduced in 1976 by Whitfield Diffie and Martin Hellman. With asymmetric encryption Bob has a "key pair" where there are two different, but related, keys. One key is "private" to Bob and the other one "public." The concept of these keys being "related" means that both keys are required—one to encrypt and the other to decrypt.

Bob can give his public key to anyone because he knows that one key does not reveal the other. His private key remains protected and is not exchanged or exposed to risk. There are several methods of asymmetric encryption. Each involves a mathematical puzzle that, as of yet, cannot be solved with current computation systems. The keys are related, but they do not reveal each other.

If Alice can unlock the cabinet with Bob's public key, then it is reasonable to assume that Bob's private key was used to lock the cabinet. Bob could try blaming Alice but his only argument would be that somehow someone was able to gain access to his private key (a key management problem). If we trust the protection of this private key, Bob has no case. This is a demonstration of the non-repudiation property of asymmetric encryption.

A major disadvantage of asymmetric algorithms is the expense of the computational effort involved with each calculation. This greatly reduces speed and performance when compared to symmetric algorithms. As we all know, time is money.

Hashing algorithms (one-way)

Using the algorithms mentioned above, one can provide secrecy, authenticity, and non-repudiation, allowing participants to trust the privacy and authenticity of a message; but how can we tell if the message itself was somehow tampered with?

For accidental corruption, various methods have been used. Parity and checksums are the most popular methods in digital communication and the formulas for both of these systems are quite simple. For deliberate corruption they are not very dependable. It is quite trivial to modify the message and to determine how to spoof the parity check or checksum.

Using cryptographic mathematics, scientists have devised systems to provide checksums that are not nearly as easy to spoof. Such formulas are known as "hashing algorithms" and the resulting checksums are more formally known as "message digests."

If Bob creates a message digest using a hashing algorithm on his message and Alice does the same thing, they can compare message digests. If the digests do not match, then something happened to the message and Alice will know that the message was not the same as Bob's. If Alice's message digest (also called "hash values," or just "hash") is the same as Bob's, Alice might not want to trust the data as she needs to validate that the hash value itself, which she received from Bob, was not corrupted along the way either.

To authenticate the hash (or message digest) Bob can use either a symmetric or asymmetric key. These special authenticated hashes are known as either "*message authentication codes*" (MAC) for symmetrically authenticated digests or "*digital signatures*" if the digest was asymmetrically authenticated.

Key Management

Key management is perhaps the most challenging operational issue with cryptography whether privacy or authentication is the objective. Consider a driver's license as an authentication system. No one can be trusted to print her own license since anyone could easily print a counterfeit. Just as we use the Department of Motor Vehicles as a trusted third party to issue driver's licenses, trusted third parties, such as certificate authorities, are used to issue cryptographic keys.

Consider what would happen if Bob lost his private key. All data encrypted with the corresponding public key would be lost. To counter this problem we could make a copy of the private key but then we lose the basic trust model granted to us by asymmetric key systems once the private key is no longer truly private. The backup administrator could easily impersonate Bob.

In symmetric systems we have to consider that an outsider could somehow guess the key value and either gain access to information that was supposed to be secret between Bob and Alice or send counterfeited or "spoofed" messages impersonating as either Bob or Alice. One way around this is to generate symmetric keys for only one use, then exchange them using a properly implemented asymmetric system. Accounting for how the integrity checks through message digests need to be signed as well, the whole sequence quickly becomes quite complicated.

Basic Attacks Against Encryption

Cryptanalysis is the science of deducing the key from available resources. Eve (the evil eavesdropper) could figure out the key just by analyzing the encrypted message to see if there were meaningful patterns found in the enciphered text. For example, in the Caesar cipher the key is that all the letters of the alphabet are shifted or "rotated" up, say three characters (A becomes D, B becomes E, C becomes F, etc.). Such a system is quite trivial to analyze as the frequency of the letters can reveal the true characters since statistically the letter E, for example, is the most commonly used letter in the English alphabet. Find the letter that shows up most often, and this is likely really the letter E.

Great steps are required to ensure that a good encryption algorithm does not reveal any patterns. But even if there is no pattern in the cipher text, Eve could try to simply guess the key. Just as in password systems, Eve could try all possible keys so long as the key word was fairly short. Even if the key was a pretty random value, given enough time, Eve would be able to arrive at the proper key. This is called a *brute force* attack.

Brute forcing works if the key word is limited in size. The key size affects the "entropy" of the system. For example, flipping a coin has a key space of 2, either heads or tails. Adding more numbers makes guessing the possible keys harder. A typical ATM PIN has 4 numbers, 0–9 or 10 to the 4th, giving the system a key space of 10,000. A key that is 128 bits long (16 Bytes) has over 340 trillion trillion *gazillion* possible keys; a very large number in other words. Considering the key size of a 4096 bit key is like trying to comprehend the number of atoms in our known universe and several other parallel ones, too. Adding just one bit doubles the key space each time.

The longer and more random the bits are in a key, the more disorder is introduced in the output. Consider the following 32 bit key:

10011011100110111001101110011011

This is considered a weak key because it has patterns within it that reduce the effective length. Every 8 bits repeat, and within that there are other patterns, too. Salt values are introduced into key generating functions to make sure true randomness occurs in the bit stream. Initialization vectors can also be added to make sure that repeated use of a key over and over does not result in the same encoding if the plain text message does not change.

The objective is to make sure the key cannot be guessed, that patterns do not exist in the output (enabling statistical analysis), and that brute forcing becomes impractical as well. However, as processor speeds continue to increase this is not such an easy task. The requirement to make up longer keys makes it harder for Bob to remember the key. The long keys, while harder to break or guess, also increase the time it takes to encrypt and decrypt messages.

Bob writes the key value on a piece of paper and tapes this to his monitor, creating a vulnerable situation. No matter how sophisticated an encryption technique is, there is often a weakness introduced indirectly. Given the difficulty of cryptanalysis, basic mistakes more commonly present opportunities for the attacker.

To minimize this risk, systems that involve all three major cryptographic techniques are implemented. A complex weave of checks and balances ensures that everything must work correctly or not at all, and that detection points and non-repudiation controls are possible as well.

In the following pages we will take a look at some popular encryption protocols (for example, SSL, IPSec, S/MIME), key management standards (like PKI and PGP), and some more cryptanalysis techniques. At the end of this section the reader should be able to understand the art and science of cryptology as a intelligent consumer and make educated decisions regarding the use and misuse of cryptographic algorithms and crypto-systems without worrying about the deeper mathematics reserved for cryptographic algorithm authors.

Know How Symmetric Encryption Works

- Substitution and transposition

  - Try it out: Research symmetric encryption vocabulary terms

- Comparing stream and block ciphers

- How stream ciphers work

- How block ciphers work

- Challenges with symmetric ciphers

Substitution and Transposition

If Bob wants to share a secret message with Alice, he can change the message in such a way as to render it unreadable to the untrained eye and tell Alice what he did so she can undo his changes to reveal the secret message. In order to do this he does need to first tell her his "secret message changing trick."

Many of us have done such things as children. I recall using a simple system as a child where we would write messages using numbers instead of letters such that A=1, B=2, etc. By substituting the valid character with the secret coded character we shared secret messages. Of course this system is easily defeated by just looking at the encoded text (ciphertext) and making a few guesses.

This can be said to be the weakness of such "substitution ciphers." Historically this was pretty much how many ciphers worked. Bob could use anything for substituting his valid characters but the result would be pretty easy to break just by looking for patterns in the output. As mentioned earlier, if Bob always substitutes the letter E with some other coded character (whether he is using my number system where E=5 or the Caesar cipher where E = H), Eve would just look for the letter that is most frequently used in the message. This is likely to be the letter E in plain text. This attack is known as "Frequency Analysis."

To mitigate frequency analysis, a scientist, Vigenere, modified this system by adding a "Key Word." Depending on the number of characters in the key word, there would be as many substituted alphabets. For example, imagine the Key Word was "Vulcan." The first character would use a substitution set where the alphabet was shifted or "rotated" up 22 characters (A=V, B=X, C=Y, D=Z, then E=A, etc.) and the second character would be rotated 21 characters so that A=U, the third letter would be rotated 12 characters (A=L), and so on.

For example, suppose we have a plain text message:

```
Hello Alice,

   I love you. Please marry me.

Yours truly,

Bob
```

The first character, H, becomes D, the next character, E, becomes A, and so on. Since there are only six letters in the key, however, the seventh character, l, would be substituted with the first set V. The net effect is that this is only six times stronger than the Caesar cipher, since we only have six different alphabets (multiple substitution sets are more formally known as "Polyalphabetic Substitution").

Another historical way to encipher messages is to scramble the message. This involves simply changing the positions of the text. For example, the same message we used in the previous example could be encrypted as:

o	a	s	E	o	u	o	b
l	l	a	m	y	r	b	
l	i	e	A	e	s	y	
e	c	l	R	m	t	l	
h	e	p	R	y	r	u	

This process of changing the positions of the letters is sometimes called "transposition" or "permutation" depending on the mathematical processes used.

Most modern encryption authors use both substitution and transposition to achieve what scientist Claude Shannon called "Confusion and Diffusion."

At this point a lot of new vocabulary terms have been thrown at you. Take a moment to summarize a few terms that have been introduced so far, and a few that will come later.

TRY IT OUT

Research Symmetric Encryption Vocabulary Terms

At this point several new terms have come your way. It would be a good idea to pause for a moment and review them. Just open a browser and type each term into a dictionary:operator search with Google. (Example: dictionary:"substitution cipher")

```
Substitution cipher
Transposition cipher
Stream cipher
Block cipher
Permutation
Confusion
Diffusion
Entropy
S-box
Asymmetric
Symmetric
```

(continued)

```
Hashing
HMAC
Salt
Nonce
Initialization vector
```

Comparing Stream and Block Ciphers

Data can be encrypted in a serial stream of bits that moves as a packet across a network host or as a block of bytes that can be loaded into computer memory and processed in multiple ways. The concepts of substitution, transposition, confusion, and diffusion explain the nature of the way plain text would compare eventually to its ciphertext representation.

Whether the encoding is done as stream or block is a matter of design choice and situational necessity. The goal is to make sure the encoded text does not reveal any details about either the key used in the algorithm or the original plain text.

There are still some ciphers that purely substitute; for example, stream ciphers such as E0 (used in Bluetooth) and RC4 (which may still be found in many crypto systems, e.g., WEP, SSL/TLS, TKIP, and more) are computationally cheap and easy to implement.

Block ciphers are considered more secure but are also more difficult to compute. Stream ciphers are much faster. The balance between availability and confidentiality must be met. Cost to reward ratio is always a consideration in cryptography.

Off loading the encryption process to a dedicated processor or ASIC (Application Specific Integrated Circuit) can speed things up considerably. Being simpler processes, it was much easier to create ASICs for stream ciphers than for block ciphers. This has changed, however, as the cost of ASICs have gone down quite a bit. Bob can now purchase a thumb drive with AES ASICs for less than five dollars.

How Stream Ciphers Work

XOR is one of several Boolean logic equations. When comparing two binary values, 0 or 1, using the XOR function, one and only one input must be 1 to return an output of 1. Another way to state this is to ask the question, "Are the inputs to a logic gate different?" Boolean logic functions are expressed in "truth tables." The truth table for an XOR looks like this:

Inputs	Result
0 0	0
0 1	1
1 0	1
1 1	0

The beauty of this system is that one can reverse the process. For example, given a plain text value in binary and a binary key:

Plain text	00100001
Key value	10100011
Cipher text	10000010

If the cipher text is XORed with the key value, we would return the original plain text.

Stream ciphers typically use a PRNG (Pseudo Random Number Generator) to create a long number that is "XORed" with the plain text to create an encrypted stream. To ensure that only the intended receiver can return the plain text, the PRNG is seeded (when a number is used as a starting point, it is known as a Seed value, or just Seed) with a secret value that only the sender and receiver know about.

For example, the number Pi is quite random, but if Bob only XORed the plain text with Pi, then anyone could decrypt the text since anyone can calculate Pi (at least to some extent). But if Bob told Alice, "XOR this cipher text with Pi, but start counting 194,672,073 (the Seed) digits in," this would be much more difficult to determine.

How Block Ciphers Work

Block ciphers also XOR plain text, just as stream ciphers, but they also change the positions of the text to achieve Claude Shannon's goal of confusion and diffusion. DES was one of the first widespread block ciphers and was very strong. In fact, when people say DES was cracked, this is somewhat misleading. DES was never really found to be vulnerable to any type of pattern matching but was simply brute-forced.

DES allowed for a key size of 56 bits. There were eight different "subkeys," each seven bits long and applied according to a "key schedule" (an additional bit per key was used for parity). Modern computing systems can guess all the possible values in a 56 bit key space in a matter of minutes or even seconds.

Block ciphers often use "S-boxes" (substitution boxes) which are logical means to infuse diffusion and confusion. It is a bit like putting several ingredients into a blender for too long. The outcome is gruel. This is the intended objective. Now consider pouring the contents of those blenders into other blenders while stirring in additional ingredients. The new stuff can be mixed in with the other stuff in a variety of ways. These combinations are the "modes" that block ciphers support. In the final result the idea is to create so much variation that tracing the cipher text backward toward the plain text is essentially impossible.

However, if you have the key and know what the encryption algorithm is, then you are "in the know."

The key determines the steps and combinations of flipping bits. Diffusion makes sure bit flipping is spread out and that one bit affects many others without regularity. Confusion ensures no patterns exist in the result. IVs (Initialization Vectors) are part of the algorithm as well and enhance the confusion properties of the encryption sequence. The sender and receiver must know a shared secret (the key), and how the algorithm works, in order to communicate.

Challenges with Symmetric Ciphers

Sometimes the key is shared out of band (prior relationship) and the IV changes are transmitted with the data. This is the case of WEP (Wired Equivalent Privacy). In other cases the IV is generated in a common fashion.

Symmetric ciphers are much more effective as far as key size (and therefore memory and processor) compared to asymmetric ciphers, but have some fundamental problems. The first issue to consider is how Bob will get Alice her copy of the key.

Bob cannot send it to her in plain text as Eve could eavesdrop and have access to the key. If he encrypts the key symmetrically, she will not be able to see it. It is similar to getting someone her initial password to e-mail. Alice would ask Bob, "What is my password to get into e-mail?" And Bob would respond, "I e-mailed it to you."

Another problem with symmetric encryption is scalability. If Bob, Carol, Ted, and Alice wanted to each encrypt messages to each other, Bob would need to share a secret key with Carol, a secret key with Ted, and a secret key with Alice. Carol would need to do the same, and so on. This number grows exponentially. The actual formula is:

```
N(N-1)/2. N = the number of participants
```

Since Bob does not need to share a key with himself, the number is multiplied by N-1. Since the secret keys are shared between participants, we then divide this number by two. In the above scenario, this becomes 4×3/2, or six keys. Add another participant and now we get 5×4/2, or ten. If the number of participants is ten, we get 10×9/2, or 45 keys. By the time we reach 1,000 participants, the number becomes nearly half a million (1,000×999/2 = 499,500).

We also have the problem of repudiation (denial). Suppose Bob sent his love letter to Alice at work and Alice only likes Bob as a friend (this is very common with men who encrypt, or men in technology in general. For more information on this issue, consult either a Star Trek or Star Wars nerd, of which I am both ;-). Alice may go to HR and file a complaint. When Bob is asked to stop sending such inappropriate messages, he claims he did not create the message and blames Alice. Since Alice also knew the secret key, there is no way for Alice to provide evidence that Bob was indeed the creator of the message, even though Alice knows Bob sent the message (she can authenticate the message, but to an outsider, Bob could claim Alice created the message).

In summary, symmetric encryption is faster than asymmetric encryption, but is limited in use as we have challenges sharing the initial key and require lots of keys as we add more users. Symmetric encryption can be used to both hide and authenticate but cannot be used to provide non-repudiation. Also, note that since symmetric encryption requires two parties to share secret keys, symmetric encryption is also known as shared or secret, or even shared secret, key systems. Test tip: If a key begins with the letter "S" it refers to symmetric keys.

Know How Asymmetric Encryption Works

- The role of asymmetric encryption

- Authentication and non-repudiation

- MiTM (Man in The Middle) attacks
- Summarizing asymmetric encryption
    - Try it out: Research asymmetric encryption vocabulary terms

The Role of Asymmetric Encryption

While symmetric encryption has likely been around as long as humans have been writing messages, the concept of asymmetric encryption is quite new (most credit Whitfield Diffie and Martin Hellman as creating the first asymmetric algorithm in 1976). The Diffie-Hellman algorithm was created to solve the first problem in symmetric encryption: how do we share that initial secret key? In this respect Diffie-Hellman is a "Key Agreement" algorithm. Bob and Alice will use asymmetric math to share a symmetrical key.

Besides being used to share the initial symmetric key, other asymmetric algorithms (notably RSA and ECC) are used to encrypt hash values to authenticate the hash. The overhead, as mentioned before, of the larger keys required in asymmetric systems make these algorithms too slow for encrypting large amounts of text or *bulk data*.

Authentication and Non-Repudiation

While there are a number of methods or mathematical processes to provide asymmetric services, the concepts are basically the same. Bob and Alice do not share secret keys. Instead Bob has a key pair and so does Alice. Each key pair is made up of mathematically related numbers.

Bob will create his pair, keep one key for himself (private key), and give out the other (public key) to anyone who wants to communicate with him. Whatever key is used to encrypt the message, the other key, and only that other key (one cannot encrypt and decrypt the same message with the same key), will be used to decrypt. This will provide three services depending on which key was used to encrypt. These services are called:

- Open Message Format
- Secure Message Format
- Mutual Authentication

Open Message Format

If Bob wants to prove he was the sender, he will use his private key to encrypt the message (usually the hash value of a larger message). This is known as the *Open Message Format*. There is no secrecy in this since anyone could get his public key, but all receivers would know that Bob sent the message (or at least his private key was used).

A symmetric key or message digest can also be encrypted with Bob's private key. This is known as "digitally signing" the document. Since his private key is not shared with anyone else he could not deny that it was his key that encrypted the message. Everyone else knows the message had to have come from Bob. This is how asymmetric algorithms provide non-repudiation.

Secure Message Format

If Alice wants to send Bob a message that only he could read, she would use his public key to encrypt the message. This is sometimes called the *Secure Message Format*. While only Bob could decrypt the message, he would not know who sent the message, only that he is the correct recipient.

Mutual Authentication

If Alice sends Bob a message, encrypted twice, once with her private key and again with his public key, then not only would Bob be the only one who could read the message, but he would also know it came from Alice. This type of service, where both the sender and receiver are clearly identified, is known as *Mutual Authentication* and is a very important and often overlooked service.

Let's consider a practical example of Mutual Authentication. Bob is using an ATM card and a PIN to access his bank account. Assuming all goes well, Bob has only proved himself to the ATM. How does Bob know that it was his ATM and only his ATM that read his account? If he encrypted his account number with his private key and again with his bank's public key, he could be reasonably assured that only his bank could see his account number and his bank could be reasonably assured that it was Bob that accessed the account. This is the idea behind SET (Secure Electronic Transaction, a very promising, but slow to come to market, system from VISA and Master Card) as well as many other protocols.

MiTM (Man in The Middle) Attacks

One way to envision asymmetric encryption is to imagine that Bob wants to share a secret with Alice, that they have never met (meaning they have no way to previously share a secret key), and, to make matters worse, that Eve is his courier.

1. Bob could put his secret message in a box and lock this box with a padlock.
2. He gives the locked box to Eve and asks her to deliver the box to Alice.
3. When Eve gives the box to Alice, she puts a second padlock on the box and asks Eve to return the box to Bob.
4. Bob then removes his padlock and asks Eve to deliver the box to Alice.
5. After Eve delivers the box to Alice, she can remove her padlock.

Assuming a perfect locking system (there is no way to break open the box or the lock), at no time did Eve ever have the box while it was unlocked. Sounds great, but there is one big problem.

Suppose Eve did not deliver the box to Alice at first but instead put her own lock on the box and returned to Bob saying, "I gave it to Alice and she put this other lock on it." Bob assumes all is normal and removes his lock. Eve can now open the lock and read the secret. She then delivers this to Alice and Alice proceeds as if all is normal.

This is a type of Man in The Middle (or in this case, woman in the middle) attack and is a fundamental issue with asymmetric encryption. The problem can be solved by authenticating Bob and Alice's locks. This is one of the functions of proper key management.

Summarizing Asymmetric Encryption

To summarize, while too slow for large amounts of data, asymmetric encryption solves a fundamental problem of symmetric encryption: the sharing of the initial symmetric key.

We can use an asymmetric system to share the initial secret. We can also provide a form of authenticity that cannot easily be repudiated (denied) since no one but Bob should have his private key.

Another great feature is scalability. Instead of N(N-1)/2, as in symmetric systems, we only need one key pair for each participant, so 1,000 participants would only require 1,000 key pairs or 2,000 keys. On the down side, we have introduced a new problem: authenticating the public keys to prevent someone from spoofing a public key to impersonate someone else. Key management systems are used to address these problems.

TRY IT OUT

Research Asymmetric Encryption Vocabulary Terms

This is another good point to pause and make sure you are comfortable with a few new concepts. Open a browser and type each term into a tool. Wikipedia also has good articles on almost each one of these phrases.

Public and private key pair

Open Message Format

Secure Message Format

Mutual Authentication

SET (Secure Electronic Transaction)

Diffie-Hellman key exchange

Digital signatures

Message digests

"Factoring large primes"

"Discrete logarithms in a finite field"

Know How Hashing Algorithms Work

- Message integrity
  - Try it out: Experiment with hashes
- Uses for one-way hashes
- Attacking one-way hashes

Message Integrity

Checking message integrity has been an issue in all communication as problems along a delivery path can create errors in a message. For digital communications, simple systems such as parity and checksums have been developed to handle such issues with reasonable assurance, assuming the corruption was due to electronic accidents. But if Eve wants to intentionally corrupt a message, it is trivial to fake the system out using either parity or checksums.

To address intentional corruption, mathematicians have borrowed cryptographic algorithms to provide checksums that would be very difficult to fake or craft. The algorithms are known as hashing algorithms and the checksums they create are formally known as *message digests*.

To create a message digest, one can run a hashing algorithm on a plain text message. For example, if we run MD5 (Message Digest version 5 from Ron Rivest) on Bob's message:

```
Hello Alice,

I love you. Please marry me.

Yours truly,

Bob
```

We would get a 128 bit message digest (frequently called a hash value or just "hash") of:

```
7928e34f8a6d230bbf492eaa6f2f3389
```

If even one bit changes in the original message, the message digest would be vastly altered. For example, in Bob's letter, by just changing the first character H to I and running MD5 again, we get a much different hash value:

```
dcf15d0673295a7d485219152144c9d9
```

If Bob creates a hash on his message before sending it to Alice, and Alice also computes a hash on the message when she receives it, she can compare values. If the hash values are different she can safely determine that the message was corrupted. However, if they are the same, she shouldn't necessarily feel safe, as she really needs to authenticate that the hash, or massage digest, was indeed created by Bob (since Eve could have changed the original message and simply created a new counterfeit hash).

As we saw earlier, both symmetric and asymmetric algorithms can be used to authenticate a message. If Bob *salts* (adds a value) his message with a symmetric value or *key*, Alice can trust that the message digest was truly from Bob. For example, if Bob salts his message with a value, say "19fd":

```
Hello Alice,

I love you. Please marry me.

Yours truly,

Bob + 19fd
```

When he runs an MD5 on this message, the new *keyed hash* (formally known as a message authentication code or MAC) value is:

```
85ef0c28ac041e9e7d1aed21bb3bef50
```

Bob now sends the original message (and only the message, not the key) to Alice along with the MAC. As with all symmetric systems, Bob will have to secretly share the key with Alice.

Once Alice has both the message and the key (which will again have to be shared with her through some secret channel or "out of band communication") she can salt the message with this key and calculate a MAC. If Alice's MAC is the same as Bob's MAC, then she can be reasonably assured that the message wasn't altered and that it came from Bob. This does not, however, provide non-repudiation, since the symmetric key or salt was known to both Bob and Alice and Bob could claim Alice created the message. A MAC provides integrity and authenticity services.

If Alice wants Bob to only send messages that can be traced to him alone, we will have to employ an asymmetric system; we now understand that only asymmetric algorithms can provide non-repudiation. So this time, Bob creates a message digest (or hash) of his message, and encrypts the hash value with his private key. Bob now sends Alice his message, the encrypted digest, and his public key. When Alice receives the message, she calculates a message digest on the message, and decrypts the digest Bob sent with his provided public key. If Alice's hash value is the same as Bob's then Alice can reasonably trust that the message:

1. Came from Bob: Authenticity

2. Was not altered: Integrity

3. Is something Bob cannot blame her for: Non-repudiation

This process is best known as *digital signing*. A hash value that has been encrypted with a sender's private key is called a *digital signature*.

As we have now seen, by using symmetric algorithms to make large messages private, hashing algorithms to provide integrity, and asymmetric systems to both agree on the secret key and authenticate the hash (strong authentication that cannot be denied or repudiated), we now see how we mix and match these algorithms to get the PAIN (Privacy, Authenticity, Integrity, and Non-repudiation) services of crypto.

Try It Out

Experiment with Hashes

If you have a Linux host handy, the command line tool "md5sum" is almost always available. Otherwise, for a Windows host visit *http://www.karenware.com* and download her "hasher" application (it's free).

Input the following string into the program and compute its hash:

```
"I just passed my CEHv5 exam today!"
```

Now change just one character and try it again. Notice the result is very different even though you made only a small change (8 bits):

```
"I just passed my CEHv6 exam today!"
```

Uses for One-Way Hashes

If it is necessary to compare two files, hashing is an efficient way to go. Simply calculate the hashes and compare them. If they are the same then the files are identical also. Even one bit difference in a 700Mb file would be enough to change the resulting hash about 60 percent. The bit flip also creates cascading changes (diffusion) throughout the resulting hash as the calculation runs through its permutations. In other words, there would be no question the two files are different.

In digital forensics, hashes are used to validate the integrity of the evidence. When a hard drive is collected, an image of the drive is created and both the drive and the image are hashed. They will match, indicating that the evidence image the investigator will be analyzing is an exact bit for bit copy of the original. Sometimes, every file is hashed and every physical sector of the drive is also hashed just to be certain.

When authenticating a document such as a digital certificate, a message digest of the file is taken and then encrypted with the private key of a trusted party—somewhat like when a notary public vouches for a document's authentic origin. But in a digital document, if there is any modification or corruption, the message digest that was signed will not match a new calculation of the hash. Attackers cannot simply replace the hash because they don't have the trusted party's private key to sign it. The receiver of the digital document will only use the public key of the trusted third party to check the signature.

When used in authentication, hashes are a way to store representations of passwords without actually storing the real thing. A user selects a password and the hash is stored in the accounts database of the system. The next time users identify themselves to the system, the hash that corresponds to their accounts is looked up and placed in memory. A hash of what they give as input during the authentication step is compared; if they match then the users are logged in.

Attacking One-Way Hashes

The fixed length characteristic of the hash limits the possible hashes that can result, even though the possible inputs to a hash function are infinite. A *collision* is the result of two different data producing the same hash, and is the primary weakness of most hashing algorithms.

You still cannot use a captured hash to determine the data, but attackers can try different combinations of input until the same hash is produced. If they know the maximum size of the possible input data—for instance, eight character passwords—then brute forcing is a lot easier. If passphrases are being used and their length could be anything from four to 40 characters or more, or if the hashing function used simply produces longer hashes (such as SHA-384), then brute forcing becomes impractical very quickly.

It might still be worth trying a guess, a dictionary, or a brute force attack, though. There is a possibility, however remote, that a short combination of characters will collide with what-ever the passphrase actually is. If the authentication system accepts the hash, then it does not matter if the data was the same or not.

Challenges, salts, and other forms of nonce values can be added to the hashing calculation to make finding collisions much more difficult. They ensure that if the same data were hashed several times it would not produce the same result unless the nonce was also added.

Know About Cryptosystems and Key Management

- Understanding "Cryptosystems"
    - Try it out: Using PGP to send encrypted e-mail
- Key management
- Public key infrastructure

Understanding "Cryptosystems"

A *cryptosystem* utilizes all three algorithm classes that we have covered: symmetric, asymmetric, and hashing. Examples include:

- For e-mail: PGP and S/MIME
- For Web-based applications: SSH/TLS
- For securing administration channels: SSH
- For remote access: IPSec (VPNs)

There are many more as well, but the basic concepts are the same for our purposes. Each of these systems requires the use of symmetric, asymmetric, and hashing algorithms to provide users with PAIN (or Privacy, Authentication, Integrity, and Non-repudiation).

TRY IT OUT

Using PGP to Send Encrypted E-mail

Most clients support cryptosystems in a way that is transparent to the user; in other words, the software does all the work. The padlock in the browser (auto)magically closes when we visit the shopping cart and we assume everything worked the way it was supposed to.

Possibly the best way to completely grasp how a whole system can incorporate many algorithms, and how key exchange really works, is to set up a scenario. Visit the following website and download PGP 6.5:

`http://www.pgpi.org`

Note: This version has a known issue so don't use it in production; however, for a lab exercise it will do just fine. The newer versions have nagware in them.

(continued)

Install the application and work through a process of the following steps. Use the documentation for guidance. Have a friend help you or use two e-mail accounts.

1. Keys are created the first time the program is run on each host.
2. Bob exports his key and sends it to Alice via e-mail attachment.
3. Alice imports Bob's key file, exports her own, and sends it to Bob.
4. Bob imports Alice's key file.
5. Bob creates an e-mail and sets Alice's address as the destination; he also tells PGP (press the encrypt button in the toolbar) to encrypt the message.
6. PGP applies Alice's key to the e-mail and sends it.
7. Alice opens the e-mail, provides her passphrase, and PGP decrypts the email.

Key Management

If we assume (and contrary to popular opinion, this is not always a bad thing) that the math behind today's encryption algorithms is pretty strong, then the hardest part of using encryption is key management. Just as we not only need to make up strong passwords, we also have to handle our passwords properly. The example of writing a strong password on a yellow sticky and attaching this to the side of our monitor (or under the keyboard) is not a very good idea. But, then again, not being able to write down passwords often means only choosing weak ones.

Mechanisms like password lockers can be used to protect these credentials, but then the locker itself must be encrypted and its key properly stowed. We also need a way to trust the authenticity of keys so only the correct identities have access to high value data.

Since we have stated earlier that the strongest algorithms for authenticity are asymmetric private/public key systems, a big challenge is how a recipient of a public key can really trust the authenticity of this key. How, for example, does Alice really know when she receives a key that has Bob's name on it that Eve didn't create the key? Or how do I know that when I download my bank's public key, that this key wasn't some counterfeit created by some thief?

Public Key Infrastructure

Just as I would not trust people to create their own driver's licenses, no one can really be trusted to validate his own public key. We use trusted third parties, as in the DMV, to create driver's licenses. Similarly, we use trusted third parties to validate public keys. These trusted third parties come in two types: public certificate authorities or, simply, another person who is trusted by both parties.

The PKI (public key infrastructure) or PKI system is the first type. In PGP, we can use the second. The primary difference between the two systems is why we trust these third parties to begin with. In PKI, we have internationally trusted agencies (do you always trust international agencies?) and in PGP, someone you know (if it is done right!) becomes the validating third party. This is also sometimes referred to as "A web of trust." It is not always what you know, but who.

PKI and PGP systems work basically the same way. The trusted third party will digitally sign the public keys of the users. As long as both Bob and Alice trust the signers, they indirectly trust each other's keys. By having trusted third parties sign each other's keys, we can mitigate any attacks that include counterfeit keys, such as the dreaded case where Eve created counterfeit keys, spoofing Bob and Alice, and performed her MiTM (Man in The Middle) attack.

Digital certificates are a common way to exchange and store collected public keys. This is simply a text file that contains three items: information about the identity of whose key this is, the public key itself, and a digitally signed message digest that authenticates the certificate file. The certificate is simply downloaded into a supporting client, such as an e-mail application or Web browser; the signature of the trusted third party is validated; and the certificate is stored until it expires or gets revoked. Revoking certificates is tricky but necessary if the private key half of the pair is ever compromised, or the identity of who the key pair belongs to is ever changed.

Know Advanced Attacks Against Cryptography

- Cryptanalysis
- "Brute force" attacks
- Pattern analysis

Cryptanalysis

Recall that "crypt" means "to hide." Whereas "graph" means "to write," "analyze" means "to solve or dissolve" or "to loosen." While the ultimate goal of a cryptanalyst is to translate the cipher text to the corresponding plain text, it can be said the most effective way to do this is to determine the encryption key. In the absence of that knowledge there might be other ways to attack the system. As a last resort, denial of service is always an option if the victim would go for an extortion scheme.

"Brute Force" Attacks

Imagine Bob buys a standard combination bicycle lock, one that contains four wheels, and each wheel has ten positions. The total number of possible keys would be ten to the 4th or 10,000 possible keys. Cryptologists typically use the term "Entropy" (the measure of chaos or randomness) to describe how many possible keys to guess. If Eve could guess 1,000 combinations per hour, then after five hours the odds are 50/50 that she would have guessed the right number. This is known as the "work factor," that is, it would take roughly five hours of work to crack such a system.

Also take some time to review the password cracking discussion from Chapter 7, "System Hacking."

Pattern Analysis

Using the same bicycle lock as in the previous example, Eve may not have to try anywhere near 5,000. Instead, she may notice a pattern. Many bicycle locks are vulnerable to such attacks. In some systems, Eve may just try the first wheel until the lock feels looser, then the second, third, and fourth. In this case, rather than try 5,000 numbers, Eve would only have to guess one in ten four times.

Four common pattern analysis attacks in cryptanalysis include:

- Cipher text only
- Known plain text
- Chosen cipher text
- Chosen plain text

Cipher text only

While Eve could try brute forcing the key (just guessing all the possible keys) she might see a useful pattern. This is analogous to trying to put a jigsaw puzzle together by either just trying to match pieces together one by one (brute force) or perhaps noticing a pattern, like identifying all the pieces with straight edges, trying pieces that have similar colors, and so on. Or imagine Bob and Alice are speaking to each other using the secret encoding scheme known as "Pig Latin" and Eve is eavesdropping. Bob says to Alice, "Appy-hay Irthday-bay." Even if Eve had never heard of Pig Latin, this obvious pattern becomes more obvious if Bob keeps talking.

Known plain text

Known plain text is a little easier for Eve to perform than the cipher text only, just as it is much easier to put a jigsaw puzzle together with access to the before picture (usually printed on the box cover). Using Pig Latin again, Eve heard Bob say "Happy Birthday" and then heard it encrypted as "Appy-hay Irthday-bay."

Chosen cipher text

In the chosen cipher text attack, Eve has no access to Bob, but can ask Alice, "Tell me what Irthday-bay means" and Alice lets her know that it translates to Birthday. This is even more powerful than the known plain text, as now Eve can choose a piece of cipher text and then, based on Alice's response, adapt her guesses. "Then tell me what Appy-hay means," and so on.

Chosen plain text

Chosen plain text is the most powerful of the four attacks. Eve chooses a deliberate set of words to see how they get encrypted. This can be done in two basic ways: batch, where Eve can create a very long message and then get access to the resulting cipher text (and look for patterns) or, even more powerful, the "Differential Analysis," where Eve can make a message, see how it is encrypted, and then alter the input slightly to analyze how this affects the cipher text. For example, Eve first tries the word "Test" and sees this encrypted as "Est-tay." Then she tries the word "Vest" and sees the new cipher text is "Est-vay."

As the math involved in today's systems has become more sophisticated, these attacks have become increasingly more difficult for Eve. But Eve can do something much simpler and yet very effective. Suppose Bob likes to watch the Philadelphia Eagles and Eve knows this. She can set up a fan site that Bob will likely visit because she is offering free videos of his favorite team. However, to watch the videos, Bob has to download a new video Codec (or driver) that requires him to allow his system to trust this new driver.

Unfortunately for Bob, he gets more than just a new driver. He also gets a bogus trusted root certificate authority (CA) and now every key Eve creates is trusted by Bob, because he trusts her bogus signing CA. Now Eve can pretend to be Bob's bank, Microsoft, or anyone she wants.

Think about how many times we are asked by hardware and software vendors to trust their software installs and how many of these vendors are in countries with governing bodies that are not very trustworthy. In fact, getting back to PKI, who should we trust to issue public keys? That is a very difficult question and one an ethical hacker must be aware of. In his great book, *The Speed of Trust,* Steve Covey says the first step in trust is to be trustworthy.

Conclusion

Before the owner of some data decides whether or not to use encryption there are some things that must be considered:

- Are you willing to lose all of this data if the key is lost or corrupted?
- Is our system accounting for both data in motion and data at rest?
- How does allowing the use of encryption impact our monitoring controls?
- How much encryption strength do I really need knowing there are performance needs to consider?
- Am I willing to take on a real key management process, permanently? What is the true cost of operating cryptosystems over time?

These questions are explored as we look at cryptanalysis in order to make this point: Crypto can be difficult to do correctly. Even though the math behind the open cryptographic standards is rock solid, there is always the possibility of a simple mistake that the attacker will be looking for. A billion dollar investment in a single sign on an authentication system supported by a strong crypto backbone is completely useless if the owner of a privileged account will trade her password for a candy bar.

The CEH exam does not require a great level of detailed knowledge about crypto; however, the contents of this chapter appear in one way or another in many information security exams and this topic should be considered as a gateway toward many other critical subjects in information security.

No matter how much you learn about crypto, the knowledge never goes to waste. Almost everything in technology is affected by or involves encryption somehow.

## CHAPTER SEVENTEEN

HACKING WITH LINUX

Introduction

Most of the focus in this class is on the Microsoft Windows operating system due to the market share and relevance it enjoys within most work environments. Linux, however, is often the tool of choice for hackers because it is free to use, flexible, and powerful, and there are many customized versions of Linux available to suit a variety of situations.

Another growing trend in the information security world is the adoption of the MAC platform, which is now at its core based on the FreeBSD code base. Since Linux is very UNIX-like in how it works, any knowledge that is gained in using command line tools is very likely transferrable.

Many students that come to CEHv6 training have not yet worked with Linux. This chapter will provide the fastest possible tutorial on getting started that can be squeezed into a few pages. The CEHv6 exam does not favor a particular version of Linux, so a broad look at a few key tools that are relevant to the security student will be sufficient to get the ball rolling.

To Pass the CEH Exam You Need to . . .

- know the origins and story of GNU/Linux
- know some important features of Linux
- know about important Linux security features
- master the CEH cheatsheets and practice questions!

Know the Origins and Story of GNU/Linux

- What exactly is GNU/Linux?
  - Try it out: Investigate Linux distribution choices
- What is a distribution?
- Which distributions should I learn?
  - Try it out: Download a Linux VM appliance

What Exactly Is GNU/Linux?

Linux started as a project to create an operating system kernel that could support hardware driver scenarios that Linus Torvalds needed to continue his work. Linus posted a message on Usenet and solicited the participation of other programmers with similar interests.

At about the same time, another programmer, Richard Stallman, was working on a UNIX-like operating system that would be "open sourced" and freely available. The FSF (Free Software Foundation) launched the GNU (GNU is Not UNIX) project and the Linux kernel was chosen instead of what they had already been working on. The GNU project then focused on necessary items for a functional OS such as command shells, as well as administrative tools that would function similarly to UNIX but would be re-written from the ground up.

The proper name of this operating system is GNU/Linux, but most of the time it is abbreviated to just Linux. Linus Torvalds owns the rights to the name, mostly as a protective measure to prevent someone else from owning it who might try to close the open development system. Richard Stallman is also very committed to keeping the FSF's contributions available to all who know how it works, modify it, and distribute it.

A Linux distribution is a collection of the kernel, GNU tools, and other specially designed administrative utilities for elements such as installation routines and hardware device detection. Presently, several hundred of these "distros" exist that have been customized for various uses.

TRY IT OUT

Investigate Linux Distribution Choices

One of the best website resources available for becoming aware of various Linux options and keeping track of the latest updated versions is "Distrowatch." Take a moment to visit the website and notice the popularity list on the front page to get an idea for what other people are using.

http://www.distrowatch.com

What Is a Distribution?

Linux is a highly customizable operating system. It is designed from the ground up to be modular and many of its important components are interchangeable. The following is a description of the broad categories of these options.

- The kernel
- The command shells
- The graphic environment
- The pre-installed tools
- The package manager
- Installed or LiveCD

The kernel

The kernel is the heart of the operating system. It manages hardware and coordinates data streams between programs. There are two types of kernels available. A monolithic kernel must be compiled to include all hardware driver support and modular kernels can be modified dynamically without being recompiled.

LKMs (Loadable Kernel Modules) are the equivalent of hardware drivers. In a modular kernel they can be installed without having to restart the system. This presents both a great deal of flexibility and risk. An attacker can rootkit a modular kernel if privileged access is achieved.

The command shells

"Shells" interpret commands and allow the user to interact with the system. Some commands are built in while others are stored in the file system as executable binaries. The shell runs in a terminal window, and putting aside a complex discussion about the differences, the phrase "open a terminal" and "open a shell" both just mean "get to a command prompt."

The Linux OS supports many shells. The most popular and common is the BASH (Bourne Again SHell) shell. Other shells have different features or scripting languages and can be installed easily when they are preferred.

The graphic environment

A Linux system can run strictly with a command line interface. Most server protocols are perfectly happy to be configured through text files and to run without the need for graphics. Applications with a "point and click" interface require a graphics server, a window manager, and "desktop," each of which has a variety of development projects creating different options. "Distros" have done all of the hard work for you. Typically, all users need to decide is what desktop environment they prefer.

There are several GUIs (Graphical User Interfaces) to choose from. KDE (K Desktop Environment) and GNOME (GNU Object Model Environment) are two of the most popular. Each has a different "look and feel" and philosophy governing how a user should interact with the system. Xfce and Fluxbox are choices that have low resource requirements.

The pre-installed tools

The pre-installed tools are the largest differentiator when it comes to determining which distro you would like to work with. Some distributions are designed to be multi-purpose desktops while others are specialized for a particular set of tasks. Some are very large while others try to maintain the smallest footprint possible.

The package manager

Should users want to install more software, the package manager is important. It keeps track of what is installed in the system and how to install updates as they become available. When installing new applications, the package manager can determine which necessary program libraries are available and, in most cases, include them as well. There are three basic families: those based on Redhat (RPM and YUM), those based on Debian (apt), and those that have a unique system (Gentoo). Some have none at all ("roll your own").

When users install their own software, sometimes the package is not available. The next best step is to obtain a "tarball." This is simply a single file that contains all of the separate files of the source code for the program. There is usually a README file that should always be read first in case there are specific instructions for installation. Then look for the "configure" script. The next exercise will walk through the steps of installing a simple program.

Installed or LiveCD

For our purposes, perhaps the most important option is between those Linux distros that run directly from CD or DVD images and those that must be installed to a hard drive first.

Installed Linux OSs are best suited for permanent implementations when hardware is available to dedicate to the OS. Most modern Linux distros, such as Ubuntu Linux, install as easy as Windows, and perhaps easier. The basics steps are similar to installing any operating system.

Linux distributions that run directly from an image are best for experimental or highly mobile uses. They are downloaded from the Internet in the form of an iso file. Most commercial CD or DVD burning software can be used to burn this image onto an optical disc. Do not just copy the data file; look for the feature that is specifically called "burn image to disc."

It is also convenient to simply load the iso file into the CD-ROM of a virtual machine. This works perfectly using either VMware or Microsoft Virtual PC. The official CEHv6 courseware includes a copy of Backtrack Linux. Make sure that during the official training class the process of using that image file is explained.

Linux can also be installed onto USB memory sticks or SD cards. This makes for a convenient "dual boot" scenario using laptops that support booting from the removable media.

Which Distributions Should I Learn?

For the CEHv6 exam the most important distribution to become familiar with is Backtrack Linux. It is a LiveCD-oriented distribution that is tailored for hacking and penetration testing. There are many tutorials and documentation resources on the Internet, even several videos on YouTube, that show users how to use this distribution. Don't wait for class; download it now and start exploring.

For a distribution that is permanently installed try Ubuntu. It is a general purpose desktop OS that has been created to be as easy to use as possible and supports most current hardware without hassles. SuSE Linux and Fedora are also excellent places to start. These variants are popular in enterprise environments because engineering support is available.

The most important thing is to pick one and get started. The upcoming Backtrack 4 distribution is now based on Ubuntu, has hundreds of important security and penetration testing tools already installed, and can be turned into a general desktop or server distribution easily by using the supported "apt" package management system. A copy of Backtrack comes with the official CEH courseware kits, but ultimately Linux is about choice and users must decide which one they like best.

You can try out a new distribution in one of four ways:

- Burn an ISO file to a CD/DVD and boot a system from it
- Install the Linux OS onto an SDCard or USB thumbdrive
- Build or repurpose an existing PC and install the Linux OS onto it
- Try a VMware product and experiment with virtual machines

Full-length tutorials on each of these topics are beyond the scope of this book. When you attend official training for CEH be sure to ask your instructor for assistance with them if you are interested. One way or another, it will be mandatory to have a Linux machine at the ready and become comfortable working with its capabilities. For now, let's focus on the quickest ways to get a Linux host up and running.

For those who have not worked with virtual machines before, the first thing to realize is that they are not "fake" computers or emulators. They are real hosts that share the hardware of your systems with other hosts. They have CMOS and BIOS, and support almost any kind of peripheral devices such as USB and sound cards. They also make it possible to perform advanced networking setups on a single hardware PC.

TRY IT OUT

Download a Linux VM Appliance

VMware offers a community website called the "Virtual Appliance Marketplace" that is full of many pre-built Linux virtual machines that are made for a variety of purposes. WMware Player or Server can be downloaded for free from their website, and a 30-days evaluation of VMware Workstation is also avaliable (registration required).

```
http://www.vmware.com
```

Once you have downloaded and installed the product of your choice, visit the community area of the VMware site and download a "Virtual Appliance" to experiment with.

```
http://www.vmware.com/appliances/
```

The following are a couple of recommended appliances to try. The URLs change frequently, so the easiest way to find them is to use the search function of the VMware website or just Google for "[name of distro] Virtual Appliance".

```
Backtrack Linux

NST (Network Security Toolkit)

pfSense Firewall

Unbuntu or Kubuntu
```

Know Some Important Features of Linux

- Know how the OS works
- Getting familiar with a new distro
  - Try it out: Manual configuration of a Linux network connection
  - Try it out: Installing an application in Linux
- Understanding the Linux file system
- Understanding the command line
  - Try it out: Using man pages
- Basic tools for using Linux
  - Try it out: Using basic Linux commands

Know How the OS Works

If you are brand new to Linux, the first step is to relax, and don't try to make it work like Windows. There are many significant differences, but once you get the hang of it things get easy fairly quickly. If you have downloaded a VM or are prepared to run a LiveCD distro, here are a few quick tips before you begin trying it out:

- Linux, in fact, is pretty simple, but like most simple things it takes a lifetime to master.
- The privileged user in Linux is called "root" and is not to be trifled with.
- Linux does not have "Drive letters" or a registry.
- You can use the GUI if you want, but will probably prefer the command line eventually.
- Linux is case sensitive, the slashes go the other way, and CR/LF are not handled the same

Linux, in fact, is pretty simple, but like most simple things it takes a lifetime to master.

The general philosophy of the Linux OS is that its job is to manage the hardware and keep users from making catastrophic mistakes that affect the system. It is not interested in enforcing licenses or phoning home to the mother-server every time you click your mouse, but it also might not care much if an installed application tried to do so.

The Linux kernel manages data streams from one place to another. For example, data is read from the hard drive and placed in memory, data is read from the keyboard and printed on the monitor, or data is read from an application and written to the network protocol stack. These streams can be redirected, of course; the user has a lot of flexibility through the use of scripting. But for the most part Linux is like a police officer that directs traffic at a busy intersection.

To some, Linux is more of a programming environment than strictly an OS. The simplicity of its design philosophy gives the programmer a lot of room to be creative, to keep costs low, and to not have to worry too much about breaking the computer along the way.

The privileged user in Linux is called "root" and is not to be trifled with.

Correction: Running as root can be very hazardous to the health of the system. Root is all powerful and it is easy to make critical errors when logged in this way. Remain logged in as a normal user and no harm to the system shall be done.

Use the "sudo" command to temporarily gain privileges for running certain tools. The password will have to be provided each time, but this helps ensure the operator thinks twice before running commands that could potentially be dangerous.

Linux does not have "Drive letters" or a registry.

Secondary storage devices can mount onto the file system anywhere the user wants them to, assuming the proper permissions are granted. Hard drives, USB keys, and CD-ROMs are accessed from directories that are chosen as mount points in the virtual directory structure.

Rather than use a registry, "package managers" keep track of the various binaries and library files on the system, but they don't keep track of tar balls that the user compiles and installs. Startup operations such as beginning services are handled by scripts. A few other important services include:

- Scheduled jobs are handled by a service called "cron."

- Log files are written by a service called "syslog."

- Services are owned by a user of the same name (usually), not necessarily by "root."
  - Domain services are called "named" (Naming Daemon) not "DNS."

You can use the GUI if you want, but will probably prefer the command line eventually.

The desktop projects such as KDE and GNOME have made significant progress in making Linux as easy to use as any other system, but the command line is often more efficient and straightforward, and the results are more predictable. The operator of the command has to tell the OS exactly what to do and it will not do any more or any less.

Linux is case sensitive, the slashes go the other way, and CR/LF are not handled the same.

The Linux command shells such as BASH (Bourne Again SHell) and others are always case sensitive. This actually leads to more power for options and arguments as well as potentially clearer self-documentation of scripts than with non-case sensitive environments.

Directory paths look like this in Windows "C:\windows\system32\drivers\etc\hosts" and like this in Linux "/etc/hosts".

If you create a plain text file in Linux and try to open it with Notepad in Windows, you will notice strange boxes where the carriage returns used to be. The problem is that Linux expects line breaks in the 'LF' format (\n), while Windows expects them in the 'CRLF' format (\r\n), both of which are hidden things in the ASCII character set. To fix it, just open the file in Wordpad and save it.

Getting Familiar with a New Distro

When beginning to work with a Linux distribution for the first time, there are three very important questions that you must answer. The information will be provided by the source of the distribution on its website.

- What is the login for the root user?
- How do I set up the network interface?
- What is the package manager?

What is the login for the root user?

If the Linux distro you have chosen is a pre-built virtual machine or a LiveCD/DVD, it is critical that you find what the root password is on the supplier's website. The username is always "root," but the password can vary.

- For Backtrack the password is "toor".
- For NST the password is "nst2003".
- For Ubuntu the default configuration involves logging in as a normal user and using the "sudo" command to access privileged tools. The password must be provided each time; for example, to run a stealth scan in nmap the command would be "sudo nmap –sS [target IP]".

Distros that you install from scratch are as easy to install as Windows. Just follow the guidance and, when in doubt, stay with the defaults. You will have the opportunity to choose a password for the root account during this process.

How do I set up the network interface?

Some distros include a GUI-based tool or "network manager" application that assists with network configuration. Many distros that are based on security or forensic use will not automatically seek out a lease for an IP configuration from a DHCP server because in these cases you may not want to give yourself away so easily.

It is important to know how to manually configure an Ethernet NIC (Network Interface Card) connection. This ensures that no matter what the distribution version, you can be up and running as long as the configuration settings are determined correctly.

TRY IT OUT

Manual Configuration of a Linux Network Connection

The following assumes you have one hardware NIC and that you know what variables to set for your location on the network.

```
ifconfig eth0 [ip address] netmask [subnet mask]

route add default gw [gateway address]
```

What is the package manager?

In order to see everything that is on the system, to receive important security updates, and to install new applications, it is important to know whether or not your distro uses RPM, APT, or some other system.

The procedures for managing applications in each of these environments vary. However, no matter what, you should always know how to work a tarball.

TRY IT OUT

Installing an Application in Linux

Visit the following website and download "xbill.src". It is a simple application that should not need additional libraries if you are running a Linux distro with a graphical environment.

```
http://www.xbill.org
```

At your prompt, type the commands that follow. The first command uncompresses and unpackages the tarball.

```
tar -zxvf
```

We then navigate into the directory that was just created.

```
./configure
```

The next three commands are the actual install sequence.

```
./configure
```

```
make
```

```
make install
```

Finally, launch the program.

```
xbill
```

Understanding the Linux File System

Linux uses a "virtual file system" that keeps the details about hardware away from the system user. The following list of directories is fairly standard among various distributions:

/	The root of the virtual filesystem
/boot	The Linux kernel and boot code live here
/dev	Special directory for device files
/proc	Special directory for system processes
/etc	System configuration files
/var	Variable data such as log files
/lib	Shared system library files

/sbin	Executable files that are available to root
/bin	Executable files that are available to every user
/root	The home directory for user "root"
/home	Location of all users' personal files

Some variations of this structure will happen from one distro to the next. Do not be surprised if on occasion it is necessary to become familiar with a new arrangement. The differences are never drastic enough to become a hindrance; it just takes a few minutes of command line exploration to get the basic idea.

Understanding the Command Line

The command line in Linux is a powerful scripting environment that provides a great deal of flexibility and efficiency. It takes practice to become comfortable with how things work, but the more effort is applied and critical thought is exercised the faster the skill will come. There is no shortcut, so you must open a shell and play.

If you ask a Linux expert a simple question and she responds with "RTFM," what she is saying is "Read the fine manual page!" "Man pages," for short, are the documentation provided by most tools in Linux, and reading them takes some practice. The more this is done, the easier it gets, so RTFM often.

Commands take the form of:

```
command [-abcdef] [-g arg] [-f arg] object
```

Use these tips as guidance:

- Anything in square brackets is optional; if there is an object, it is mandatory.
- The options   `-abcdef`   are the same as

    `-bcafde`   or

    `-fedcba`   or

    `-a -b -c -d -e -f`

    Order usually does not matter.

- Options that have args must be followed by the arg. The man page will describe the arg for each option.
- Some options have both long names and short names. Two hyphens means long name. Consider this example from IPTables:

    `-sport` is actually `-s -p -o -r -t`

    But `--sport` means "Source port"

To get the hang of it faster, practice reading options out loud as though the command is an expressive sentence. For example:

The command "`nc -l -p 3210 -e cmd.exe`" sounds in English as: "Using the netcat tool, start a listener on port 3210 and execute cmd.exe when there is a connection."

TRY IT OUT

Using Man Pages

Practice reading the man pages for a few commands that are relevant to the CEH exam (Note: some pages do not exist on some systems, so just try). Use the space bar to scroll through a whole page. Press the letter "q" to quit. Use the "/" character to begin a forward search.

```
man nmap

man hping2

man nc

man ettercap

man snort

man iptables
```

The CEH exam does have some questions that involve knowing some command line options, but do not get too overwhelmed by these pages. Just look them over to get a sense for them.

Basic Tools for Using Linux

Now that we know the basics of using tools and interpreting the manual pages, let's look at some of the common everyday commands that every Linux user must know. Of course, this is not comprehensive; it is just a handful to get started with and assist in being more comfortable before attending the formal CEH training class.

TRY IT OUT

Using Basic Linux Commands

Run the following commands and observe the results. Man page each command to read the description and learn about the options. Play around with the commands in different combinations until they are mastered.

```
mkdir pookie

cd pookie

pwd

cd ~

ls

rmdir pookie
```

(continued)

TRY IT OUT (*Continued*)

```
ls -l
touch foopie
chmod 666 foopie
ps aux
ps -aux | tee procs.dump
ls
file procs.dump
cat procs.dump
rm procs.dump
ls
cat /etc/passwd | tee users.dump
ls
head /var/log/messages
tail /var/log/messages
cat /var/log/securetty | more
```

TRY IT OUT CHALLENGE

• It might seem a little strange to be asked to play around with some random tools. However, this is a necessary first step. Experiment, play around, and be random at times. This is the shortcut to learning Linux. Figure out things that can be done with these commands and add many more into the mix.

Know About Important Linux Security Features

• Defense mechanisms in Linux
• Tools for hacking with Linux
  • Try it out: Tools for hacking with Linux
• Using Backtrack 4 and Ubuntu

Defense Mechanisms in Linux

Now that the world's shortest basic tutorial on getting a start with Linux is about through, we need to continue full speed ahead and discuss some things that are very much in the specific context of an information security course.

The Linux operating system has several built-in mechanisms to defend itself from attack should the operator choose to configure them, including:

- IPTables
- TCP Wrappers
- PAM

IPTables

IPTables is the built-in firewall for Linux kernels version 2.6 and forward. It supports packet filtering, NAT (Network Address Translation), SPI (Stateful Packet Inspection), and can plug into IDS (Intrusion Detection Systems) to create a powerful IPS (Intrusion Prevention System).

Kernel version 2.4 previously used IPChains. For the CEH exam, don't worry about the differences even if the terms might get used interchangeably. The official source of information on IPTables is at the Net Filter project (*http://www.netfilter.org*).

TCP Wrappers

TCP Wrapper is an ACL (Access Control List) system for services that use TCP as their transport protocol. It sits between incoming services and the daemons themselves, allowing for both monitoring of the connection activities as well as control over connectivity at the IP address level.

Two files are used to configure TCP Wrappers: the /etc/hosts.allow file, which indicates who can access what, and the /etc/hosts.deny file. This allows easy configuration of either a default permissive or a default restrictive policy.

PAM

PAM (Pluggable Authentication Modules) is a set of binary files that can be called from a configuration file to provide authentication services for applications.

The idea is that the Linux OS doesn't normally want to be in the business of authorizing anything but users onto the system itself. It wants to let the basic RWX (Read Write Execute) rules included within the metadata of each file govern access rights. Some application developers want more control than that. Therefore, so rather than create their own authentication subsystem from scratch, they can call on the PAM libraries.

Advanced ACLs (Access Control Lists) for directories and files exist in Linux but depend on the underlying file system of the data volume. In other words, if a partition on the physical disc has been mounted on the /home directory and was formatted with ReiserFS, then the available ACL style permissions that can be assigned are dependent on the metadata that ReiserFS supports. Other file systems include "EXT2" and have different capabilities and support for security features, error recovery, and efficiency.

Tools for Hacking with Linux

Linux has seemingly endless tools available for security practices and forensics. The forensics tools are discussed in the EC-Council CHFI course and other critical security tools are introduced in the CEH class. Both categories of tools are collected in distros like Backtrack and Helix, among many others.

TRY IT OUT

Tools for Hacking with Linux

The following tools are important to know for the CEH exam. Read their man pages and try them out. There are other commands that have been discussed throughout the book as well that are not mentioned here. This is a short list just to get going.

#command	#Description
lsof	List open files
file	Determine the data type of a file
rpcinfo	Enumeration tool for queries to portmapper
finger	Should not work, but it might
dd	Create a bit for bit image of a data volume
ifconfig	View current network statistics
route	View current routing tables
iptraf	LAN monitor
chrootkit	Trojan horse detection

Using Backtrack 4 and Ubuntu

As of this writing, Backtrack Linux version 4 is available for download. It is based on Ubuntu Linux and, as such, there are a few important differences that must be pointed out that vary from other common distributions.

A security feature of Ubuntu is that there are extra steps needed to access the root privileged account. This helps avoid potentially critical errors that could be made when an operator has forgotten he is logged in as root and issues a command that can cause system-wide damage. You have to think twice in Ubuntu before making such mistakes.

The root user account is not accessible until a password is set for it. Until then, the "sudo" command can be used to access privileged commands. It is probably a good idea to keep it this way on most systems, but for a security application so many tools require the root account that it might be more convenient to set the password and switch the context to the root user some of the time; just make sure to exit back to the standard account as soon as possible.

Here is an example process (Ubuntu-based Linux systems only):

Trying to run a stealth scan with nmap, the normal user will be told that "You requested a scan type which requires root privileges. QUITTING!"

```
nmap -sS [target IP]
```

This can be overridden by issuing the command like this:

```
sudo nmap -sS [target ip]
```

If you get tired of doing this try:

```
su root
```

```
{enter your current password}
```

```
passwd
```

```
{Enter a root user password}
```

```
{Retype the password}
```

```
exit
```

Now anytime it is necessary to be root for awhile (do this with caution):

```
su root
```

```
{enter the recently configured password}
```

Conclusion

The first step in working with anything is to master a few basics, to notice some patterns, and to try what you have learned in some situations that include unknowns. It is impossible to learn and memorize everything, but it is absolutely reasonable to work with unfamiliar materials using existing knowledge as a base to figure things out. This is perhaps the most powerful skill that Linux teaches.

Linux is an operating system based on open systems of ideas and contributions. This can seem somewhat chaotic at times, but the basic fundamentals are based on time-tested designs and practices. The best hacking tools are those which are flexible and can be used without fear of intellectual property violations and similar distractions. Everything a student can learn about Linux and working with tools in this environment will come in handy at some point.

The CEHv6 exam does not favor a particular version of Linux, so a broad look at a few key tools that are relevant to the security student will be sufficient to get the ball rolling. On the exam, do not debug scripts or argue with examples. Do not feel intimidated by the amount there is to know; the important thing is to get started and pick up one new piece of knowledge each day. It adds up fast. The idea is to practice, practice, and practice.

## Chapter Eighteen

IDS, Firewalls, and Honeypots

Introduction

Up to this point in the CEH methodology, there have been a variety of attacks that may or may not work in particular situations. The skilled attacker realizes that the steps can be modified and that the variables are simple. The other side of the attacker's challenge is to understand the major countermeasure products. With this information the attacker can engage in a precise attack.

The final step in the CEH methodology is "clearing tracks." This step is as much about evading detection or leaving behind evidence as it is about manipulating the downsides of countermeasures.

The CEH course is a defense-oriented course that explores attack scenarios. It is essential to bring critical thinking to this module. We present examples of the basics because this is not meant to be a complete course in these products; however, if the entire picture this class attempts to demonstrate is considered, there is much room for creative thinking. Enter this chapter with this attitude in mind.

To Pass the CEH Exam You Need to . . .

- know the classes of firewalls
- know the classes of intrusion detection systems
- know how to deploy honeypots
- know the testing and evasion techniques
- master the CEH cheatsheets and practice questions!

Know the Classes of Firewalls

- Understanding firewalls

- Classes of firewalls

- Example: Basic operation of IPTables

  - Try it out: Learn more about IPTables

Understanding Firewalls

Firewalls are hardware and software technologies that assist with the enforcement of security policy. They filter traffic based on a set of matching rules as traffic passes through them.

Firewalls are not routers. The concept of routing traffic for delivery is an entirely separate discussion. Network-based firewalls often do eventually route traffic, but only if the policies allow. Host-based firewalls can protect single hosts from both incoming and outgoing traffic. All firewalls can cause troubleshooting nightmares if they are not configured carefully; this is why a business objective-driven policy is always the first step.

Firewalls do not lend to improvised configurations. They must be carefully thought through and the impact of all policies should be studied before the firewall is implemented.

Firewalls cannot prevent social engineering or physical attacks. Default configuration attacks and careless implementations are the most common weaknesses an attacker can find. It is important to understand both the benefits and limitations of firewalls and not be lulled into a false sense of security by their very presence.

Classes of Firewalls

There are many different types of firewalls on the market and each has its place on the network. Many commercial products, sometimes referred to as "Internet-in-a-box" appliances, combine each of these types including infrastructure features such as routing and DMZs (Demilitarized Zones). However, it is critical for CEH that we take some time to understand the separate concepts.

- Packet filters

- Circuit level gateways

- Application level firewalls

- Stateful multilayer inspection firewalls

Packet filters

Packet filters look for protocol information in the delivery and transport layers. The idea is to get rid of the easiest and obvious stuff first.

Every packet is a discreet single logical unit, much like the way an envelope that is received in the "snail mail" box is just one single package. Packet filters only look at one delivery at a time. They are computationally cheap and very efficient.

Circuit level gateways

This is a unique class of firewall that protects the integrity of each end of the session without invading the confidentiality of the data that is exchanged. It is a socket-level proxy in that it creates entirely new connections based on the synchronizing of IP addresses and ports.

It takes the concepts of network address translation a step further by including a new translation of the sequence numbers that are tracked by TCP to help the receiving host reassemble all of the segments of data. This prevents session hijacking and helps obscure the true endpoints of any observed conversation.

Application level firewalls

Application firewalls look at the content of each network packet, otherwise described as "Layer 7." This data includes all client server requests and information content that is delivered on the network.

This form of firewall is computationally expensive. Many factors that ride far beyond simple string pattern matches must be incorporated. Context is a factor as well as policies such as user profiles and time of day constraints. If a violation of policy is encountered, it must be considered whether or not to log the evidence in a forensically sound manner, redirect the user to another source, or simply log an alert and let human management make the call regarding appropriate actions.

Stateful multilayer inspection firewalls

This firewall class combines the aspects of the other three types. They filter packets at the network layer to get rid of the easiest stuff first and then send the remaining packets to the "deep packet inspection" engine.

Example: Basic Operation of IPTables

IPTables is the firewall that is built into the Linux kernel starting with version 2.6. A similar firewall that might be mentioned is IPChains, which was included with Linux kernel 2.4 and previous versions. For the purposes of the CEH exam they are the similar enough not to worry about it.

"Chains" of policy rules are linked together from a main set that sorts network packets to make analysis more efficient. For instance, if we need a set of detailed rules to filter FTP traffic, there is no need for 99.9 percent of all the traffic that is totally unrelated to FTP to have to be put through this chain. Therefore, we sort the FTP traffic out first and only put those packets through that set of rules. The rest of the packets could end up in other chains or simply could be accepted or dropped right away.

There are three default chains to start with: INPUT, OUTPUT, and FORWARD. The INPUT and OUTPUT chains are engaged whenever traffic is sent to or generated by the host itself, and the FORWARD chain is engaged only if the host is a router and is passing the traffic from one interface to another.

All firewalls can be configured initially either to pass all traffic or to block all traffic. Rules are then designed either to deny only certain packets or to accept only certain packets. Either way, once a packet matches a rule, action is immediately taken. The only time a packet will go through every rule or chain is if it matches nothing. The default policy then governs what happens.

If a Linux host is under attack, a fast way to block the incoming traffic is to set the default policy of the INPUT chain to DROP. If a host is spitting out traffic due to a virus infection or botnet activity, one quick way to stop all traffic is to set the default policy of the OUTPUT chain to DROP. In both cases, the situation can be investigated and normal operation restored by putting the policy back to ACCEPT once the threat is mitigated.

Let's look at a very brief example of a Linux host that is also a router. The CEH exam does not require that you become an expert in IPTables, so this example will be kept short and simple. What is important is to get the basic idea of firewall configuration and the process of implementing a set of rules. No matter what kind of firewall is in place, the basic steps are:

1. Understand the business objectives clearly
2. Pseudo-code the objectives into technical phrases
3. Document a configuration proposal
4. Backup the current configuration of the firewall
5. Implement the configuration proposal
6. Test the firewall
7. If the test goes wrong, restore the original configuration and repeat the steps until it is made right

The business objective for our example is that we wish to block all traffic except web surfing from the internal network. We know this will involve the following details:

*   The default policy of the FORWARD table will be set to DROP all traffic.
*   We need to allow HTTP outbound from the internal network.
*   We need to allow the responses to HTTP requests to come back through.

The next step is to "pseudo code" these business policies into something closer to what the rules must actually be. For instance, what exactly is "internal network"? Are there any special considerations for HTTP traffic? Are we going to use the Stateful Packet Inspection features of IPTables or keep it simply as a basic packet filter?

We decide that the internal network is 192.168.1.0/24. We are going to allow SSL along with the HTTP requests. HTTP is port 80 and SSL is port 443; both are based on TCP transport. We also realize that the DNS server is on the outside so that traffic (UDP port 53) will also have to be allowed. Our pseudo code looks something like this:

*   Change default policy of forward chain to drop all traffic
*   Allow UDP from 192.168.1.0/24 to any network port 53
*   Allow TCP from 192.168.1.0/24 to any network port 80
*   Allow TCP from 192.168.1.0/24 to any network port 443

The next step is to convert the pseudo code into the actual syntax required by IPChains. The script would look like this:

```
# set the default policy (-P) of the FORWARD chain to DROP
iptables -P FORWARD DROP

# Append (-A) the FORWARD chain with a rule to jump (-j)
# to ACCEPT when traffic is coming from (-s) IP address and
# is going to protocol (-p) and destination port (--dport)
iptables -A FORWARD -j ACCEPT -s 192.168.1.0/24 -p udp --dport 53
iptables -A FORWARD -j ACCEPT -s 192.168.1.0/24 -p tcp --dport 80
```

The final step is to test the firewall and we find it doesn't work. The problem is that the return traffic is not accounted for, so we cannot get back any responses to these requests. Another problem we forgot to consider in the pseudo code is that 192.168.1.0 is a private address and therefore not routable beyond our own internal networks. We are going to have to use NAT to fix this unless another router downstream does that for us. We go back to the drawing board and update our proposal.

We are going to have to turn on NAT, no problem. Fixing the "return traffic" problem is a bit trickier. We do not know what port our clients will send their requests from; they will pick something above port 1023. Traffic will return to (destination port) something above 1023. If we create a rule to allow this, we have just opened the firewall wide open. The next best thing is to only allow traffic to return if it comes from port 80 or 53. Here is our new configuration:

```
# Turn on NAT (masquerading) on interface eth0
iptables -t nat -A POSTROUTING -o eth0 -j MASQUERADE

# set the default policy (-P) of the FORWARD chain to DROP
iptables -P FORWARD DROP

# Append (-A) the FORWARD chain with a rule to jump (-j)
# to ACCEPT when traffic is coming from (-s) IP address and
# is going to protocol (-p) and destination port (--dport)
iptables -A FORWARD -j ACCEPT -s 192.168.1.0/24 -p udp --dport 53
iptables -A FORWARD -j ACCEPT -s 192.168.1.0/24 -p tcp --dport 80

# Allow traffic to return to the internal network (-d)
# if it is coming from the allowed source ports (--sport)
iptables -A FORWARD -j ACCEPT -d 192.168.1.0/24 -p udp --sport 53
iptables -A FORWARD -j ACCEPT -d 192.168.1.0/24 -p tcp --sport 80
```

It is time to test again, and this time it works. The problem is that if you only test this configuration for functionality, then security risks are overlooked. A proper penetration test should also be conducted. By using scanning techniques and other tests it might be discovered that traffic can get in from an attacker if he is coming from another internal network (such as 192.168.2.0/24) and set the source port of all their traffic to 80. Getting into this completely involves more information we have not provided in the example, and we have gone far enough for now to make the point that firewall configuration is not easy. However, understanding how it works can help the details of scanning techniques make more sense. A hacker should learn both offensive and defensive skills.

Another consideration for firewall configuration might be limiting the number of connections that can be established through this firewall. For example, the following line would allow only two Telnet connections per host (should be all one line):

```
iptables -A INPUT -p tcp -syn -dport 23 -m connlimit
-connlimit-above 2 -j reject
```

TRY IT OUT

Learn More About IPTables

If you have a Linux host available, open a shell terminal and read the man page for IPTables. Try to find each of the options that were discussed in the previous examples.

```
man iptables
```

Find answers to the following questions:

How do you list the rules that are currently in place?

How can you clear all of the rules and return the default policy to ACCEPT?

What are the protocols that are supported?

Can you delete or insert new rules?

TRY IT OUT CHALLENGE

Learn More About IPTables Scripting

Putting together complex chains is a real challenge and it is best left up to those who specialize in firewall administration. Perform an Internet search for support websites that provide chains you can use. Read through the examples thoroughly; this is the best way to learn more about firewall configuration.

Know the Classes of Intrusion Detection Systems

- Classes of Intrusion Detection Systems
- Interpreting alerts
- Events to look for during analysis
- Example: Basic operation of snort
  - Try it out: Learn more about snort

Classes of Intrusion Detection Systems

Intrusion detection is a critical aspect of network monitoring. It is considered a "passive" technique in that detection only informs us that an event has occurred, but it does not by default prevent or correct the situation.

Intrusion prevention systems exist that take this monitoring to an "active" level. Attackers can sometimes use false positives to turn these systems against their owners. The configuration and testing of these devices is critical and might be something a CEH professional is asked to do.

There are several different methods for intrusion detection. Each has its own benefits and drawbacks. Placement of detection agents also plays a role in the type of system that is chosen. There should always be an agent in the DMZ, and one just to the inside of the firewall that screens all internal networks. Let's take a quick look at the following techniques:

- Signature recognition
- Anomaly detection
- Statistical detection
- Network-based intrusion detection
- Host-based intrusion detection
- Log file monitoring
- File integrity checking

Signature recognition

Signatures are simply recognizable characteristics of a packet; for instance, a particular series of bytes or characters. The position (offset) of particular bytes can also be of significance, as can field values or flag combinations.

Signature detection happens in real time. Alerts can be placed in a log file immediately after a suspect packet is detected. Notifications can then be sent. Alternatively, if the IDS is running in "in-line" mode, it can interact with firewall software to implement new policy rules to block the attack. This is an IPS (Intrusion Prevention System).

The drawback to signature detection is in the complexity and amount of the rule set that must be used. It must be updated constantly, and will not detect 0-day exploits.

Anomaly detection

This type of IDS looks for events that are unusual. This means that knowing what normal traffic is becomes critical. A baseline metric of typical and expected traffic is given to the IDS. It then provides an alert when events other than what the baseline predicts take place.

The advantage of this form of monitoring is that certain types of attacks that would evade signature analysis might be noticed. Attacks such as ARP poisoning or heavily fragmented packets will cause unusual traffic that can be noticed. The drawback is this IDS is only as good as the accuracy of its baseline.

Statistical detection

This form of IDS can notice attacks that take place over time. If an attacker tries to scan very slowly, for instance, it has been proven that even one packet per day at random times and with random values could trigger an alert. The drawback is that the analysis takes time; attacks may not be discovered until they have been completed, but at least we will know they have happened.

Network-based intrusion detection

This type of IDS is considered passive as it just "listens on the wire." Any form of analysis engine can be used.

Host-based intrusion detection

This type of IDS is considered active as it can be invasive in order to monitor the behavior and actions of a host. For example, if a host sends out three e-mails within a fraction of a second that all have blank subject lines and empty contents, this could be considered suspicious. The HIDS will pause all e-mail activity and ask the user if this activity was intended or not before continuing.

Log file monitoring

Log files are a challenge to analyze because there are thousands of formats and each one is unique to the service being monitored. There are commercial tools that know about many popular formats and can make reporting much easier. They can even be used for real-time intrusion detection.

File integrity checking

SIVs (System Integrity Verifiers) are a class of IDS that keeps a database of hashes computed from critical files or directories on the system. It recalculates these hashes either periodically, or whenever the file is accessed, and presents an alert when changes have been detected.

This IDS discovers files that have been replaced, altered, or corrupted; therefore, files that change often are difficult to monitor. Operating system files and program libraries do not commonly change, and new hash databases must be computed after accepting patches or other security updates.

Interpreting Alerts

Whenever alerts to events are logged, it is up to a human analyst to determine if a response action is appropriate and exactly what that response should be. Knee-jerk reactions, overcorrections, and time wasted in response to non-issues are not only a waste of time but can create new problems.

It is important to keep in mind that IDSs only look for what they have been told to. They do not make subjective decisions. Just as the case with firewalls, a strong policy is at the heart of any monitoring and incident response program.

For analysis, IDS alerts can be sorted into the following categories:

False positive	We thought it was an attack, but it wasn't.
False negative	We didn't think it was an attack, but it was.
True positive	Yes, it is really an attack!
True negative	No, it is not an attack.

Events to Look for During Analysis

The best monitoring program will include redundancy and many different methods of detection. Each threat category has its own risk factors to the organization which determine how the asset should be monitored.

A simple way to look at it is to consider the difference between a public web server and a database. The web server should be accessed a lot—at least, we hope many customers are visiting us—but certain types of access such as obvious directory traversals indicate one of our visitors is trying to scrape us for documents or detect other flaws. It could also just be a search engine spider. Regardless, if we know from our thorough testing there is nothing to find, most of that activity is expected and will be ignored.

The database server, on the other hand, should only be accessed by authorized processes, and only when those processes are running correctly. They should only attempt to perform certain actions. If anything outside of that is taking place, it may indicate that an attacker may have gained a better position on the network. The source of the queries has been compromised, and the database must also be analyzed for any successful breaches.

Know the threats and do not overreact. Just because a host reboots doesn't mean it has been invaded; it could just mean the RAM needs to be reseated on the motherboard.

Attackers will try to cause diversions and waste the administrator's time with false positives. False negatives will only be detected by redundant IDSs that are using different methods of detection. True positives must be responded to by a tested plan or team such as a CSIRT (Computer Security Incident Response Team).

The following is a brief list of items to consider monitoring for. As you read the list, consider which form of detection would be best, and how an attacker might trigger a false positive or evade detection altogether.

- Modifications to systems software and configuration files
- Gaps in accounting systems
- Unusually slow performance
- System crashes or reboots
- Short or incomplete logs
- Logs containing strange timestamps
- Logs with incorrect permission or ownership
- Missing logs
- Abnormal system performance
- Unfamiliar processes
- Unusual displays or text messages
- The presence of new, unfamiliar files or programs
- Changes in file permissions
- Unexplained changes in file size
- Rogue files on the system that do not correspond to your master list of signed files
- Unfamiliar user names
- Missing files
- Repeated probes of the available services on your machines

- Connections from unusual locations
- Repeated login attempts from the remote hosts
- Arbitrary data in log files

Example: Basic Operation of Snort

Snort is one of the most common and popular NIDS in use. It uses signature detection and has a "pre-processor" engine that allows for the triggering of dynamic rules. This helps snort avoid getting overwhelmed when processing large amounts of traffic. It often comes by default in Linux distributions or can be easily installed. It has also been ported to the Windows environment.

Getting snort up and running in its default configuration is easy. For many quick and simple implementations, the default configuration is sufficient. For more permanent or finely tuned installations, the "snort.conf" configuration file is used to make the necessary adjustments. These include setting values for rule variables, setting rule update parameters, and arranging for a few performance tweaks.

Rule updates can be purchased from Sourcefire (*http://www.snort.org*) or a free community set of rules can be used that is not as up to date. Rules can also be written on site. For the CEH exam, it is important to know how the snort rules language works, although you do not have to be an expert at snort in total. This brief tutorial is enough to get started.

Let's first take a look at the most basic rule. It would catch all TCP traffic:

```
alert tcp any any -> any any (sid:1000000; msg:"Test rule";)
```

The rule is divided in two parts: the rule header and the rule options. Options are in the parenthesis and the part that comes before it is the header. The header is made up of the following:

```
[action] [protocol] [source address] [source port] -> [destination
address] [destination port]
```

- Actions can be: alert, log, pass, activate, or dynamic.
- Protocols can be IP, ICMP, TCP, or UDP.
- Addresses and ports are source and destination if the direction operator is used ("->"); otherwise, the operator "<>" can be used instead to indicate the addresses and ports are in either direction.

There are many options that can be used with snort. They are separated in the options field by a semicolon. The following is a brief list of common options:

sid:number	Rule id. Custom rules start with 1000000
msg: message text	Shows in the alert file to describe the event
content:"string"	String content in the packet we are looking for
content:"|AB CD EF 12 34|"	Hex values in the packet we are looking for
reference:"[reference number]";	Example: "CVE 4001-1234"

Example rule: Let's say we wanted to detect an attempt to access a certain software pirate website. The access is coming from an internal host, and the pirate site could change its IP address often, so we do not want to hard code its IP. We are expecting the site to use common HTTP ports.

1. Open snort.conf in a text editor and set the variable for $HOME_NET (we could just use the internal IP address in the rule, but variables make the set of rules more portable to other snort agents on the network):

   ```
   var HOME_NET 192.168.1.0/24
   ```

2. Open the local.rules file in a text editor and add the following (all one line):

   ```
   alert tcp $HOME_NET any -> any 80,81,8080 (content:"serialz.cx";
   msg:"Pirate site accessed"; sid:1000000;)
   ```

3. Start snort using a command like:

   ```
   snort -vde -l /var/log/snort -c /etc/snort/snort.conf
   ```

The "-vde" options will cause snort to display in the window all traffic including Layers 2 and 7 that it sniffs. This is a lot of extra work for snort and wouldn't normally be done. Only packets that match rules will be in the alert file (located at /var/log/snort). A binary version of the captured traffic will also be provided and can be opened in Wireshark for analysis (remember only the "alert" file is text and can be viewed directly; a file whose name is something like "snort.log.10232424032" should only be opened by a protocol analyzer).

The –c option sets the configuration file. It will specify that the local.rules file is included along with all of the other rule sets. If you want only your local rules to be used, just specify that file as the configuration; for example, the simplest way to start snort using only your own rules is a command like "snort -c rules.local".

If your rules are not typed correctly snort will not start. Open the file up again and double check your syntax. Don't forget the trailing semicolon after the last option.

Dynamic rules allow one packet to trigger another rule. This is helpful when detecting scans or attack methods that depend on a sequence of traffic events. A dynamic rule looks like this:

```
activate udp any any -> any 69 (content:"GET hacktool.exe";
activates: 1;)
```

```
dynamic udp any any -> any 69 (activated_by:1; count:100;)
```

If someone uses TFTP to try to upload hacktool.exe, we will log the next 100 bytes so we can perhaps see what the tool was or where it was coming from.

The hardest part about creating snort rules is determining the proper signature. You want to find the traffic if it really happens (true positive) but avoid falsely identifying the attack (false positive) as much as possible. Only solid testing by either running the attack yourself or using a packet crafter such as hping2 to simulate the traffic can help you determine if the rule is efficient or not.

Sometimes it is easier to accept some traffic first before letting that traffic be analyzed by additional rules. In other words, a host that regularly runs vulnerability scans on the home network would fill your logs with false positives unless you tell snort to pass all traffic it generates. If the IP address of the scanner is 192.168.1.10 then the rule would look like this (all one line):

```
pass tcp 192.168.1.10 any -> $HOME_NET any (msg:"Pass from the
nessus scanner"; sid:1000000;)
```

TRY IT OUT

Learn More About Snort

The users manual for snort is only about 100 pages and can be worked through in a single day. Snort is included with Backtrack Linux, so there is no need to install it. At the very least, look over the snort man page and the snort configuration file.

```
man snort

cat /etc/snort/snort.conf
```

TRY IT OUT CHALLENGE

There is an excellent virtual appliance called NST (Network Security Toolkit) that already has snort and several plugins that create a nice web-based front end for administration and log viewing. Just search for "NST VMware appliance" and it will show right up. Take an hour or two to get it up and running, perhaps monitor some Internet noise for a day or two, and see how your humble home router is constantly being pounded on.

Know How to Deploy Honeypots

- Understanding the nature of honeypots
- Honeypot types
  - Try it out: Learn more about honeypots

Understanding the Nature of Honeypots

Honeypots, honeynets, and honeytokens are all designed to attract attackers with the idea that monitoring systems will allow the attacker to be observed. The terms are a matter of scale; a honeypot is a host, a honeynet is a network, and a honeytoken is a piece of monitored data. "Honeypot" is a generic term we will use inclusively.

Before organizations can deploy a honeypot, they need to verify this tactic will not violate the privacy rights of the attacker. The covert honeypots deployed by third party projects rest in a different category.

There is an art to setting up a decoy victim. It must look legitimate. It must not stand out or seem unusual or the attackers will notice it and avoid it. Honeypots are therefore not necessarily entirely exposed to risk. The term "bastion host" is used to describe one that is. A bastion host is completely exposed and therefore must be completely hardened because it is getting no help.

A honeypot cannot create additional risk; otherwise, it might become a weapon against its owner. If the honeypot is compromised in a manner that evades the monitoring systems, and at the same time gives the attacker an enhanced perspective, the "tables are turned," as the saying goes.

Honeypot Types

Given the challenges of deploying honeypots, a variety of products exist. The choice is largely about a balance of risk, accuracy, and administrative distraction from the production hosts personnel are supposed to be paying constant attention to.

Given this, there are different levels of honeypot products available.

- Physical honeypots
- Virtual honeypots
- Low interaction
- High interaction

Physical honeypots

Physical honeypots can be as simple as an unlocked bicycle leaning against a wall. Just because it is there and unlocked does not mean permission has been given by its owner to take it. Theft is still theft regardless of how weak or nonexistent the countermeasure is.

Physical honeypots can be considered psychological tests. They are full-on configured systems with value that are heavily monitored.

Virtual honeypots

A sacrificial host can be set up on the network that has real services running on a real operating system but contains only fictional data, if any at all. This could be the most convincing form of honeypot, but it introduces great risk.

Without formalized configuration, release, and change management processes in place that communicate such efforts, the honeypot will appear as rouge infrastructure and cause internal time wasting wargames.

If the physical honeypot is compromised while remaining undetected, it can become a weapon against the network. IDS systems may have been told to pass all traffic coming from the honeypot; this is clearly a big mistake.

Low interaction

This form of honeypot appears to a scanner as an access point, but only logs probing activity. Since this is a host of no production value, all access attempts are considered suspicious.

There is little to no risk involved with this decoy because it is not capable of interaction.

High interaction

This form of honeypot is a risk. It can be fully compromised and must be separated from any network segments that have production value. The monitoring capabilities of this type of honeypot facilitate the gathering of information that would not be noticed by NIDS. If the attackers managed to evade the network-based intrusion detection, then we hope they find this diversion and attack it. With diligent monitoring, detection of the larger picture plan of the attacker is possible.

TRY IT OUT

Learn More About Honeypots

There is an entire community that supports various honeynet projects. The efforts of these defense-minded hackers help both independent individuals and commercial researchers. Take a few moments to look over these resources.

`http://www.honeynet.org`

Know the Testing and Evasion Techniques

- Scanning for firewalls, IDS, and honeypots
- Simple evasion techniques
- Packet crafting
  - Try it out: Explore the hping tool
- Changing signatures
- Creating tunnels and reversing shells

Scanning for Firewalls, IDS, and Honeypots

For the attacker, figuring out where the filters are is critical. This is also a primary difference between the white hat penetration test and true attacks; the filters and monitoring systems are often moved out of the way for simple assessments.

Attackers want to know what their barriers are, and this also plays a major role in the scanning phase of an attack. Not to repeat this too much, but the reconnaissance and scanning phases are often the difference between attacks that are graceful and never discovered, and those that cause an explosion with a fast escape.

Fingerprinting firewalls involves some basic techniques:

- Traceroute
- Banner grabbing

- Look for any open port that can be accessed
- Port scanning
- Firewalking

Traceroute

Knowing the path to the target host is critical when interpreting the results of all other scans.

Traceroutes help the hacker make sure she doesn't inadvertently attack hosts that don't belong to the target organization. It also helps distinguish hosts and gateways, which each demand different scanning techniques.

If two or more hops appear with the same IP address, that suggests a load balancer or cluster. Logically, several hardware things cooperating as one logical machine might not make a difference to the attacker, or it might. Either way it is good information.

Banner grabbing

Using a client as Telnet, attackers can try to connect to any access point that has been discovered and attempt to get information. Correct instructions must be sent relative to the expected service to achieve full interaction, but even those that return only errors often reveal important information.

Look for any open port that can be accessed

Regarding a routing firewall, there are two major issues: the firewall itself and the hosts that can be reached beyond it.

Certain ports that are showing as open give away clues about the nature of the possible routing firewall itself. IP protocol ID 47 reveals support for GRE (Generic Router Encapsulation). This often is accompanied by TCP ports 1723 or 1701 and could reveal a potential VPN gateway.

Traceroute is the most common way to find a series of routers, each of which can also be a filter. It is important to be able to use a variety of scanning techniques including the basic ICMP type 8 as well as methods such as ACK scans. If the output of the traceroute tool shows two hosts with the same IP source address, this can be an indication of a NAT (Network Address Translation) server or a load balancing device.

Port scanning

Port scanning is conducted against both of the routing firewalls and hosts that are possibly running firewall software themselves. The point of view the security practitioner holds is complex and filled with policies and paperwork. The attacker just cares about what she can access.

Firewalking

A firewalk scan requires three hosts: the scanner, the gateway, and the destination.

The scanner sends traffic to the destination and informs the firewalk tool what the gateway is. Firewalk then sets the TTL (Time to Live) value of each packet it sends to one hop past the gateway to the destination. If the gateway passes this traffic, the destination will respond with an ICMP type 11 (Time exceeded) and the attacker knows the port is open. If not, the packet is dropped at the gateway.

Simple Evasion Techniques

Real time IDS systems such as signature-based analyzers can be fooled if they aren't set up correctly or are not installed on hardware that is robust enough to handle the load on their segment. Simple command line tools can play havoc in these circumstances.

- Fragmented traffic
- Encryption
- Decoy traffic
- Denial of service

Fragmented traffic

"Fragrouter" is a command line tool available for Linux that allows the attacker to ensure that all packets sent to a particular host will be fragmented to the size the attacker can specify. IDS must reassemble these fragments before the full analysis can take place. This keeps the IDS busy and might cause it to let other packets through during times of high network load.

Do not confuse this tool with "fragroute" which is capable of being an inline packet modification tool, otherwise called a "packet shaper."

Encryption

Security policies must specify when encryption is mandated and when it is forbidden. This is the only way attack traffic can at least be flagged as suspicious even when a determination cannot be made as to what the attack is exactly.

Encryption countermeasures can sometimes be used to create covert channels for attackers. If the host end points that have established tunnels are compromised, the attacker might not need to even care about encryption. If anything, it is sometimes a benefit to them. IDS tools cannot analyze encrypted traffic unless they are given the ability to decode the packets. This exposes the keys to more risk or further complicates key issuance and management.

Decoy traffic

Tools such as nmap include options for generating packets with random IP addresses and port numbers that can be mixed in with the actual attack packets. The IDS might register a lot of false positives, and the analyst must figure out what is real and what isn't.

Denial of service

As a last resort, the IDS might be denial of service based on the underlying operating system or on a flaw in the IDS code itself. The problem will be fixed quickly if there is someone paying attention, such as personnel in a SOC (Security Operations Center) However, it might buy just enough time for the attacker that is conducting the access step to plant the maintaining access code.

Packet Crafting

There are many ways to craft packets. Programmers that use languages such as PERL can automate the creating of traffic they have complete control over. A packet amounts to a series of bits. These bits can be captured, manipulated, parsed, adjusted, created, and sent in any way attackers might need as long as they know what is required for a given attack. Understanding how this works is central to the entire CEH course.

The command line tool Hping is one of the coolest and easiest to use packet crafters for testing firewalls and IDS. It comes with Backtrack Linux. As a side note, there are different versions of this tool and the associated manual pages. If entering "hping" doesn't work, try "hping2" or "hping3". One of them will be there.

Let's discuss one example of hping to get started. The rest is all about reading the manual page and applying the skills discussed throughout this book.

```
hping3 -I eth0 --spoof 1.2.3.4 -p 80 -S 192.168.3.6
```

This command says: "Use the eth0 interface to send traffic that sets the source IP address to 1.2.3.4 with the SYN flag set in the TCP header and targets this packet to port 80 on host 192.168.3.6".

TRY IT OUT

Explore the Hping Tool

Take a moment to view the manual page for hping. Remember that it might be called hping2 or hping3 as well. Open a shell terminal in your Linux distro and issue:

```
CDT man hping
```

Notice how the command options match up to the RFCs that previous "Try It Out" exercises have recommended you read. Consider the hacking possibilities this tool offers.

Changing Signatures

If packet crafting will take too much time, another approach is to attempt to change the signatures of all traffic that is sent. Signatures based on sequence of bytes in the data layer can often be circumvented if the bytes under analysis are changed.

Injection attacks involve adding bytes to the data. If the signature is too strict, an attacker might be able to change values that have nothing to do with the signature but would cause the analysis rule to decide on a false negative. Some tools that attempt these techniques are listed below:

- SideStep
- ADMutate

- Fragrouter
- NIDSBench

Creating Tunnels and Reversing Shells

Any packet can be enveloped in another one. Also, protocols that specify arbitrary data in the payload area can also be used as tunnels.

An ICMP type 8 message (Ping request) does not specify what should be echoed. The RFC just says "data. . . ." The tool "loki" is capable of taking a message, splitting it up into pieces, and sending each piece as a part of the echo request in a type 8 message.

Enveloping packets is even easier. Consider the following:

|IP 1| TCP 1 | Data 1| can be encapsulation as a data payload for:

|IP 2| TCP 2 | .... Packet 1 ....|

The catch is that something on the receiving end must understand the encapsulation. The point is that the same principle that applies to VPNs (Virtual Private Networks) can also be applied to covert attack channels.

Reverse shells happen because there are SPI firewalls. This type of firewall prevents incoming connection attempts, but allows the return of traffic generated from requests. This principle tells the attacker that in simple terms the victim must ask to be attacked.

Social engineering now enters the game. At the same time, technologies such as Skype, public video conferencing services, and commercial license schemes all use technologies specifically designed to ask the victim to volunteer.

Conclusion

We have just about completed the picture. The EC-Council model for attack has been outlined: "Reconnaissance, Scanning, Gaining Access, Maintaining Access, Clearing Tracks." There are many other aspects of these phases that don't fit conveniently into rigid categories. These are the optional modules that are included within the official courseware.

The next step is to take a break, consider the previous chapters in a bigger picture view, and make sure you are comfortable with the material; then read the next two chapters.

Chapter 19 describes the optional chapters and includes some critical highlights that are relevant to the CEH exam, in spite of the fact that these are optional chapters.

Chapter 20 describes the professional context of this course. It addresses the question of how a CEH can professionally apply these skills in a defensive and professional matter.

SUMMARY OF OPTIONAL MODULES

Introduction

In the official CEH courseware, several modules are included on the DVDs that come with the printed materials along with about 13Gs+ of tools, source code, and research papers. There is not enough time in the approved training format to cover all of these modules, and the exam is not supposed to cover this material. However, the author has experienced that some of this information is in fact on the exam.

Care has been taken to include the overlap material in the other chapters of this book. The idea behind this chapter is simply to describe each of the optional chapters, make a comment or two about each, and provide important information that should not be overlooked. This chapter also provides some text taking tips for dealing with those questions that seem to come from nowhere. Usually, there is a way to answer them even if you are not completely familiar with something you see.

To Pass the CEH Exam You Need to . . .

• Approaching the weird questions

• know the basics behind the topics in the optional materials

Approaching the Weird Questions

EC-Council has taken great lengths to future proof the material and the core of the CEH class covers basic fundamental skills. The variables within attack steps are always present; the most recent exploit tools can be interchanged with the older "proof of concept" well-known stuff. The steps remain essentially the same.

If you can master the core materials, you will have the skills to master the optional material as well. Apply your instincts, then choose the correct tool or technique now that you know what all is out there.

As is the case with all credible certifications, about 10 percent of the questions are considered "control questions," or those that seem to come from random places or have paradoxical choices. The latest version of the CEH exam is well written and fair. The control questions should not make the difference between passing and failing. However, it would be a wise strategy to be able to pick a few of them up just in case it makes a difference.

This author has seen far too many students get a 69.9 percent (70 percent is passing) for one of three reasons:

- Not taking time
- Not meeting prerequisites
- Not knowing some current events

Not taking time

You get four hours to take the exam. You paid for this time. There are no extra points for being the first to finish. Logic then dictates that a sensible person would use up as much of the four hours as necessary to fully commit to and believe that she has solved the entire exam as a whole. It is a complete puzzle.

Taking any multiple choice, technical exam allows you to mark questions and to return to them. (CEH does, truly evil exams from other vendors might not.) In this way, you can reduce the size of the test on the first pass. Answer the questions that you absolutely know the answers to, and mark the others for a second pass.

By now the test is smaller, and some of the questions can be answered based on what you know from the explanatory material within the others. Take a break. Then pass through the marked questions with a finely tuned point of view. Mark the control questions and keep an even pace that is a bit slower than the first go around; reduce the exam further.

Now you might already have passed. DO NOT TAKE THIS FOR GRANTED! Put your best effort into the remaining questions and pick up one or two more; it might be the difference. The bottom line is that a prepared student will pass this test. The tricky questions will not be a valid excuse because if you score a 69 percent or less it will be from questions that could have been answered correctly or from careless test-taking efforts.

The control questions are a psychometric "psych out" to make sure you focus on the wrong things after the exam is over. It is hard to remember what you just experienced while obsessing over a question that had two equally correct answers. This is a common tactic to prevent "braindumps" and other methods of exam compromise. Even the smartest and most observant people fall for the illusions and diversions of professional magicians. It is human nature. But now you know the trick.

Prepare and you will pass. The control questions will not be the difference in your score. It is a fair test. Knowing this going in is the shortcut.

Not meeting prerequisites

It is possible to pass this exam without the assumed knowledge, but your comfort level will be greatly enhanced if the following criteria are met. Keep in mind that the spirit of the CEH is to begin a journey, not to mark the end of one. An adventurous attitude will make the entire process both enjoyable and ultimately more beneficial. The prerequisites of this class are basically the following:

- A thorough knowledge of the OSI networking model
- An instinctive ability to covert binary, hex, and decimal numbers
- An understanding of network addressing
- An understanding of fundamental network administration
- The equivalent of a CompTIA Security+ certification or a CISSP

Not knowing some current events

The CEH exam is a mix of hacking fundamentals and new ideas. Information technology is a discipline, and most disciplines have basics. Even experienced veterans forget the basics now and then due to arrogance or false assumptions. Attackers are waiting for such opportunities.

Take the ideas in the CEH curriculum and apply them to the situations of tomorrow and you will find they fit quite well. This is the attitude of the defensive hacker; Respect for the fundamentals mixed with critical thinking and a creative application.

No set of "practice exams" can ever replace this preparation. This is not a test with answers to memorize. However, if you understand the material, you can pass it.

Know the Basics Behind the Topics in the Optional Materials

- Discuss the optional CEH modules
  - Try it out: Investigate VoIP hacking tools

Discuss the Optional CEH Modules

This and the next chapter will discuss some of the less-than-direct knowledge that can provide an edge on passing the CEH exam. Complete slide presentations are provided on the official courseware kits, but they may not be required to be covered during the live class.

Some basics have already been covered. As pre-study or review, use this list as a guideline for topics that information security practitioners should keep an eye on while moving forward in their career.

- Covert hacking
- Writing virus codes
- Assembly language tutorials
- Exploit writing
- Reverse engineering
- MAC OS X hacking
- Hacking routers, cable modems, and firewalls
- Hacking mobile phones, PDA, and handheld devices
- Bluetooth hacking
- VoIP hacking
- RFID hacking
- Spamming
- Hacking USB devices
- Hacking database servers
- Cyber warfare hacking Al-Qaida and terrorism
- Internet content filtering techniques
- Privacy on the Internet
- Securing laptop computers
- Spying technologies
- Corporate espionage
- Creating security policies
- Software piracy and warez
- Hacking and cheating at online games
- Hacking RSS and Atom
- Hacking web browsers
- Proxy server technologies
- Preventing data loss
- Hacking GPS
- Computer forensics and incident handling

- Credit card frauds
- How to steal passwords
- Firewall technologies
- Threats and countermeasures
- Case studies
- Botnets
- Economic espionage
- Patch management
- Security convergence
- Identifying terrorists

Covert hacking

A covert channel is a mechanism for sending or receiving data between hosts without alerting any firewalls or intrusion detection systems. Covert channels are undetected by monitoring devices and, therefore, are not mitigated.

Cryptography and steganography are two common forms of techniques for creating covert channels. Tunneled protocols can provide covert data in movement while other technologies can provide secrecy for data at rest or in processing. This can be as sophisticated as hidden processes and semaphores within computing systems or as simple as piggybacking on the payloads of legitimate traffic.

Writing virus codes

The art of creating viruses is controversial even when it is studied from a defensive mind-set. The goal is to cause the effect in the fewest bytes of instructions, while spreading effectively and evading detection. This is a lot to consider in what sometimes amounts to only a few hundred bytes or even less.

Virus writers and security researchers are playing a perpetual game of strategic dominance. Opportunities range from flaws within applications and operating systems to manipulation of common protocols as they are designed to work. The possible dangers are only limited by the skill and creativity of the creator.

Assembly language tutorials

While it is not necessary to be an assembly level programmer to pass the CEH, for those who are interested in exploring this skill, the official courseware provides an excellent tutorial to get started. Prepare for hours of concentration and focused thinking.

Exploit writing

After completing the assembly tutorials, it is a good idea to learn how exploits are written and then how to disassemble them for reverse engineering. This is the approach for learning how to reverse engineer malicious code that is captured in the wild. It takes years of practice and insight to be effective, but there is always a way to start anything and there is no substitute for diving in. If this is something you want to do, you just have to work at it.

Reverse engineering

This module goes along with several previous modules and describes some of the tools such as IDA Pro and OllyDBG that are used to convert machine language to assembly so the activities of the code can be understood and reconstructed.

Decompilers are also discussed. These tools attempt to reproduce high-level language code, which is sometimes easier to understand than the assembly. Decompilers are valuable for troubleshooting and for getting a better "sense" of what a program or library is meant to accomplish.

MAC OS X hacking

The Macintosh operating system is fast becoming a favorite among penetration testers and hackers alike. While it has yet to enjoy deep market penetration in the business world, many students and other individuals are adopting it along with the many other mobile devices that Apple has produced.

The MAC OS has a reputation for being extremely secure. This is driven in part by its use of the BSD code base. Some argue that it is relatively untested in relation to Windows- and Unix-based platforms. There are some vulnerabilities, however, that have been used and demonstrated in public environments. Sometimes, these are mistaken for third-party hardware issues, and this is one of the reasons Apple is so insistent on being a closed technology.

Hacking routers, cable modems, and firewalls

This module focuses more on the home user than on enterprise or backbone class routers. Home routers are not expected to handle a lot of traffic yet are constantly scanned and bombarded with attacks. Most of the tools that hit these targets are automated crawlers that simply go from IP address to IP address looking for easy hits.

Some home routers are opened for experimentation and can be "flashed" with new operating system images. A hobbyist market exists for exploring the possibilities of the relatively inexpensive hardware. Most exploits, however, come from default configuration weaknesses or the lack of critical updates. If attackers can gain access to the administrative interface of a home router, then they own the whole house.

Hacking mobile phones, PDA, and handheld devices

Mobile phones are often the business lifelines of many professionals. They are increasingly tied to web-based data access and are at the same time used as authentication tokens to extremely confidential and critical services.

The hardware and operating systems are different than all-purpose, personal computers. There must be a delicate balance between memory storage, processing power, form factor, and battery life. Each device carries with it potential vectors of attack; mostly, however, physical attacks will always be the easiest angle.

Bluetooth hacking

Bluetooth has proven to be a fairly secure protocol but there are a few ways it can be repurposed by a hacker. PANs (Personal Area Networks) are essentially the domain of Bluetooth technology, and the occurence of such applications is increasingly common in public places. The need for speed, distance, and more "automagic" (configures) pairing is desired by consumers and will continue to present interesting opportunities for the hacker.

VoIP hacking

VoIP (Voice over Internet Protocol) is fast replacing common analog telephone systems. Digital convergence of voice, data, and multimedia on the same network is enabling a powerful set of opportunities for communication and collaboration that were, only a short time ago, considered science fiction.

Since this is all essentially data, attacks that are network based apply. Denial of service, sniffing, and injection attacks are attractive to attackers who can access a network that is known to carry VoIP traffic. Many sniffing tools such as Cain and Able can reconstruct captured VoIP data into MP3 format for listening.

TRY IT OUT

Investigate VoIP Hacking Tools

Take a look at the following open source tools from noted developer Jason Ostrom.

Voice Hopper

`http://voiphopper.sourceforge.net/`

UCSniff

`http://ucsniff.sourceforge.net/`

RFID hacking

Radio frequency ID (RFID) gadgets are showing up everywhere. For years they have been embedded in consumer products. More recently they have been used in passports and other identification devices.

Eavesdropping and denial of service attacks have received the bulk of media attention, but a far deeper risk includes the privacy concerns. If chips the size of a grain of sand (or smaller) can hold enough data to personally identify you, your every movement can be registered by larger equipment and stored in a database. If that grain of sand or molecular-sized device were misplaced, what could you be liable for?

Considering the unfortunate fact that individuals are not the inherent copyright owner of data about themselves, the implications of RFID go far beyond catching shoplifters or purchasing gasoline conveniently or driving through a roadway toll booth without having to stop.

Spamming

Unsolicited e-mail has been dramatically reduced by sophisticated filtering products, but those who send spam are too motivated to give up that easily. They adapt their tactics to evade the filters or simply come up with other ways to convince users to visit a site or view a message.

Irrelevant or deceptive notices on usenet, bulletin boards, and forums are also considered spam and are not usually filtered effectively because we trust the page that is loading.

The underground network of spammers, 419 scams, and spear fishers have mature business models and know how to find resources. Rogue ISPs, free hosting services, and botnets are all used in the distribution of this material.

Hacking USB devices

USB devices range from HIDs (Human Interface Devices) such as keyboards and pointing devices to high speed external storage. Speeds up to 4.8Gbps (USB 3.0) and the decreasing physical size of high capacity storage makes it easy to copy large amounts of data quickly.

USB thumbdrives can be considered as essentially "high capacity floppies" in the sense that "sneakernet" has once again become a convenient way to exchange files. This also means that virus activity has found an old-new way to become active again.

Some USB devices act as "dongles" or authentication tokens. The credentials are stored in firmware on the chip inside of the device and can be attacked through electronic probing. Other devices have been discovered to have buffer overflow problems in the embedded drivers that allow the USB device to run on a system.

Hacking database servers

Everything is about data these days. Cheap storage and faster connections have sent the trend toward collecting anything and everything that can be learned about customers. Databases are also the heart of most commercial applications in one way or another. All forms of databases are vulnerable to attack, whether they are simple text files or complex enterprise level products.

Many attack vectors against databases are possible. They include:

- Direct connection via the Internet
- Vulnerability scanning
- Enumerating the SQL resolution service
- Cracking passwords of default accounts
- Direct exploits against the database manager
- SQL injection
- Blind SQL injection
- Reverse engineering
- Google hacks or discovery queries
- Source code analysis

Cyber warfare hacking Al-Qaida and terrorism

Cyber-terrorism comes in the form of three attacks: physical attacks, EA (Electronic Attacks), and CNA (Computer Network Attacks). When the attacks are sponsored by a government, covert corporation, or terrorist group, the resources are almost unlimited. Communications that are reliable and readily available, such as twitter, can be used to plan elaborate physical attacks while all members retain anonymity even to each other.

Hacktivism also plays a role in the sense that the objective of the attacks might be influenced by particularly unique motivations. The goal might not be to gain something, but to cause damage and disruption, including, at times, the loss of human life.

On a more individual level, bullying and stalking are also major problems because it is so easy to do and physical proximity is not necessarily required. Due to the permanence of data on the Internet, once a person's reputation has been attacked, even when it is completely unfair, it is next to impossible to remove the information and repair all perceptions.

Internet content filtering techniques

Content filters can be installed as host-based or network-based firewalls. The host-based variety limits the ability of the web browser to make queries for certain content. Pornographic images and advertisement blocking are common uses for these tools.

Internet content filtering on the network is conducted by a class of firewalls that can look inside Layer 7 data, not just protocol information. This is also sometimes called "deep packet inspection." The primary purposes for content filtering include enforcing acceptable use policies and collecting forensic evidence.

One of the challenges of content filtering is context. Certain words or phrases are passable in some situations but not in others. For this reason, reporting and user profiles are configured so possible violations of policy can be accurately analyzed.

Privacy on the Internet

There is none. It is that simple.

Securing laptop computers

Mobile devices are increasingly common in today's "never unplugged" business world. Netbook class computers are as capable as any laptop needs to be, in most cases, and their low cost and high portability makes it increasingly attractive to take important data on the road. It seems as though once a month another story hits the news regarding a stolen laptop, netbook, or cell phone that reveals thousands of sensitive documents or database records.

Operating systems such as the Palm WebOS and the open source "Android OS" make transparent and constant integration with backend services as easy as entering an address and a password. These credentials are usually stored and automatically used, and the phone itself has no idea who is operating it. Even though the technology in terms of connectivity might be secure, the fact that a misplaced device can be picked up and used by anyone is a major concern.

Hard drive encryption is one solution, but sometimes there are ways to get around this. Plus, the more secure the system, the greater the risk of using everything if the password is forgotten.

GPS devices can be embedded in the hardware as a tracking device. Another approach using tools such as "PAL PC tracker" sends an e-mail whenever the laptop connects to the Internet, and the source IP address can be used to locate the attacker.

Spying technologies

This module focuses mostly on hardware solutions. The bottom line is that cameras and sound recorders can be hidden in almost anything, and obtaining them is easy for anyone as these devices are sold on the Internet.

Corporate espionage

Espionage is defined as, "The use of illegal means to obtain information." This is another reason the insider threat is the most dangerous, as accomplishing espionage often requires a level of access that only an insider would have.

There are several different categories of insider threats:

- Pure insiders (example: user with privileged access)
- Insider associate (example: a repair technician)
- Insider affiliates (example: spouse or family member posing as the insider)
- Outside affiliates (example: breaking in or just walking in through a door)

Techniques for conducting industrial espionage include:

- Social engineering
- Dumpster diving
- Information extraction
- Network leakage
- Cryptography
- Steganography

Creating security policies

Writing good policies is one of the most important skills of the security practitioner. Communicating the policy is the most crucial step of enforcement. The lack of solid, well-designed policies presents potential liability issues for publicly traded companies, and government-driven organizations are almost completely run off of them.

Policies must be clearly written, enforceable, and completely supported by senior management. Risk management, contingency planning, and system management processes are all affected by security policies. It is also important to design the right level of policy to fit the situation. Security policy levels include:

- Paranoid (locked down tight)
- Prudent (sensible and balanced)
- Permissive (relaxed with minimal protections)
- Promiscuous (wide open)

Software piracy and warez

Sometimes referred to tongue-in-cheek as "extended evaluation" software, there are those who believe copyright enforcement is not moral, and that a service is being performed when license enforcement techniques are reverse engineered and broken.

Software that has been purchased often involves entering a license key to register the application after it has been installed. One of the inherent problems with this type of SAS (Software Authentication Service) is that the routines that check the key for a particular format must be in memory and can be tracked down using a disassembler such as OllyDBG or IDA Pro. Once the check of the key is figured out, a "keygen" is created, which is simply a tool that generates license keys that will be considered valid by the application.

Some vendors have adopted a system that requires the application to have Internet access and must "phone home" to present the key to an online SAS. It is occasionally possible to circumvent this by telling the application that you have no connection and must use a fax machine or perform a manual registration over the phone. The pirate simply creates a type of keygen that would give the same type of number anyway. The practice of "phoning home" is controversial, as some companies take liberties to send usage information and other data the user may not be aware of.

Many sites on the Internet offer "warez," "keygens," and "serialz." It should be expected that these sites will attempt to compromise the visitor's web browser and that whatever is downloaded will be trojanized. It simply is not safe even to look for this software. Other methods of distribution include bittorrent sites and even auctions on eBay.

The BSA (Business Software Alliance) provides legal support to software vendors when it is suspected that a company is not observing the constraints agreed upon in the license. Anonymous tips are often provided by former or disgruntled employees.

Hacking and cheating at online games

Online games often include entire multiplayer virtual worlds where participants can interact with each other from anywhere in the world. There is even real world monetary value given to virtual objects and property. Additionally, some games provide an API (Application Programming Interface) that allows the game environment to be extended by independent programmers.

Common attacks are the basic stealing of login passwords using malicious infections such as keyloggers, screen capture tools, and proxy servers. Denial of service attacks and various forms of cheating, such as collusion and automating tasks that are supposed to be played, are also common.

Hacking RSS and Atom

RSS (Really Simple Syndication) and Atom are XML document formats that deliver micro-content collected from websites. Many news and content-driven sites provide these feeds as a service to their viewers to make it easier and quicker to peruse the latest headlines and stories that have been posted. Multimedia such as podcasts can also be distributed this way.

RSS is also used in software version management systems such as CVS (Concurrent Versions System) and "Subversion." Open source projects hosted by sites such as *http://www.sourceforge.org* can be tracked using the project feeds.

When feeds are used as input to web applications, XSRF (Cross Site Request Forgery) and XSS (Cross Site Scripting) attacks might be possible. Since RSS feeds can contain multimedia, the risks of unsecure ActiveX controls is also present. Additionally, problems in the XMLHttp and XMLHttpRequest methods that are used in Ajax applications can be exploited; the XML document structure of RSS and Atom feeds are ideally suited for these applications and are increasingly common.

Hacking web browsers

Web browsers have been continuously changing and adding features in an effort to impress users and compete for market share. Firefox supports a plug-in architecture, and third-party developers have created some amazing utilities that can be used for page analysis and application testing.

Don't make the mistake of assuming that only IE (Internet Explorer) has exploitable vulnerabilities. Many attacks, such as stealing passwords from the cache object, have been demonstrated. Cookie stealing and Session ID hijacking are also possible in almost all browsers that support JavaScript.

In the case of IE, several vulnerabilities have been found in the way it handles URL protocol handlers (example: *html:// mhtml:// telnet://*) and in the rendering engines of BHO (Browser Helper Objects) such as the .jpeg viewer and .vml viewers. Objects such as "History" and "Default Home Page" settings are exposed to JavaScript and attackers have used these to serve advertisements or to redirect the user to malicious sites.

Proxy server technologies

Proxy servers broker connections on behalf of a client request. Using the Socks5 protocol (TCP port 1080), proxy servers can be chained together and, if they do not keep any logging records, provide anonymity for the original client source.

The drawback of proxy servers is that the client application must realize it is connecting to a proxy server. This is not a problem for web browsers but could be for other applications. Speed is another issue; a performance decrease is often noticeable.

There are several types of proxy servers:

- Caching servers (serve requested documents from a local location)
- Web proxy (serves frequently requested web pages from a local location)
- Anonymizing proxy (keeps the client source hidden)
- Hostile proxy (used to eavesdrop on the data flow between a client and server)
- Intercepting proxy (enforces acceptable use policies)
- Forced proxy (combination of intercepting and hostile proxies)
- Open proxy (accessible to anyone on the network or Internet)
- Split proxy server (two software proxies installed on two different hosts)
- Reverse proxy (can be used to hide the server rather than the client)
- Circumventor (allows a user to bypass other proxies and view blocked content)
- Transparent proxy (doesn't change the request or response)
- Non-transparent proxy (does change the request or response)

Open proxies on the Internet are provided by several companies as well as by individuals, and the addresses can change constantly. The TOR (The Onion Router) network was once supported by the EFF (Electronic Frontier Foundation) but is now a standalone project (*http://www.torproject.org/*) and access is available to anyone.

Preventing data loss

Data loss can occur through intentional actions, unintentional actions, or hardware failure. An efficient and well-tested DRP (Disaster Recovery Plan) must exist in order to safely recover if data loss should occur.

Basic fundamental security practices must be implemented to prevent data loss. These include using updated anti-virus scanners, timely backups, and a secure physical environment.

EC-Council provides training products called E|DRP (EC-Council Disaster Recovery Planning) and CHFI (Certified Hacking Forensic Investigator), which both cover the topic of data recovery extensively.

Hacking GPS

The Global Positioning System (GPS) is run by 24 satellites positioned 11,000 nautical miles above the earth's surface. The system is comprised of these satellites, of monitoring and control stations on earth, and of the GPS receivers utilized by users that lock into the satellites that are available from their current position. Coordinates in three dimensions (latitude, longitude, and altitude) provide an accurate location anywhere in the world to an unlimited number of people.

GPS can be used for amazing purposes including the WAAS (Wide Area Augmentation System) that can provide support to aircraft for all phases of a flight including take off and landing. When used for navigation, waypoints (coordinates combinations) can be set into the GPS receiver to plan a navigation path or to find the way back to the original position.

One problem with the dependence on GPS is what to do if the system isn't working. Jamming signals are sometimes used as a DoS attack against receivers in the area. Other factors in the GPS satellite system can cause temporary errors or inaccurate positions. Also, some receivers cannot lock onto satellite signals if there are too many obstructions, such as occurs with the levels of a parking garage.

Computer forensics and incident handling

Recovering an evidence image is all about accuracy and making sure the original materials are not altered or compromised during the recovery. It is important to approach this perfectly every time because it is never known until the investigation is conducted what will have been collected.

CSIRTs (Computer Security Incident Response Teams) are assembled and will test and rehearse all incident response scenarios in order to prepare for the real events that occur. The practice of the forensics portion of the response plan includes:

- Preservation
- Identification
- Extraction

- Interpretation
- Documentation

Forensics is a growing, high-demand area that is its own discipline apart from information assurance, but many CEH professionals will crossover at different times in their career.

Credit card frauds

E-Crime is a constant problem in a world that is increasingly dependent on Internet-based communications. "Skimming" machines are used by "Carders" to capture and reproduce the information held on the magnetic strips most credit cards use. While the exact way that credit card numbers are generated is an industry secret, many attempts at reverse engineering this process exist and both websites and standalone tools provide simple credit card generators.

Fraud control techniques use sophisticated data mining techniques to reduce fraud to less than 0.5 percent of all transactions. This number is still too high, but this is one example of a positive use of data mining and collection. The company "Maxmind" provides a service called "minFraud" that can detect possible fraud in real time and distribute the data across a network of partners in real time.

How to steal passwords

Without the use of multi-factor authentication, passwords are still the dominant method of authentication because they are cheap and easy to implement. Unfortunately, no matter how solid the encryption technologies are behind the scenes, passwords are often the weakest part of any authentication service.

Firewall technologies

The Firewalls, IDS, and Honeypots chapter in this book covers this material, but the additional information provided in this module might answer remaining questions and provide some overview information about the configuration of a few specific firewall products.

Threats and countermeasures

Weighing in at 906 slides, this module provides a checklist of policy and security settings that can be used for an audit or pentest.

Case studies

This module is an interesting collection of news stories taken from various sources about attacks on both large and medium scales. These case studies are worth reading because they provide some context for the entire CEH knowledge base, and illustrate how much of this material has been used in actual attacks.

Botnets

Botnets (Robot Networks) are collections of compromised hosts that communicate with each other or can be controlled from a central location called the C&CC (Command and Control Center). The agents that belong to the botnet are commanded to steal information, to distribute additional malware, or to conduct DDoS (Distributed Denial of Service) attacks.

One of the primary benefits of the botnet approach is that it can overcome stateful inspection firewalls by establishing outgoing connections.

Research companies deploy honeypots on the Internet to aid in the tracking and observation of botnet activity. As a result, the botnets themselves are constantly evolving to include encrypting commands, and spreading the C&CC out to distributed architectures to avoid being located. Some of the most infamous botnets that have been discovered in the wild include:

- SDBot
- RBot
- Agobot
- Spybot
- Mytob

Economic espionage

Economic espionage is generally considered a white-collar crime. Insider knowledge and theft of secrets that produce an economic advantage can circumvent an entire economic system of checks and balances. Trade secrets include: formulas, designs, prototypes, and engineering information.

The difference between industrial and economic espionage is the potential participation of governments. Economic espionage is conducted between nations, and as the world becomes more and more "flat" in the economic sense, governments sometimes find themselves at war with the corporate layer of authority that sometimes influences governing decisions.

Disruption of the economic systems of a nation can cause incalculable damage.

Patch management

Patch management is a critical part of securing any network. Tools such as SAS (Server Automation Systems) or Microsoft SUS (Software Update Services) can be used to help with this process as well as standalone tools like Qfecheck, HFNetChk, and UpdateExpert. This module explains in detail some best practices such as:

- Test patches, and make sure only tested patches are installed
- Have a proper change management, configuration management, and release management process in place to roll out patches
- Only get patches from the proper sources and verify them using digital signatures, checksums, and integrity checks
- There are also hotfixes, roll-ups, and service packs. All the best practices apply to these as well
- Make sure to patch not just operating systems but also all applications and services

Security convergence

Security convergence describes the process of blending technologies, security processes, and people to create new or improved capabilities. Programs and recommendations for security convergence include

- RAMCAP (Risk Analysis and Management for Critical Asset Protection)
- OSE (Open Security Exchange)
- ESM (Enterprise Security Management)
- Log collection (log shipping)

NOCs (Network Operation Centers) and SOCs (Security Operations Centers) are established both to make sure things run smoothly on a moment by moment basis and to monitor and analyze security events.

Identifying terrorists

As defined by the FBI, terrorism is "The unlawful use of force or violence against persons or property to intimidate or coerce a government or civilian population, or any segment thereof, in furtherance of political or social objectives is terrorism."

Two major categories are recognized: domestic and international.

What actually causes terrorism is a subject of fierce debate. Poverty is most often a wellspring of terrorist groups because it is easier to recruit people that have nothing to lose, are frustrated, and are capable of being influenced. Terrorist groups can provide them with jobs and the means to escape poverty, unless death comes first.

The FBI also identifies the following categories of terrorist behavior:

- Political (attempts to further a political objective such as stealing an election)
- Psychological (targets the fears of a person, community, or entire population)
- Coercive (the use of violence and destruction)
- Deliberate (carefully planned activities with discipline and patience)
- Dynamic (attempts to bring about revolution and alter the status of a nation)

Conclusion

The optional modules in the CEH official courseware are full of interesting and important information. In this chapter we just took a quick tour, but after passing the exam you will definitely want to read more.

Now that the model of an attack has been explored along with a variety of possible attack vectors, it is time for the white hat professional to consider what the professional approach would be that allows for monetizing these skills and conducting safe and ethical penetration attacks.

The next chapter covers the basics as well as provides a preview of the course that follows CEH. The ECSA/LPT (EC-Council Certified Security Analyst and the Licensed Penetration Tester) programs are the next step for those who wish to make the hacking mindset a livelihood.

Whether this is your ultimate goal or not, passing the CEH exam requires some familiarity with these ideas. Interpretation of the scenario-based questions will depend on having the correct attitude.

## CHAPTER TWENTY

PENETRATION TESTING

Introduction

People become CEH certified for different reasons. One major reason is to become a professional that manages IT departments or administers systems and wants to better understand the inside attacker and how various tools and attack processes work. Another major reason is to become a professional in the security field that performs assessments or works in a certification and accreditation capacity. In both cases, the subject of penetration testing will eventually arise.

There is a wide range of test types that can be ordered for different reasons. All tests, however, need to address legal issues, run as an organized project, and produce a deliverable that the client or customer has confidence in. The results of a test are expected to be put to a valuable, business-related purpose.

In other words, the penetration test is a professional manifestation of hacking skills, and is a way to make a living with the CEH certification and a defense-oriented mindset. If the reader should decide to go on to the ECSA/LPT program after CEH, make certain the training involves an intense hands-on experience. Talking about this process is not good enough. As it is with hacking, there is no substitute for having to perform each step of the test. This includes documenting and report writing.

In this chapter we will provide a very basic thumbnail sketch of the penetration testing process. It is meant to provide context for safely applying the skills that are acquired during the CEH process as well as a look ahead to the ECSA/LPT training course that follows it.

To Pass the CEH Exam You Need to . . .

- know general penetration testing methodologies
- know the basic requirements of an engagement
- know how to write an effective report
- know how to stay current with information
- master the CEH cheatsheets and practice questions!

Know General Penetration Testing Methodologies

- Reasons for conducting penetration tests
- Types of penetration tests
- Basics steps of the engagement

Reasons for Conducting Penetration Tests

The types of penetration tests range from simple tests of a single vulnerability to complex engagements that can last for months. The important thing is to have a clear business objective for ordering the test. Without this understanding, the scope of the test will not be defined and the appropriate documents that charter the project cannot be drafted.

Penetration tests might be performed for a number of reasons. They include:

- Research for risk management data
- Compliance
- Test incident response plans
- Verification of a false positive

Research for risk management data

Risk management is an ongoing process in an organization. When threats are analyzed, defenses that are already in place must be considered. The risk management team might not feel it has sufficient or accurate data on the true effectiveness of a risk plan, and a test to determine the true exposure level of a possible weakness can be ordered.

The web application, for example, might be protected by a WAF (Web Application Firewall) that the salesman said would block all XSS attacks. Being a newly certified CEH professional on the risk management team, you are skeptical. You suggest that the risk cannot be considered 100 percent mitigated until a thorough test of the web application is conducted.

The results of your test show that the WAF is effective against some threats but only partially effective against this one. A plan is set in motion to actually fix the application itself instead of relying solely on the WAF, and you receive a promotion and a raise.

Compliance

"Organizations are interested in compliance, not security" is a statement often made in information security circles.

Both assessments and penetration tests are part of this process and are valuable tools for measuring both the current state of security and the effectiveness of configuration and process changes that are made in order to achieve required security goals.

Stated in simple terms, assessments and penetration exams are a way to test policies and policy enforcement.

Test incident response plans

No plans are worth anything until they are tested. Incident response, business continuity planning, and disaster recovery planning are core responsibilities of any organization. For publicly traded companies, negligence issues can result if there is a lack of effort in this area.

Verification of a false positive

Assessments are sometimes just rough sketches of the current state of security levels within a network. Whenever the report shows critical vulnerabilities there is often a question of whether or not the vulnerability scanner simply reports a false positive; that is, something that looks like a vulnerability but really isn't.

Assessment tools like vulnerability scanners have three major caveats: They produce a lot of noise on the network, they do not perform vulnerability linkage, and they are considered prone to false positives.

Vulnerability scanners send specially crafted traffic to target hosts and then analyzes the responses. They will trigger alarms in intrusion detection systems, and scans can involve dangerous tests that can possibly cause a DoS (Denial of Service).

Some vulnerabilities on the network require multiple steps to demonstrate a confirmed exposure; for example, gaining access to one machine to 'pivot' from it and attack a target on a better point of view. Vulnerability scanners do not typically take the scan to this level, but there are several tools such as Metaspolit, Canvas, and Core Impact that can.

Scanning tools have improved over the years, and the old reputation of being prone to false positives is often a dangerous assumption. More often than not, the assessment is proven correct, and remediation of the vulnerability is required or heavily advised.

Types of Penetration Tests

There are several ways to categorize the different type of tests and the descriptions can be organized in different combinations. To restate, the most important thing is to select the correct type of test for what the client truly needs.

- Announced vs. unannounced tests
- Internal vs. external tests
- Black box vs. grey box vs. white box tests

Announced vs. unannounced tests

Announced tests occur when everyone, especially the administrators of the network, are aware the test is being conducted. Getting caught is not a concern nor is it part of the analysis of the results. Maintenance windows are typically determined to minimize the effects of the test on resources and services.

"Unannounced" tests occur when monitoring and incident response plans are being assessed. No one but the project sponsor and system owners (typically senior management) is aware of the test. The "get out of jail free" card is critical in this type of test because if the tester does get caught the sponsor of the project must step in and be responsible.

Internal vs. external tests

Internal tests and external texts describe the position of the simulated attacker. Sometimes the goal is to start the exam on the outside of the organization and attempt first to infiltrate to an inside position, and then continue to prove potential weaknesses.

Black box vs. grey box vs. white box tests

A white box test, or "Blue Teaming," is typically more of an assessment class test, and the information-gathering steps have been skipped to save time and cost. Black box, or "Red Teaming," tests are more time consuming and costly, but they simulate something much closer to the true attack scenario.

Grey box tests are those with a limited scope. The tester is given enough information to establish a very clear objective, but all of the information required to achieve the objective might be withheld. For instance, "audit the user accounts for passwords that an attacker might obtain" is a simple objective. Whether this is done through social engineering, obtaining local hashes, sniffing hashes, guessing, using fake websites, and so on is up to the tester and might not be specified.

Basic Steps of the Engagement

The best way to view the process of a penetration test is to modify the CEH methodology of attacks to fit a format penetration test. (This material was covered in Chapters 1 and 3.) Here is a quick refresher with the extra steps we discuss in this chapter.

- Initiating the engagement
- Project scope and charter
- Reconnaissance
- Scanning
  - Unearth initial information
  - Locate the network range
  - Ascertain active machines
  - Discover open ports and access points
  - Detect operating systems
  - Uncover services on ports
  - Map the network
- Vulnerability assessment

- Gaining access
- STOP!!

It is almost always unacceptable to maintain access or gain complete control of a system when performing a defense-oriented test. This is, of course, always a matter of negotiation with the client and expectations must be clear and in writing.

The steps change slightly depending on the type of test that has been ordered. The most important thing is not to breach the rules of engagement, control what does not belong to you, or violate the confidentiality of data, and also to make a best effort to avoid denial of service. The point is to prove the vulnerability is there and to document supporting facts to explain how it was discovered, why it matters, and what can be done about it.

An example would be a XSS attack. Once a proof of concept "Hello There!" type alert() box can be delivered across the vulnerability, the problem is proven. The rest is simply a matter of the skill an attacker would have with JavaScript to do more damage. Take a screen shot of the alert() box in the middle of the vulnerable page and provide it in the final report along with the URL that contains the code. Then move on.

Know the Basic Requirements of an Engagement

- Setting up the engagement
- Planning and management
- Initial documentation

Setting Up the Engagement

The most important step in setting up the penetration test is to plan the correct test for the needs of the client. The sales engineer must be able to advise the customer on what type of test will fit the situation best and to establish clear expectations and exit criteria. Once these agreements are made, it is time to assemble the talent.

A small engagement might be conducted by a single person with a wide range of advanced skills. Time and cost can be saved by using sophisticated penetration testing tools that go beyond the assessment level. These situations are typically insider-announced tests because the tools can trigger tens of thousands of alerts in the intrusion detection agents. It is necessary to run scans during maintenance windows with the coordination of the incident response teams.

Larger tests may involve a team of professionals. There should be a mix of skills that covers the whole OSI model: a physical tester and social engineer, a network and scanning expert, a very creative programmer, researchers, and a customer liaison. The liaison might be the only person the client ever actually meets (or knows she meets) and must be comfortable in both business and technical discussions.

Planning and Management

A professional penetration test is managed as a project no matter what its size. It must be successful and repeatable from a metrics and control perspective. This is a business abstraction of the real experiences of the testers that must improvise and be creative. As counter intuitive at this relationship might be at times, it really does work out because both the technical talent and the business processes are necessary for this machine to work.

The following is perhaps the world's shortest explanation of the project management principles that drive the management of a penetration test. There are five distinct phases:

- Initiation
- Planning
- Execution
- Control
- Closure

Initiation

There must be a reason to do the project. There must also be an understanding of what effort and impact tolerance this will really take to accomplish.

The initiation phase is about commitment. A definition of the problem and solution, the estimates of time and financial budgets, and the impact of surrounding operations and emotional or political support are all gathered. A sponsor steps up to fund the idea and take responsibility.

A charter is signed to kick off the project. It includes a clear definition of exactly what the sponsor wants, which is in theory the same thing the customer wants. In fact, the sponsor and customer might be the same person.

Planning

At this stage there is no option to fail because the project has begun. No excuses will be built into the plan; only contingencies and risk management options will be accepted. The project definition will be broken down into manageable and assignable parts. Schedules will be calculated and assignments will be delegated.

Execution

This is the actual doing of the plan. The best advice that can be given at this point is to follow the plan and take good notes along the way. Documentation is difficult to reconstruct after too many things have happened, but if the pentester takes good notes then the next phase can be almost painless.

Control

Control is about being able to make adjustments that are well informed and not counterproductive to efforts made by other members of the team. It is about handling "unknown unknowns" gracefully. This phase is also about maintaining the confidence of the sponsor and client that, while the world isn't always perfect, we know what is going on and we have a solution to keep things on track.

Status requests are inevitable. The answer "I don't know" will only cause panic and stress. The members of the testing team must be able to explain at all times and at any random moment what they are doing and why. What they have done should always be in the document heap and will eventually be aggregated into the final polished report.

Closure

The deliverables (also called exit criteria) of the project have been met. In a penetration test this would be the report. "Administrative close" is also an important part of this phase and includes formal acceptance of the results, agreements to finite support regarding clearing all tracks of the test, and payment.

The pentesting team will celebrate yet another successful engagement and conduct a lessons learned (post mortem) meeting to review the project as a whole and support a continuous improvement culture.

Initial Documentation

Before the execution and monitoring phases of the engagement begin, it is mandatory that certain agreements be made in writing and the understanding between the client and tester is perfectly clear. The final outcome of the test depends upon this, and the process of the test is potentially too dangerous to allow any sloppiness in the cooperation that must exist between the testing team and the project sponsor.

The following is a list of the core documents that make up the initiation of a penetration test:

- Project scope
- Indemnity clause
- "Get out of jail free" card
- Rules of engagement
- Communications plan
- Non-disclosure agreements
- Exit criteria

Project scope

The scope document defines the test from a high-level view. It also provides start and end dates, budget estimates, and a list of the people that will participate in the project. These "stakeholders" include the project sponsor on the client side, the person that will represent the testing team, and the members of the team. It is important that if any members of the team change in the middle of the engagement, the client is informed.

Terms such as SOW (Statement of Work) and "Project Charter" are associated with this step as well. The point is that this document is the official beginning of the engagement and from this point on, failing to finish the task is not an option.

Indemnity clause

This is a legal statement that protects the testers in case something goes wrong. The client is completely informed of all risks prior to the start of the penetration test. The indemnity clause makes the client responsible for the decision to move forward and releases the testing team from liability.

"Get out of jail free" card

It cannot be emphasized enough that the person that represents the client and is the project sponsor of the test is actually authorized to order and pay for the project. If the test is unannounced, there is a chance the tester will be caught. The sponsor must step in at that point and reveal that this exercise was approved and all responsibility lies with this decision maker.

Rules of engagement

This is the document that restrains the testing team and protects the client. It makes sure that none of the activities of the test will exceed the comfort zone of the project sponsor. A comprehensive checklist of activities is negotiated, line by line, as to what tools and techniques the team is allowed to use and explicitly not allowed to use.

For example: Social engineering might be allowed over the phone but not in person. DoS tools are likely not allowed at all. Rootkits, viral code, and illicit servers obtained from unknown sources might not be permissible because they cannot be completely controlled or cleared up by the testing team.

If scripts are written by the team during the test, is this proprietary intellectual property of the pentesters or does all of the source code need to be disclosed to the client? The rules of engagement process is vital to the final outcome, and the team must remain within these boundaries if the other legal protections are to hold up.

Communications plan

Occasionally the testing team will encounter a vulnerability that requires immediate attention; the risk is so great that reporting this issue to the customer cannot wait until the end of the project. A proper procedure for this must be in place. At the same time, if the testers affect a service and must stop what they are doing, there must be a way the customer can contact the team and ask for a pause (this usually also involves providing an explanation, too).

The communication plan will have to fit the scope and type of test that has been ordered. Too much communication is not only dangerous but might also diminish confidence in the testers themselves. A skilled liaison that can exercise good judgment in this area is valuable. The individual consultant must wear all of these hats.

Non-disclosure agreements

The distribution of the results of the test will be tightly controlled. A method of providing the report will be agreed to, as well as the proper destruction of any copies of the notes that were taken along the way.

The customer will want assurance that the information learned by the penetration testers is sacred and protected. The business that provides the testing service wants referrals and positive word of mouth, yet cannot always reveal their clients due to the nature of this sensitive information. This is a real "catch 22."

This is the essence of the value of the LPT. When experience cannot be explicitly discussed, it is helpful when at least a baseline of knowledge can be communicated and a global organization can back up the endeavor that was undertaken to earn the credential.

Exit criteria

The report, a debriefing, and a follow-up discussion regarding a schedule of future tests are part of the exit criteria. The project must have a defined end, but good business people will always establish what the next step should be. The next project might be a routine repeat of the previous one or become a whole new service based on the results of the test that is being closed.

In project management terms, the meeting of the exit criteria is both an end to the current project and a milestone in a larger picture program. It is a chance to draft a new charter and start all over again.

Know How to Write an Effective Report

- Style and tone
- Elements to include in the report
  - Try it out: Research some common vulnerability databases
- Delivering the report

Style and Tone

The report is a major part of the exit criteria. It is what will help customers reach the objective that caused them to order the test in the first place. It is also the lasting impression clients will have on the work of the team. It is written in business language, meaning straightforward and to the point, without excessive detail.

If the test revealed many problems, be sure the explanation of these issues is dry, empirical, and fact-based. Do not insert opinion and be careful not to be offensive. Do not make the report sound like a resume for the brilliant work of the team. Do not use words like "I." Try to make the test itself be the source of the information; the testers themselves are not the object that should have readers' attention.

There are many ways to arrange the information. It can be by IP address of affected hosts or by vulnerability, listing the affected hosts for each. The customer might have a preference and this should be communicated in the project plan. The summary information should be accurate, but easily digestible. If there is a way to make 876 vulnerabilities across 918 hosts look manageable, do it. The final report is not the place for FUD (Fear, Uncertainty, and Doubt). In fact, it is exactly the opposite. It has value and it is helpful.

In the case of situations where the test was somewhat uneventful, realize that there was not necessarily an explicit expectation that huge gaping holes in the network would be found. In fact, sometimes customers are very much on the ball with their security and the test will show this. The tester should never give away free testing services or feel guilty about not finding vulnerabilities. The testers should never violate the rules of engagement in their frustration over not finding anything to put in the report.

Proper documentation and justification of each action during the test is the team's best opportunity to demonstrate the value of the test. The report should honestly and accurately explain to the client what took place. The customer will make the ultimate decision about whether or not the proper effort and diligence was performed.

Elements to Include in the Report

Writing a report is a true skill and is harder than most people think. You have to do it to truly appreciate the tasks. The report will be how the entire effort of the team is judged. It will also sometimes make the difference between repeat business and a customer that is not convinced the product was what he paid for.

Customers are not always right. They purchase expertise because they lack something. This can place the hired expert in precarious situations at times when battling sales and marketing pressures. There is a trust involved that must be fulfilled along the way.

In a penetration test, the final report is an opportunity to show the customers they made the right decision. This can be uncomfortable at times, but through observing a few basic principles this can be a healthy process that supports all parties. A report should contain the following elements:

- Executive summary
- Definitions and conventions
- Rated vulnerability on criticality or an accepted scoring system
- Index numbers of industry recognized vulnerability databases (when applicable)
- Description of the vulnerabilities found (or activities conducted looking for them)
- Summary and conclusion

Executive summary

Acknowledge the audience and respect their time. The executive summary tells readers what they are reading and what the big picture conclusion is. If this is compelling, the rest of the paper will be read with interest and critical thought. The information will be communicated.

Without a good executive summary it is likely the report will end up in the "circular file" and no matter how good the information is nobody will read it. This step sells the document.

Definitions and conventions

Some jargon is hard to avoid. For example, the term "rootkit" summarizes about an hour's worth of explanation that barely scratches the surface. In the context of the report, it is just better to simply use the word and keep going. Separated from the context, it is possible to give a simpler definition.

The challenge of writing is putting non-linear ideas into a linear form. (Even the act of writing requires some hacking.)

Rated vulnerability on criticality or an accepted scoring system

Discovered vulnerabilities should be assigned a metric that helps the consultant and client collaborate on a set of priorities. Every issue that is observed should get a score that can assist in prioritization. This is very subjective, and all commercial assessment tools provide a system of their own.

In the "Definitions and Conventions" section, explain the scoring scale. Do not give a nonsensical scale of something like an undefined 1–9 type of thing that tries to play the psychology smoke and mirrors of the situation. The pentest report must have real definition.

If you decide the scale is 1–5, then tell clients exactly what a "1" is and exactly what a "5" means to them. They should also know what a 2, 3, and 4 are. Keep it straight-forward, and explain it.

Some vulnerability assessment tools have a built-in scoring system that might be the requirement to use. There is also a tool called CVSS (Common Vulnerability Scoring System) that takes into account several factors relating to true risk. For example: How available are the exploit tools, how much skill does the attack require, what is the impact of the exploit if successful, and how much does the attacker need to have under control in order to perform the exploit? A description of the system can be found here: *http://www.first.org/cvss/*

Index numbers of industry recognized vulnerability databases (when applicable)

The report should inform the customer as best as possible about the vulnerabilities, what causes them, how to reproduce them if needed, and how to fix them. If the vulnerability is already cataloged in one of the industry recognized databases, provide the index number and a link in the report so customers can do further research on their own.

If the test is a black box style, keep the description you write in your own words, and focus on what the testing did specifically to discover the vulnerability. Let the customers choose to research further using your references if they want to, and make sure your writing style remains "business language."

If the test is white box, it might be acceptable to just use the reports your assessment tools created automatically. The important thing is to make sure that value is added to the report that serves clients specifically; they do not want to pay thousands of dollars and be handed a stock Nessus report they could have done themselves. Make sure there is expertise and service applied in the way clients are informed of the test results.

TRY IT OUT

Research Some Common Vulnerability Databases

Many of the popular repositories offer RSS feeds that allow the pentester to remain informed of the most recent additions to the database. Make these sites part of a regular routine.

CVE (Common Vulnerabilities and Exposures Database) `http://cve.mitre.org/`

OSVDB (Open Source Vulnerabilities Database) `http://osvdb.org/`

Milw0rm `http://www.milw0rm.com/`

Description of the vulnerabilities found (or activities conducted looking for them)

The title of the vulnerability is like a newspaper headline. It is short but gets attention.

Keep the hidden observer (the reader of the report) focused on the risk, not on the tester. There must be a reason this vulnerability is important. Describe how the weakness was found, including tools and discreet actions used, but keep the flow of the text going. Defer details such as lists and screenshots to an appendix. Give the executive the choice to pursue the "nuts and bolts" or just take your word for it and continue with the thought process.

Provide enough evidence to be convincing and provide guidance to an experienced administrator in terms of reproducing the problem without getting into a full blown tutorial. This is to remain in business language, but it must have substance, too.

Summary and conclusion

Sometimes it can be hard to write the conclusion in a way that does not involve opinion. Accuracy in the assessment is not the same thing as insulting the client. A statement such as, "The testing team discovered several vulnerabilities that will require immediate attention" along with proper communication of risk to back up that claim is appropriate. A statement such as, "This poorly designed network has many issues and clearly shows a lack of competency" is clearly not acceptable. The customer will be frightened or bullied into hiring you for remediation or follow-up tests.

There are other ways to communicate value and professional work during the conclusion statements. Assure customers of actions taken to protect their intellectual property. If it was an internal test, make sure they know what was brought in the building during the test and how you made sure not to allow anything of theirs to leave. Explain how any tools that were used were removed and will not leave residual issues. Occasionally, refer to the fact that these practices were agreed to in writing beforehand and were followed by the team.

Delivering the Report

Arrangements must be specified in writing as to how the customer wants the final report. This critical document cannot be seen or found in the hands of the wrong people.

Sometimes it is acceptable to provide the report in password protected .pdf format and send it by encrypted e-mail, but .pdf passwords are not that difficult to crack with the *right* tools. If .pdf is used, there must also be a stated expectation of how long the testing team will keep a copy. For their own protection, the testers will want to destroy those files rather than be responsible for the security of them. The customer should know how long this time period will be and should be certain not to lose her own copy beyond that time. That report might be all that is left of an engagement that cost tens of thousands of dollars.

Other times the best way is to make a single printout of the report in the customer's building and deliver it directly to the project sponsor. A debriefing meeting might be asked for to explain the basics of the report, and if PowerPoint slides are created for this purpose, they too must be properly handled and destroyed.

Know How to Stay Current with Information

- RSS Feeds, blogs, podcasts, mailing lists, and social networks

  - Try it out: Gather a few good resources

RSS Feeds, Blogs, Podcasts, Mailing Lists, and Social Networks

Between the CEH and the ECSA/LPT courseware; encyclopedic reference material is provided that can be used to ensure no stone is unturned during your pentests. CEH provides tools and technical theory and ECSA/LPT provides analysis, staging, and checklists for ensuring a thorough and safe test every time. It is still important, however, to adopt a daily routine of staying informed; as new vulnerabilities are found, test results can become obsolete within hours of being delivered.

Just 30 minutes a day and a few time-saving tools can make a large difference in the long term. You will be surprised now and then that you know something without realizing where it was learned, and this knowledge will come during an engagement just when you need it. The manageable daily effort of keeping up to speed has a powerful accumulative effect. Do not feel like you have to wade through all of it all the time. Set a time limit, and be consistent.

RSS feeds are a way to aggregate headlines and articles from websites and blogs. They are also used to deliver podcasts that can include sound and video. Many security conferences publish videos of their breakout sessions via an RSS feed.

Google Reader is an easy-to-use application for managing and viewing feeds. Most current browsers now support RSS bookmarks, and there are many other freeware utilities available as well.

Look on a webpage for a little orange logo that says "RSS." It might also say "XML," "Atom," or "Feedburner" and, in fact, there are many others out there. Just copy the link into your reader and the summarized information will be at your fingertips each day.

Mailing lists can be a bit noisy, but some of the best information is still leaked out this way. Subscribe to the daily digest or RSS feed if available and lurk (view without contributing) for awhile until you get a feel for the culture and level of information the long-time participants are expecting.

TRY IT OUT

Gather a Few Good Resources

The following is a short list of RSS feeds the author recommends. Take some time to find others as well once you get the hang of it.

The Register

`http://www.theregister.co.uk/security/headlines.atom`

Slashdot

`http://rss.slashdot.org/Slashdot/slashdot`

US-CERT Technical Bulletins

`http://www.us-cert.gov/current/index.atom`

Microsoft security bulletins

`http://www.microsoft.com/technet/security/bulletin/secrss.aspx`

Cisco Advisories

`http://newsroom.cisco.com/data/syndication/rss2/SecurityAdvisories_20.xml`

Full disclosure mailing list

`http://seclists.org/rss/fulldisclosure.rss`

Buqtraq mailing list

`http://seclists.org/rss/bugtraq.rss`

Dark Reading

`http://feeds.feedburner.com/darknethackers`

Schneier on Security

`http://www.schneier.com/blog/index.xml`

Certisfaction – The IT Training and Certification Blog

`http://intenseschool.blogspot.com/feeds/posts/default`

With the growth in popularity of social networks like Facebook and Linkedin, many groups exist that are hosted by someone trying to build a community of like-minded people in the information security community. LUGs (Local User Groups) sometimes form from these efforts or might already be available in your area. If not, consider starting one if the commitment is possible. Some can be too active, while others amount to very little. Do a little research before joining.

Conclusion

The CEH class is an encyclopedic view of technology with a bias toward critical thinking rather than configuration and engineering. Baseline knowledge is necessary to begin formulating creative questions. Attackers don't care about making things work; they care about reaching their objectives.

Attacks can be widely dispersed as in phishing, or blunt and clumsy as in brute force. They can also be precise, patient, and disciplined. The motivation of the attacker and the preparation level of the adversary will determine the strategy.

Attackers will not confine themselves to rules of engagement, deadlines, or approved tools. They don't have to respect intellectual property. They don't dismiss opportunity because it's an old trick; they are just grateful the administrators were so careless and that they can move on to the next challenge. They will be imaginative and resourceful when the old tricks aren't working.

Attackers do not stop working at exactly 5:00 or refuse to work weekends or complain about their conditions. They can do their thing from airports, parking lots, coffee houses, classrooms, dumpsters, and cubicles.

A penetration tester must be formal, repeatable, and must observe whatever constraints the customer requires. The objective is never to control what does not belong to them, to compromise confidential data, or to cause a denial of service. They must clean up after themselves and make it seem as if they were never there. The endgame is not personal gain, but value in the information that can be communicated to decision makers that will, in turn, fulfill a chosen business objective.

Penetration testers get paid nicely and stay out of prison. They can use their CEH knowledge within a defense-motivated framework. Through genuine curiosity and respect for the practice of applying technology, they can do more than just focus on security.

Good Luck and See You in Class!

Practice Exam Questions

Chapter 1: Ethical Hacking

1. Your employer has asked you to perform an audit of the passwords for the user accounts for a particular server. What type of test have you been assigned?

   a. White box test

   b. Grey box test

   c. Black box test

   d. Grey hat test

2. Which of the following phrases is a derogatory term and would only invite retaliation?

   a. Script kiddie

   b. Hacker

   c. Attacker

   d. Consultant

3. Webhosting services often offer free scripts for customers that pay for minimum level services. Occasionally there are security flaws in these scripts that are never fixed even though thousands of customers might be using them.

   This is an example of what type of threat category?

   a. PHP

   b. SQL injection

   c. Cross site scripting

   d. Shrink wrap code

4. Neil is conducting security research on a popular software application and discovers a buffer overflow. He considers reporting his finding to the vendor but realizes the EULA (End User License Agreement) forbids this kind of research. What should Neil do?

   a. Neil should sell his exploit on eBay. There is nothing wrong with making an honest dollar this way since the software itself should have been free in the first place.

   b. The laws that protect the right to full disclosure are in higher standing than the EULA. It is a constitutional issue regarding speech and expression. Neil can reveal his findings without worry.

   c. Report the finding to a neutral party such as a CERT coordination center.

   d. Anonymously report the finding to the bugtraq or "full disclosure" mailing lists.

5. Which of the following represents the greatest danger to enterprise networks?

   a. Disgruntled employee

   b. Black hat hacker

   c. Negligent management

   d. The burdens of government regulations

6. When finished footprinting the network, the next step attackers would take is:

   a. Launch a vulnerability scanner

   b. Enumerate as much as possible about the policies of each system

   c. Attack!

   d. Take the information they have gathered and start searching Google

7. Which of the following types of hosts are completely exposed to risk?

   a. A Windows 2000 server

   b. Honeypot

   c. Bastion host

   d. An open source operating system

8. Which of the following types of hosts are placed on a network to attract the attention of a malicious attacker and allow the administrators to observe their actions?

   a. Honeypot

   b. Bastion host

   c. Intrusion detection system

   d. A Windows 98 machine

9. Hosts can often be attacked in layers. If the target service is not vulnerable then what else should the attacker try? (Choose up to two)

   a. Annoy the administrator of that host with a denial of service attack

   b. If the target service is secure there is nothing else that can be done

   c. Convince a user to accept a malicious file into one of the clients on the host

   d. Attack a service on one of the other open ports

10. Another way to describe risk is:

    a. A positive or negative event that can impact a resource or process

    b. A negative event that can cause damage to a resource or process

    c. Bungee jumping

    d. A management technique that measures certainty

11. Which of the following is considered to be the most dangerous vector of security threats?

    a. Unpatched operating systems

    b. Natural disasters

    c. DDoS (Distributed Denial of Service)

    d. Social engineering

12. When attackers have gained and then maintained access to a system it is said they have installed a:

    a. Backdoor

    b. Rootkit

    c. Maintenance hook

    d. Trojan

13. An attacker wants to make changes to a log file to clear his tracks. Instead of erasing the logs, he just makes changes to some of the entries. What is he trying to do?

    a. Throw off the timeline to confuse the investigator

    b. Create the appearance of decoy traffic

    c. Make an extremely unusual event so it wouldn't be looked at

    d. Taunt the administrators

14. If a white hat researcher discovers a vulnerability in a software product, what should she do with the information?

    a. Create a tutorial complete with screenshots and submit the finding to digg.com and slashdot.org

    b. Call the vendor and offer to keep quiet if they pay you a finder's fee

    c. Prove the exploit works, then sell a script on eBay

    d. Report the vulnerability to a regional emergency response organization

15. Someone downloads a tool from the Internet and uses it to experiment with an idea she got from a YouTube video. Another exam you recently passed considers this unethical and inappropriate. A friend of yours just considers this person to be a "script kiddie." You have your own opinions. What is the most defensive way to respond to this scenario?

    a. Lecture the person about ethics and appropriate behavior. Make certain she realizes the trouble she is causing the industry as a whole.

    b. Avoid insulting the person, enforce policy in a professional yet objective manner, and consider the idea that this person can be an asset if properly mentored.

    c. Explain "Script kiddies are l00s3rs" and agree with your friend that if this l@m3r can't write her own buffer overflow shellcode then she isn't worth a slice of pizza.

    d. Shrug your shoulders in indifference and get on with your day knowing your network is so secure that this person poses no possible threat.

Chapter 2: Hacking Laws

1. What is the threshold for the amount of damage an organization must sustain before federal law enforcement will get involved?

    a. $1,000

    b. $5,000

    c. $10,000

    d. There is no lower limit

2. Which of the following statutes says that attempts to circumvent copy protection are illegal, regardless of how weak that protection might be?

    a. Copyright and Patent Protection Act

    b. Freedom of Information Act

    c. Digital Millennium Copyright Act

    d. It is not illegal; if a protection can be broken it is a right to break it

3. Which of the following statements are most true? (Choose up to two)

    a. The law recognizes a difference between a computer being used in a crime and when a computer is the target of a crime

    b. The Freedom of Information Act guarantees the fair use and exchange of all information materials

    c. The law has definitive distinctions between what is "important" versus "unimportant" information

    d. Penalties increase dramatically if human life has been put in danger

4. If attackers experimenting with the latest botnet tool decided to seize control of some federal computers for the purposes of committing a fraud utilizing symbolic data such as credit card information they would be in violation of:

    a. Computer Fraud and Abuse Act Section 1030

    b. Federal Computer Breech Act of 1985

    c. The Bush Cheney Act of 2006

    d. Symbolic Data Protection Act of 2001

5. You want to determine the web server and host operating system of a target. For legal reasons, you worry about getting caught. A passive reconnaissance technique that cannot be detected might be a good idea.

    Which of the following choices holds the least risk of detection?

    a. Use the netcraft website to look up the target's host

    b. Use Telnet to perform a banner grab

    c. Use a common scanner in "paranoid mode"

    d. Call them and ask

6. You are researching an adversary and are certain that you saw some incriminating information on their website about six months agout it isn't there now. What resource below might be the quickest way to check for this data?

    a. Look through the websites that the target has partner relationships with

    b. Use Google to look through their cache database

    c. Learn to program in PERL and create a webcrawler of your own

    d. "The Wayback Machine"

7. Which of the following statements is the most correct about the DMCA?

    a. Circumventing copyright protections is permissible if they can be defeated. The responsibility lies on the rights holder to enforce protection adequately.

    b. The "Librarian of Congress" can issue exceptions to the circumventing of copyright protections that the DMCA addresses.

    c. The DMCA stands for the "Digital Mandates for Circumvention of Assets" Act. It implements treaties established by WIPO (World Intellectual Property Organization).

    d. The DMCA protects the attacker by defining reverse engineering as "The legitimate act of research" and "an inherent right of each user."

8. Hayley decides to circumvent the copy protection laws by taking an entire movie she recorded on her cell phone in the theatre and appending it with an insightful review. She claims this is journalism and free speech. She still gets sued and loses. Why?

   a. She didn't have enough money to hire a good attorney.

   b. This was an injustice. She should have won the case.

   c. She used too much. A clip or two with proper attribution would have been better.

   d. It was a flip of the coin; the case could have gone either way.

9. Which of the following protects the rights of individuals in regard to the disclosing of information? (Choose up to two)

   a. The Human Rights Act of 1998 (UK)

   b. The Google Act of 2003

   c. The Privacy Act of 1974

   d. There are no such rights

10. "Port scanning" is considered what form of attack?

    a. Illegal and highly prosecuted

    b. Information gathering

    c. Rude and impolite

    d. Denial of service

11. In the United States, attacks on financial institutions are handled by:

    a. The GLBA (Graham-Leach-Bliley Act)

    b. The FBI

    c. The Secret Service

    d. A free market society has no such crime. It is a moral imperative that to the winner "goes the spoils." If you can work the system then it works for you.

12. "Periodic assessments of the risk and magnitude of the harm that could result from unauthorized access, use, disclosure, disruption, modification, or destruction of information

and information systems that support the operations and assets of the agency;"

Which act mandates a security program be implemented in a federal agency that meets the above criteria?

a. Directive 8570

b. FISMA

c. FISO

d. The Homeland Security Act

13. Which of the following statements describes a provision of FERPA?

a. Organizations that provide educational services and receive funding from the Department of Education must have certain controls over student records, including disclosure to third parties.

b. Organizations that provide financial services must have certain controls over client records, including disclosure to third parties.

c. Individuals that receive TARP funds must protect the identities of the financial officers that brokered their benefits.

d. FISMA and FIDO must not collude to compromise, sell, or distribute information that reveals financial details about a citizen of the United States.

14. Which of the following acts of the UK parliament makes it illegal to modify the contents of a computer with the intent to impair its operation?

a. Computer Operation and Protection Act of 1989

b. Computer Hacking and Modification Act of 1990

c. Computer Fraud and Abuse Act Section 1029

d. Computer Misuse Act of 1990

15. Which of the following acts were meant to protect the illegal use of computers by unauthorized parties, although many argue that they in fact had the opposite effect? The laws could enable unsolicited e-mail and usage monitoring (choose two).

    a. CAN-SPAM Act

    b. SPY Act

    c. Intellectual Properties and Protection Act

    d. Free Speech in Advertising Act

Chapter 3: Footprinting

1. Which of the following tools can an attacker use for almost all footprinting needs, including whois, HTTP banner grabbing, and traceroutes?

   a. Google Earth

   b. My IP Suite

   c. Neotrace

   d. Sam Spade

2. Which of the following tools runs under Windows, has a GUI, and can be used for footprinting web servers?

   a. Nitko

   b. Wikto

   c. Dogpile

   d. Web Ferret

3. Which of the following commands would be used to request a zone transfer?

   a. nslookup; server ns1.example.dom; ls –d example.dom

   b. dig @ns1.example.dom - -zone-transfer

   c. host –t ZONE example.dom ns1.example.dom

   d. dig@ns1.example.dom example.dom IXFR

4. Which of the following are valid RIRs?

   a. LACNIC, LAPNIC, AFLAC

   b. ARIN, LAPNIC, RIPE NCC

   c. ARIN, APNIC, LAPNIC

   d. ARIN, LACNIC, AfriNIC

5. When attending a hacker meeting for the first time, John was asking about purchasing domain names. He was told in order to avoid identity theft or other forms of harassment, it is a good idea not to put correct information in the whois record when buying a domain name. (Select the best statement)

   a. He was given bad advice. Incorrect information is a violation of the IEEE and IETF terms of service.

   b. He was given bad advice. Incorrect information is a violation of the ICANN terms of service.

   c. He was given good advice. Domain poachers use the contact information to steal domains all the time.

   d. He was given good advice. You never want to put a personal address in the whois, and proxy services that will hide the information are outrageously expensive.

6. Which of the following tools will help the attacker learn how long a web server has been up for and what type of server it's running (indicating perhaps it has not been updated in awhile)?

   a. This cannot be determined remotely

   b. BidiBlah Suite

   c. http://uptime.netcraft.com/up/graph

   d. www.archive.org

7. When looking at some log filesasey noticed some strange entries that involved a request to TCP port 53 and the string "AXFR." What was the attacker attempting?

   a. It was a common virus scan

   b. Directory traversal

   c. Verify the accounts on a mail server

   d. Zone transfer

8. How long will the secondary server wait before asking for a zone update if the regular update hasn't yet been answered?
   lab.dom. IN SOA ns.lab.dom. (200030432 7200 3600 1209600 1800)

   a. 2 hours

   b. 60 minutes

c. 14 days

d. 1 week

9. **What is the name of the tool that will show old versions of websites that might reveal e-mail addresses or other information that could be harvested?**

a. Web the Ripper

b. Black Widow

c. The Wayback Machine

d. HTTrack website copier

10. **Which of the following are ways to footprint e-mail addresses or systems?**

a. Send an e-mail to a domain that will bounce back and analyze the headers

b. Telnet into port 25 and issue the VRFY command on names collected from the company directory

c. Embed a "web bug" in the HTML e-mail and spam it out to everyone

d. All of the above

11. **Dave used the engine at http://www.kartoo .com to footprint his competitor's domain. What was Dave trying to accomplish?**

a. Pinpoint targets for a denial of service attack

b. Assemble competitive intelligence

c. Find press releases or negative stories

d. Find the names of company officers

12. **While researching a public company, Tony wanted to figure out the names of important company officials and what they paid for the business. Which resource is best used for this research?**

a. The Edgar database

b. Findlaw.com

c. cnbc.com

d. Finance.yahoo.com

13. **When performing a traceroute, Gregory notices that the last two entries are the same IP address. What does this mean?**

a. There is a cluster or load balancer on that segment.

b. Traceroute is a buggy and defective tool.

c. One of the two hosts is a honeypot.

d. Gregory needs to try a Layer 4 traceroute since this result is impossible.

14. **Which of the following is the best statement in terms of footprinting a network?**

a. Map the network, discover live hosts, discovery open portsiscover services

b. Discover live hosts, discover open ports, discover services, map the network

c. Find the network block, traceroute to the web server, scan all hops looking for segments

d. Call the front desk and ask to talk to the network administrator. Tell him that network topologies must be a matter of public record for investors and you want a copy mailed right away.

15. **If the standard traceroute tool is not working, the attacker can then try which of the following?**

a. Call the front desk and ask them to ping you, since traffic coming from them will be successful

b. Telnet to various ports and run a packet sniffer to watch the backscatter

c. "lft" is an advanced traceroute tool that can incorporate various Layer 4 techniques and it might work instead

d. Post a message on the nmap hackers mailing list and ask someone else to try it from their address

Chapter 4: Google Hacking

1. **Based on the following command, which of the following statements are true? (Choose up to two)**

    lynx –dump http://www.google.com/ search?q=site:eccouncil.org+ceh > ceh_ search.txt

a. Lynx is a command line browser. We are passing in a URL that contains a search and dumping the results to a text file for further review.

b. Lynx is a command line browser and is extremely useful to the attacker that only has a remote shell on a system (no GUI).

c. Lynx is a little known tool in the Google API. It provides access to undocumented functions and can access even Darknet data.

d. Lynx is an internal Linux command that tunnels an HTTP connection across a firewall and permits access to data anonymously. Since we do not want to be caught searching for a hacking class, this is the best tool to use.

2. **What is the difference between the inurl: and the allinurl: operators?**

a. Using inurl: is like a logical OR and using allinurl: is like a logical AND.

b. There is no difference; the allinurl is not listed on the help page because it has been discontinued.

c. With inurl: only the first keyword must be in the URL and additional keywords can be anywhere on the page. The allinurl: operator means all of the keywords must be in the URL.

d. With inurl: only the first keyword must be in the URL and additional keywords can be anywhere on the page. The allinurl: operator means any of the keywords must be in the URL.

3. **What is the difference between the filetype: and ext: operators?**

a. Filetype: looks for executables where ext: looks for data files.

b. They are synonyms of each otherut the ext: is intended more for negation.

c. There is no such thing as a filetype: operator.

d. There is no such thing as an ext: operator.

4. **What would a search for the string "#include <stdio.h>" produce?**

a. Nothing as the # (hash0 character comments out the remaining string)

b. Library files from Visual Studio

c. Source code for scripts written in "C"

d. A well-known vulnerability in the IIS ISAPI for IPP (Internet Printing Protocol)

5. **What is the following search trying to accomplish?**
intitle: "This page cannot be found" and "Please try the following"

a. Broken links produce these errors and indicate a malfunctioning server that is exposing weaknesses.

b. Server errors that provide valuable information about what went wrong with the script.

c. 404 errors produce pages that include these phrases as a common matter; the search doesn't really tell the attacker anything.

d. The first phrase produced too many results. The second phrase was added to refine the search.

6. **When playing around Chuck tries to run a search for "intitle:index.of" because he saw it in a hacker book. The first entry was for a site called Ibiblio and it looked interesting. What should Chuck do next? (Choose all that apply)**

a. Since Google hacking is anonymous; Chuck should start hacking away at the Ibiblio site. Who knows what this thing isut it looks fun to attack.

b. Ibiblio is a popular host for downloads; they present a directory listing routinely and this target is not something Chuck should bother with because directory listings are not always a problem.

c. Chuck should look further into the results or perhaps add the site: operator to his search.

d. Stupid Google is only showing useless results that aren't even web pages. The hacker book must have had a typo as usual and Chuck should just move on to something else.

7. Janet read on the Internet that free hosting services will offer scripts to customers that have security holes. It is possible that these holes are not always patched. She also read that Matt's PERL scripts are quite popular.

   What would Janet do next? (Choose up to two)

   a. Use Google to locate Matt's script archive, guess on a popular script like formmail.pl, and use Google to look for vulnerabilities. Pop a code string into Google again and try to find vulnerable sites.

   b. Use Google to search for webhosts that use these scripts and sign up for a free account. Download the scripts and analyze them for vulnerabilities.

   c. These scripts are old and outdated. No one uses stuff like this anymore so Janet should ignore the article and move on.

   d. Webhosts would not release vulnerable code, particularly the free services. They recognize their responsibility and invest a lot of money in ensuring the safety of their products. Janet has no angle here and should move on.

8. The "title" of a web page (for instance, that is used in the intitle: Google search operator) is located where in the web documents?

   a. Name of the physical file on the web server

   b. `<head><title>` This is the title`</title></head>`

   c. Mapped in a configuration file on the web server

   d. In the status bar of the web browser

9. Which of the following is a hacking tool for automating Google searches?

   a. Bing

   b. GoogleGet

   c. AutoGoo

   d. Goolag Scanner

10. Brian wants to demonstrate an example of hacking Google's adsense system. He decides to setup a "splog". What is Brian trying to illustrate?

    a. Articles full of keywords but with dubious content value

    b. Splurging on a burst of advertising on high cost, high impact traffic sites

    c. Posting comments on trendy, spur of the moment type blog articles that have timely and up to the minute reporting

    d. A network of connected sites that promote high click through actions. Example: "Click here" results in a sentence or two of promotion copy only to require yet another click to hopefully one day view some content.

11. Sean hears about the practice of "Web Scraping," and realizes this could be a good way to make some extra cash.

    What is Sean going to do?

    a. Run a series of "Make money online" workshops and tell people to do what he is doing—look for things to sell online

    b. "Scrape" information from other information sources and add his own insightful commentary

    c. Steal other web pages, place them under his own domains, place Google adsense onto those pages, and rake in the money when the keywords cause search hits

    d. Purchase domains that have recently expired, then sell them to their previous owners for a profit, even if he had no intent of ever using those domains for anything

12. What will the following search phrase ask for? [CDT]site:example.com -ext:html -ext:htm -ext:asp -ext:php

    a. All indexed pages on the example.com site including those with extensions html, htm, asp, and php

    b. All non-indexed pages on the example.com site expect those with extensions html, htm, asp, and php

c. All html, htm, asp, and php pages on every site other than example.com

d. All indexed pages on the example.com site other than those with extensions html, htm, asp, and php

13. Using automated tools to search Google violates their terms of service. Searching known Google appliances, however, is a different matter.
Which of the following tools is designed to work this way?

a. GoogleGather

b. GScanPlus

c. GooApp

d. Gooscan

14. Claire wants to sabotage her rival's latest adsense campaign. She reduces the CTR (Click Through Rate) of her competitor by viewing pages on whcih their ads are shown, then is careful not to click the ads. To make enough of a difference, fake pages are setup with keywords that attract the ads, then bots automate clicking the pages by the thousands.
What is this an example of?

a. Good old fashioned competition

b. Impression fraud

c. Click fraud

d. Can't be done

15. "Google Zeitgeist" is a project that does what?

a. It is a Slashdot hoax

b. Legal issues brought on by privacy concerns in Germany

c. A project that is meant to demonstrate "The spirit of the times"

d. A conspiracy of Google to own all of the world's information

Chapter 5: Scanning

1. Amberlee attempts a UDP scan into a DMZ and no results are returned. What could be the possible reasons? (Choose up to four)

a. The network segment is down.

b. ICMP Type 3 messages are being filtered on the way back.

c. She is only scanning UDP ports that are open, like 53.

d. The filter is blocking all UDP traffic.

2. While DNS walking during the recon phase, Ryan discovers two hosts that should exist and have available servicesut when he performs an inverse scan on them he gets confusing results. He can reach them through a web browseronfirming they have HTTP services runningut the scan produces only RST, ACK responses. Why?

a. Ryan is inverse scanning a Windows host.

b. Ryan is inverse scanning a Linux host.

c. The filter is returning the RST flags to discourage the scan.

d. The HTTP server always responds with a RST if the browser agent is not Mozilla or IE.

3. Larry doesn't want to learn how subnetting or routing works, and just wants to take a wild guess at a scan. He has an inside position so scanning private addresses is OK. He downloads Angry IP and puts in a range of 192.168.0.0/16.
What is the best statement in regard to what Larry is doing?

a. Seems like Larry is taking a reasonable approach. He expects the scan to take awhile, and he can do other things while he waits.

b. 192.168.0.0/16 is an RFC 1918 compliant rangeut this scan will attempt to reach over 65,000 hosts and there are better ways of doing this.

c. RFC 1918 specifies 192.16.1.0/24 as a private range, and Larry is trying a class B mask. Larry is wasting his time.

d. He should get the network block from ARIN and scan from the outside if he wants to make sure he sees every inside host.

4. When attempting an operating system fingerprinting scan, NMap requires which of the following?

a. An open port

b. Specific services like HTTP on the target since OS detection is basically a banner grab

c. A packet filtering firewall between the scanner and the target

d. One open port and one closed port

5. Which of the following tools is best used for passive OS fingerprinting?

a. Cheops

b. Queso

c. NMap

d. p0f

6. Clement is running a sniffer while performing a scan. He noticed a few ICMP Type 3 Code 13 messages. What does this mean?

a. Timestamp requests

b. Administratively prohibited

c. Destination unreachable; the network is down

d. Time to live has expired

7. Which of the following commands would successfully conduct a UDP scan of ports 1 through 100?

a. nc –u –v –w3 [target ip] 1-100

b. hping3 -8 –S –p 1-100 [target ip]

c. nmap –sU –v –v [target ip] 1-100

d. uscan –p 1-100 [target ip]

8. Which of the following represents a stealth scan?

a. SYN; SYN/ACK; ACK; RST

b. SYN; SYN/ACK; RST

c. SYN; SYN/ACK; FIN

d. SYN; SYN/ACK

9. Ted is looking at packet dumps of a scan and notices the flags UPF are set. He also notices the target port is always 31337. What does Ted conclude?

a. He is watching normal traffic.

b. Someone is scanning for subseven.

c. This is a harmless UDP scan.

d. Someone is scanning for back orifice.

10. Monty wants to check a block of phone numbers for rogue infrastructure. What tool or technique would he use?

a. War dialing with Ettercap

b. War dialing with THC-Scan

c. Dialing for Dollars with Cold-Call Pro DX

d. Robo-dialing with DialDick.exe

11. In addition to the TTL field, which of the following can be analyzed during OS fingerprinting to identify the target OS? (Choose up to five)

a. The setting of the DF bit

b. Window size

c. IPID incrementing

d. ToS bits

e. Initial NACK field

f. Datagram size

12. Which of the following is not one of the states of a port?

a. Half-open

b. Listening

c. Filtered

d. Established

13. Frank's boss wants to start performing vulnerability scans and a golf partner recommended SAINT. He sets up a Windows machine and asks Frank to get started but immediately Frank runs into a problem. What is wrong?

a. SAINT only runs on UNIX.

b. Frank's boss needed SATAN; he bought the wrong product.

c. SAINT only scans wireless networks.

d. Vulnerability scans only tell the attackers where the weaknesses are.

14. Bart is running an NMap vanilla scan and believes the results are inaccurate. He decides that slowing down his scan might increase the accuracyelieving that latency or congestion is causing some dropped responses.

    Which of the following choices will help Bart get the job done?

    a. nmap –sT –v –T5 [Target IP]

    b. nmap –sT –v –T0 [Target IP]

    c. nmap –sV –v –T0 [Target IP]

    d. nmap –sT –v --slow [Target IP]

15. Sean is trying to scan a network using the evasion technique of fragmenting his traffic with the –f option in NMap. What is the MTU (Maximum Transfer Unit) for an Ethernet network?

    a. Depends on the speed of the link

    b. 53

    c. 65,535

    d. 1,500

Chapter 6: Enumeration

1. **Which example is the correct syntax for establishing a null session?**

    a. net use \\IPC$\[target ip] "" /user: ""

    b. net use \\[target ip]\IPC$ "" /user: ""

    c. net use \\[target ip]\IPC$ ' /user: ""

    d. net use \\[target ip]\NULL$ "" /user: ""

2. **Which of the following lists of tools are used in a Linux system to gather information locally about what is running?**

    a. netstat, pstools, nbtstat, procmon

    b. top, netstat, lsof, ps

    c. ps, top, nbstat, net use

    d. rpcinfo, ldap, nbstat, ps

3. Sara has managed to get access to the passwd file in the Linux system. Which of the following entries shows a user that is in the root permissions group?

    rkuby:x:1001:1001:Ron Kuby:/home/rkuby:/bin/bash dhcp:x:1002:1002::/home/dns:/ bin/bash monticore:x:1003:0::/home/monticore:/bin/bash awright:x:1004:500:Amber Wright:/home/awright:/bin/bash

    a. awright

    b. monticore

    c. dhcp

    d. The group cannot be determined in the /etc/passwd file

4. Which of the following Linux permissions will allow the owner to have full access, the members of the group to have RX access, and the world to have only R access?

    a. chmod 764 foo.sh

    b. chmod 664 foo.sh

    c. cacls u+rwx g+rx o+r

    d. calcs ./foo.sh /G owner:RWX /G group:rx / G world:R

5. Which of the following represents an OID?

    a. S-1-5-7-341656734543-512

    b. S-1-5-7-545632867586-1001

    c. AD3424FDA31404EE

    d. 1.2.1.1.1.2.1.3.1.4.6

6. **What are LSASS and GINA?**

    a. On a Linux system they are responsible for logins, much like PAM is for Windows.

    b. On a Windows system they manage SIDs and user account databases.

    c. On a Linux system they govern access to TCP-based services along with Inetd and TCPWrappers.

    d. On a Windows host they comprise part of the authentication subsystem.

7. Password hashes are stored on a Windows machine in several locations. Sometimes only the system account has accessut because this is data at rest booting to an alternate OS or remotely accessing via a call with system rights could work. Where could password hashes be stored on a Windows host? (Vhoose up to four)

   a. The registry

   b. The SAM file

   c. A repair file

   d. In RAM

8. You are poking around in a Linux box, run the ls –l command, and notice a curious entry:

   _rwsr_xr_x 1 root users 381 2009-02-29 6:32 yes

   Which of the following statements is true? (Choose up to two.)

   a. The octal equivalent of these permissions is 755 + SUID.

   b. The answer to the command was "yes" and the file requested does exist.

   c. The octal equivalent of these permissions is 4755.

   d. The SGID bit is set and the file "yes" is executable with the root UID.

9. Shalicia wants to find all of the currently open connections on a Windows host. Which command would provide this information?

   a. netstats –an

   b. netstat /an

   c. nbtstat –an

   d. nmap –sT -P0 –v [target ip]

10. Edward is trying to locate the computers on a network by their computer names. What command line tool can he use? (Choose up to two)

    a. Windows doesn't have a scanner that will help with discovery.

    b. He needs to install a tool first.

    c. He could use "net view" with no arguments.

    d. He could use the nbstat tool with the –r or –c or –n options to at least see names of machines he might have discovered via natural protocol behaviors.

11. Kevaun wants to find file shares on a remote system. Which of the following commands would provide this information?

    a. netstat /an

    b. nbtstat –A

    c. net view \\[servername]

    d. nbstat –shares [target ip]

12. Chris is using a Linux box and is also attempting to enumerate the network for computer names and shares. What command below would he run?

    a. smbclient –L [target ip]

    b. nbtstat –L [target ip]

    c. net view \\[domain]

    d. Linux doesn't support Windows file sharing, so Chris is wasting his time

13. From his Linux host, Kempton wants to connect to an unprotected share he has discovered. What should he do next (assuming he has a credential)?

    a. smbclient \\\\[target ip]\\c$ -U administrator

    b. nbtstat \\[target ip]\c$ -u administrator

    c. net view \\\\[target ip]\ipc$ "" user:""

    d. Kempton cannot have a credential yet. He needs to read the system hacking chapter in the CEH courseware and try some of those techniques first.

14. Joe extracts a SID using the tool "SIDExtracter." Which of the following SIDs has administrator privileges?

    S-1-5-21-1147638176-875867241-945   Fred
    S-1-5-21-1147638176-875867241-134 Paul
    S-1-5-21-1147638176-875867241-777 Steve
    S-1-5-21-1147638176-875867241-500 Liz

    a. Fred

    b. Paul

    c. Steve

    d. Liz

15. **What is a "NULL" user in the context of the Windows operating system?**

    a. An account with no user name or password

    b. A user that has been disabled

    c. The system user of the "NULL" service

    d. An internal "loopback" user

Chapter 7: System Hacking

1. **Which of the following are valid ways to disable the storage of LM hashes on a Windows host? (Choose up to three)**

    a. Use group policy

    b. Edit the registry

    c. Use a password that is at least 15 characters long

    d. LM hashes cannot be disabled because of legacy support

2. **Curtis is looking over a SAM file he captured using PWDump3v2. He is looking at the LM hashes for a password he might be able to crack rather quickly. Which of the following users has a password that is less than seven characters?**

    a. E390B1995922152FAAD3B435B51404EE

    b. 4097A469B4C52C1D1D71060D896B7A46

    c. FB4138BA5EB0FA6AF56EE607BD78827B

    d. E52CAC67419A9A224A3B108F3FA6CB6D

3. **Which of the following is the static string that is encrypted with the DES key in LM?**

    a. M!cr0s0ft

    b. Lm@uth

    c. LmH@sH

    d. KGS!@#$%

4. **An attacker writes a script similar to the one given. What is he trying to accomplish?**
   FOR /F "token=1, 2*" %i in passlist.txt do net use \\target\IPC$ %i /u: %j

    a. Send a virus disguised as "passlist.txt" to the target

    b. Password guessing from a list

    c. Backdoor the target host with an undocumented feature of Windows

    d. Access the IPC$ share with a strong authentication token

5. **What is the feature supported by all NTFS volumes that allows forked data to be associated with a file in a way that will not affect the size of the original data?**

    a. Alternate data streams

    b. Steganography

    c. Cryptography

    d. FAT32 hidden streams (for legacy support)

6. **There is a windows tweak that allows the storage of different login credentials using the "Stored Usernames and Passwords" applet.**
   Which command will allow access to this tool?

    a. runas passmgr.exe

    b. net use \\server\ShowKMgr

    c. rundll32.exe keymgr.dll, KRShowKeyMgr

    d. runas winpassmgr.bat

7. **Bill seems to be connected to every marketing project that has had information leaked to the same competitor. Someone notices on a Myspace page some photographs of Bill socializing with some executives of that competitor. Bill is sent on vacation for a week, and a supervisor accesses Bill's e-mail and notices repeated e-mails with silly documents attached like jokes, random lists, or cooking recipes.**
   He asks you if this seems suspicious and wonders if these are coded messages. You tell him it is even easier than that, and suspect which of the following techniques?

    a. ADS streams are being used to smuggle documents using a USB key.

    b. Steganography is being used to tunnel the secrets through the VPN.

    c. This host was compromised by foreign hackers and Bill is the real victim.

    d. snow.exe could be used to hide data inside the attached documents.

8. Your father just purchased a new computer and brings it to you to look it over. He wants to make sure he can safely use the Internet and a few other applications. You show him the necessary steps for preparing a Windows computer fresh out of the box.

   What did you teach your father to do? (Choose up to three)

   a. Make sure the antivirus scanners are updating

   b. Make sure all applications have security patches updated

   c. Download a free anti-toolbar blocker application from secure-updatez.ws

   d. Make sure his Explorer settings are set to the maximum security levels for all websites

   e. Enable Windows Update and the personal firewall

9. Blair receives permission to audit the passwords on a critical server. The server is joined to a domain and is therefore "Kerberized," but Blair decides to try the simplest approach first anyway. He uses pwdump to successfully obtain the hashes and "John the Ripper" to crack them.

   Blair's supervisor is stunned. He says, "I made sure every password was at least 10 characters long." Why did the audit fail?

   a. Blair used a terabyte-sized dictionary file he downloaded from the Internet.

   b. The effective length of the passwords was only seven characters.

   c. Blair used "AllCrack2008" the most powerful cracking tool available.

   d. Blair used a hacked version of "John the Ripper" that is "forensic" strength.

10. KC comes into work about 30 minutes early to start an ARP poisoned attack to sniff traffic between the workstation of a fellow coworker, Greg, and the domain controller. His boss compliments him for being so early and likes his work ethic.

    KC waits until Greg comes to work and then logs in to the domain. He sniffs the passwords and spends the rest of the afternoon cracking it. What tool can be used to perform this entire sequence?

    a. Rainbowcrack

    b. L0phtcrack

    c. Kerbcrack version 6

    d. Cain and Abel

11. April is noticing in her network monitoring software that an unusual amount of UDP traffic is being sent to ports 1026 and 1027 toward various hosts. She sets up a honeypot by opening a port and listening in case any of this traffic heads in her direction.

    A few minutes later she sees text appear on the command console that reads and recognizes this as messenger spam.

    "Windows has discovered 31 critical errors. The following steps must be taken immediately: [the rest goes on to recommend a download and other destructive suggestions]"

    What did April do to receive and view this message?

    a. Used Netcat with the command: nc –l –p 1026 –u -v

    b. Used Netcat with the command: nc –l –p 31 –u -v

    c. Used Windump with the command: windump –l –p 1026 –u -v

    d. Sent a message back to the source asking for clarification

12. As a technique, rootkits hide processes and the resources that start them. What is the primary objective of a rootkit?

    a. Open access points (backdoors)

    b. Replace important system files with corrupted versions

    c. Prevent diagnostic tools from operating correctly

    d. Privilege escalation

13. Marco wants to encode data into a music file. Since it is text, he isn't sure this can be done. After searching the Internet he comes across a promising tool. What tool did he find?

    a. Mp3stego

    b. Snow

    c. Camera Shy

    d. S-Tools

14. Ernest finds a laptop that seems to have an encrypted drive. He knows the owner of the laptop works for a company that requires 15 character strong passwords. With a good quality password cracker, how long will it take Ernest to brute force this password? (Choose the best answer)

    a. 5 minutes

    b. 30 seconds

    c. 12 million years

    d. 2 days

15. In order to speed up the process of breaking a password that is pretty strongarney decides to use DNA. What is the best description of this technique?

    a. Decremented notation algorithm is a super-efficient way to break passwords. The more random the password, the better the technique works.

    b. Distributed nonce algorithm increases the analysis of seed values to 1,000 times normal rates. This allows more key space to be covered in a short time.

    c. Distributed network architecture allows multiple computers to calculate possible hash values in parallel.

    d. Distinct nuance alternatives can get "close enough" hash collisions in a short amount of time using minimal processing power.

Chapter 8: Trojans and Backdoors

1. Which of the following is the best definition of a Trojan horse?

    a. Unauthorized software that performs unwanted functions

    b. Authorized software that has been embedded with malicious code that performs unwanted functions

    c. Unauthorized features in an application that perform authorized but hidden functions

    d. Authorized software that includes rootkit functionality to protect it from being detected as a false positive

2. In terms of information security and malware classification, a RAT is a:

    a. Remote Authentication Terminal

    b. Someone that reports the activities of a coworker to management

    c. Remote Access Tool

    d. The Reveal–Access–Target model of malicious activity

3. Tayzia notices that her IDS logs are showing repeated access attempts to the $EXTERNAL_NET toward a range of ports 6662-6667. Luckily, the connections were unsuccessful. What is the bad news?

    a. Tayzia will have to work overtime trying to figure out where all the MP3s are being hidden on the network.

    b. Clearly someone is using BitTorrent to download the first season of "Star Trek: Deep Space Nine."

    c. Something on her network is trying to access IRC, and it might be an infected host.

    d. These are common administrative ports for Citrix or Oracle or something. She doesn't remember because during that discussion in her training class she was answering an e-mail instead of listening. Either way, there is no need to investigate; it is probably just a false positive.

4. Which of the following is an example of a UNC link?

    a. \\server\share

    b. UNC://server.com/share

    c. file:\\unc.server.com\share

    d. UNC shares can only be accessed via drive mapping, not addresses

5. Your company's sales manager, nicknamed "Zig," is looking for a creative way to advertise and grow the business. He accesses a popular technical forum website and asks a question he knows many in the group will be able to answer. He thanks them for their help "in advance" (TIA) while suggesting everyone visit his site for more information about his question.

One poster responds back with a link to a page called http://www.superdupersalesleadsUSA.cx and compliments Zig on his fantastic website. He says he can assist better if Zig could fill out the contact form on that page, and will also refer a number of new clients in case Zig is interested.

The sales manager gets suspicious and asks you for advice. What can you say to him?

a. It looks like a promising link, and he should try it out.

b. You tell him the site is not from the USA and would probably not have leads he can use anyway. He should respond to the poster by calling him a jerk for wasting our time.

c. You offer to click the link from your workstation insteadcause it is safer.

d. You advise this is not considered good netiquette and that this type of advertising does not present the best image for the company. You ask Zig not to click on the linko not respond further, and please don't do this again.

6. Which of the following keys can be configured to "autostart" an application when a Windows system boots up?

a. HKEY_LOCAL_MACHINE\Software\Microsoft\Windows\CurrentVersion\RunServices

b. HKEY_LOCAL_MACHINE\Software\Microsoft\Windows\CurrentVersion\RunStart

c. HKEY_LOCAL_MACHINE\Software\Microsoft\Windows\CurrentVersion\Startup

d. HKEY_LOCAL_MACHINE\Software\Microsoft\Windows\CurrentVersion\StartOnBoot

7. Larry notices in his log file that a lot of TCP traffic with the UPF flags set are targeting various internal hosts on port 31337. He suspects this traffic is unusual but does not quite know what to make of it.

Knowing you just passed your CEH exam, Larry decides to ask what you think. What would be a possible conclusion?

a. UPF scans are common license tracking mechanisms and should always be ignored. The port belongs to an old tool no one uses anymore and therefore poses no threat.

b. Larry should download the 27001 spec and pour through it word for word until it tells him what to do.

c. Larry should run "Zombie P0wn3r," a tool he got from the last Defcon security conference he attended that was guaranteed to wipe out all malicious servers.

d. The traffic is being sent from a tool, and based on port 31337, the assumption could be this is a back orifice scan.

8. Which command line tool can be used to detect all ports currently available on a system?

a. netstat –an

b. nbtstat –an

c. netports –all

d. Ipconfig—open–ports

9. Greg is using his laptop computer one day and the screen suddenly flips upside down. He remembers his old computer used to change resolution suddenly and for no reason and that his coworker told him it was a virus and told a horror story about identity theft.

What should Greg do now?

a. Assume it is a virus again and go buy a new computer.

b. Call Microsoft and demand they fix their stinking operating system because he is tired of this garbage.

c. Check to see if his laptop has a keyboard shortcut for rotating the display, since he may have accidentally hit it.

d. Download every freeware scanner he can find and spend the next three days looking for the malicious code.

10. Kumar wants to maintain access to a remote machine. He knows he can "drop a shell" that will be usable across his firewall using port 80. Which of the following tools will give him this capability?

a. Monkey shell

b. STunnel

c. HTTrack

d. Loki

11. A tool that can combine two executables together is called:

a. Wrapper

b. Masher

c. Squisher

d. Flux capacitor

12. Willard wants to use the tool "Qfecheck" to scan his network to see if the latest updates are yet installed. In order to make sure it runs correctly, permission on what registry key will have to be set properly?

a. HKEY_LOCAL_MACHINE\ SOFTWARE\Services\Microsoft\Updates

b. HKEY_LOCAL_MACHINE\ SOFTWARE\Microsoft\ServicePacks

c. HKEY_LOCAL_MACHINE\ SOFTWARE\Microsoft\Patches

d. HKEY_LOCAL_MACHINE\ SOFTWARE\Microsoft\Updates

13. Krya is an intern that has been planted to commit economic espionage. It is too dangerous to risk physical access twice to the CEO's computer. She wants to collect information and e-mail the data once a day in an encrypted zip file. What sort of tool would she need to use?

a. RPC-SMTP Trojan

b. VNC remote desktop

c. Hardware keylogger

d. Screenshot spytool

14. A tool that is part of the "sysinternals" collection can scan the Windows registry and can help detect unusual events. What is the name of this tool?

a. Regmon

b. Rootkit Revealer

c. Registry Revealer

d. Registry Baseliner

15. Code that has been posted online and given away for free, such as librariesan themselves be backdoored and propagate the security hole whenever they are used in other applications. What is the name for this type of risk?

a. Rootkit

b. Trojan horse

c. Shrink-wrap code

d. Illicit server

Chapter 9: Viruses and Worms

1. Which of the following virus types is capable of eluding signature detection by reordering its code at the machine level?

a. Multipartite

b. Metamorphic

c. Polymorphic

d. Stealth virus

2. What are the three phases of a viral outbreak?

a. Releaseetection, Removal

b. Invention, Releaseetection

c. Infection, Spreading, Attack

d. Spreading, Attack, Infection

3. Which type of virus hides itself in the unparsed areas of a binary file?

a. Cavity virus

b. Polymorphic virus

c. Metamorphic virus

d. File descriptor virus

4. What type of scan best detects a virus or worm based on behavior characteristics when the signature-based approach will not work?

   a. Heuristic

   b. Anomaly

   c. Host based

   d. PUP analysis

5. Applications that clean viruses from systems are sometimes called "Virus Scrubbers." One drawback is that they are only as good as their last signature update, and even at that, many types of malware could be undetectable if there is no signature.

   Another approach is to detect corrupt files, or at the very least, files that have been modified that shouldn't be. What type of tool performs this technique?

   a. Rootkit revealers

   b. Firewalls and virtual private networks

   c. Anti-phishing, anti-malware, etc.

   d. File integrity verification tools

6. A virus that XORs a keystream with the shell-code, uses loader code to decrypt the shellcode, then executes the decrypted code is called:

   a. Metamorphic virus

   b. Polymorphic virus

   c. XOR virus

   d. Stealth virus

7. Chandler is having a conversation with Benjamin, the present IT administrator. Benjamin is convinced his network is rock solid secure and impenetrable. He has each and every technology-based countermeasure installed. Chandler mentions there is always a weak link, and that somehow, someway a weakness will be present somewhere.

   What principle of defense is Chandler talking about? (Choose the best answer)

   a. Viruses such as polymorphic and metamorphic are too sophisticated to be stopped.

   b. Nuisances such as spam will never go away and the attackers are always one step ahead.

   c. "Zero-day" exploits are constantly being discovered and cannot be defended against.

   d. People are always the weakest link. Untrained usersareless users, and inside attackers are always a risk.

8. Which of these types of viruses primarily attack Windows systems?

   a. Boot sector

   b. System level viruses

   c. Multipartite viruses

   d. Macro viruses

9. What is generally considered to be the first worm?

   a. Elk Cloner

   b. Morris

   c. Strange Brew

   d. FU

10. Which of the following viruses had five infection methods and spread around the world in an estimated 22 minutes?

    a. Blaster

    b. Slammer

    c. Code Red

    d. Nimda

11. Dora is examining her log files and notices several access attempts with the following string:
GET/default.ida?NNNNNNNNNNNN
NNNNNNNNNNNNNNNNNNNNNNN
NNNNNNNNNNNNNNNNNNNNNNN
NNNNNNNNNNNNNNNNNNNNNNN
NNNNNNNNNNNNNNNNNNNNNNN
NNNNNNNNNNNNNNNNNNNNNNN
NNNNNNNNNNNNNNNNNNNNNNN
NNNNNNNNNNNNNNNNNNNNNNN
NNNNNNNNNNNNNNNNNNNNNNN
NNNNNNNNNNNNNNNNNNNNNNN
NNNNNNNNNNNN%u9090%u688%u
cbd3%u7801%u9090%u6858%ucbd3%u7
801%u9090%u6858%ucbd3%u7801%u90
90%u900%u8190%u00c3%u0003%u8b0
0%u531b%u53ff%u0078%u0000%u00=a
HTTP/1.0

She opens a browser to visit her own website and notices the front page had been defaced to say the following:

"HELLO! Welcome to http://www.worm.com! Hacked By Chinese!"

What may have happened?

a. Code Red got to her web server.

b. An attacker used a fuzzer to overflow the query string.

c. Class case of Michelangelo.

d. The Nachi worm found her site and successfully exploited it.

12. Microsoft knowledge base bulletin MS03-026 describes an RPC (Port 135) vulnerability that has been exploited time and again even though a patch exists. Which of the following worms exploited this vulnerability?

a. Pretty Park

b. Storm

c. Nachi/Welchia

d. I Love You

13. What are the six steps of the virus lifecycle?

a. Design, Replication, Infectionetectionon-tainment, Elimination

b. Design, Replication, Monitoringetection, Incorporation, Elimination

c. Design, Replication, Launchetection, Elimination, Incorporation

d. Design, Replication, Launchetection, Incorporation, Elimination

14. Kelly sent an e-mail out to the entire staff warning of a new vulnerability in Outlook that would expose the entire contact list. She explains that several versions of the e-mail have been foundut they all contain the words "Sales Lead" or "Service Request" in the subject line. These e-mails must be deleted without being opened for the next 72 hours while a patch is released.

What statements below are the most true? (Select up to two)

a. Kelly is being helpful. Coworkers watching out for events like this and helping one another is critical to any working security program.

b. This looks like a hoax. If Kelly is even a real person she should be fired on the spot, since hoaxes are considered as dangerous as actual viruses.

c. Hoaxes are considered as dangerous as actual viruses and this could be an indication that training is in order for more people than just Kelly.

d. An investigation should be conducted to find out if Kelly was attempting a hoax or was herself socially engineered.

15. Melissa receives an e-mail that comes from a random e-mail address. She has many friends that use their online "handles" like sillyputty321@yahoo.com, for instance, so she isn't really surprised by that. There is an attachment on the e-mail called "Iloveyou.txt" which looks intriguing even if she doesn't remember knowing this person. What is about to happen?

a. She will open the attachment and it will be from a long lost partner she has been hoping to get back in touch with for years.

b. The file is really named "iloveyou.txt. vbs" and is a well known classic trick to spread a macro virus.

c. Her boss sent her this as a practical joke to see if she would open it, but it's likely harmless.

d. Windows will pop open to a command shell and a lot of noise will come from her speakers. The shell will say "Will you marry me?" The e-mail was from her fiancée.

Chapter 10: Sniffers, Spoofing, and Session Hijacking

1. What would the following command accomplish?

    windump –nes 0 –w C:\dump.txt tcp[28]=0x72 or tcp[28]=0x73 or tcp[40]=0x72 or tcp[40]=0x73

    a. Sniff all TCP traffic that has certain flag combinations.

    b. Sniff the file "dump.txt" if it is sent across the network.

    c. Sniff cheatcodes on nes (Nintendo Entertainment System) traffic.

    d. Sniff SMB challenges.

2. To use a sniffer on a Windows machine you first need to install a promiscuous mode driver. What is this package called?

    a. Ethereal

    b. Promiscap

    c. Winpcap

    d. Libpcap

3. How many possible values can be generated in the sequence number field of a TCP header?

    a. 2 billion

    b. 3.4 million

    c. 4.3 billion

    d. 16.7 million

4. Which of the following forms of attack depends on an already established connection between hosts?

    a. Smurfing

    b. Spoofing

    c. Man in The Middle

    d. Session hijacking

5. One possible way to defeat a switch is to flood it with spoofed MAC addresses until it fails into "hub mode." Which of the following tools can accomplish this?

    a. Macof

    b. Dsniff

    c. Sniffof

    d. Sniffit

6. Quincy runs the L0phcrack tool which has a feature that sniffs SMB passwords and stores them for offline cracking. He tries for hours and picks up nothing. What could be the reason?

    a. L0phtcrack does not do this, he needs to use 0phtcrack.

    b. He is sniffing on a segment that is using only IP security traffic in ESP mode.

    c. He is sniffing on a fiber optic network.

    d. His network interface is in promiscuous mode.

7. Which of the following tools allows for the easy capture and analysis of data that has been captured during a TCP connection?

    a. TCPFlow

    b. TShark

    c. Mergecap

    d. Text2pcap

8. Bruno wishes to carry out a session hijack attack between hosts "Jaguar" and "Puma." They are in an established state. Puma has a receive window of 300 and Jaguar has a receive window of 350. Jaguar has just received byte 500 from Puma and Acknowledged. What is the range of sequence numbers that Jaguar will now accept from Puma?

   a. 501–851

   b. 500–850

   c. 350–500

   d. 501–801

9. Which of the following display filters will only show TCP traffic with the URG, PSH, and FIN flags set?

   a. tcp.flags == 0x12

   b. tcp.flags = = 0x29

   c. proto.flags == UPF

   d. tcp.flags == 29

10. LaDanian is sniffing some traffic and notices a frame that is sent with the source MAC address of: 34:A3:02:68:AF:D4. The third byte in (from the left), which is the least significant byte of the vendor code section of the address, is 02. This is what he thinks is weird. Why?

    a. The second bit (from the LSB) is set, which means this is multicast, and a single frame cannot come from multiple hosts.

    b. The first bit (from the LSB) is not set, which indicates this frame is sent from a logical network interface.

    c. The second bit (from the LSB) is set, which means this is a virtual machine interface.

    d. The first bit (from the LSB) is not set, which indicates this frame is sent from a logical network interface.

11. ARP spoofing works in part because Ethernet hardware has no way of knowing if there is another NIC on the network with the same MAC address or not. True or false?

    a. True

    b. False

12. Which of the following protocols are not vulnerable to sniffing due to clear text credentials being sent?

    a. FTP

    b. POP3

    c. MAPI

    d. IMAP

13. Janet is reading about the "Pass-the-Hash" technique to access a Windows host. She thinks she can use Wireshark to sniff an SMB session between two hosts if she can capture the password hash and user name, and simply send them as credentials anytime she wants in a "Replay Attack."

    What are other true statements about this attack? (Choose all that apply)

    a. This can also be done using a modified smbclient tool that does not hash an entered password; it will just directly send the hash that Janet captured.

    b. Janet can also use a tool such as smbrelay to become an SMB proxy and capture credentials that way.

    c. The traffic that Janet sniffed did not include a challenge; if it did, the technique is still not impossible, it just involves more steps.

    d. Because Microsoft uses techniques such as SMB Signing, Kerberos Timestamps, and Challenges that are used to create unique MACs (Message Authentication Codes), the "Pass-the-Hash" technique is mostly a proof of concept that works in theory but not in practice.

14. Which of the following attacks are not considered "Active Sniffing"?

    a. ARP poisoning

    b. MAC flooding

    c. MAC spoofing

    d. SMAC fueling

15. Assuming your own address is 192.168.1.1, what display filter could be used to show all traffic other than web and mail?

    a. Host 192.168.1.1 and not (port 80 or port 25)

    b. Host 192.168.1.1 and not port 80 and not port 25

    c. Ip.addr 192.168.1.1 && ! tcp.port == 80 && ! tcp.port == 25

    d. Ip.addr 192.168.1.1 & ! tcp.port = 80 & ! tcp.port = 25

Chapter 11: Social Engineering

1. Dave wants to steal the contact database from a rival sales person. He calls his rival's secretary and pretends to be from the IT department. He says, "The sales tracking system just crashed, at least we think so. We are hopeful that we saved everyone's dataut we need Mr. Shiver's username and password in order to log in and check." What type of attack is Dave conducting?

    a. Identity theft

    b. Identity faking

    c. Identity spoofing

    d. Identity pre-texting

2. Karen gets hired on with disrupttheprocess.org to organize interference in public political events. Her real purpose, however, is to figure out where the real funding for these events is coming from so she can inform the media. She figures out how the power structure works and spies a contact list on the desk of a fellow coworker.

    Karen recognizes that this person also handles finances and works out at a gym that Karen belongs to as well. Karen arranges to bump into her one day and suggests they do spin class together for awhile. Long story short, this friendship trust eventually results in Karen achieving access to a database of sponsors, which she then provides to the local newspaper.

    What type of social engineer is Karen?

    a. Insider associate

    b. Insider affiliate

    c. Outsider affiliate

    d. Outsider associate

3. Which of the following are ways to overcome insider threats? (Choose up to seven)

    a. Separation of duties

    b. Rotation of duties

    c. Restrict privileges

    d. Controlled access

    e. Logging and auditing

    f. Legal policies

    g. Archiving critical data

4. It is considered that 60 to 70 percent of all attacks come from insiders. Which of the following groups or individuals is not an insider?

    a. Disgruntled employee

    b. Suppliers and vendors

    c. CEO

    d. Business partners and consultants

5. What is the most common method of social engineering?

    a. LANs

    b. E-mail

    c. In person

    d. Telephone

6. Easton is hired by a materials company to investigate why a competitor seems to be able to apply for patents for exactly the same technologies faster than they can. The competitor doesn't even produce or make anything; they seem to exist only to sit on patents.

    Easton finds John, a proud father and dog owner who is always bringing new pictures into the office on a USB key. He loads them onto his computer each morning, tries to show them to coworkers as they walk past, then copies them back onto the USB key in the afternoon. Since they are just pictures of his children and his dogs, no one thought anything of it.

At the very least, John might be abusing company time editing his photos, but there is no such software on his system.

What activity does Easton suspect John is up to?

a. Picture fuzzing

b. Steganography

c. Cryptography

d. Reverse social engineering

7. Tom sees Jerry walking quickly up to a door that is protected by a proximity card. Jerry looks like he is in a hurry and has something on his mind. Tom runs up alongside him and starts a distracting conversation. As Jerry opens the door, his body language suggests that he wants to get away from Tom but Tom just gets more aggressive and walks in behind him through the door. Once inside, he gives up and tells Jerry to have a nice day.

What has Tom done?

a. Clever talking

b. Door jamming

c. Tailgating

d. Mantrapping

8. Devon has been "dumpster diving." He went through his target's garbage and recycle bins getting all he could. What is the term used to describe what he will most likely do with these documents?

a. Paper pilfering

b. Trash tracing

c. Green grabbing

d. Document grinding

9. Lucas is an e-mail administrator. He is extremely sick and tired of spam and convinces his boss to let him focus entirely on the e-mail system for awhile. He puts into place a list of countermeasures that include: Spam prevention software at the edge of his networkNSBLs (DNS Based Black Lists), and Mail Exchanger Callbacks. Still the spam comes in.

He decides the next best thing to try is a system that slows down connections to known spam relays to at least reduce the volume of traffic that just gets blasted in. What is this technique known as?

a. SPAM Cannibal

b. Sender policy framework

c. Teergrubbing (Tar Pit)

d. SMTP Cannonball

10. What are the six principles of social engineering?

a. Authority, Scarcity, Liking, Reciprocationommitment, Intimidation

b. Authority, Scarcity, Liking, Reciprocationonsistency, Social Validation

c. Authority, Scarcityomplimenting, Reciprocationonsistency, Social Validation

d. Intimidation, Scarcity, Liking, Reciprocationharisma, Social Validation

11. Sean is having a conversation with a friend, making fun of how foolish spammers are. Clearly, he says "These e-mails are just sent by the millions and look like it. Only an idiot falls for them." In the meanwhile Sean is reading an e-mail addressed to him. It says:

Dear Sean,

I understand you did some work awhile back for an orfanage in Brazil. Sorry to bother you, sir, we have never meet, but I am a 13-year-old boy whose parents were taken the the States. I need some money to get them to return safely or, if I can, greet them there in the States, too. Can you help?

Sean remembers his trip to Brazil and thinks of a boy he met there (He met hundreds, but the mind plays tricks like this on the best of us). He wonders for a moment if this might be him. What technique is Sean about to fall prey to?

a. SPAM & scam sandwich

b. Brazilian online cartels

c. Spear phishing

d. South American 419 scam

12. Which of the following are best practices when securing a relay so it is not "open"? (Choose up to two)

    a. Disable MX zone transfers

    b. Filter VRFY and EXPN commands

    c. Filter VRFY and ESPN commands

    d. Configure SMTP-AUTH

13. An attacker sends e-mail to a domain toward an invalid address intentionally. A bounce back is sent and the attacker uses the header to determine internal mail relays. How is a header read to determine the path the bounce took?

    a. From the bottom up

    b. From the top down

    c. With a sniffer

    d. Headers are not useful; the source of the e-mail is always spoofed

14. Once efforts to set up blacklists were created and high profile spammers were starting to receive prison sentences, one would think they would be discouraged. Nope. Which of the following is a technique that is now used to distribute spam and to cloak its sender?

    a. Social networks

    b. SMS, Skype, and IM SPAM

    c. Spear P

    d. Botnets

15. What are the three steps of reverse social engineering?

    a. Sabotage, Advertising, Assisting

    b. Advertising, Sabotage, Assisting

    c. Sabotage, Assisting, Advertising

    d. Assisting, Sabotage, Advantage

Chapter 12: Denial of Service

1. Sergio wants to get back at his competitor for winning the gold medal in a town fair BBQ contest. He pays his nephew to attack their website. The competitor doesn't realize this until they notice it is not accessible—there is an error message about the authentication system, and a simple reboot is not enough to fix it. What type of attack is this most likely? (Choose the best description)

    a. Distributed denial of service that relies on accidental traffic

    b. Denial of service based on a well-known LSASS vulnerability

    c. Distributed denial of service that overloads resources

    d. Denial of service that requires human interaction to restore service

2. Clive notices that one of his hosts keeps getting DoS'd. A quick view of the traffic on the wire shows a lot of traffic that has both the destination and the host address the same as the victim. What type of attack is this?

    a. Land

    b. Fraggle

    c. Smurf

    d. Ping of death

3. Which is the best description of an unnamed attack?

    a. A 0-day attack that researchers have not yet identified

    b. An attack that has not been identified by the IDS

    c. Reducing offset values to cause a short packet on reassembly

    d. Increasing offset values to cause a long packet on reassembly

4. Mary notices her machine has Internet access for about ten minutes then it seems to slow down. She reboots, and everything is fine for another ten minutes. What is the most likely problem?

    a. Her Internet filter is metering her usage and throttling her down.

    b. Her ISP is traffic shaping.

    c. The website she is visiting is down.

    d. Her host is vulnerable to slammer.

5. Tony wants to clear his afternoon to play a video game. He needs to manufacture an emergency and tells his boss that the servers are vulnerable to an "Evil Bit" attack, and it will take all afternoon to fix them. This sounds bad, so the boss tells him to get right on it. What is Tony really talking about?

   a. He is referring to a character in his video gameut the boss doesn't realize this.

   b. He just gave the boss a simple explanation for a real attack knowing he wouldn't understand the right one.

   c. The high order bit in the fragment offset field is setut it is supposed to be reserved with a value 0, and most IP stacks have not been updated to understand it. It crashes the system.

   d. This is an IT inside joke.

6. Which of the following tools is not a demonstration of an asymmetric attack (or a tool)?

   a. Tribe flood network

   b. Trinoo

   c. C2myazz

   d. Stacheldraht

7. A host is bombarded with packets intended to exploit stateful network protocols. Every time it gets a packet, it allocates memory for the expected connection. The connection is never fully established by the sender. What form of attack is this?

   a. SYN flood

   b. Smurf

   c. Ping of death

   d. Stachledraught

8. Which of the following tools means "Barbed Wire" in German?

   a. Zertifizierte

   b. Stacheldraht

   c. Barbenkwier

   d. Zschwiedlfenken

9. Knowing her company is about to spend 45 percent of its marketing budget for the year on one commercial during the Super Bowlontessa decides to test the load of the servers. This way, Capacity problems won't cause the site to go down if the commercial is successful. What tool can she use?

   a. UDP flood

   b. Jolt2

   c. Blast

   d. MStream

10. What is a possible countermeasure for SYN floods?

   a. SPI firewall

   b. SYN cookies

   c. Block all flags with the SYN flag set, in or out

   d. Disable outgoing SYN traffic

11. Which of the following tools is known for having a menu of choices available to the attacker?

   a. TFN2K

   b. Targa

   c. Kismet

   d. Wikto

12. Blair and Lee work in the NOCs (Network Operation Centers) of two different ISPs. They are on the late shift and bored. Blair sends a series of packets that are 65,537 bytes in length to try to irritate Lee. What is he doing?

   a. Ping of death

   b. Invite of death

   c. Generate false positives on the IDS that Lee will have to explain

   d. Nothing. Packets can be up to 2^{32} in size because the datagram length field is 15 bits and the 16th bit is a multiplier.

13. Sterling sends a flood of UDP traffic toward port 19 on an old UNIX mainframe, spoofing the broadcast address of the subnet and source port 7. What is he trying to do?

    a. Smurf attack

    b. Fraggle attack

    c. FrickaFrack attack

    d. SmallService attack

14. Gary assembles an ACL for his Cisco router that looks something like this:
    access-list 111 deny ip 10.0.0.0 0.255.255.255 any access-list 111 deny ip 172.16.0.0 0.15.255.255 any access-list 111 deny ip 192.168.0.0 0.0.255.255 any access-list 111 deny ip 127.0.0.1 0.255.255.255 any access-list 111 deny ip 224.0.0.0 31.255.255.255 any access-list 111 deny ip host 0.0.0.0 any

    The list is applied to an outside interface. What is this list trying to accomplish?

    a. Defining private IPs

    b. Defining internal networks

    c. Anti-NAT attacks

    d. Anti-spoofing

15. Landon sends a "Chernobyl Packet" into a network. What does this mean?

    a. A packet that causes a kernel panic

    b. A packet that causes a broadcast storm

    c. A packet that contains a virus

    d. A packet that causes a BSOD

Chapter 13: Buffer Overflows

1. What is the term used to describe the space in memory that stores a set of instructions that are meant to be running temporarily?

    a. Stack

    b. Page

    c. Heap

    d. Pile

2. What are the terms used to describe the loading and unloading of a stack of instructions?

    a. Load/Unload

    b. Push/Pop

    c. Get/Put

    d. Retrieve/Return

3. Which of the following are dangerous functions in C? (Choose up to four)

    a. strcpy

    b. strcat

    c. wcscpy

    d. fgets

4. Four bytes are used by programmers to terminate string operations. They can also check these bytes when a function returns to see if an attempt has been made to overwrite them, and if so, an alert can be generated and a message sent to syslog. These are called the "Canary Bytes." If a message does show up in syslog indicating a problem, what happened?

    a. An overflow has been attempted.

    b. An overflow was successful.

    c. The stack has crashed.

    d. The host-based IDS caught the event.

5. The terms "overflow" and "overrun" mean the same thing.

    a. True

    b. False

6. If you have the following pseudo code, what is the most accurate natural language description?

    If (i >= 300) then exit

    a. If we have written 300 characters to the buffer variable, the function should stop because it cannot hold any more data.

    b. If we have written more than 300 characters to the buffer variable, the function should stop because it cannot hold any more data.

c. If we have written less than 300 characters to the buffer variable, the function should stop because it cannot hold any more data.

d. If we have written less than or equal to 300 characters to the buffer variable, the function should stop because it cannot hold any more data.

7. It is hard to be precise with the offset value that gets placed into the return register when an overflow is deliberate, as in during an attack. A NOOP sled can be placed at the beginning of the shell code to create some margin for error. Which of the following looks like a sled?

   a. 0xA4\0x23\0xFE\0x65\0xA5\0x65\0xAE\0x5B

   b. 0xFF\0xFF\0xFF\0xFF\0xFF\0xFF\0xFF\0xFF\

   c. 0x00\0x0D\0x0A\0xFF\0x00\0x0D\0x0A\0xFF\

   d. 0x90\0x90\0x90\0x90\0x90\0x90\0x90\0x90\

8. Which of the following registers will be overwritten in a buffer overflow exploit?

   a. EIP

   b. ESP

   c. ERP

   d. EXP

9. The following four bytes represent what?
   NULL (0x00)R (0x0D), LF (0x0A), EOF (0XFF)

   a. Bytecode

   b. Shellcode

   c. NOP Sled

   d. Canary bytes

10. Which of the following languages is less vulnerable to buffer flow attacks?

    a. ActiveX

    b. Assembly

    c. Java

    d. C++

11. You just embedded an Active X control in your webpage that has malicious code. It exploits a well-known buffer overflow exploit in Internet Explorer. If a casual home user drops by to visit your site and accepts the plugin, what privilege will you likely have on the affected host?

    a. Whatever the user was when they visited the page

    b. IUSR_[compuer name]

    c. System or Administrator

    d. Internet_Explorer

12. You just attacked an IIS server and managed to exploit a buffer overflow in the .printer ISAPI. Turns out there are several tools to choose from. Which of the following tools does not perform this attack?

    a. Jill.c

    b. iishack2000.c

    c. iis5hack.zip

    d. john the printer

13. There is a "Chunked Encoding Transfer Heap Overflow" vulnerability in IIS. You Telnet into port 80 of a possible target and enter the following commands:

    [CDT]POST /iisstart.asp HTTP/1.1
    Accept: */*
    Host: acme.com
    Content-Type: application/x-www-form-urlencoded
    Transfer-Encoding: chunked

    10
    PADPADPADPADPADP
    4
    DATA
    4
    DEST
    0
    [enter]
    [enter]

What is the vulnerable script that you are targeting?

a. acme.com

b. iisstart.asp

c. PADPADPADPADPADP

d. Not enough information to tell

14. You are looking at some code and notice something that concerns you. What is the dangerous function in the code below?

```
void myMethod(char * pStr) {
char pBuff[10];
int nCount = 0;
strcpy(pBuff, pStr);
}
void foo()
{
}
```

a. void foo()

b. myMethod

c. strcpy

d. fgets

15. When successfully executing a buffer over-flow, what level of privilege will the attacker have?

a. Buffer overflows always have system

b. Buffer overflows always have root, or admin

c. The same context of the service or application that was running

d. It's undetermined; depends on the exploit

Chapter 14: Hacking Web Servers and Web Applications

1. When testing a website you enter the following into a field on the login form:

<script>alert ("oops")</script>

When you submit the form an alert box pops up as the next page loads. This is a demon-stration of what type of attack?

a. CSS

b. XSS

c. Buffer overflow

d. Code injection

2. Which of the following tools cannot be used to perform a dictionary guessing attack on a web application?

a. THC-Hydra

b. John the ripper

c. Brutus

d. Nikto

3. What is CGI?

a. A set of specifications for creating web-based applications

b. A way to create enhanced special effects for movies

c. A language used in the logic layer of a web application

d. A set of standards that govern the design of databases for web applications

4. Which of the following URLs looks like an SQL injection attack?

a. http://www.example.dom/msadc/..%5c. ./..%5c../..%5c/..Á_../..Á_../..Á_../winnt/ system32/cmd.exe

b. http://www.example.dom?search. pl?lname=doe%27%3bupdate%20 usertable%20set%passwd% 3d%27%P0wn3d−−%00

c. http://www.example.dom?search.pl?lnam e=%3Cscript%3E%alert("P0wn3d")3C %2Fscript%3E

d. http://www.example.dom/scripts/. .%2f. .%2f. ./winnt/system32/cmd.exe?c+dir

5. Which of the following tools are web vulner-ability scanners/testers? (Choose up to six)

a. Whisker

b. Burpsuite

c. N-Stealth

d. HTTrack

e. Nikto

f. Kismet

6. You just hired a new graphic artist to work on your website. You are cheap, and don't want to spring for a programmer because web design is all the same anyway. The new guy you hired is an expert at Photoshop, but hates coding. Tell him, "Look, this makes no sense. Just follow a few of these pointers and you will be fine." In the interest of security, what is one of the things you will tell him?

a. Visitors enjoy it when one page of content is broken up into five pages. They get to click often and we get to show more advertisements. It is the best way to avoid making enemies.

b. Never decorate text with the color blue or green as visitors will think these are links and spend all day trying to click them; they will get angry and DoS us.

c. Most application vulnerabilities stem from a lack of sanitizing input. They will be his faultut no pressure.

d. Section 508 details all security best practices. It will get him up to speed.

7. An attacker is testing out the login page of a website. He notices that after five failed attempts he is redirected to a different page. He assumes this logs his IP address, and if this redirect continues, it could lead to being blocked. How can he avoid this from happening?

a. He can turn on SSL support in his browser; that way the encrypted requests will be hidden from the IDS.

b. He can send his requests from random spoofed IPs so the server wouldn't think they are all coming from the same source.

c. He can create a persistent cookie that tells the web server to ignore failed logins.

d. If there is a hidden form field that stores the "retries" count, he can modify the source code to avoid the threshold.

8. Ned is testing a web application. He visits a page that seems to have some features that can be customized by the userut not all of them. He uses a cookie viewer to take a look at how his settings are stored and notices the following name value pairs:

Colorscheme=ocean
layout=newspaper
admin=false

He changes the admin variable to true, and reloads the page. This time he can change more items on the page. What is the name of this attack?

a. Parameter manipulation

b. Cookie triangulation

c. Cookie hijacking

d. Cookie stealing

9. You have successfully completed a buffer overflow attack against an IIS server. You have a shell. Now what, you wonder. First, what permissions do you have at this point?

a. IUSR_[computer name]

b. Administrator

c. The user that installed IIS

d. The permission you have when launching the attack

10. Dylan found a vulnerability on a web application that let him copy the sessionID out of a local cookie and place it into another cookie, thus assuming the identity of the original user. The problem is that the server also associates the originating IP address. Dylan simply spoofs that addressut he then finds he cannot establish an interactive session with the server. Why?

a. The attack should work as stated.

b. There is a NAT firewall preventing this activity.

c. Dylan cannot spoof his address over HTTP.

d. The server will send all replies back to the spoofed IP.

11. Mike is trying to recover his password from a site. It asks for his e-mail address. Just then, his cat walks across the keyboard and enters an extra character. He ends up entering into the form mike.portnoy@silverlinings.com' and the return page shows an error was returned from the server.

    What is the cause of this on the web server?

    a. User input is not sanitized.

    b. The e-mail address is not valid.

    c. The database server on the backend of the site is down.

    d. The ISP is traffic shaping again and made a mistake.

12. You see an e-mail in your box that looks suspicious. It has typos and seems to be preying on a current event that is volatile and has a large audience of passionate people that want to believe its message. This is classic social engineering spam. It reads:

    . . .

    Stop them from setting up death panels!!!! Only when the government interferes do things go terribly wrong. Sign our petition to put an end to this madness and recover your constitutional rights! While you are there, join in the fight by purchasing a t-shirt for only $29.95. Its slogan reads: Government is the only disease I have!! Wear it at the next town hall meeting to let them know you are paying attention.

    http://0x7F2D52DB/stophealthcare.ee

    (The address is encrypted to protect your identity. They are collecting enemy lists; we are making sure you are safe.)

    . . .

    What is the real IP address of this site?

    a. 127.45.83.218

    b. 127.45.82.219

    c. 127.44.83.219

    d. 127.44.83.218

13. You have a website that is not meant for everyone, only for a particular audience. You do not want certain directories to be crawled by a spider. How can you limit (in theory at least) what search engines will index?

    a. .htaccess file

    b. Robots.txt file

    c. Set permissions on the directories to deny spiders read access

    d. Require a login page

14. Janet wants a no-cost solution to blocking certain applications from launching pop-up windows while she is surfing the web. She has tried everything her old Windows XP computer can run. Alternative browsers, freeware spyware scanner, nothing helps.

    a. She needs to understand that these pop-ups are part of using the Internet and that it is impolite to block them because the sites she is visiting for free depend on them for revenue.

    b. SP2 upgrade with the windows firewall enabled.

    c. She needs to use Linux instead.

    d. She needs to modify the hosts file daily to point all addresses that generate the pop-ups to 0.0.0.0 to keep them from resolving.

15. You notice the following in your log files. What attack is being attempted?

    GET /scripts/root.exe?/c+dir
    GET /MSADC/root.exe?/c+dir
    GET /c/winnt/system32/cmd.exe?/c+dir
    GET /d/winnt/system32/cmd.exe?/c+dir
    GET /scripts/. .%5c. ./winnt/system32/cmd.exe?/c+dir
    GET /_vti_bin/. .%5c. ./. .%5c. ./. .%5c. ./winnt/system32/cmd.exe?/c+dir
    GET /_mem_bin/. .%5c. ./. .%5c. ./. .%5c. ./winnt/system32/cmd.exe?/c+dir
    GET/msadc/. .%5c. ./. .%5c. ./. .%5c/. \xc1\x1c. ./. .\xc1\x1c. ./. .\xc1\x1c.\./winnt/system32/cmd.exe?/c+dir
    GET /scripts/. .\xc1\x1c. ./winnt/system32/cmd.exe?/c+dir

GET /scripts/. .\xc0/. ./winnt/system32/cmd. exe?/c+dir

GET /scripts/. .\xc0\xaf. ./winnt/system32/ cmd.exe?/c+dir

GET /scripts/. .\xc1\x9c. ./winnt/system32/ cmd.exe?/c+dir

GET /scripts/. .%35c. ./winnt/system32/cmd. exe?/c+dir

GET /scripts/. .%35c. ./winnt/system32/cmd. exe?/c+dir

GET /scripts/. .%5c. ./winnt/system32/cmd. exe?/c+dir

GET /scripts/. .%2f. ./winnt/system32/cmd. exe?/c+dir

a. XSS

b. Directory traversal

c. Showcode.asp

d. Nimda

Chapter 15: Wireless Networks

1. Zachery sees a video on YouTube that describes a wireless hacking technique. He must capture a packet then inject it over and over again into the network stream. The target MAC of this frame will ensure it goes to the correct WAP. The idea is to speed up the process of acquiring new initialization vectors for the purposes of cracking a WEP key.

   What is this portion of the attack called?

   a. Replay attack

   b. Injection attack

   c. Spoof attack

   d. WAP attack

2. During an attack you set up an access point with a stronger signal than those around you. You also set the SSIDs to be the same as the one you are targeting. You capture authentication frames.

   Which of the following is the best name for this attack?

   a. Rogue WAP

   b. Drive-by

c. WEP attack

d. Denial of service

3. Arianna wants to implement 802.11b for a series of hotels that her employer won a contract on. Her boss says that one of the customers was concerned that if TCP error checking was part of the configuration, the network would be slower. Arianna pauses, and explains . . . . (Choose the best statement)

   a. TCP error checking effectively speeds up the network. Since there will be fewer retransmissions the speed will surpass the speed of the wired network.

   b. The resulting speed will be about 6 Mbps. Since the Ethernet in the hotel is 10 Mbps, accounting for several users at the same time, a throttle speed makes sense.

   c. Error checking is part of the TCP protocol already. Network speed measures bits; the overhead that gets delivered are bits, too.

   d. Her boss is correct, and the whole project should just get scrapped. Let someone else deal with these difficult customers.

4. Jack is worried about the FUD (Fear Uncertainty Doubt) he has heard about wireless networks. He also does not want to learn about WPA2 and how easy it is to implement. He sets forth a policy of no wireless networks allowed, period. What else should he do? (Choose up to three)

   a. Train users in the new policy.

   b. Implement signal jamming technology.

   c. Survey the area using tools such as WiSpy and AirPcapreate a baseline, and investigate the rest.

   d. Disable wireless protocols at the firewall.

   e. Set penalties for those who create WAPs without approval.

5. What is the highest possible speed of 802.11n?

   a. 600 Mbps

   b. 54 Mbps

c. 108 Mbps

d. 11 Mbps

6. An SSID is: (Choose the best statement)

a. Secure Set Identifier Determination

b. Secure Service Identification Detection

c. A security vulnerability

d. A password

7. Howard wants to control access to his wireless network. Which of the following would not be of assistance to him?

a. WEP

b. A Layer 2 firewall

c. MAC address filtering

d. Proper placement of the antennas

8. Keith is setting up a Wifi network and wants to use highly directional antennas that do not require precision. Which of the following would be best?

a. Yagi

b. Reflector

c. Omnidirectional

d. King/Hanneman

9. A one-time, unique value that is added to an algorithm to ensure a truly random output is called:

a. Nonce

b. IV

c. Salt

d. Seed

10. Dean is repurposing an old Dell Axim PDA (Personal Digital Assistant) as an easy to use walkabout tool for scanning Wifi networks in his area. This PDA is based on Windows Mobile and he has a compatible CF Card Wifi radio. What software can he use on this device to meet his objective?

a. Ministumbler

b. Netstumbler

c. Kismet

d. Kismac

11. Karen sets up a wireless network that is open and includes WEP. Which acronym accurately describes this configuration?

a. TCP/IP

b. OSA/AES

c. WPA/FSK

d. OSA/PSK

12. WPA is vulnerable to brute force if the password is easy and short. What tool attempts this attack?

a. WEPCrack

b. coWPAtty

c. WPACrack

d. Airfart

13. You have been asked to set up a wireless intrusion detection system. Which of the following products fills this function?

a. Airsnort

b. LIDZ

c. WIDS

d. WIPS

14. You are a wireless hobbyist. A few years ago it was novel to find wireless networksut these days it is commonplace. So you get more creative and try any other transportation mechanism possible to find accessible hosts. What is this called?

a. Warxing

b. Bored

c. Flexible

d. Diligent

15. Leo wants to secure his wireless network. He implements WAP2, installs directional antennas, and implements rogue infrastructure testing. What else does he need to consider? (Choose up to four)

a. Denial of service attacks are always a threat but they are hard to prevent. A proper incident response plan must also be established.

b. Associating with a WAP only secures the hosts. The users operating the hosts are a whole separate issue.

c. WEP provides similar functionality to a network switch. Sniffing is then improbable, so that is one threat that is no longer an issue. Key distribution is the most important challenge at this point.

d. Interference with other items within the 2.4 Ghz band might cause issues. It is important to select a channel within the range that is less populated.

Chapter 16: Cryptography

1. **What is a hash?**

   a. Single key algorithm used to protect data at rest

   b. Non-reversible representation of the data

   c. Private key encryption that is used as a counterpart to the key

   d. A mechanism to protect the exchange of a public key

2. **Which of the following is the best description of a "weak key"?**

   a. A key that defines its own IV

   b. A key that is easy to guess

   c. A key that is too short

   d. A key that makes an encryption algorithm behave in a particular way

3. **Some versions of Windows servers use a feature called "syskey" to enhance the protection of the database where user account hashes are stored. What level of encryption does syskey use in Windows 2000?**

   a. 128b

   b. 56b

   c. 256b

   d. 40b

4. **Nick wants to protect data as it moves across a network by using a tunnelut he cannot implement a full VPN solution. Which of the following is his best option?**

   a. MD5

   b. RSA

   c. SSH

   d. PGP

5. **Kalyna implements a strong system to protect her network communications. It involves DSA (Digital Signature Algorithm) and also uses elliptic curve cryptography to enhance the efficiency of the system. What is this technology called?**

   a. ELGamal and DSA

   b. ECDSA

   c. RSA-PSS

   d. SHA-1 with RSA

6. **If the hash of a password is sent across the network, it might be possible to capture and replay it without ever having to attack the hash itself. In order to prevent this, and also to keep the hash from being transmitted in the clear, what method can be used?**

   a. Challenge/response

   b. SSL

   c. Cryptographic authentication

   d. Cross realm authentication

7. **Tabatha wants to implement a two-factor authentication that includes the use of hardware devices but she doesn't have the budget for smart cards. Which of the following is her next best option?**

   a. OTP (One Time Passwords)

   b. Security token

   c. Proximity cards

   d. Biometric devices

8. **ExampleFinancial got attacked by a group of hackers from Elbonia. Forensic analysis shows that a home user's machine was infected with a spreading Trojan that got into the corporate network through the VPN. The attackers wanted to use it to capture important source codeut they also ended up using it to obtain information from the dataset of customer information.**

What policy can ExampleFinancial implement to avoid this in the future?

a. Enable a 25 character password for all VPN access

b. Do not allow VPN access from home computers

c. Use only dial-up connections for VPN access to a segmented gateway

d. Require biometric authentication

9. Which of the following is not a block cipher?

a. DES

b. Blowfish

c. RC4

d. Rijndael

10. What is the best definition of a covert channel?

a. A server using an unusual port for connections

b. Repurposing a protocol for a use other than intended

c. Multiplexing on a communication link

d. Control channels used in technologies such as WiFi or DSL

11. What statement best describes the way to prevent a key generating algorithm from creating the same keys, weak keys, or a batch of keys that have a lot in common?

a. A different algorithm should be used each time to confuse the cryptanalyst.

b. The algorithm should be salted with a one-time random value before each key is made.

c. Only one-time keys should be used because it is impossible to prevent a computer from repeating a process.

d. Keys should always be created offliney a dedicated system.

12. Caden is considering an e-mail encryption technology. It must be available for multiple types of systems. Which one is his best choice?

a. S/MIME

b. SSH

c. PGP

d. Yahoo

13. One of the disadvantages of symmetric key encryption is key management. For instance, if there are 10 people who wish to exchange data with each otherut maintain confidentiality at the same time, how many keys must be issued?

a. 1,000

b. 10

c. 1

d. 45

14. Which of the following is not correct in regard to one-time pads?

a. They are the same or greater lengths than the message being encrypted.

b. The pad itself must be exchanged out of band.

c. A truly random pad is considered unbreakable.

d. If the pad is generated the same way by each party, they don't need to exchange it; therefore, it is never exposed to risk.

15. A method for verifying that a message is being exchanged only by two members with a prior association and that its integrity has also been maintained is called:

a. Diffie hellman

b. Message digest fingerprint

c. Message authentication code

d. Digital watermarking

Chapter 17: Hacking with Linux

1. From the following log entries, what are the affected user accounts?

mkdir – p /etc/x11/applnk/internet/.etc
touch -macr /etc/x11/applnk/internet/.etc
mkdir – p /etc/x11/applnk/internet/.
etcpasswd

touch -macr /etc/x11/applnk/internet/.
etcpasswd
adduser dns –d /bin –s /bin/bash –u 0 –g 0
passwd nobody –d
passwd dns –d

a. dns, nobody

b. nobody, macr

c. dns, IUSR_

d. mkdir, touch

2. **A common technique when compromising Linux hosts is to make sure that if it is used as a sniffer, the command _____ is replaced with a modified version that will not show the _____ flag in its output. (Fill in the blanks)**

a. ipconfig, PRMISC

b. ifconfig, SNIFFER=1

c. ipconfig, PROMISC=On

d. ifconfig, PROMISC

3. **Where are password hashes stored on a Linux system?**

a. /etc/credentials

b. /etc/passwd

c. /etc/shadow

d. /etc/sam

4. **Darren wants to run a stealth nmap scan that will require root privileges. Observing best practices, he does not want to be logged in as root. What is the best way to run the command?**

a. root nmap -sS

b. runas nmap -sS

c. sudo nmap -sS

d. start nmap -sS

5. **Doug was just told about a set of tools known as the "dsniff" suite that runs nicely under Backtrack Linux. Which tool can he use to capture a file transfer that took place over NFS?**

a. filesnarf

b. urlsnarf

c. mailsnarf

d. nsfsnarf

6. **What does the following command do?**
   Hping2 –I eth0 –a 2.2.2.2 –s 1020 –p 22 --syn –c 1 –d 0xF00 –setseq 0x0000000F 192.168.100.2

a. This command will generate multiple SYN packets from address 192.168.100.2.

b. This command will generate a UDP packet from 22 spoofing address 2.2.2.2.

c. This command will generate one TCP segment from 2.2.2.2 port 1020 with sequence number 15.

d. This command will generate one TCP packet destined for 2.2.2.2 port 1020 and coming from 192.168.100.2.

7. **Cedric is troubleshooting his Linux system because a hardware component has stopped working properly. He wonders if another admin has installed a non-approved LKM. He runs a check and is relieved to find at least that is not what is wrong. What command did he run?**

a. cat /var/log/drivers.log

b. cat /proc/hardware/LKM

c. cat /proc/kernel/LKM

d. cat /proc/sys/kernel/tainted

8. **William wants to check his Linux system for rootkits. Which of the following tools can he use? (Choose up to two)**

a. chkrootkit

b. rkhunter

c. rootkit revealer

d. Sophos anti-rootkit

9. **It is possible to run critical services on a Linux machine in such a way that the root directory for that service seems to be different than the root of the actual system. The purpose is to prevent access to any files outside of that directory structure.**
   What is this technique called?

a. Chroot jail

b. Tar pit

c. tcpwrappers

d. Pluggable authentication modules

10. Which of the following Linux tools can be used for not only detecting port scans but for taking action to prevent them?

    a. Portsentry

    b. Port Knocking

    c. Port-Auth

    d. PortSentinel

11. Peter is worried about the possibility of software on his system being vulnerable to "stack smashing" attacks. He always compiles from source.

    What other precaution can he take?

    a. Never use the ./configure script the developer provides either

    b. Compile with "Stackguard"

    c. Only use SELinux kernels

    d. Patch his kernel every time an update is released

12. Zachery remembers someone mentioning a tool called "Bastille Linux" that he could use for hardening the configuration of his system after install.

    Which of the other tools is also an option?

    a. LSAT

    b. LIDS

    c. chkrootkit

    d. Sara

13. Carter is evaluating ways to detect intrusions on his Linux system. He has log file analysis under control as he needs to be able to easily create status reports for his boss. He is looking for tools that monitor modifications to files.

    Which of the following is an option?

    a. Firewalk

    b. Whisker

c. He should write his own scripts using the find command

d. AIDE

14. Which of the following allows a safe environment for developers who wish to work on code using normal permissions but ensure they are still isolated from the rest of the system?

    a. XEN

    b. SELinux

    c. UML

    d. Kernel mode

15. The IT manager of a large corporation is a bit reluctant to allow the use of Linux systems on users systems because he has been told they come with many hacking tools that are either pre-installed or easy to obtain. For example, he cites tools like ettercap that can create havoc on a local network.

    Which of the following can also be used for a session hijack or arp poined attack?

    a. Hunt

    b. T-sight

    c. Pragroute

    d. P0f

Chapter 18: IDS, Firewalls, and Honeypots

1. Jacob finds the following packet dump in his log file:

   05/20-17.06.45.061034   192.160.13.4.3465
   -> 172.16.1.101:80
   TCP TTL.44 TOS.0x10 ID.242
   A* Seq. 0XA1D954BD Ack. 0x0
   Win. 0x400.
   05/20-17.06.58.685879   192.160.13.4.3466
   -> 172.16.1.102:80
   TCP TTL.44 TOS.0x10 ID.242
   A* Seq. 0XB7C5627D Ack. 0x0 Win.
   0x400

   What is likely happening?

   a. ACK scan to port 80

   b. Snort alerts noticing strange events

c. Sequence numbers are random, indicating custom packets

d. TTL of 44 is too low, this is a firewall scan

2. **What do the following IPTables commands accomplish?**

   Iptables –A FORWARD –j ACCEPT –p UDP --dport 53 iptables –A FORWARD –j ACCEPT –p TCP --dport 80

   a. Allow web requests to be routed

   b. Accept only packets that are destined for port 53 and port 80

   c. Append the FORWARD table with a jump (-j) rule that send this traffic to the IDS

   d. Nothing, since –p is the option for port number and that is not how these commands were written

3. **You wish to capture a set of data for about 10 minutes for a host that you only have command line access to. You use TCPDump for the captureut find it is hard to work with. You aren't so much interested in the data within the packets but in statistics about how much data and of what type is being sent.**

   Which of the following tools can be used along with your sniffer to collect this data?

   a. IDS Wakeup

   b. TCP Slice

   c. Win Dump

   d. WinpCap

4. **What is the most accurate statement below regarding the following snort rule:**

   alert tcp any any -> any 111 (content:"|00 01 86 A5|"; msg: "mountd access";)

   a. An alert is generated when a packet originates from anywhere and is destined for any IP and port 111.

   b. An alert is generated when a packet originates from port 111 and is destined for any IP and port.

   c. An alert is generated when the string 00 01 6 A5 is seen in the payload.

   d. An alert is generated when the command mounted access is seen in a packet that is destined for port 111.

5. **Using HPing, you wish to enumerate the rules of a firewall. You direct the traffic to a confirmed host and set the TTL value to one hop past the firewall, also incrementing the destination port by one with each packet. Return ICMP type 11 messages will tell you what the firewall allowed to pass. What is this technique called?**

   a. Firewall footprinting

   b. Firewalking

   c. Firewall enumeration

   d. Bounce scanning

6. **During a traceroute, you notice that the last two hops reveal the same IP address. What is a possible explanation?**

   a. Application proxy is in use

   b. A stateful inspection firewall

   c. A load balancer or cluster

   d. A honeypot is returning deliberately confusing results

7. **Curtis works for a small company. His boss isn't too interested in security issues as he isn't certain the risk is high enough. Stillurtis wants to implement something that can collect data about just how often they are attacked, and from this, perhaps create a business case for why security must be taken seriously. He needs to know even when a simple scan is taking place.**

   What tool can he use?

   a. GFI guard

   b. NMap

   c. Genius

   d. Snort

8. **Steve is suspicious that someone in his company is attempting to access folders that are unrelated to his or her job or projects. His first step is to create groups and solidify permissions to prevent this sort of access. He then creates a folder project called**

"New Netbook OS Project – Do Not Leak to Media" and places fictitious documents inside of it. He then monitors the gadget sites for information and, when he sees somethinghecks what employee accessed that file.

What has Steve done?

a. Created a "honeypot"

b. Setup a network "tar pit"

c. Configured a "black hole trap"

d. Created a "honey token"

9. Which of the following tools can be used to collect webpages for offline browsing?

a. Url snarf

b. Mget

c. Wget

d. Black spider

10. NIDS operates at Layer 2. Raw traffic is observed by the hardware and the packets are provided to software that analyzes it. It can be possible to confuse the detection engine of the NIDS by modifying the packets in stream. Which of the following tools accomplishes this?

a. Fragroute

b. Tcpfrag

c. Rcpdump

d. Fragtraf

11. When evaluating possible NIDS, you are concerned that an attacker might detect the presence of your monitoring agent. Which of the following techniques can be used to hide the NIDS? (Choose up to two)

a. NIDS will not respond to scans by default; detection is not possible.

b. Set the IP address of the tap to be the same as the gateway.

c. Have two NICS, and make sure the tap is not bound to the IP stack.

d. Use a receive-only cable on the tap.

12. Jeremy knows that the network has been breached and several important files have been modified. After analyzing the access and firewall logs, he can't come to any sort of conclusion about exactly what happened. In the future, he wants to make sure he can detect when certain files change, then maybe use honey tokens to catch the intruders.

Which of the following will accomplish this task?

a. Kismet

b. Strataguard

c. Snortsam

d. Tripwire

13. ARP spoofing can be used to perform "Man in The Middle" attacks and should be monitored against. Which of the following techniques can be used to defend against this? (Choose up to three)

a. Use arpwall to block ARP spoofing attacks

b. VLANs

c. Static ARP configurations

d. Detection of large amounts of ARP traffic

14. You are considering using a host that has Linux kernel 2.5 installed as a firewall. What is the built-in firewall for this distro?

a. IPTables

b. IP Chains

c. IPfw

d. Net filter

15. Which of the following snort rules looks for FTP login attempts?

a. alert tcp any any -> any any 21 (content:"user root"; msg:"FTP Login attempt";)

b. alert ftp -> any port 21 (content:"user login";)

c. A INPUT –j LOG –dport 21 –p TCP

d. tcp.port == 21 && host eq any

Chapter 19: Summary of Optional Modules

1. Using the HTTP/S Connect(), an attacker can create a(n)

   a. Covert tunnel

   b. E-Commerce site

   c. SQL connection

   d. Send e-mail

2. Viruses can be described as having three parts: replicatoroncealer, and payload. In the payload portion, there is a trigger mechanism and destructive code. When the trigger is based on events such as keystrokes, what class of malware is that considered?

   a. Hoax

   b. Timed destruction

   c. Keystroke bomb

   d. Logic bomb

3. Cisco devices use a protocol called CDP (Cisco Discovery Protocol) that allows routers to share information about each other. These messages can sometimes be sniffed. What is the destination MAC address for a CDP message?

   a. 00-00-00-00-00-00

   b. FF-FF-FF-FF-FF-FFF

   c. 01-00-0C-CC-CC-CC

   d. 01-46-02-7B-45-AD

4. Which of the following is not a valid mobile phone technology?

   a. GSM

   b. GPRS

   c. GPS

   d. CDMA

5. The type of attack that sends unsolicited messages to a target Bluetooth device is:

   a. Blujacking

   b. Bluesnarfing

   c. Bluesniffing

   d. Bluesmurfing

6. The ITU protocol for sending audio-visual data across any packet-based network is called:

   a. H.323

   b. H.636

   c. X.500

   d. X.509

7. The act of stealing information from a victim's magnetic strip is called:

   a. Sniffing

   b. Carding

   c. Skimming

   d. Bump and run

8. A mechanism that RFID devices use to be rendered inoperative is called:

   a. Kill switch

   b. Denial of service

   c. Tracking disable

   d. Cannot be disabled

9. USB Hacksaw is a tool that can be used to:

   a. Automatically download files and e-mail them to the attacker

   b. Disable the USB drivers preventing other devices to work

   c. Log the USB mouse movements and clicks, then combine them with screenshots

   d. Prevent unauthorized access to a PC by acting as a dongle

10. Programs such as NetNanny can be installed to monitor and control the Internet use on a computer, including keeping logs of chats. To prevent the sites themselves from knowing who visited them, a different tool is used. Which of the following will accomplish this purpose?

    a. GoToMyPC

    b. Free Agent Pro

    c. NetSeive

    d. Anonymizer

11. There are many products that take a variety of approaches to protect laptops from being stolen. They range from physically altering the laptop to make it impossible to resell, to biometric controls, to complete drive encryption. Which of the following places a tracking device that can help with locating the physical location of the stolen or misplaced laptop? (Choose up to three)

a. Stop-lock

b. PAL PC tracker

c. Inspice trace

d. Ztrace gold

12. Using Internet Explorer settings, it is possible to set a security level. High security disables JavaScript and Active X controls. Which zone are all of the websites that are visited placed unless they are specifically listed in other custom zones?

a. Internet

b. Trusted

c. Custom

d. Default

13. At any given time there are thousands of free proxy servers available on the Internet that can be used to keep certain activities anonymous. What protocol has been designed to allow the chaining together of proxy servers?

a. SOCKS5

b. ProxyChain

c. FreeGate

d. TOR

14. When logging into an IRC server, what two commands must be passed by the IRC client?

a. USER, NICK

b. PING, USER

c. USER, JOIN

d. QUERY, JOIN

15. Onan wants to install a biometric reader to control access to a server room. He knows there will only be about five people that will ever need access. In regard to storage of the user account credentials, which of the following systems will be the easiest and most efficient to install?

a. One to one

b. Many to one

c. One to many

d. They should not be stored in or near the device itself

Chapter 20: Penetration Testing

1. Cade ran a scan on a system and could not identify the operating system. There does seem to be a web server running, though. How can that fact help Cade figure out the rest of the system?

a. Telnet to the open port and grab a banner

b. Use a browser to view the web page

c. Use an FTP client to connect to port 80 and observe the error messages

d. View the source code of the index.html page

2. When performing a pentest, Russell has been asked to perform a thorough network footprint for a small company of about 50 hosts. He checks the address of his own machine and notices that it is a class c. Knowing there are multiple network segments, he runs the following command:

Nmap –sS –p 0-65535 –P0 –O 192.0.0.0/8 >> /root/footprint.nmap

Which of the following statements describes what Russell has done?

a. The –sS scan looks for "Services" and this is not compatible with the –P0 (Do not ping first) option.

b. He shouldn't run a dangerous scan like this as root, otherwise it's OK.

c. He is being thorough just as his boss asked him to. This range will be sure to notice everything.

d. He tried to scan 65,536 ports on about 16 million addresses. This is excessive traffic and is not a good approach.

3. Sara has been asked to perform a port scan on a number of servers to check for access points that should not be running but would have elevated privileges. She is not familiar with port numbers and isn't sure how to scan only those that we know meet the scanning criteria.

    What advice would you give her?

    a. She should scan 1-1023.

    b. She should scan 0-63535 just to be sure.

    c. She should scan 1-49151.

    d. She should consult the network documentation and avoid the scan altogether.

4. During a pentest, you retrieve a USB key from a box of discarded hardware that was just sitting by a number of other items. You check the key for files and it turns out to have a number of .pdf documents that could have sensitive information. If this information were to get leaked it would be a great risk to your client. In your report you point this outut the customer doesn't see the problem as all of the documents were password protected.

    Why isn't this enough to prevent the information leakage?

    a. Without knowing the original user of the file, the information could be inaccurate or not relevant; however, if someone thinks it is they would still try to use it during a social engineering attack.

    b. Many tools that are easy to obtain can brute force the passwords. It is also common for documents of this nature to use easy to remember dictionary words that are also often the same for many files.

c. Since the password must always be stored in the file itself, it is fairly easy to use a common hex editor to analyze the file and extract the credentials.

d. The passwords are usually stored using a very strong encryptionut notepad will usually open the files in clear text anyway.

5. A business manager is arguing with a compliance officer that a pentest would never be necessary for this company since it uses single sign on authentication throughout. You are asked for your opinion, and say, "If I can access a network physically I can own it." This sounds a little extremeut what is not true about this assertion?

    a. Booting up to an alternative operating system might allow you to circumvent the local authenticationompromise a credential store, or steal critical data.

    b. Not being able to login would prevent your host from obtaining network configurations such as an IP address, routing, and DNS settings. But sniffing is still possible.

    c. There are ways of detecting the presence of new systems on the network such as rogue infrastructure. These techniques should still be tested regularly.

    d. Physical security is always critical and, along with user training, should be a constantly run program.

6. During an internal pentest, you set up a fake website that offers some documentation and useful resources. You create a link and send it via e-mail to a few key people. When they visitode is run on their own machines that compromise their systems.

    What form of attack is not taking place?

    a. Cross site scripting

    b. SQL injection

    c. Browser drive-by

    d. Social engineering

7. During a pentest, you notice the organization uses different domains for various internal departments. What phase of the test would this have been discovered?

   a. Project scoping

   b. Rules of engagement negotiation

   c. Vulnerability analysis

   d. Passive information gathering

8. Knowing ports is important for attackers, pentesters, and analysts. On a windows system, what are the port numbers for the following protocols (in order)?
   Kerberos, WINS, RPC, SMB SessionIFS

   a. 82, 42, 139, 135, 445

   b. 88, 445, 42, 445, 139

   c. 42, 88, 135, 139, 445

   d. 88, 42, 135, 139, 445

9. Using netcatryptcat, or ncat to transfer files across a network is a common practice for a pentester because any port that will pass through the filters between the target and tiger box can be used. Which of the following commands will transfer a binary file on a commonly unfiltered web port?

   a. nc –l –u –p 8080 > /home/tiger/foo.txt

   b. nc –l –u –p 8080 < /home/tiger/foo.txt

   c. nc –l 8080 –u –p < /home/tiger/foo.txt

   d. nc –l 1080 –u –p < /home/tiger/foo.txt

10. During the network footprinting phase it is often helpful to get information from DNS that can reveal hosts, which in turn reveal network segments, and traceroute can reveal even more. Obtaining records like CNAME, MX, and A are examples of this. Of the following answers, what is the best way to describe what the attacker is looking for?

    a. Zone harvest

    b. Zone poison

    c. Zone transfer

    d. Zone estimate

11. Systems that have default configurations are common targets during a pentest. Which of the following is not a default configuration?

    a. Setting up a web server that uses a secondary port that only invited users will know about

    b. Keeping the directory structures the same as installed, for easier maintenance

    c. Allowing the sample pages of the web server to remain so as not to confuse anyone until the real site is built

    d. Keeping the default user accounts to make sure access is always available

12. Milo is trying to learn all he can about a network. He is looking for easy things he can do that might reveal information. Eventually, he can collect all of that data and after analysis learn, perhaps, enough to have a complete picture. One technique is to send e-mail to e-mail addresses with different status, such as valid users, non-existent addresses, users on vacation, employees that are no longer there, as well as commonly named e-mail groups.
    What would be a reason for doing this?

    a. To verify information about the e-mail administrator

    b. Gather information about internal hosts

    c. To see how the IT department responds to a denial of service attack

    d. To learn about the internal policies for handling such events

13. Gary is using an e-mail system that allows web-based access and is popular among employees of the company he is attacking. He is testing this system to see if there is a way to gain access to other users' accounts. He signs up for an account and begins to use it. He notices in the URL that information about his account name is present:

    http://mail.exampleco.com/inbox.aspx?lang=en&mailbox=Gary+Tennenbaum

He replaces his name with someone else's name in the target company that he gathered from a job posting site. What attack is he attempting?

a. URL obfuscation attack

b. Directory traversal attack

c. Query string parameter manipulation attack

d. A path string attack

14. **Maureen returns from lunch and notices her PC has a BSODut the hard drive activity light is still flashing. What tool is possibly being used?**

    a. Nessus scans can cause BSODs; she just needs to reboot.

    b. Her computer is enumerating the network with dumpsec.

c. Her computer is using floppyscan.

d. A USB key was inserted and caused an IRQ conflict

15. **You are conducting a test and got caught. What document will ensure that you are protected from negative consequences within the target company?**

    a. Indemnity clause

    b. "Get out of jail free" card

    c. Rules of engagement

    d. Non-disclosure agreement

Practice Exam Answers

Chapter 1: Ethical Hacking

1. **B.** A grey box test is specific but not all of the information needed has necessarily been provided. It is a limited test.

2. **A.** There is a famous story behind this question. Start by reading this wiki article at: http://en.wikipedia.org/wiki/WkD_Bot

3. **D.** This is an example of reusing code and spreading a security risk.

4. **C.** Neutral third parties exist that will protect the anonymity of the person or organization that submits an incident or vulnerability. From there, the proper vendor can be notified. There is philosophical debate within the security community regarding whether or not to leak the information out after the vendor has been given fair time to respond but has chosen not to. Most agree, however, that immediate full disclosure is a grey area at least.

5. **A.** While black hat hackers may have the skills to pull off an attack, they may not have the best position in the network. Disgruntled employees will have been insiders and likely have many contacts that are willing to collude with them. The most common form of disgruntled employee attack is to report the former employee to the BSA (Business Software Alliance) and claim they are using unlicensed software.

6. **B.** A vulnerability scanner is too noisy to use in most cases, even though common tools such as Nessus will do most of the footprinting work for the attacker. It is safer to pick the interesting machines one by one and try to find out as much as possible about them, as it might be possible to choose an attack strategy without a vulnerability scan at all.

7. **C.** Bastion hosts are fully hardened machines designed to withstand any kind of abuse because they will have no help. It is usually a matter of access; for instance, a web server in the DMZ (De-Militarized Zone) might need to be fully exposed on port 80 to the entire world, so at least where that port is concerned it needs to hold up to attack.

8. **A.** Honeypots are hosts with no production value that serve to attract the attention of an attacker. When designed properly, they blend in with the other hosts on the network, including not having exaggerated levels of weaknesses. While a honeypot is accessible, it is not necessarily completely exposed to all risks.

9. **C, D.** It is often best to begin attacking from the lowest layer of the OSI model that can be accessed. If possible, a physical attack is always best. Remote attacks against enabled services might allow access to the OS. Then attack the application either as a remote client or from within using social engineering. There are many ways to get in.

10. **A.** Risk is sometimes called a "measurement of uncertainty." It is neither positive nor negative until the impact is determined. Opportunities can sometimes be identified and if the plan is right in the end, risk management improves an organization overall.

11. **D.** All of the answers present dangerous possibilities, but social engineering is always considered the most exposed and hardest to completely countermeasure. Training is considered to be the most cost effective solution. (Running security awareness seminars counts for your continuing education units!)

12. **A.** The maintaining access step is about installing backdoors so access can be gained at anytime. A backdoor can be a privileged user account (noisy), or an illicit server (installed via a Trojan), or a variety of processes that were hidden by a rootkit.

13. **A.** Be careful on the wording here: If false entries looked like decoy traffic it would only show someone is in there messing around. Unusual events are often false positives but should be confirmed. The timeline is the most valuable thing an investigator can determine when tracking down events. Part of the clearing tracks phase of an attack is to take investigators off the scent, ideally without them realizing they are even playing the game at all.

14. **D.** Reporting vulnerabilities can be tricky. There is a fear of retribution for doing the research in the first place, there is the desire to be given recognition and credit, there might be financial incentives for using the exploit, and there is always leverage; trying to force the vendor to respond under threat of full disclosure. The question specified "white hat" and CERTs often provide a way to report vulnerabilities in a way that reduces risks to all parties as much as possible.

15. **B.** Hopefully no further explanation is required here.

Chapter 2: Hacking Laws

1. **B.** $5,000 is considered the threshold. Be aware of "Salami Attacks" which are those kept intentionally under the damage limit. It would be necessary to forensically prove a connection between the separate attacks through log files and other monitoring mechanisms.

2. **C.** Demonstrating the intent to protect copyright is enough, and however weak that protection might be is no excuse for cracking it in the eyes of the courts.

3. **A, D.** These are two important statements when interpreting legal matters when it comes to ethical hacking. Computers contain data which is often a valuable target. They can also be used as tools to disrupt other systems. In both cases, when human life or rescue services are affected the penalties increase dramatically.

4. **A.** Section 1030 (a) (1) states in part: *"having knowingly accessed a computer without authorization or exceeding authorized access...."*
   Section 1030 (a) (2) (A) states in part: *"information contained in a financial record of a financial institution, or of a card issuer as defined in section 1602(n) of title 15, or contained in a file of a consumer reporting agency on a consumer, as such terms are defined in the Fair Credit Reporting Act (15 U.S.C. 1681 et seq.);"*

5. **A.** http://www.netcraft.com keeps track of the uptime and version information of Internet accessible websites. They send a periodic request to the server that will produce an error. The banner grab that results is collated into a searchable database.

6. **D.** The site at http://www.archive.org has a feature called "The Wayback Machine" that archives old version of websites.

7. **B.** The "Digital Millennium Copyright" Act does allow exemptions when an access of the properly purchased technology affects access during a non-infringing act.

8. **C.** The "Fair Use Doctrine" has been challenged on many occasions and. The best bet for low risk is to understand that while it is okay to cite sources and then comment on them, the less used is better.

9. **A, C.** The Privacy Act of 1974 prevents the disclosure of personal records without written consent for census data. The Human Rights Act of 1998 discusses the privacy rights of an individual, such as the drivers of cars not having to reveal their identity in a photograph.

10. **B.** Port scanning might be considered an attack by internal policy standards, but in general it is only an information gathering attack.

11. **C.** The Secret Service does more than most people think, but it this is a secret. (Shhhh!) The GLBA deals with the handling of financial information.

12. **B.** FISMA (Federal Information Security Management Act) drives a lot of United States federal requirements. Directive 8570 drives proper training and certification requirements for individuals as a part of FISMA.

13. **A.** FERPA is the "Family Educational Rights and Privacy Act."

14. **D.** The Computer Fraud and Abuse Act of 1990 also criminalizes unauthorized access with the intent to use the computer to commit a crime.

15. **A, B.** Critics argue the CAN-SPAM Act does not require advertisers to get permission before sending the UCE (Unsolicited Commercial E-mail), and that it provides a legal definition for what is not SPAM exactly, thus enabling the sending of UCE if the advertisers go about it the right way. The SPY Act tries to prevent computers from being used as spam spreaders, but gives specific protection to vendors that install software that monitors usage for license enforcement. With not much creativity, it can be imagined how Trojans can be created that are now legally protected, as long as they go about things in just a certain way.

Chapter 3: Footprinting

1. **D.** Sam Spade has been a reliable and popular tool for years. This is a great tool to have on your tigerbox.

2. **B.** Nikto is a website scanner that runs under Linux and does not have a GUI. When you download Wikto, also grab the HTTrack (for website mirroring) and the HTTPrint (for web server fingerprinting) plugins to use all of the available features.

3. **A.** The semicolon in the statement is meant to show there are multiple commands involved. First, an nslookup shell is invoked and then the other two commands are issued. IXFR is an incremental transfer and the other answers are not valid.

4. **D.** There are no registrars named LAPNIC or AFLAC.

5. **B.** If a regional CERT needed to get in touch with the owner of a domain they would use the POC (Point of Contact) information. Therefore, it is necessary that the information is correct and a domain can be immediately forfeited if a false record is discovered. Proxy services will keep the real POC anonymous for only a few dollars a year.

6. **C.** Be sure to visit this link, and while you are there also try out the Netcraft Phishing Toolbar (another possible test item).

7. **D.** For the CEH exam, be sure you can recognize certain items within log file or packet dumps. "AXFR" always means "All Zone Transfer." Verifying accounts on an e-mail server would be "VRFY."

8. **B.** The fields on an SOA record are: Serial, Retry, Refresh, Expiry, TTL, and the values are given in seconds. There is a calculator provided on the CEH exam, but it is not scientific.

9. **C.** The "Wayback Machine" is located at http://www.archive.org. The other answers are all website copiers that allow offline browsing of the current version of the site, or whichever one was copied.

10. **D.** All of the answers mentioned are important techniques for footprinting e-mail.

11. **B.** Kartoo is a search engine with a graphical interface that can help determine links and partners. It can be helpful in competitive intelligence gathering to understand the immediate network of resources a business is using. Determine who is driving traffic or business their way, what external partners they support, and who their large customers are. Look for the names of organizations in marketing materials such as testimonials and Kartoo search them as well.

12. **A.** The EDGAR database provided by the SEC (Security Exchange Commission) is the best resource. While there might be other financial websites that provide research on a company, these are the actual legal filings.

13. **A.** Load balancers and switches that are performing Layer 2 routing can cause traceroute to show hops that live on the same segment. P2P networks often cause a mismatch between logical and physical topologies as well. A good explanation of this is located here: http://eprints.ru.ac.za/12/03/chapter.3.html

14. **B.** On the CEH exam, the longest answer is not the most correct. Forget those multiple choice tricks.

15. **C.** LFT (Layer 4 Traceroute) may not be installed by default in your Linux system. It is, however, in the debian and yum repositories source, which is also available. Read about it here: http://pwhois.org/lft/

Chapter 4: Google Hacking

1. **A, B.** Lynx is an important tool to get to know. It is ported to Windows and is usually available by default in most Linux distributions. Command line equivalants of important QUI-based tools are handy for times when all the attacker has is a shell on a remote machine.

2. **D.** The difference between two of the answers is only one word. "Any" or "All". Be careful about this sort of question on the CEH exam.

   There are also "allintitle" and "allinchache" operators.

3. **B.** Usually the ext: operator involves a – (dash) character before it to negate the string from the results. Otherwise, there really isn't much difference and Google describes them as synonyms.

4. **C.** To pass the CEH exam it is not necessary to be a programmer but it is necessary to be able to recognize languages and certain specific strings as they might relate to an attack. The string in this question is standard for scripts written in "C" and does not indicate any kind of risk on its own.

5. **D.** Be creative about combining the Google syntax to refine searches. Start broad then narrow it down.

6. **B.** Not everything that looks like an attacker's dream is.

7. **A, B.** Finding some vulnerable websites requires knowledge of a programming language, but Google can help quite a bit if the attacker follows the steps of Google hacking.

8. **B.** The title of a web page is in the head section of the source code. It is also often found in the title bar of the browser window.

9. **D.** "Goolag scanner" (http://www.goolag.org/), originally released by members of "The Cult of the Dead Cow," makes custom and automated Google searches easy.

10. **A.** A "Spam Blog" is a web page based on highly searched-for keywords in an effort to skew adsense metrics or simply to drive traffic to these MFA (Made For Adsense) pages in hopes of generating revenue.

11. **C.** Even open content that the author intends to give away for free, but only under certain conditions of the spirit behind its use, must be protected by a proper license.

12. **D.** The "-" character is a negation operator.

13. **D.** Gooscan is a tool that might be hard to find these days but is in the Official CEH kits.

14. **B.** Impression fraud occurs when a company resorts to unfair means of gaining an advantage by reducing the ranking of a competitor. In this case, Claire's ads show more often when her bid price and click through rate are favorable. Messing with this metric causes Claire increased expense with less actual page views. Eventually she could be paying a lot for very little exposure.

15. **C.** Search data is collected and shown in a summarized view to show "What is on the mind

of the people." A complete list of Google Apps is maintained here: http://en.wikipedia.org/wiki/List_of_Google_products

Chapter 5: Scanning

1. **A, B, C, D.** Often the most challenging aspect of scanning is interpreting results, and wondering if your tool worked in the first place. Using more than one scanning tool and being familiar with how protocols work is often the best way to double check your results. Having good information collected during the recon phase will also make a large difference.

2. **A.** A Windows host will always respond to inverse scans with a RST whether the target port is open or closed. Ultimately, inverse scans might be helpful in determining basic filter rules or for discovery of live hosts, but will only produce meaningful port scan results if the target of the scan is a Linux host.

3. **B.** Read RFC 1918 thoroughly. Also, don't cheat on your scans. A skilled attacker will use proper techniques like DNS walking and traserouting to make sure their scans are targeted deliberately. It is part of the clearing tracks phase not to create excessive traffic.

4. **D.** NMap has an extensive database of signatures for the peculiarities of various operating systems. An OS detection scan performs a series of tests that involve sending packets to an open and a closed port and then analyzing the return traffic against the signature database.

5. **D.** p0f is a passive fingerprinting tool while the others are considered active stack fingerprinting tools.

6. **B.** Type 3 is destination unreachable. There are several reasons this could be the case, so the codes are used to modify the type. In this case, a code 13 is administratively prohibited, likely sent back from a firewall that dropped the packet.

7. **A.** Netcat, hping3, and NMap can all be used for a UDP scan but this is the only choice that is written correctly. For the CEH exam, pay attention to command line switches for the following tools (discussed throughout this book): NMap, netcat, hping, ettercap, iptables, and snort.

8. **B.** In a stealth scan, the handshake is not completed, but the half-open port is reset to avoid SYN flooding the target.

9. **D.** For the CEH exam there are a few illicit server ports that you should memorize including:
31337 = Back Orifice
27374 = Subseven
7777 = Tini
12345 = Netbus

10. **B.** Wardialing is the technique of automatically working through a set of telephone numbers looking for modems. "The Hackers Choice" scanner is a popular tool for this purpose.

11. **A, B, C, D, F.** All of these are used in active stack OS fingerprinting except for the initial NACK field, which doesn't exist.

12. **C.** The states of a port are: Listening, half-open, established, closed.

13. **A.** SAINT runs on UNIX, but there are many other vulnerability assessment tools to choose from. Visit http://sectools.org/vuln-scanners .html and be familiar with these tools for the CEH exam.

14. **B.** The timing option for NMap scans has a range of 0-5, with 5 being the fastest. A vanilla scan is another name for a TCP Connect scan, which is the –sT option.

15. **D.** An IP packet should be neither smaller than 64 Bytes nor larger than 65,535 Bytes. But the packet must be placed into a frame at Layer 2 before it can be placed on the link. Ethernet specifies a maximum size of 1,500 for the framed packet, allowing up to 22 bytes for the frame header. (18 is typical, but 22 could happen if the frame has a VLan tag.)

Chapter 6: Enumeration

1. **B.** In general, do not debug the scripts or command syntax on the exam. Look for what statement makes the point logically in terms of what the question is really asking. However, in the case of null sessions, do practice this and make it work.

2. **B.** Some of the tools listed in the choices are found in Windows or are not considered native tools. A default installation of Linux will include those listed in the correct answer by default.

3. **B.** The passwd file is a database of comma delimited entries. The first column is the user name. The second column is the user id and the third column is the group id. A group id of 0 is the root group. Not all fields need to have data in them; two consecutive colons just means the field is empty.

4. **A.** Linux uses a simple octal system to denote file permissions. There are three digits representing Owner (user), Group, and Others (world). Each binary position of the octal number represents rwx respectively. Octal 764 is 111110100 in binary; split the digits into three sets and you have rwxrw_r__.
   The tool "calcs.exe" shows up in other questionsut in reference to NTFS (Windows) volumes be sure to look it up.

5. **D.** Be prepared to recognize elements in packet dumps and log file entries.

6. **D.** LSASS (Local Security Authority Subsystem Service) is a process that enforces security policy and GINA (Graphical Identification and Authentication library) is part of the Windows authentication subsystem. The sasser worm attacks LSASS in unpatched systems.

7. **A, B, C, D.** All of these locations store credentials. Syskey is no help if the attacker knows how to use the right tool.

8. **C, D.** Being able to do binary, octal, and hex numbers is a prerequisite for the CEH. Understanding how Linux permissions work is also critical. The "4" in this case is in binary 100, which will set the UID bit for the User.

9. **B.** For the CEH exam it is important not only to know the tools and a few of their switches, but it is also important to know some of the quirks involved between the Windows and Linux command shells. In Windows, a forward slash "/" is a way to express an option, but in Linux a hyphen is used. Many tools in Windows will accept a hyphen also, so don't be surprised if you see it. In Linux the forward slash is a directory path character.
   Also, only netstat would work for this objective anyway.

10. **C, D.** Try them out, but this might not reveal the most information possible. Get creative with the options.

11. **C.** Try it out on a Windows host.

12. **A.** Smbclient is the command line tool for Samba.

13. **A.** Assuming the credentials, this command will mount the root of the system drive and allow access. If Kempton does not yet have the credentials he needs to get them he will need to try some of what is in the modules that follow.

14. **D.** The RID for Liz is "500" Local administrator.

15. **A.** The NULL user logs in to access the IPC$ share on Windows hosts for file sharing protocols.

Chapter 7: System Hacking

1. **A, B, C.** All of these are valid ways to disable LM hash support, but legacy systems must be considered before doing so.

2. **A.** Look for the "404EE" (you don't have to memorize the whole thing) on the end of the hash. It is easy to remember and always happens when the second half of the LM hash is only NULL characters.

3. **D.** This is part of the reason that a set of seven NULL characters will always result in the same ciphertext.

4. **B.** The file "passlist.txt" contains a list of usernames and passwords in two columns. Each row in the list will be inserted into the net use command and applied to the target machine.

5. **A.** ADS allows data to be placed into a file attribute named "$DATA. It is a feature of NTFS that supports the applications originally written for the HPFS (High Performance File System).

6. **C.** The rundll32.exe application allows access to functions within .dll files. Dynamic Link Library files are shared by many applications but are not directly executable. In this command, we are calling KRShowKeyMgr within the keymgr. dll by using rundll32.exe

7. **D.** Data can be hidden in many different file types including photographs, tunnels, and streams. The only statement that is correct and relevant to the question mentions snow.exe, which is a tool for hiding data in text files. On the CEH exam, even if you have not heard the name of a tool that gets mentioned, it is usually still possible to

reason out the best answer from the other information given.

8. **A, B, E.** Unfortunately, setting his browser settings to their strongest setting will result in him calling several times a day complaining that "the Internet doesn't work."

9. **B.** Even when hosts are joined to a domain, it must be verified that LM hashes are not being stored.

10. **D.** This attack is possible if the Kerb-PreAuth key is captured. This one time a credential is exposed on a Windows network login attempt. The ARP poisoning was to defeat a switch and allow sniffing. Intrusion detection systems could have detected this part of the attack before it was successful.

11. **A.** Netcat is the "Swiss army knife" of tools and, in this case, was used to open a "listener" (-l) of the correct port, expecting UDP traffic(-u) and displaying the data received in the console window (-v).

12. **A.** Rootkits are part of the maintaining access step of an attack. Once the host has been compromised the rootkit is installed. It opens ports for access, and some can initiate connections to remote hosts.

13. **A.** The other tools are also steganography tools, but use different media.

14. **C.** It is impossible to know exactly how long something like this will take. On the test, look for extremes. Strong and long passwords take a long time, while short, weak, or dictionary words take the shortest time.

15. **C.** Internet wide distributed computing efforts exist for a variety of complex projects. It is also possible to do this on a private network.

Chapter 8: Trojans and Backdoors

1. **B.** A Trojan horse is a form of social engineering. Victims think they are installing authorized or "safe" code. It has, however, been modified to provide malicious capabilities such as keylogging.

2. **C.** This class of tool includes such classics as Netbus, Back Orifice, and SubSeven. Modern RATs have evolved into commercial programs as well.

3. **C.** Internet Relay Chat is commonplace for the Command and Control Centers of botnets. It is also where the DCC (Direct Client to Client) protocol is used to transfer files. People visiting chatrooms are duped into accepting these files, which can be Trojan horses.

4. **A.** Universal Naming Convention is used in the Windows file sharing protocols to identify a resource on the network. For Linux systems, the slashes going in the wrong direction sometimes require escape slashes. The UNC would look like \\\\server\\share.

5. **D.** Spamming in forums is almost always frowned upon and will incite flame wars (exchanges of insults). At the same time, social engineering is a common practice as attackers post links hoping to attract visitors to their malicious sites.

6. **A.** A malicious application that intends to restart on every reboot of the host has many options in the Windows environment. In Linux, the "rc" scripts can be modified and the changes could possibly go unnoticed.

7. **D.** The URG, PSH, FIN flags all set at once look like an Xmas scan. Regardless of what sent it, this combination would not happen during natural protocol behavior and is therefore created by a hacking tool.

8. **A.** Netstat is for network statistics, the –an options say "all connections and listening ports, show numeric values."

9. **C.** It is easy to get so focused on malicious security issues and forget the basics. Don't always assume the worst; apply proper troubleshooting and diagnostics.

10. **A.** The term "drop a shell" or "shovel a shell" can be used to describe a connection that returns shell stream back through a firewall that would block the connection in the forward direction. Monkey shell sends the data within XML traffic which disguises it as normal web traffic.

11. **A.** The terms "Wrapper" or "Binder" might be used to describe this process. A tool such as "elitewrap" makes creating Trojan horses easy.

12. **D.** For more information on using this tool visit: *http://support.microsoft.com/kb/282784*

13. **D.** A hardware keylogger is visually detectable and requires at least two physical access

opportunities (install and retrieval). A screenshot tool can take period screenshots that show all activity on the host including sensitive files.

14. **B.** This tool was used in the famous "Sony Rootkit" discovery. For information visit the information page at: *http://technet.microsoft.com/en-us/sysinternals/bb897445.aspx*

15. **C.** It is important to obtain code only from trusted sources; since that is hard to do, the better step is to use only source code that you can inspect first before using.

Chapter 9: Viruses and Worms

1. **B.** Metamorphic viruses change code, and polymorphic viruses encrypt themselves.

2. **C.** The question wasn't asking about incident response or monitoring. It was referring to the actual outbreak itself. Vulnerabilites are exploited, resulting in the infection. The virus then spreads to other hosts, and once it makes a home, it inflicts its damage.

3. **A.** A cavity virus hides inside of binary files and can perform the attack from that location. Stealth viruses store themselves inside of files, but remove themselves to run, then to hide again.

4. **A.** "Heuristics" deals with problem solving, learning, and deduction. It is experience based. A heuristic scanner looks for smaller samples of a larger behavioral problem and attempts to alert the user before the viral or malicious activity has a chance to complete its exploit.

5. **D.** FIV tools might also be called SIVs (System Integrity Verifiers). They create a database of the hashes of critical system files, then monitor them for changes. They also track MAC times (Modify, Access, Change).

6. **B.** The question contains a brief description of how the polymorphic virus works. The XOR process is used because it is fast and easy "bit oriented" encryption.

7. **D.** It is arguable that all of these principles are risks that can be minimized or mitigated to a degree. Attacks that are not stopped can usually be detected and the damage can be contained. The best answer in this case is the one element that security professionals will have the least control over: what people do every day.

8. **D.** A macro virus targets the scripting languages present in Microsoft Office products. There are cases of macro viruses for the Open Office and Star Office products as well, but this is still traditionally considered to be a Microsoft issue.

9. **B.** Morris was the first worm, Elk Cloner the first virus, Strange Brew the first to attack Java, and FU is a rootkit.

10. **D.** Blaster and Slammer are both known for spreading very fast, but they are considered worms and are not capable of a variety of infection and spreading vectors. Nimda is also "Admin" spelled backwards, another common trivia reference.

11. **A.** Code Red and Nimda were both very successful at spreading via directory traversal vulnerabilites in the IIS 4.0 and IIS 5.0 servers.

12. **C.** Nachi, also known as Welchia, used similar vectors as the more recent Blaster worm. The Welchia worms actually tried to patch infected systems and uninstall itself after 120 days.

13. **D.** The entire virus lifecycle is not to be confused with the three steps of an outbreak. Learning steps for an exam is always about two things: conceptual walk-through of the list and practice. The author designs the virus, it infects and spreads, then launches an attack, it gets detected, response teams are activated and the threat is elliminated.

14. **C, D.** Remember that on every defense-oriented test (no matter how "attack" oriented the material is), cooler heads always prevail if there are incident response, training systems, and communications for the security policy in place.

15. **B.** The hidden extension trick is a time honored classic and no exam involving viruses would be complete without at least one question about it.

Chapter 10: Sniffers, Spoofing, and Session Hijacking

1. **D.** The filter "tcp[28]50x72" says "look for the value hex 72 at byte 28". This is where the SMB challenge is. Obviously there is a lot more than can be explained here. But this is a well-known filter string when using a simple command line sniffer like windump or tcpdump to grab credentials.

2. **C.** Promiscuous mode drivers allow received packets to be available to the sniffer application which operates at Layer 7 rather than be discarded at Layer 2 if the destination hardware address did not match. The package libpcap is used for Linux.

3. **C.** The sequence number field is 32 bits in length. 2^32 would give (rounded up) 4.3 billion decimal values.

4. **D.** The order of steps in a session hijack attack are: tracking the connection, desynchronizing the connection, and injecting the packets.

5. **A.** The CAM table (Content Addressable Memory) stores the MAC addresses that a switch learns about in memory. If that limited space is full and it cannot learn new addresses, every frame becomes "unknown unicast." This would cause the switch to forward all frames out every interface.

6. **B.** IPSEC in ESP (Encapsulated Security Protocol) mode is an encryption tunnel.

7. **A.** All of the other tools are command line utilities that come with Wireshark. TShark is the command line sniffer, Mergecap and Editcap both allow combining or slicing of existing capture files, and text2pcap takes an existing hex dump and turns it into a capture file.

8. **A.** If byte 500 was just received (it was the last byte in the previous packet), then the next byte 501 will be acknowledged for. Since the receive window is 350, 501$\rightarrow$3505851, the range of sequence numbers that will be accepted before the next acknowledgement.

9. **B.** The flag field is 8 bits (two unused bits, then UAPRSN). In binary the UPF flags would look like: 00101001 which is hex 29.

10. **A.** The first two bits of the vendor ID (first 3 bytes) have special meaning: The first bit set to "0" indicates this MAC address is the one burned into the hardware, whereas a "1" means it is a logical address configured by an administrator. The second bit set to "0" means the address references a single host, whereas a second bit set to a "1" indicates a multicast or group.

11. **A.** Ethernet is a "logical bus" architecture. Whether or not a switch is involved, Ethernet is designed to work as if every NIC sees every frame and simply checks to see if the destination hardware address is a match to its own.

12. **C.** Using tools like "sniffpass" or "dnsiff," many cleartext protocols are vulnerable. MAPI (Messaging Application Programming Interface) is a Microsoft protocol that Outlook uses to communicate with Exchange and protects the credentials.

13. **A, B, C.** Core security offers the "Pass-the-Hash" toolkit for the more advanced situations. There are also metasploit modules now available for this.

14. **D.** No such thing. SMAC is a tool for MAC spoofing, though.

15. **C.** The examples that begin with "host" are capture filters and are equivalent. The other one is incorrect.

Chapter 11: Social Engineering

1. **C.** Spoofing is a temporary situation. IP addresses, sources of e-mail, usernames, and, in this case, a person can easily be spoofed in a packet or phone call. Attackers can distance themselves from the act immediately afterward. Identity theft or faking is more long term and involves actively assuming the identity of the victim for a period of time.

2. **A.** Insider associates begin with limited authorized access, and escalate privileges from there. Insider affiliates are insiders by virtue of an affiliation, and they spoof the identity of the insider, while outsider affiliates are non-trusted outsiders that use an access point that was left open.

3. **A, B, C, D, E, F, G.** These are all ways to mitigate insider threats.

4. **C.** CEOs are not considered insiders so much because they are usually the owners of the information; therefore, this is the party being attacked.

5. **B.** The telephone used to be the best answer, but now it is e-mail. However, as filtering policies get more effective, the trend in more targeted social engineering can always swing back to telephony.

6. **B.** Sometimes social engineering principles are used to keep people from becoming suspicious. If John wasn't so willing to share his pictures and was more private about it, suspicion may have come sooner.

7. **C.** This is classic tailgating; sneaking in through a door when someone else opens it with their credentials. This is one reason to log all people that enter. If someone is in the building but there is no record he swiped his card, then it bears investigation.

8. **D.** After enough documents are collected, they could be scanned into OCR (Optical Character Recognition) software and then searched or parsed into information that might be usable to the attacker like a dictionary file for password cracking, list of user names, e-mail addresses, and so on.

9. **C.** Teergrubbing is the German word for Tar pit. This concept relates to the general technique of slowing down connections between hosts to deter abuse. SPAM Cannibal is software that can do this, and the feature is built into Windows 2003 Sp1 (disabled by default). The question did not ask for a specific product, just for a technique.

10. **B.** The ISOC model and the Gartner Group's explanation are basically the same with slightly different words. Do not let slight variations throw you off. Learn the principles themselves first and foremost.

11. **C.** The attacker might have gotten this information from a Facebook posting or twitter message that Sean was using to share the experience with his "friends." Spear phishing targets specific elements about a victim.

12. **B, D.** SMTP_AUTH mitigates open relay related SPAM. VRFY and EXPN are SMTP commands that an attacker can use to determine e-mail addresses.

13. **A.** While it is true that the sources of a message can be spoofed, they aren't always. Headers are worth looking at just in case; if the bounce doesn't work, attackers can also try to get someone in the company to send them an e-mail.

14. **D.** The other answers are used to collect information or are the targets of spam. Botnets are distributed networks that can be used to carry the spam, causing it to come from so many directions that it becomes difficult to filter or trace.

15. **A.** Cause a paper jam, tell everyone you can fix it, and then, while fixing the paper jam, ask the office manager when the weekly payroll report

is printed. (She thinks it is so you can help; you intend on being there to read it.) When the time comes, she invites you.

Chapter 12: Denial of Service

1. **B.** Seems like a strange question, but be prepared to consider scenarios and describe them to a level of detail that is similar to the question. LSASS is the access control subsystem for Windows, and if it is crashed it will result in a denial of service. It did take human interaction to restore, but "B" is a better answer.

2. **A.** A land attack is when the attacker sends traffic toward a host spoofing its own address as the source. Its ACK counter does not increment the way it should (because it didn't send the traffic in the first place), causing it to "re-ack" for the same sequence number over and over.

3. **D.** Decreasing offset values is a teardrop attack. The other two answers have specific terms: 0-day and false negative.

4. **D.** Slammer exploited a problem with Windows SQL server desktop edition which is present in Windows XP machines and forward. It was only memory resident, so a reboot would remove it; however, a vulnerable machine would likely be re-infected within minutes.

5. **D.** Read RFC 3514 and the Wikipedia article here: http://en.wikipedia.org/wiki/Evil_bit

6. **C.** C2myazz is malware that steals passwords. The other tools are DDoS tools, which are asymmetric in nature.

7. **A.** The attacker sends packets with the SYN flag set to an open port. The server responds with a SYN-ACK, but the attacker never sends the final ACK to complete the handshake. In the mean time, the server has allocated memory for the connection and eventually runs out.

8. **B.** There might be some trivia questions on the real exam. This is to make sure you actually have read the material, but is not enough to make the difference between pass or fail for the prepared. In other words, if you get the trivial questions wrong that won't really be the reason for not passing. Don't let them get to you.

9. **C.** Blast is a TCP stress testing tool. Jolt2 is a fragmentation reassembly exploit. UDP flood would not apply to the TCP oriented web service and MStream is a DDoS tool. Never perform asymmetric tests on your network from the Internet.

10. **B.** The other answers might work, but they would go too far or not be applicable in all situations. SYN cookies allow the receiving host to dump its SYN queue as it sends out the SYN-ACK. If nothing comes back, no harm done. If an ACK is returned, the original SYN queue can be reconstructed based on the SEQ number the receive host chose in its first response.

11. **B.** Targa is capable of several "protocol based" attacks including: Nestea, Syndrop, Teardrop, Bonk, and Ping of death.

12. **A.** The multiplier concept has to do with the way window sizes in TCP work. IP packets cannot be larger than 65,536 (0–65535) according to RFC 791. Attempting to send a larger one might result in a denial of service, crashing the IP stack on the receiver. An invite of death is a type of VoIP attack.

13. **B.** This is a description of the UDP version of a Smurf; traffic is sent to the chargen port of the UNIX mainframe, which will respond back to the echo ports on all of the other machines, who would all then echo the chargen traffic until the network itself is flooded.

14. **D.** There is never a time when it makes sense for packets to come from the outside that have a source address of an inside segment. This might also be the anti-Smurf and anti-Fraggle countermeasure. Read RFC 2827. (http://www.ietf.org/rfc/rfc2827.txt)

15. **B.** A Chernobyl packet is so named because it "meltsdown" the network segment. There is a Chernobyl virus that affected the CMOS of individual hosts; close answer, but different attack.

Chapter 13: Buffer Overflows

1. **A.** The CEH exam deals only with stack-based overflows, but the term "heap" (where the main part of the program runs) might be mentioned, too.

2. **B.** Push instructions onto the stack, and pop off when executed.

3. **A, B, C, D.** Remember these dangerous functions when viewing code. The CEH does not require that you are a C programmer, but you must be able to recognize a few basics. For a great introduction read this article on the OWASP Wiki: http://www.owasp.org/index.php?title5Dangerous_Function&setlang5en.

4. **A.** The idea is to be able to halt the operation of a program and tell the programmer why. This is a tricky question because the attack was certainly attempted and successful in the sense that the canary bytes were overwritten, but that is not the objective of the attacker. Hopefully, the program halted before the shellcode was able to launch.

5. **A.** The term "overrun" also refers to CD-ROM read errors, but for this class it is OK to interchange the two terms. You might say, "The buffer was overrun causing an overflow condition of the register."

6. **A.** Off by one, errors are nerve racking. Watch out for a pseudo code question or two that cause you to make an intuitive read. Just follow the logic. This statement means "greater than or equal to".

7. **D.** Detection of a buffer overflow attempt will involve 0x90, NOOP, or NOPS. Be careful about the last one. NOPS can also just mean "No OPtions Set" if you are looking at a packet header. Context matters a lot on this exam.

8. **A.** The EIP register is the instruction pointer that is overwritten to hijack the execution sequence.

9. **D.** These are the bytes that are used to terminate a string operation (Null, Carriage Return, Line Feed, End of File) and also serve as canary bytes to detect a buffer overflow.

10. **C.** Java converts its instructions to bytecode which runs in a virtual machine in memory. The virtual machine handles all memory management so the programmer does not have to. C++ is object oriented C, and ActiveX controls can be written in C.

11. **A.** Most casual home users are administrator. On the production network, this should never be the case.

12. **D.** There are also modules for Core Impact and Metasploit. Remember the names of these tools and what attack this is.

13. **B.** The first line tells the server you want to use the POST method to communicate with the iisstart.asp file. You then pass it the rest of the data. Many remote exploits work simply by accessing the open port using telnet or netcat and knowing what to type.

14. **C.** Strcpy is the dangerous function in this script. The fgets function is also dangerous, but it is not in the example code.

15. **C.** Whatever context the owner of the process has is what the attacker gets.

Chapter 14: Hacking Web Servers and Web Applications

1. **B.** Cross site scripting is abbreviated as XSS because the other acronym, CSS, stands for cascading style sheets, which is part of the family of web languages. When you see JavaScript, whether clear like this or in URL encoded form, lean toward XSS as the answer, but as always, read the question carefully and don't jump to conclusions.

2. **B.** John is a cracking tool, assuming you have obtained the encrypted form of passwords. The three other tools are capable of throwing combinations of usernames and passwords from dictionary files at the web application.

3. **A.** Common Gateway Interface is not a language, but a way to describe how web applications should be written. They must handle the exchange of client/server data and the concept of stateful sessions differently than desktop applications.

4. **B.** Amidst the encoded characters you can see an SQL statement: "update usertable set passwd P0wn3d." What are the other answers indicating? One is XSS, another is directory traversal, and the remaining one is a Nimda scan. Make sure you can identify all of them for the test.

5. **A, B, C, E.** "Choose up to n" doesn't mean always pick that many. A HTTrack is used for tunneling through port 80 and Kismet is a wireless analyzer. Be familiar with the top ten web vulnerability scanners as listed on this site: http://sectools.org/web-scanners.html

6. **C.** Input on forms should always be checked for data types and special characters. The code cannot be in the source of the page, however,

as this is easily bypassed. It must be checked on the server. Section 508 deals with access for visitors with disabilities and is a good idea, but is not related to security. The source of avoidable vulnerabilities is often a well-intentioned professional placed in an unfamiliar situation.

7. **D.** Hidden form fields might also get mentioned in the context of changing prices on an order form although that vulnerability is extremely rare (we hope). Changing hidden form fields for a variety of reasons is still very much a threat. They must be used carefully.

8. **A.** Although there are a number of valid attacks that involve cookies, this one is a simple matter of changing some values. Most cookies are encrypted to minimize this and other risks.

9. **C.** IUSR [Computer Name] is the account of the anonymous user that visits the website. As with any installation, the security context of the application or server will be whatever account installed it.

10. **D.** The sessionID and other HTTP commands are passed between client and server at Layer 7, but they are encapsulated by a Layer 4 transport that must establish a socket. The socket also involves Layer 3, spoofing an IP address prevents traffic from returning, and the socket is never set.

11. **A.** It is easy to miss the tick character that trails the e-mail address. It is not a speck on your monitor or a typo. Look carefully for it. This character is often used to test for the possibility of SQL injection vulnerabilities.

12. **B.** Open a command window and ping it. Before the exam, however, make sure you can do hex, octal, decimal, and binary conversions. If you have to convert a decimal number to a dotted quad form, just divide the decimal number by 16,777,216. The result is the first octet; the remainder is then divided by 65,536 to get the next octet. The result is the second octet and the remainder is divided by 256 to get the third octet. The remainder is the fourth octet.

13. **B.** Robots.txt file is placed at the root directory of the website. The .htaccess file is used in apache web servers as an authentication feature and was at one time placed in the root directory but is no longer with newer versions. Login pages sometimes protect "The dark net" but search engines might still be able to reach the files.

14. **B.** Her pop-ups may not be related to browsing at all. They could also be Windows Messenger spam. The firewall will block them.

15. **D.** Look at line 2. If you see MSADC, think Nimda. If you see it with showcode.asp, that is a vulnerability that allows attackers to view source code on the server. Directory traversal is happening also, but Nimda is a better answer in this case.

Chapter 15: Wireless Networks

1. **A.** Captured packets can be resent over and over again to a host. If they elicit a response, there are several things that can be learned. In the case of WiFi traffic, new IVs need to be collected.

2. **A.** Rogue infrastructure along with spoofing is a real problem in WiFi.

3. **C.** Users perceive network slowdowns, but in reality the bit rate remains the same.

4. **A, C.** The role of the security professional is to advise, not to set consequences. Firewalls typically handle Layer 3–7 and WiFi is not part of the equation. Signal jammers exist and are not that expensive, but they may have additional undesirable effects. The best approach is to train users and survey the area.

5. **A.** The current proposal of 802.11n supports speeds up to 600 Mbps.

6. **D.** This is a password. The fact that it is not terribly secret is not the point. The fact that software makes the exchange easy is also not the point. It is a data that is known to parties that wish to establish a trust.

7. **B.** There is no such thing as a Layer 2 firewall. Even with proper placement of the antennas, the signal cannot be completely controlled. But, it is still a best practice to try.

8. **A.** A Yagi antenna is highly directional. A reflector is as well, but is harder to aim as its power increases.

9. **A.** A nonce is a one-time value that can be used to seed or salt an algorithm. An IV might also be a nonce, but is used during the encryption process to ensure stronger characteristics of the key.

10. **A.** Ministumbler is a tool designed for Windows Mobile devices. The other answers are all valid WiFi scanning tools, but built for other operating systems.

11. **D.** Open systems authentication and pre-shared key best describes this scenario.

12. **B.** For WPA to be secure the passkey has to be long and complex. The tool can be found here: http://sourceforge.net/projects/cowpatty/

13. **C.** A wireless intrusion prevention system can sense rogue infrastructure and take preventative measures by monitoring the radio spectrum for anomalies compared with a baseline. Airsnort is for WEP cracking; it is not an intrusion detection tool.

14. **A.** Look for anything with a "war" in front of it: Wardriving, warwalking, wardriving, warflying, warspying, warteabagging . . . and so on. Try this site: http://www.waraxe.us/ftopict-44.html

15. **A, B, D.** When WAP2 is implemented, there is no WEP.

Chapter 16: Cryptography

1. **B.** Hashes are not reversible, but, due to collisions, they are vulnerable to brute force attacks because hashes for a data set are computed until a match is found.

2. **D.** Weak keys can cause predictable results in an algorithm. When a weak key is used, and the algorithm is also known, it might be possible to predict the outcome. IVs can also be weak; the way that IVs are implemented in WEP (Wired Equivalent Privacy) leads to a large vulnerability.

3. **A.** Syskey is discussed in this class to illustrate a critical point about cryptographic controls: There are sometimes bugs in implementations that are exploited in spite of the encryption itself being strong. There are times when the data must be held in a decrypted state outside of the protection of the encryption system. Also, in order to protect against offline brute forcing, some algorithms introduce a variable at the time of decryption that, it could be predicted, would leave the data still vulnerable to attack.

4. **C.** Secure shell is a common choice for establishing secure tunnels between protocols such as telnet and ftp. It is not considered to provide a full VPN solution.

5. **B.** Elliptic curve digital signature algorithm.

6. **A.** A challenge is a set of random data that can also be encrypted then sent as a question that must be answered as a response. If the challenge is answered correctly, it is assumed this could only happen if the client requesting authentication is, in fact, the correct party.

7. **B.** OTPs are often generated using security tokens or smart cards. But they can also be implemented through devices such as cell phones. Security token is a more specific answer in terms of a product choice to implement. Biometric devices are considered expensive and proximity cards are rarely two-factor.

8. **B.** "Split tunneling" should not be allowed from home users. If a data or process is accessed from a less secure source, while at the same time that same client is accessing a more secure source, unintentional exposure can result. If the VPN can be accessed from home, all other network activity should be disabled, or the access should not be allowed to the VPN at all.

9. **C.** RC4 is a stream cipher.

10. **B.** Protocols that are encrypted are good targets for overt channels due to the difficulty of monitoring or filtering the payloads of each packet. If the protocol itself can be sensed, there isn't necessarily a reason to suspect it is being used in some way other than intended, giving the attacker double the protection of being noticed.

11. **B.** Computers are ideal for repeating a process with great accuracy of steps. If a one-time random value is made part of the calculation, the same steps can be repeated but with different results each time.

12. **C.** S/MIME is built into the Microsoft Outlook/Exchange products, and in a domain is the easiest to implement. PGP, however, is a better choice because supporting other operating systems and e-mail clients is necessary in the scenario.

13. **D.** The formula $n(n-1)/2$ is used for this calculation. In this case $n = 10$. Therefore, $10 \times 9 = 90$ then divided by $2 = 45$.

14. **D.** One-time pads are generated once only.

15. **C.** A message, such as an e-mail, can have a symmetric key (pre-shared or exchanged with the other party) added to the e-mail before it is hashed. Only someone who has that same key would be able to append the e-mail and check the hash for integrity. MACs are also used in authentication systems such as challenge response.

Chapter 17: Hacking with Linux

1. **A.** The nobody account is commonly used for anomymous access such as visitors to the web service. The account "dns" is a ruse that is more commonly known as "named" (as in Naming Daemon); it is given root privileges and the attacker is hoping this account would simply remain unnoticed.

2. **D.** The ifconfig command shows the present configuration of the NIC. If it is running the LibPcap drivers for sniffing mode, the attacker would not want this to be detectable.

3. **C.** Hashes were originally stored in the /etc/passwd file which was readable to the world and vulnerable to password cracking attacks. These hashes were moved to the /etc/shadow file that can only be read with root privileges.

4. **C.** The sudo (Switch User and Do) command is used in Linux to elevate the privilege of a single command. The "runas" command can be used in Windows.

5. **A.** NFS (Network File System) can be used in the Linux world to share directories and files across the network. Default implementations do not provide for encryption, so the files can be sniffed on the network. Two other tools, "urlsnarf" and "mailsnarf", are also valuable tools for specifized sniffing.

6. **C.** HPing is one of the tools you want to know some options for going into the exam. The –a option spoofs an address, the –c option counts packets to send, and the –setseq option sets the sequence number. Hex 0000000F is the same as decimal 15.

7. **D.** Non-approved kernel modules will taint the running kernel and will result in the vendor of the distribution to be reluctant to provide support. In true open Linux distros, this might include any LKM that is not GPL licensed.

8. **A, B.** The other two tools are for Windows systems.

9. **A.** The security of a system can benefit from placing exposed services in chroot configurations. TCP Wrappers controls network access to session-oriented protocols, Tar pits slow down connections intentionally to discourage repeated attempts at unauthorized access, and PAMs allow administrators to configure application access.

10. **A.** Since being scanned is often a precursor to other forms of attack, Portsentry works with the TCP Wrappers service to block the incoming IP address by adding it to the /etc/hosts.deny file.

11. **B.** Stackguard protects against buffer overflows (Smashing the stack) by using canary byte techniques.

12. **A.** Linux security auditing tool and Bastille both help determine configuration issues and provide ways to fix them. SARA is a vulnerability scanner and chrootkit is a way to run a service securely.

13. **D.** Advanced intrusion and detection environment is a replacement for Tripwire, which is the tool that is also mentioned often regarding this activity.

14. **C.** User Mode Linux is a way to partition user space memory to isolate applications. Kernel mode is used for privileged access, XEN is a virtual machine technology, and SELinux is a security enhanced kernel capable of implementing mandatory access controls.

15. **A.** Hunt is a session hijack tool that specializes in ARP poisoning. Juggernaut is another one. T-sight is designed for Windows systems. P0f is an OS detection tool, whereas fragroute can modify packets on the fly and is used in IDS evasion testing.

Chapter 18: IDS, Firewalls, and Honeypots

1. **A.** The ACK bit is set, the destination host address is not changing, and the traffic is aimed for port 80. This is a simple ACK scan looking for live hosts on this segment.

2. **A.** This is of course a very incomplete set of rules. On the CEH exam it is important to remember

not to debug; it is a test, not a specification manual. Do not complicate your thoughts with material that is not even present in the question. In this case, even not knowing some of the command options, the answer can be guessed effectively.

3. **B.** Reviewing from the sniffer chapter, know the command line tools that work well in Linux for sniffing and analysis as this activity often goes hand in hand with tuning IDS and firewall products. IDSWakeup and NIDSBench are two tools you should know about for testing IDS as well as hand-crafted packets with HPing.

4. **A.** Practice any command line tool or rule by converting it into plain natural language. "I would like snort to alert me whenever tcp-based traffic coming from anywhere going to any hosts port 111 contains the hex values 00 01 86 A5, and label it in the log as 'Mountd Access'."

5. **B.** The tool "firewalk" can also be used for this purpose. HPing and NMap are both capable of it as well. For other questions, remember that if nothing is returned at all, then the firewall is blocking the return ICMP messages.

6. **B.** There are other hosts behind the one address, but their configuration is hidden or obscured. Read the following explanation: http://www.exit109.com/~jeremy/news/providers/traceroute.html

7. **D.** Genius was a multi-purpose tool, and the other tools are used for assessments and footprinting. Snort is also available in a pre-built virtual machine which includes additional software such as ACID and Barnyard for graphical reporting. Look for "NST Virtual Appliance."

8. **D.** A honey token is when bogus information is placed in a system that should never be accessed and is then monitored. A honeypot does not target a specific problem like information leakage. It is meant to be watched, but the researcher does not know what will happen.

9. **C.** Wget is a great tool for downloading multiple documents from a website. Many sites will blacklist an IP if wget is detected.

10. **A.** Be careful on the real exam with the tool names. Frageroute captures packets and allows them to be modified and replayed. Fragrouter

causes packets to be excessively fragmented, which is also an IDS evasion technique.

11. **C, D.** A receive-only cable prevents the NIC from responding in any way to a scan. The next best thing is to make sure that no protocol stacks are bound to the interface.

12. **D.** Tripware keeps a database of hashes for critical system files. Kismet is a wireless analysis tool and the others are IPS (Intrusion Prevention System) products that can make changes to access points on the fly.

13. **A, C, D.** An ARP poisoning attack only works on a single VLAN; the members of it are vulnerable. The other techniques are all valid monitoring or prevention tools.

14. **A.** IP Chains is used in kernel 2.6 and forward. IPTables is used in 2.4 and 2.5. Be aware, the minor numbers for production kernels are even, meaning 2.5 is not really a good choice in the first place if the machine has production responsibilities.

15. **A.** The syntax of snort rules, ipchains acls, wireshark display filters, and tcpdump capture filters are all covered on the exam. You do not have to memorize the full languages; just become comfortable with what they look like.

Chapter 19: Summary of Optional Modules

1. **A.** The most common methods found for the submitting of web forms are GET and POST, and all servers must implement them. The HTTP protocol supports other methods as well including: PUT, DELETE, TRACE, OPTIONS, and CONNECT, which is used to create a tunnel for SSL.

2. **D.** Logic bombs are triggered by events such as a keystroke combination, time and date of day, or file access. Inside attackers can plant logic bombs that can be disabled for use during extortion attacks.

3. **C.** The first byte denotes this as a multicast. Also, the repetition of the character "c" would make that a good guess.

4. **C.** GPS is global positioning system.

5. **A.** During the initiation phase of two Bluetooth devices, information is sent from one device to the other and this data can be modified to include an unwanted message. Bluesnarfing involves the theft of data using the OBEX protocol.

6. **A.** H.323 is designed to provide telephony over TCP/IP networks and is used by many teleconferencing products.

7. **C.** Credit card skimmers are easy to obtain and is a risk from dishonest merchants. With a writing device and blanks, these cards can be reproduced (carding). Visa and MasterCard have systems that conduct the payment process without it being necessary for the merchant to retain any of this data. RFID devices that customers use for payment are also vulnerable to skimming.

8. **A.** Customers should be given the choice to disable the RFID devices used in theft prevention, otherwise, "tracking" attacks would be possible against customers; for example, if a vendor in shopping malls wants to collect data on what stores shoppers go to after making purchases.

9. **A.** USB Hacksaw is an extension to the USB dumper tool that can automatically retrieve system files such as the SAM.

10. **D.** Their products also protect against advanced attacks such as "evil twins" (attackers posing as legitimate Wifi spots).

11. **B, C, D.** Stop-lock is the tool that makes the laptop unsellable, removing the motivation for theft if the data was not the target.

12. **A.** Placing the Internet zone to high is the safest approach but makes many sites virtually unusable.

13. **A.** SOCKS is the protocol and the other answers are either proxy tools or networks. Beware that many of the free proxies on the net are actually honeypots that are placed there by either black hats or white hats for research.

14. **A.** When logging into an IRC server, a username is provided to the system but then nick is used to identify the user in chatrooms. The nick must be unique within the entire network.

15. **B.** For only a small number of people it is sufficient for the system to find out "who the person is"; meaning, the biometric data can be compared with many entries in the database to find out if this person is in the group of authorized users. If there were, for example, hundreds of possible users, it would be better to ask for a username then compare that biometric to only the template in the database that matches that user.

Chapter 20: Penetration Testing

1. **A.** Banner grabbing is a basic activity on a pentest. Each protocol requires different commands; therefore, this is also a good way to verify services on the open ports.

2. **D.** A good footprint and fingerprint approach is a balance to having an accurate scan, not creating excessive traffic, and finishing in a reasonable amount of time. The example command does not meet these objectives.

3. **A.** The keywords here are "elevated privileges" and "known ports." This is the range 1–1023.

4. **B.** The password must be stored in the file, but a strong key can be generated from it to protect the data from being visible to alternative readers. It is possible, however, to brute force the file; tools such as those from "Elcomsoft" make short work of most file formats.

5. **B.** If packets can be sent and received there are countless forms of attack that can be attempted. This is true regardless of the type of network, wired or wireless.

6. **B.** The keywords in this attack are "runs code on their own machines." The pentester created a website with deliberate vulnerabilities, then placed the attack in the URL. There could also be the downloading of images or media that exploits the browser. By now, the tester likely knows the version of browsers being used in the environment. SQL injection works against the web application.

7. **D.** Project scoping and rules of engagement happen before the test actually begins. The vulnerability analysis comes later in the test, after as much information as possible has been gathered.

8. **D.** Port numbers are considered pre-requisite assumptions for this class. The trick is not memorizing, but rather about noticing them as they are mentioned while you study the material. Exposure to them alone should be enough to understand them in practice.

9. **B.** Using nc, setup a listener to receive udp traffic on port 8080 and direct the data to a file called foo.txt. Other common "web ports" are 80, 81, and 443. Port 1080 is for the socks protocol.

10. **C.** Using tools like nslookup, dig, and host, full transfers might be possible. They likely will not be; however, if the command only takes five seconds and could save hours, it could be worth a try. Be aware that it is a TCP transfer and attempts to obtain zones all at once can be detected and logged. The alternative is to attempt to get the records in a way that looks like simple client requests, one at a time.

11. **A.** There are many reasons hosts are used in a production network with default configurations. Lack of training and being distracted by too many projects are common reasons along with not having a configuration standard that is part of an appropriate risk management, incident response, and disaster recovery management program.

12. **D.** Sending e-mail to non-existent addresses might reveal addresses of internal mail relays, but it also tells the attacker about policies for handling such mail including how to handle bounces, full in-boxes, vacations, ex-employees, undeliverables, and, of course, spam.

13. **C.** If the system authenticated the client via the browser, then changing the name being passed to the account might allow the attacker to assume the identity of the target account. If the parameters are not in the query string, they could be in the http header and Paros could be used to change and resubmit them. Instead of something simple like names, session ID values are commonly used in these attacks.

14. **C.** Floppyscan is a tool that can be configured to automatically footprint a network and e-mail the results to a predetermined address. While it is scanning, it presents the BSOD so that the computer looks busy.

15. **B.** Make sure the person that issues this document actually has the authority to do so. The penetration test should be sponsored by senior management, who should also issue the other legal documents as well.

Index